DESERT WIND
AND TROPIC
STORM

DESERT WIND AND TROPIC STORM

An Autobiography

DONALD HAWLEY

WITH A FOREWORD BY
LORD CARRINGTON

MICHAEL RUSSELL

© Donald Hawley 2000

First published in Great Britain 2000
by Michael Russell (Publishing) Ltd
Wilby Hall, Wilby, Norwich NR16 2JP

Printed and bound in Great Britain
by Biddles Ltd, Guildford and King's Lynn

ISBN 0 85955 258 6

TO
RUTH, SARA, CAROLINE,
SUSAN & CHRISTOPHER

Map Key

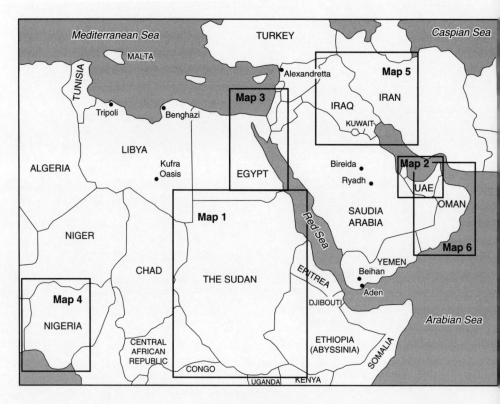

LIST OF MAPS

Contents

Foreword

Some people appear to think that the life of a diplomat consists of cocktail parties, receptions and a life of ease and relaxation, striped trousers, short black coats and formality. Anybody who reads this book will find Donald Hawley's experience very different. Wartime soldier, called to the Bar, long career in the Foreign and Commonwealth Service and a very active so-called retirement. In his many postings, he somehow contrived to be where the action was.

In the Sudan, he saw and was involved in the transition to Independence and was a notable member of the elite Sudan Political Service. In Cairo he had to deal with the aftermath of the Suez operation. In Nigeria, as Head of Chancery and often Deputy High Commissioner, he was involved in the turbulence which led to the Biafran War; in Baghdad with the emergence of the Baath Party and the delicate relations with the oil companies. In Oman, as the first Ambassador, Sir Donald saw the beginnings of the remarkable transformation of that country into a modern state and became a firm friend of Sultan Qaboos, its wise monarch.

Finally, in Malaysia he showed not only his love for that country and its people but an acute awareness of the feeling that Malaysian and British were each taking the other for granted. He even managed to find excitement when in London, supervising some rather dull departments such as the Passport Office, by leading a mission to President Amin of Uganda. He was involved in the aftermath of the invasion of Cyprus by Turkey and, on a more modest scale, was instrumental in preventing the Treasury, in their usual passion for economy at any cost, from selling the splendid British Embassy in Rome.

Naturally, Sir Donald became acquainted with many world figures who influenced events in the countries in which he served. He noticed and remarked on the powerful and sinister presence of Saddam Hussein, not at that time in the front rank of the Iraqi Government. Many and various politicians crossed his path – not least George Brown, who put on one of his more extrovert performances in Baghdad.

Certainly for Sir Donald life was never dull and, though his book is a model of restraint, reading between the lines it can be seen that he sometimes seems to have found his instructions from London mystifying, though carrying them out with the tact and flexibility which a good diplomat always achieves.

In his retirement, he is as active as ever, and his service to the University of Reading is something of which he should be especially proud. If these memoirs lay to rest the misconceptions about the Foreign Office, so much the better; and they are a good read as well.

CARRINGTON

Preface

In writing this book I have drawn not only on memory but also the diaries I kept from the age of thirteen and the weekly letters I wrote to my parents until my father's death in 1973 – which fortunately they kept.

Lord Carrington has come into my life in a number of ways from time to time, notably as Chancellor of the University of Reading and earlier when he was Secretary of State for Defence and later for Foreign and Commonwealth Relations. I am, therefore, delighted and honoured that he kindly agreed to write a foreword.

My wife Ruth has shared my experiences over the last thirty-six years and I am deeply grateful not only for her constant support but also for her reading, and contributing ideas for, the manuscript.

A number of others have also given me valuable assistance and encouragement. Ivor Lucas, Jim Hodges and members of the Research Department of the Foreign and Commonwealth Office have made helpful comments on the text and saved me from at least some errors. The maps have kindly been provided by Heather Browning and Professor Brian Goodall of the Department of Geography at Reading University. Furthermore these memoirs could not have been completed without the help of Joanna Buckley, who not only typed the final manuscript but also made numerous editorial suggestions and compiled the index. To all these, I extend my hearty thanks.

Little Cheverell, 2000   DONALD HAWLEY

I

Early Days

Fame and infamy alike eluded my immediate Hawley forebears, who were modest people with no great name among them. Earlier Hawleys were of mixed reputation. John Hawley of Dartmouth, who died in 1408, was perhaps the original for Chaucer's Shipman with the 'great number of ships to his use', inspiring the rhyme:

> Blow the wind high. Blow the wind low.
> It bloweth good to Hawley's hoe.

An early diplomat, Thomas Hawley, Clarenceux King of Arms in Henry VIII's time, treated with the Scots, French and 'northern rebels', but his addiction to gaming and the bottle might have disqualified him from appointment to regular service in a later age. He was in fact 'so distempered' when the Heralds were at Windsor for the funeral of Jane Seymour in November 1557 that 'he fell downstairs' as he was leaving the Treasurer's chamber. Sharing lodgings with the Somerset Herald, he 'kept such rule' that his servant – 'as naughty a fellow as ever was' – broke his head with a pewter pot, whilst his companion 'would have ravished the maid and wrang her throat so that she could not get her breath'. A sixteenth-century administrator, Francis Hawley, Vice Admiral of the Island of Purbeck, who held Corfe Castle for Sir Christopher Hatton, was likewise no saint and appears to have been in league – fashionably – with the pirates and smugglers in what was one of the most lawless parts of England.

The famous mathematician and astronomer Edmund Hawley was a man in a different mould. Though better known as Halley, after whom the comet was named, he often spelt his name 'Hawley', as Pepys did in commenting on his three voyages in the *Paramore*: 'Mr Hawley . . . may be said to have the most competent degree of the science and practice of navigation.'

These may or may not have been related ancestors but it seems that General Henry Hawley was not. He was a cavalryman who fought at Dettingen and Fontenoy, and was defeated at the Battle of Falkirk in 1746, though he led the cavalry in Cumberland's victory at Culloden.

He was said to have been a severe disciplinarian, known as 'The Chief Justice', and he wrote oddly in his will: 'As I never was married, I have no heir . . . I have taken it into my head to adopt one . . . after the manner of the Romans.'

Two fairly prominent Hawleys could have had connections with our family. Frederick Hawley, a distinguished Shakespearian scholar and actor, bore the same Christian name as members of my family have for five generations, and Colonel William Hawley, to whom I am said to bear a close physical resemblance, was an antiquary who excavated Old Sarum, Stonehenge and Avebury in the earlier years of the twentieth century. My family also claimed some kinship – unproven – with the Hawley baronetcy and so Sir Joseph Henry Hawley, the third baronet who was notable for winning the Derby four times[1] and advocating Turf reform, could also have been distantly related. The Hawley peerage, however, which was created in 1645, became extinct in 1790 and no one has claimed it successfully since.

We are on more certain ground with my father's immediate family, who came from Buckinghamshire and Northamptonshire and stemmed from yeomen farmers, minor gentry and craftsmen. A cousin of my grandfather, Alfred Hawley, having founded the Sketchley Dye Works, made a great deal of money and was renowned for openhandedness, generosity and an easy manner. In 1922 he became High Sheriff of Leicestershire, with which county there were many Hawley connections, and Arthur Hawley was High Sheriff of Rutland in 1941.

My paternal grandmother's family, the Webbs, came from earnest reformers in the City of Bristol, one of whom was Master of St Peter's Hospital in the early nineteenth century. My mother's family, the Hills, were Londoners making their living as pianoforte and musical instrument manufacturers, and Robert Hills, the watercolourist, appears to have been one of them. My great-aunt Elizabeth Hills brought European influence into the family by marrying a son of the Mayor of Prague, and my maternal grandmother had Huguenot and Scottish ancestry – and was proud of it. She was a wonderful lady and a great favourite of mine as she spoiled me. My mother's father, a quieter man than my paternal grandfather, was dignified but had a twinkle in his eye.

There were several pedagogues amongst the Hawleys and Webbs, and my father's father, Frederick Thomas Hawley, was a very musical

1 In 1851, 1858, 1859 and 1868.

schoolmaster with an ever-present sense of fun. Organist at the same church for forty years, he subtly – but shockingly – worked music from Gilbert and Sullivan operas into his voluntaries, peering out from the organ loft to see if he had been detected. His talents won the praises of the organist at Westminster Abbey and, after his death, Goss Custard, the celebrated – if improbably named – organist, played at the dedication service for the improved organ endowed by my father and aunt in their father's memory.

My aunt, May Hawley, might have become a concert pianist had my grandfather approved but, an excellent linguist, she devoted forty years to teaching modern languages and music at the North London Collegiate School – a school of high academic repute founded in the last century by Frances Mary Buss who, with Miss Beale of Cheltenham Ladies' College, provoked the jingle:

> Miss Buss and Miss Beale
> Cupid's darts do not feel.
> How different from us
> Miss Beale and Miss Buss.

May Hawley had been an undergraduate at Newnham College, Cambridge and had taken a good degree in modern languages in 1909 – though it was not until the 1920s that the University formally recognised degrees for women. A suffragette, though a milder one it would be difficult to imagine, she knew Rupert Brooke at Cambridge and described him as 'very beautiful'. Music was in her very being and she worshipped it as a divine art.

My father's mother, Lily Webb, who died sadly young in 1904, had followed her own father into teaching and in her early years ran the village Church school at Shermanbury in Sussex with her younger sister, for which they were warmly commended by both the Schools Inspector and the local vicar. The large family of Webbs claimed distant relationship with the Colston family[2] and numbered amongst their forebears not only educationalists, musicians – including the organist of Brecon Cathedral – public servants, an endower of almshouses and farmers, but also a seventeenth-century Governor of Bombay and a Consul in Manila, William Hacker Webb. His despatch to Earl Russell dated 17 September 1864 was perhaps the most publicised of any ever

---

2 Edward Colston was a major benefactor of Bristol in the seventeenth and eighteenth centuries.

sent to the Foreign Office, for every bottle of Dr Collis Browne's Chlorodyne, the popular remedy distributed throughout the world, had wrapped round it:

Extract from a despatch from Mr Webb HBM's Consul in Manila dated September 17th 1864:
'The remedy most efficacious in its effects in epidemic cholera has been found to be Chlorodyne and, with a small quantity given to me by Dr Bark, I have saved several lives ... Earl Russell communicated to the College of Physicians that he had received a despatch from Her Majesty's Consul at Manila to the effect that Cholera had been raging fearfully, and that the ONLY remedy of any service was Chlorodyne. (see *Lancet* December 31st 1964).'

My father was a chartered accountant, placed fourth in the United Kingdom – second in England, the Scots taking the first two places – when he passed his finals in 1912. He was a keen member of the Territorial Army and, whilst serving in the Middlesex Yeomanry in the Great War, was seriously wounded at Gallipoli and had to be invalided out. One wound affected his left arm so badly that, always a good tennis player, he developed a unique style of serving, holding balls in the racket hand and throwing one up as he swung the racket back. Despite this handicap, he won a formidable number of tennis tournaments. Always a friendly and helpful father, he shared the family sense of fun and also had a fine baritone voice.

My mother, who was both beautiful and clever, always dressed immaculately and was rare in her generation in taking a degree in science at London University in 1916. This had the slight disadvantage that, if she did not agree with my approach to something, she accused me of 'not being scientific'. She was a loving and always interested mother, though, who created a very happy home. I had only one sister, Enid, to whom I have always been devoted, even though she once boxed my ears when I teased her in our teens – hastily apologising for her 'reflex action'.

We grew up in an environment which was a little academic, mildly intellectual and also musical. As a family, we sang and played a lot together and were devotees of Gilbert and Sullivan as well as Edward German, who had been a friend of my grandfather's. Any tendency to an insular approach to life was avoided by the French, German and three successive Egyptian girls whom Aunt May taught at school and to whom she was *in loco parentis* before they qualified as the vanguard of women doctors in Egypt.

My connection with the Middle East, which was to continue throughout my life and career, began even before birth. I was carried *en ventre de ma mère* in Persia, Iraq, the Gulf and Egypt when my parents were on a business visit in 1920 on behalf of the Anglo-Persian Oil Company. The London staff of this company, which became BP, numbered only eighteen, including the typing pool, when my father joined it, and he served it all his working life, eventually becoming a director. The store of oriental objects around our home perhaps also biased me subconsciously towards a career largely spent in the Middle East and Islamic oil-producing countries.

Fortunate in my parents and family, I was lucky – after a false start – to be generally equally happy in the schools to which I was sent. This was not the case at St Cyprian's, Eastbourne, and I was not consoled even by winning a boxing cup. My parents, therefore, sent me to Elstree, the headmaster of which was Edward Lancelot Sanderson – E.L.S as he signed himself in all the books which he vetted before they were allowed into the school. He was a scholar of Harrow, where he was a contemporary of Winston Churchill, and King's, Cambridge where he won a Half Blue for athletics. Much more remarkably, he had been sent to sea to recuperate from a weak chest and sailed on a schooner with Joseph Conrad, who dedicated his second book, *An Outcast of the Islands*,[3] to him. When later he succeeded his father as Headmaster of Elstree, he retained Conrad's friendship and was also a close friend of John Galsworthy. A very kindly though strict headmaster, he found patent errors committed by boys in his top form excruciatingly painful as I discovered one day when I stood up in class at his command to read some lines of Ovid. There was a sudden explosion and E.L.S, breathing heavily down his nose, exclaimed, 'Nasty little boy. False quantity!' I had pronounced a syllable short when it was supposed to be long. Despite this, I much admired him and kept up a correspondence with him until his death.

His son, Ian Sanderson, introduced a breezy element when he succeeded E.L.S. after retiring from the Navy as a lieutenant commander. He had been at the Battle of Jutland only seventeen years before as a midshipman of sixteen, and he regaled us with stories about it, which we often pressed him to repeat.

Mrs E. L. Sanderson, a lady of sweet, gentle and slightly ethereal disposition, had spent part of her earlier life in Kenya and often talked of

3 Published in 1896.

it. She mothered us and always read to us in small groups in her drawing room on Sunday evenings. When boys left, she asked them to name
their favourite hymns, and made a collection of them.

We were on the whole fortunate in our masters at Elstree. J. F. Walms-
ley, brother of a distinguished wartime Air Marshal, became a close
family friend. Brian Hewitt, who married one of the mistresses, Miss
Winterton, remained at the school from 1928 to the 1970s and, after
retirement, became a governor. A Chips-like character with a Pickwick-
ian manner, he had an armoury of distinctive phrases like 'Boy, you are
on speed and not on accuracy!' and, on the football field, 'Shoot man!
You're in the area'. Another staff marriage was between Miss English
and the diminutive, tubby chaplain, Mr Hardy, who was counter-
balanced in height, at six foot seven, by the inappropriately named Mr
Littlewood.

Miss Davies taught music and musical appreciation with infectious
enthusiasm but her Welsh religious upbringing could not allow 'Cin-
quering kongs their titles take' as a diverting Spoonerism. Robert
Stainton, a double Oxford Blue – for soccer and cricket at which he also
captained Sussex – succeeded E. L. Sanderson as classics master and
was a brilliant teacher. It was not difficult for a boy to respect such a
man, who also looked like the Hermes of Praxiteles, and he too became
a family friend with whom I maintained a correspondence for many
years. One evening in July 1934 the evening paper reported the assassination by Nazis of Dr Dollfuss, the Chancellor of Austria, and he
remarked to us gravely and memorably, 'Oh dear. We shall all be back
in the trenches again.'

Our first matron was known as Hecate or the Queen of the Night,
and dosed us with iodine for anything external and rhubarb and soda
for anything internal, consigning us to 'Egypt', the sick room, if we
were worse and 'had the plague'. Her successor, Miss Stewart, was a
glamorous arrival from New Zealand, whose attractions were plain
even to young boys. It was not long before a stir of speculation and
excitement arose as a change in her manner was detected. The denoue-
ment was swift and breathtaking, for she married the Lord Chief Justice
of England, Lord Hewart.

Dwin Bramall, the future Field Marshal and President of the MCC,
though two years my junior, played in the same First XI in which I was
known by the sports master as 'The Merry Cricketer' – perhaps because
of my lighthearted unclassical strokes. When we met again many years
later in Malaysia, Dwin recalled that, as a prefect supervising the boys

going in to supper and noticing him scuffing along, I had said, 'Pick your feet up, Bramall.' I replied that the advice had not served him badly!

Rather to the chagrin of E. L. Sanderson, who often wore the blue cornflower in his buttonhole, I sat for an entrance scholarship to Radley instead of Harrow in 1935.[4] I was fortunate to gain fourth place immediately after Pat Nairne who in later life became a distinguished civil servant, a Privy Counsellor, Master of St Catherine's, Oxford and Chancellor of the University of Essex, as well as being a good artist. He remained a life-long friend as did Michael Barbour, the second scholar, with whom I went up to New College in the same term. His academic career as Professor of Geography took him to the Sudan and Nigeria, and part of our time in both countries coincided.

The Warden for my first two years was the Reverend W. H. Fergusson, a fine man with the mien and standards of a kindly Old Testament prophet. An excellent musician, who later became Canon Precentor of Salisbury Cathedral, he insisted on the highest standards of singing by the whole school and personally took a 'congregational practice' every Saturday. His inspiration led to impressive results generally, and in particular the loud and confident singing in chapel which everyone enjoyed. I was in A Social[5] first with J. G. McPherson as Social Tutor and then Stephen Paton, a short man who was a brilliant modern linguist, philosopher and teacher, though he had difficulty with his 'r's and was renowned for his idiosyncratic rendering of one of his favourite phrases, 'Can't you say the ordinary English word "orange"?'

I enjoyed Radley, playing for three years in the First XV, though I just missed a cap in the first year. In one match, I played against Adrian Stoop, who had been captain of the England XV before the First World War and, playing fly half at the age of fifty-two, was forcibly leading a formidable team of Harlequins. We had an annual match against Downside, which was always a needle fixture carrying religious overtones, which seemed strange to me as Radley itself was a High Anglican school.

Life in the Upper Sixth was civilised. We sat in the beautiful library around a large oval table covered by a green baize cloth, and were taught by excellent scholars, especially the new Warden, John Vaughan Wilkes, who had been Master in College at Eton and, at thirty-four, was one of the youngest headmasters in the country. Art was

4 My mother wondered whether the public school system would last. My father accurately predicted that it would.
5 A house was called 'a Social' at Radley.

expounded by an eccentric and amusing artist, T. B. Huskisson, who aroused our interest in Whistler, Fragonard and Boucher, among others. Another remarkable man, Hans Koeppler, who had come to England as a refugee in the early 1930s and to the end of his life always spoke with a strong guttural German accent, occasionally taught us long before he became famous as the Principal of Wilton Park, re-educating Germans in democracy. In my last year I entered the competition for the major speaking award, the Birt Speech Prize. To my own astonishment – and I think that of everyone in the hall apart from the adjudicator – I won, and was presented with a number of handsome books inscribed by the Warden.

In the Christmas term of 1938, war began to seem inevitable and we were all issued with gas masks. The prefects had to help the smaller boys to fit theirs for practice, though fortunately the masks never had to be used. War declared on 3 September 1939 and, then a corporal in the OTC, I went to the depot of the Oxfordshire and Buckinghamshire Light Infantry in October to 'join up'. I took the King's Shilling and was told that I would not be required until I was twenty in about eighteen months' time. I therefore went up to New College, Oxford to read law. Meanwhile, life for a prefect took new forms with such additional prefectorial duties as enforcing the blackout.

Unwittingly, if pompously, I made a prophecy at the end of my last term at Radley in December 1939, when interviewed by the editor of *The Emergency Ration*: 'I intercepted Rugger Secretary D. F. Hawley passing rapidly between Big Side and the Music School. I asked him with what emotions he faced the prospect of leaving. He replied, "I ... look forward to reaching the world's wide open spaces."' I did not realise that this would lead to my spending thirty-one years overseas, of which twenty-six were in the Arab world.

In my last year I played in the annual hockey match between Radleians and Marlburians at Fulham Palace, arranged by Bishop Winnington-Ingram, the Bishop of London, an Old Marlburian and Visitor of Radley. A pitch had been marked out at the Palace, though the lines were obscured by light snow. The Bishop was eighty-two but the weather did not deter him, particularly as it was to be his last match. Hockey stick in hand and clad in brown plus-fours, a tweed cap, white sweater and a white woollen muffler round his neck, he cried in a high-pitched voice as we took the field, 'Come on us Old Marlborough boys!' It was customary for the Bishop to score a goal but this was not easy to contrive with any semblance of authenticity as the snow continued to fall. Indeed we were principally anxious that he might hurt himself. In the event, he scored two goals, much to everyone's satisfaction. We then repaired to the Palace for tea and, after changing, each of us was summoned to see him individually. He told me he was about to retire and people thought he was going to die, but he had no such intention; rather he proposed to make a voyage round the world. He invited me to kneel for his blessing, after which we all enjoyed a generous tea provided by the benevolent old man.

At New College, where I arrived in January 1940, I had joint tutorials with James Comyn, later a celebrated QC and judge, with our formidable bursar, Dr G. R. Y. Radcliffe, who was probably the leading authority on the law of real property. At the end of term he congratulated us both because he had only lost his temper with us once, though on one occasion he did say, 'There you go into it again Comyn – arse over tip!' My first rooms, meanwhile, were in Garden Quad near the magnificent herbaceous border along part of Oxford's ancient wall. My next rooms in 'Pandy', named for its varied architecture, were immediately above Anthony Meyer's who, unusually for an undergraduate in those days, was already married. Like me, he joined the Diplomatic Service and later, having abandoned diplomacy for politics, boldly but vainly challenged Margaret Thatcher in 1989 for leadership of the Conservative Party.

The Liberal Club was reputed to have the prettiest girls. I joined it – not solely for that reason – and even served on the committee. The Club attracted distinguished political speakers, including Lord Samuel, the first British High Commissioner in Palestine, who recounted how General Allenby, the Military Commander, had insisted on some form of documentation when Samuel arrived in Jerusalem in 1920. The new High Commissioner wrote a receipt reading, 'Received one Palestine. E and OE'[6] – sadly descriptive and prophetic words.

Later there was to be a debate on Regulation 18b made under the Defence of the Realm Act which enabled the Government to detain aliens without trial. The committee discussed who would propose the motion condemning the measure and Ken Jones, the Chairman, who later became a judge, looked round the table from behind his horn-rimmed spectacles and asked the most powerful speakers, one of whom was Basil Wigoder, later to be a Lord of Appeal, to propose and second the motion. He then asked for someone to oppose it. Out of perhaps misguided loyalty, I volunteered and was asked to find my own

6 Errors and omissions excepted.

seconder. I persuaded Kemmis Buckley who had been at school with me
and was also at New College. The ensuing debate was strong but predictably we lost and the motion of condemnation was carried by a
handsome majority. At the next elections for the committee I was not
re-elected. Asking my close friends the reason, I was told that my views
– as expressed in the debate – were too conservative!

At Oxford my other preoccupations included singing in the Bach
Choir, playing games for the College and reaching the finals of 'Cup-
pers' in hockey and tennis, doing air raid watch duty and becoming an
instructor in gunnery in the OTC, on which we spent a day and a half a
week, as well as working at my books and essays. Having satisfied the
examiners for a War Degree, I prepared for my military service.

A new factor arose, however. New College had connections with the
Anglo-Egyptian Sudan and Christopher Cox, one of the dons, had
recently returned after a distinguished tour as Director of Education
there. Encouraged to apply for the Sudan Political Service, I did so on
the basis of serving until the end of the war as a soldier with Sudanese
troops, who were then fighting in the Abyssinian campaign against the
Italians. The Sudan was then said to be a 'country of Blacks ruled by
Blues' and, though I did not get a Blue, my rugger, hockey and tennis
were insufficiently bad to cause me to be blackballed when interviewed.
Selection boards were believed to select people in their own image. I do
not know whose image I matched but two genial interviews with senior
members of the Political Service were enough to open the way for me to
join a very prestigious service.

First, however, I went to the Officer Cadet Training Unit, OCTU, at
Ilkley where the Battery Commander, addressing us on our first
evening, advised us to go out that very evening to measure our capacity
because subsequently drunkenness in any form would not be tolerated.
Our troop drill sergeant accused us of wandering round the parade
ground like a lot of snakes but eventually pronounced himself proud of
us. Other cadets there included Hugh Montefiore, later Bishop of Birm-
ingham, and Howard Hartog whose spectacular collision with the only
tree in the middle of a field where we were learning to ride motor bicy-
cles scarcely foreshadowed his subsequent versatility as an impresario.

After being commissioned at Larkhill, where officers who had earlier
served in the Sudan Defence Force (SDF) envied me my posting, I was
sent out on a voyage lasting two and a half months round the Cape to
Suez. My recently acquired knowledge of contract law did not avail to
prevent a taxi driver from breaking his agreement over the fare to

Cairo. Arriving in Khartoum at the end of December 1941 after the four-day journey by train and Nile steamer from Cairo to Khartoum, I became a bimbashi[7] and immediately wore a crown and star on my epaulettes like a colonel rather than the subaltern I was. No British officer held a rank below this in the SDF.

7 Turkish terminology was used in the Sudan Defence Force as in the Egyptian Army for ranks, and a bimbashi was literally 'commander of 1,000 men'. Wearing an Egyptian crown and star like a lieutenant-colonel, in practice British bimbashis might be the equivalent of major, captain or even lieutenant.

2

The Sudan

It was a pleasure and a privilege to serve with Sudanese troops. Smart, efficient, brave and loyal, they were full of humour and fun. Retaining the hospitable customs of their villages, they liked to entertain their officers to tea in the lines and on return from home leave would bring small presents like dates or locally made slippers. Shaking hands in greeting they would, with smiles and endearing flattery, express the virtually vain hope that their particular officer would become Kaid.[1] As soldiers, Sudanese seldom displayed a trait common among their countrymen – the *ahsan fikr*. Told to carry out a particular task, a Sudanese official saluted smartly and replied 'Yes sir.' Asked two days later if the job had been done, he might retort, 'No, sir, I had a better idea.'

For the most part flat with the exception of some isolated mountainous regions, the Sudan is a country of about one million square miles – ten times the size of the United Kingdom and the rough equivalent in area of British India – with a population in 1941 of some eight million. It is also extremely hot with temperatures reaching over 120 degrees fahrenheit in the shade.

A vast marshy area of the middle White Nile, through which river navigation is very difficult, effectively separates the Northern and Southern Sudan. This Sudd proved as significant to nineteenth-century explorers, soldiers and administrators as to Roman centurions sent by Nero to explore the sources of the Nile nearly 2,000 years before. To this day it remains a barrier – emotional and cultural as well as physical – and accounts for the very different history and development of the two regions. Along the Nile the North, ruled by early Egyptian dynasties from about 2000 BC, was later known as the Land of Kush. From about 750 BC until the beginning of the fourth century AD, a strong civilisation centred on Napata and Merowe controlled the northern Sudan and at times ruled even Egypt itself. It was characterised by pyramids and temples – albeit not on the scale of Egypt's.

1 Commander-in-Chief of the Sudan Defence Force.

Later, converted by early Eastern fathers from Alexandria, Christian kingdoms and monastic institutions[2] flourished in the North for a thousand years, but from the thirteenth and fourteenth centuries Arab incursions and settlement led people to adopt Islam. The important Sultanates of the Fung on the Upper Blue Nile and Darfur in the West also practised Islam. The South remained a region of simpler tribal societies, based on herding, fishing or basic agriculture, and the people remained pagan or animistic. Destiny has now decreed that Christianity should flourish and grow among southerners – introduced only in the nineteenth and twentieth centuries by Western Christian missionaries. Largely through them, and devoted British administrators known as 'bog barons', the South was exposed to the modern world.

The Sudan first began to resemble a unified modern state when in 1821 Ibrahim Pasha, the son of Mohamed Ali Pasha the Ruler of Egypt, conquered the whole country. The Turkiya administration, however, was far from benign and the slave trade scandalised European consciences. The Khedive of Egypt, Ismail Pasha, therefore appointed General Charles George Gordon as Governor-General and he governed with Christian conviction and passion to right wrongs. His murder in Khartoum in 1885 a few hours before the arrival of the British relief expedition had a profound effect in Britain and the Prime Minister, Gladstone, previously affectionately known as the GOM (Grand Old Man), was blamed for the failure to rescue Gordon in time and subsequently called MOG (Murderer of Gordon). The assassins were followers of Mohamed Ahmed who had established an Islamic theocracy based on his claim to be the 'Expected Mahdi' foreseen before the final end of the world. He had apparently not sanctioned the murder, but the death of the Christian hero at the hands of his troops gave strong emotional overtones to the reconquest of the Sudan. This was achieved between 1896 and 1898 by Anglo-Egyptian forces under the command of Kitchener and, as Gordon had come to be thought of as almost a saint, a Gordon Memorial Service was held every year in Khartoum Cathedral.

The Sudan became an Anglo-Egyptian Condominium, a constitutional device invented by Lord Cromer, then the hugely powerful British Consul-General in Egypt. Its aim was to preserve the joint rights acquired by conquest on 'reoccupation', to ensure a British-dominated administration and to secure the ultimate sovereignty of the Sudan in

2 Monophysites like the Copts in Egypt and the Ethiopians.

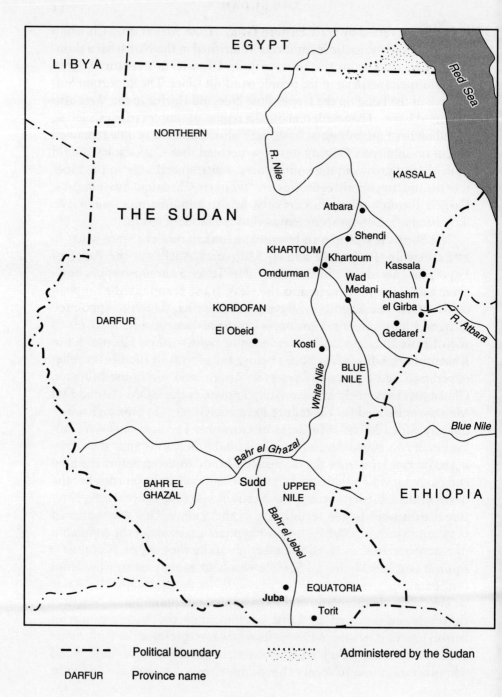

| --- · --- · --- | Political boundary | ⋰⋰⋰⋰ | Administered by the Sudan |
| DARFUR | Province name | | |

The Sudan

trust for the Sudanese. Kitchener himself became the country's first Governor-General under the new dispensation and his authority prevailed over roughly the area of the modern Sudan.

The capital in 1941 was Khartoum, where the White and Blue Niles meet before running northwards to Egypt and the Mediterranean. There were then nine Provinces, six covering the Arab and Muslim North and three the pagan or Christian South. The Governors of Provinces and the District Commissioners were British administrators from the Sudan Political Service, which numbered only 393 in all over the whole 58–year period of the Condominium from 1898 to 1956. The welfare of the Sudanese was a paramount pillar of British policy and those who served in the Sudan were in the main idealistic, believing it to be their duty to provide a benevolent administration – the modern generation do not have the monopoly of idealism in overseas countries! Personal relations between the British and the Sudanese were close and often full of humour. There seemed to be a natural affinity between us.

Exciting events took place just before my arrival in the Sudan. Commanded by General Willie Platt as Kaid when Mussolini brought Italy into the war in 1940, the Sudan Defence Force consisted of some 5,000 Sudanese troops with a handful of British officers and technical warrant officers. Faced by Italian troops in overwhelmingly superior numbers on the Abyssinian and Eritrean fronts, they convinced the enemy by daring tactical raids that their numbers were far greater than they were. When the East African campaign got properly under way, the SDF fought with the 4th and 5th Indian Divisions both in Abyssinia and Eritrea, and played their part in the victory at Keren and the surrender of the Italian opposition in 1941 – attended incidentally by Bimbashi John Kenrick,[3] because he was the only officer who matched the Duke of Aosta, the Italian Commander, in height! My sea journey round the Cape, however, took so long that, to my disappointment, the fighting was over by the time I arrived in Khartoum in December of that year.

Joining the Sudan Artillery Regiment, whose officers had a rather wild as well as gallant reputation, I was first given a very brief course in Arabic. This was a necessary preliminary as all orders were given, and business conducted, in that language. Sudanese troops would meet a young officer more than half way in understanding but, though many Sudanese officers spoke English fluently, other ranks customarily never

3 A member of the Sudan Political Service and later Assistant Adviser on Constitutional and External Affairs to the Governor-General.

did. Shendi was the headquarters of the regiment which was mainly recruited from the Shaigiya and Gaaliyin tribes, and there the Commanding Officer Ged Palmer[4] greeted me very kindly. I was also introduced to polo, though I did not have time to become much good. After a few days I was posted to Kufra, an oasis in the middle of the Libyan desert captured from the Italian colonial regime and a *point d'appui* for Long Range Desert Group patrols to gather intelligence.

Later Kufra became a base for raids notably by the newly-formed SAS under David Stirling, a frequent visitor to our mess with fellow officers including Paddy Mayne, whose personal exploits in the surprise destruction of enemy planes and equipment in the North of Libya became legendary. An Irish rugger international, he had a special connection with us having played against Dick Guest, one of the three Bimbashis in our battery – an England wing three-quarter himself before, and also after, the war. The raids carried out on Benghazi and other targets, including the oasis of Gialo in which the SDF participated, deceived the Germans into believing that they were seriously threatened on their right flank and consequently withdrawing divisions from the front line facing the British at Alamein in October 1942.

On leave in Cairo after Kufra I spent some days in the famous old Shepheard's Hotel, and there at the long bar met Wilfred Thesiger for the first time; he was later well known for his explorations in Arabia and elsewhere. There too I fell into conversation with a young American who, bemused by the bimbashi's crown and star on my epaulettes, blurted out, 'Say, just how old are you?' When I replied I was twenty-one, he gasped, 'My! Twenny one and a lootenant-coinel. I'm only a rooky caught in the draft.'

After Alamein my battery retrained in the Sudan on Bofors guns and I wrote the Arabic version of the gun drill. Sent then to Tripoli in Libya, we were adjudged by a British instructor in gunnery to be fully up to a British battery's standard in drill and effectiveness and I was looking forward to soldiering further west in North Africa. Suddenly, however, much against my will and in defiance of my written protests, I was recalled to the Political Service in the Sudan and firmly told that my duty lay there. The country was then short of administrators, many senior and middle-grade officials having been sent on secondment to work with the Occupied Enemy Territories Administration (OETA) in Eritrea and North Africa. After a brief spell in Wad Medani in the Blue

4 El Miralai G.M. Palmer Bey.

Nile Province, where George Bredin was Governor, I was posted as Assistant District Commissioner under Philip Broadbent in Kosti on the White Nile.

The Political Service had its origins at the beginning of the century in a military administration and our uniforms remained military in style. The duties, however, were very different from soldiering. Pitched straight into District work, I was involved in direct administration, magisterial duties and supervision of local authorities – governmental duties having been devolved wherever possible to local traditional and tribal administrations. In Kosti District the chief local figure was Shaikh Mekki Ahmed Asakir the Nazir of the Baggara Confederation, a group of largely cattle-owning tribes, with regional Shaikhs called *omdas* and village and sectional Shaikhs under them.

A good District Commissioner or Assistant was expected to spend ten to twelve days a month on trek among the people, staying either in simple rest houses of straw or mud brick provided by the Shaikhs, or in his own tent. I did some long camel and horse treks both in Kosti and later in Gedaref Districts, but more often we journeyed by car. A moving home – consisting of bed-roll, wash basin, canvas bath, table, chair and tent – was packed up neatly into the back of the grey Sudan Government Ford truck, driven by a smartly uniformed Blue Nile Province policeman. One police escort also rode on top of the luggage piled in the back and perched with him was my *suffragi*[5] - the beaming, capable and honest Mustafa Murgan, who stayed with me throughout my whole military and civilian service in the Sudan. Thus we travelled over flat savannah covered with spiky acacias; over gravel desert or sand dunes; or over rocky, hilly places, visiting even the remotest parts of the District. Once we arrived at a rest house, Mustafa would set out my trek equipment and, as a gesture of hospitality, the Shaikh of the area frequently brought a sheep and had it slaughtered at my feet. Some of the meat would later appear for my dinner but happily the greater part was eaten by the Shaikh's family and retainers. We sometimes ate together but the sheep's eye was never offered, though raw liver and other delicacies were. Rain during a visit was a good omen and I was often thanked for 'having a wet foot' – somewhat akin to a Roman general being nicknamed 'Felix'.

On trek I not only visited the Nazir, Omda or Shaikh, but would hear any petitions and frequently hold a small local concourse to gather

5 Personal servant.

people's views or explain aspects of Government policy and administration. Sometimes I would sit long into the night talking with the Shaikh and his entourage about almost everything under the sun. Sometimes, too, a dance would be arranged with groups of young men dancing in a line to the accompaniment of drumming, ever increasing in intensity, opposite a line of girls. If invited to participate I often did. The Baggara girls were very good-looking and well shaped with beautiful teeth which made their smiles, framed in chocolate brown faces, extremely attractive. They did not wear veils like the townswomen and often went topless. Their hair, painstakingly woven into small plaits, was dressed with rancid butter; this made their custom of shaking their hair in the faces of male dancers rather less appealing than it might otherwise have been.

Always perforce using Arabic and continuing to study under a local teacher in preparation for the law exams – which involved translation in both directions, reading petitions and an oral – I gradually grew stronger in the language. Nonetheless I have subsequently regretted I did not study the Koran, Islamic culture and the Arabic language itself more deeply and that I was never sent to MECAS – the Middle Eastern Centre for Arabic Studies in the Lebanon. Two years after arrival in the Sudan I took both the Arabic and Law exams in Khartoum and stayed, as I had on first arrival, with John Willie Robertson and his wife Nancy. They were always extremely kind to me. A Scot of great stature and a Balliol man who had also played rugger for Oxford, he was a strong, able and kindly administrator – qualities which led to his becoming Civil Secretary of the Sudan Government during the critical period leading up to Independence and later the last British Governor-General of Nigeria. Celebration with friends after the relief of finishing the exams was such that the sun was high in the sky on the roof of the Robertsons' house when the head *suffragi*, Hamed, woke me next morning saying with quiet but forceful emphasis, 'His Excellency wants breakfast.' Dressing extremely quickly I appeared and tried my best to look alert at the breakfast table. In the event I obtained a distinction in Arabic.

Our hand was light in administration, the task often more diplomatic than directive, for no people can be governed without broad consent unless under overwhelming force. After pacification, however, force was not in the general spirit of the Administration. Nonetheless, as representative of a Government held in great respect, largely for bringing peace and relative prosperity to the country after the terrible

Sudanese losses in Turkish and Mahdist periods, it was common to hear Sudanese say admiringly, '*Wallahi al Hukuma shedida*' – 'By God this is a strong Government.' In fact, we only had some seventy police for a district of 10,000 square miles with 40,000 inhabitants. Our houses at Kosti were never guarded, though a prisoner with a very good conduct record was employed as gardener and allowed to sleep out of the gaol. On one occasion when my cook, who left next morning, was absent through 'illness' – a euphemism for drunk – the *syce* Nuh[6] aided by the 'guaranteed prisoner' rallied to my aid. At the shortest notice they prepared a dinner party for a visiting VIP, who was fortunately neither gourmet nor gourmand.

As administrators we did not have the complication of settlers in any part of the country. One of Kitchener's first acts as Governor-General was to decree that foreigners should not hold land in the Sudan, thus emphasing philosophically that our work was based on a trust for the benefit of the Sudanese, whose ultimate independence was envisaged even then. The question of how long this Trusteeship might last was another matter. I asked three senior officials soon after my arrival when they thought the Sudan might become independent. One remarked it was an extraordinary question for a young man to pose and he had never really considered it; it might take a hundred and twenty years. Another put it at eighty years and the most daring put it at sixty. In fact the Sudan was independent fourteen years after I put the question but, in fairness to the prophetic powers of these devoted officials, the Sudan was at that time very quiet, the people felt involved in the war on the side of the allies and new nationalist manifestations had not begun.

Things were to change rapidly but in Kosti District I saw no signs of desire for early independence, except among a handful of the best educated, the Effendia class. Some years later on the other hand, a British friend, Bill Carden, asked a secondary school boy, when they found themselves cycling side by side from Khartoum to Omdurman, what he would do when he grew up. The boy believed it would be easy to get a job when the British had gone – which he regarded as a shortly to be fulfilled forgone conclusion. He would merely don the uniform of a DC, sit in an office and govern a District as the British did. If he achieved his ambition he no doubt discovered the real implications as well as the family and political pressures to which he could become subject.

---

6 Nuh is the Muslim equivalent of Noah. My *syce* (driver) came from the Hamed, a horse-breeding tribe in the Western Province of Kordofan.

One of the country's two leading religious figures, Sir Sayyid Abdel Rahman – known as SAR – the posthumous son of the Mahdi, spent much of his time on Aba Island on the White Nile in Kosti District. There and on the neighbouring banks of the Nile he had a large cotton-growing scheme irrigated by water pumped from the river. In order to prevent a resurgence of Mahdism, which despite its idealistic origin had earlier brought catastrophe to the Sudan, Sayyid Abdel Rahman and his family had not been permitted, since the earliest days of the Condominium, to travel west of the White Nile, in view of his enormous influence with Western tribes. Some even believed he was the *Nabi Isa* – the prophet Jesus who, according to their belief, was to come as successor to the Mahdi. Aba was therefore a place of pilgrimage for people from Nigeria and other parts of West Africa and some settled there with their families, forgoing the orthodox *Haj* to Mecca. Philip Broadbent and I frequently visited this attractive and engaging man on Aba and from time to time he would come to lunch with us.

The local official community of a District was not large. Of our senior Sudanese colleagues the Mamur was, under the District and Assistant District Commissioners, the senior District Administrator – a very solid citizen, wise through experience though not as highly educated as those who went to school later. The Sub-Mamur was usually younger and a product of the School of Administration – with a tendency to greater polish and knowledge of English. The District Judge had been educated at the Law School in Khartoum and the Kadi, also trained specially for his role, was responsible for the administration of Sharia law in all personal cases involving Muslims. Two doctors, graduates of the Kitchener School of Medicine, made up the local team together with senior officials of the Sudan Government Railways and Steamers Administration, Kosti being the port where steamers began or finished their fortnight-long voyage up and down the White Nile from Juba. The station was therefore an important one on the line between Khartoum and the western terminus in El Obeid.

The District Judge, Mohamed Ahmed Abu Rennat, later became the first Sudanese Chief Justice and a well-known international jurist; the Kadi, Shaikh Ali Abdel Rahman, became the first Minister of Justice in the Government of Ismail al Azhari, the Sudan's first Prime Minister – a disadvantageous appointment in some ways because of his extreme pro-Egyptian nationalist sentiments and actions. All were very agreeable colleagues, however, and Philip Broadbent and I had frequent social contact with them at tea parties, a form of entertainment beloved of the Sudanese, and dinners.

When left in charge of the District I persuaded a member of the rather dreary Kosti Town Band to teach me to play the cornet. Discovering a large store full of unused brass instruments I had them cleaned and tried to play each in turn – from cornet through the euphonium to the trombone. Inquiry also revealed that there were other musicians locally who had played in the brass bands of the Sudanese battalions of the Egyptian army, disbanded in 1924 after the mutiny and murder of the Governor-General and Sirdar of the Egyptian Army, Sir Lee Stack, in Cairo. One such man had fought under Kitchener when, at the Battle of Firka on 7 June 1896, he defeated the troops of the Khalifa Abdullah, the successor to the Mahdi who had died in 1885. These men, all well-trained musicians who read music well, were recruited into the band, who only needed a little inspiration and direction from Philip Broadbent and me to make their playing really lively. The instruments rescued from oblivion shone with polish and attention, and the band appeared proudly in smart new uniforms. Their weekly concert and special performances such as on Empire Day were popular with the public, who enjoyed their repertoire, a mixture of oriental and occidental music. I was very moved on leaving Kosti to find, to my surprise, the Town Band drawn up on the station to play 'Auld Lang Syne'.

A young man's first District would always make the deepest impact on him and I still remember with affection the names and faces of most of the Shaikhs and personalities in Kosti. So my transfer in 1946 to Gedaref District in Kassalla Province in the East at first saddened rather than elated me. In Gedaref I worked under two immensely hardworking District Commissioners but was instructed personally by John Willie Robertson, by then Civil Secretary, not to be intimidated and to keep my head. At first I had a semi-autonomous 'command' as Assistant District Commissioner Butana, the huge plain between the Nile and Athara rivers, largely dominated by the Shukria tribe. Living in Khashm el Girba on the Atbara river, I started a boarding school for the sons of nomadic tribes and organised the first tribal gathering to be held in the area for more than a decade – a combination of Durbar, race meeting and Bath and West Show, with an impressive parade of tribesmen, camels, horses and other animals.

This could have been seem a solitary life but, in constant conversation and contact with the people, I found it absorbingly interesting. I shot for the pot, mainly sand grouse on the Atbara and guinea fowl, which abounded. The nationalist politics in the capital and large cities, which after the war were rapidly gaining significance for the future of the whole of the Sudan, seemed very remote but, after a few months, I was moved into Gedaref, the District Headquarters. I retained a special interest in this Northern area and over the next two years settled the boundary between the Shukria and Batahin tribes whose animosities resembled those of the Montagues and Capulets.

I was also Deputy Chairman of the Rural District Council, in which capacity I was filmed by a visiting news team from England and appeared on the news shown in the cinema at home, much to my parents' surprise. Our main leisure activity was playing polo on rather rough ground. I also taught the police ju-jitsu to minimise the force they used to deal with violent and drunken offenders, and in doing so threw the Sergeant-Major, much to the amusement of his juniors. Other highlights were catching an elderly Shaikh in my arms when he leaped from a moving train on which he had inadvertently stayed too long, and compensating with £E5 an old man who insisted that, as he always created a disturbance when the Governor-General came to Gedaref, he should be temporarily incarcerated for the duration of the visit in return for 'the usual'!

Canon Harper, 'Uncle', came from Khartoum to take a Unity Service – an annual event in Khartoum with all the Christian denominations participating and ranging from the well-known liturgy of the Anglican Church to the strange chanting of the Copts and Armenians. This was the first such service held in Gedaref where the small Christian congregations – mainly Copts, Syrians and Armenians living among a big Muslim majority – were largely Arabic-speaking. 'Uncle' Harper had two translators for the occasion. The first soon got out of phase with the responses and was promptly 'sacked'. The replacement coped admirably until the end of the service, when 'Uncle' with customary benignity expressed his delight about the whole event. He hoped there would be an even larger congregation next time. The translator rendered this: 'His Honour the Priest is angry there are so few people here today,' bringing loud spontaneous shouts from the back of the church, 'No, he's very happy, my brother.'

Both in Kosti and Gedaref I did a considerable amount of magisterial work supervised by the Province Judge. Promoted from second class to first class magistrate, I was to preside, with two Sudanese members of the court, at the trial of serious criminal offences including murders. Presiding at a murder trial was a very heavy responsibility and pronouncing the death sentence, as I had to do several times, awesome.

The full record of such cases had to be submitted not only to the Province Judge but also to the Chief Justice for confirmation or otherwise and, in cases of murder, the Legal Secretary had to make a submission to the Governor-General on whether the prerogative of mercy should be exercised or not. In as many cases as was possible it was.

Growing experience combined with my law degree perhaps prompted the Legal Secretary Tom Creed[7] to invite me to join the Legal Department. His prognosis that I would become one of his successors, though flattering, was frustrated by political events – destroying, incidentally, my faith in detailed career planning for ever. It did not move me that I 'would get away from all that saluting and so on', as I enjoyed my work in the Political Service enormously, but having always contemplated a legal career, I could not look a gift horse in the mouth. I therefore joined the Legal Department in 1947 and this gave me a broader perspective. The three 'funnels' to the Governor-General were the Legal, Civil, and Financial Secretaries, who were represented on every Central Government committee and, sitting on a number of these, I gained some insight into the inner workings of Central Government.

When Sir Robert Howe succeeded Sir Hubert Huddleston as Governor-General in 1948, the two noted religious leaders Sir Abdel Rahman el Mahdi, whom I had known from Kosti, and Sir Ali el Mirghani – known as SAM – called on him. Nominated as the official interpreter on both occasions I was fortunate at a young age to participate in high level talks. It was not until after Independence that I was given a similar role when President General Abboud, who headed the moderate military regime lasting from 1958 to 1965, paid a State Visit to London in May 1964. I knew him well when we served together in the SDF and, by then in the Foreign Office, found myself appointed official interpreter for the formal dinner at Lancaster House given by Rab Butler, the Foreign Secretary. However, President Abboud and Ahmed Kheir, the Sudanese Foreign Minister whom I had first met when he was an Advocate in Kosti, both spoke excellent English and I was able to dine well without being overly taxed.

My first appointment in the Legal Department in 1947 was as Police Magistrate. The cases varied from prostitutes' peccadilloes and traffic offences to serious indictments against politicians and journalists. By

---

7 Later to become the Vice Chancellor of London University.

the late 1940s the political pace was palpably quickening. The Egyptians pressed their claims to the Sudan at the Security Council and the politically aware Sudanese, still very far from the majority, were divided into two broad groups. The Ashigga (Brothers) and National Unionist Party, both closely linked with the Khatmia sect and Sayyed Ali el Mirghani, supported close ties with Egypt. The Umma, believing in the aim of complete independence, were closely associated with the Ansar and Sayyid Abdel Rahman el Mahdi.

Inevitably political passions led some politicians into clashes with the law and I became involved in one capacity or another in a number of 'political' cases. The pro-Unionists were most inclined to trail their coats. On occasion there were large crowds of white-clad figures in the streets outside the court shouting slogans like 'Long live the Unity of the Nile Valley' and 'Down with Imperialism'. There were sometimes anomalies between protest and policing in these situations. A young Sudanese Police officer with a degree might well have been a university student a year before, shouting and shaking his fists in the same sort of crowd as that which he now had to disperse. Sudanese police and those who served in the Administration were labelled the 'Tails of the Colonisers', a designation which at first they found highly amusing, but this verbiage, invented in Communist Russia and eagerly taken up by Egyptian and nationalist propagandists, gradually began to have effect.

In this situation it was perhaps remarkable that all the politicians were at pains to respect – and often to speak out in approval of – the independence of the Judges, British or Sudanese. They sometimes, however, unfairly criticised District Commissioners acting in their magisterial capacity, though the respect for the Judiciary was, perhaps strangely, not diminished by the fact that nearly all the British Judges had previously been in the Political Service.

A group of eleven men, two of whom later became Ministers, appeared before me accused of causing a serious riot at Atbara. The leading accused, Mohamed Nur el Din, was sentenced to six months' imprisonment. At the end of proceedings, he asked for leave to make a statement and then astonished me by thanking me warmly, and clearly without irony, for giving all the accused a 'very fair trial'. Like other Sudanese, he bore no animosity towards British officials doing their duty according to their own lights and I maintained friendly relations with him for several years afterwards. This trial had a curious postscript. Mohamed Kheir Bedawi was one of those convicted. Many years later his daughter, Zainab el Bedawi, became a well-known TV presenter in Britain. and he himself was a BBC World Service journalist. It was he who in the early 1990s urged on me the necessity of strengthening British-Sudanese relations and trying to revive the moribund Anglo-Sudanese Association.

My most notable 'political case' was in July 1949 and it involved Ismail el Azhari, the leader of the Ashigga Party and later first Prime Minister of the Sudan. His co-defendant, Mohamed Amin Hussein, was the editor of a leading Unionist newspaper *Sawt es Sudan* (Voice of the Sudan). Acting on behalf of the Advocate-General, I prosecuted both successfully before a Major Court presided over by the senior Sudanese Judge of the High Court, Mohamed Ahmed Abu Rennat. Both were convicted of having published a seditious libel bringing the Government into 'hatred and contempt' by falsely affirming that the Government had deliberately caused a famine to kill people in the Kassalla Province. Azhari received a gaol sentence of four months and Mohamed Amin Hussein of two. This, however, did not affect my personal relations with them and I exchanged friendly messages with Azhari up to the time of his death several years after Independence.

After my initiation as Police Magistrate in 1947/8 I was moved to other legal duties. As Deputy Assistant Legal Secretary, I was a sort of legal Pooh-Bah working directly to the Legal Secretary, representing him and devilling for his submissions to the Governor-General and other senior administrators. During another period, I assisted the Advocate-General on legal opinions and court work and then became Assistant to the Commissioner of Lands, helping draft legislation and regulations for the control and disposal of Government lands. All the while I was studying for the Bar exams in England.

I passed the Bar finals in 1951 and was called at the Inner Temple. Some months later on 'study leave' in Fountain Court I became the last pupil of Harry Phillimore, later to become a High Court Judge and a Lord Justice of Appeal, before he took silk. I learned much from his clarity of mind and brilliant pleadings. James Comyn, my fellow student at New College, was in the same chambers. The head was Edward Pearce.[8] Another member was Robin Dunn, who also became a Judge of the High Court and a Lord Justice and it was through his kindness that in February 1952 I became Marshal to his father-in-law, Mr Justice (Sir Toby) Pilcher, accompanying him on circuit to Liverpool. The other judges on that Assize were Mr Justices 'Owlie' Stable, William Macnair

8 Later Lord Pearce, a Lord of Appeal in Ordinary.

and Seymour Karminski, a very varied body of judicial talent and wit, from whom I learned much both in court and at table in the Judges' Lodgings.

One afternoon I sat with Owlie Stable when he was trying a civil case of negligence. The plaintiff's claim alleged an unsafe system of work causing him injury because the lowest rung of the ladder on the machine he operated was too high off the ground – two foot six. The Judge, hitching up his red robe and placing his foot on the table in front of him, which was higher than two foot six, exclaimed, 'I can do that easily!' The hearing continued but I do not recall the outcome. Toby Pilcher and Owlie Stable were keen racing men and we were lucky to be in Liverpool for the Grand National in March and to see it from Lord Sefton's box overlooking the Canal Turn. I was uncertain where to place my money but Legal Joy seemed fortuitously appropriate and, backing him both ways, I was well rewarded. He came in second.

When I returned to the Sudan I became Chief Registrar of the Judiciary and Registrar-General of Marriages, which prompted me to write my first book on the complicated nature of permissible intermarriage between different non-Sudanese communities, previously recognised as distinct under the Ottoman system of Millets. Under the Self-Government Statute which came into force on 9 January 1954, the Judiciary was established as a 'separate and independent Department of State', which was also specifically charged with the 'custodianship of the constitution'. My role was mainly administrative and it was to set in place the organisation and regulations necessary to support both the Civil and the Sharia Divisions. I worked first with the Legal Secretary, Cecil Cumings and – when he retired and that office was abolished with the new constitution – with the Chief Justice, 'Wob' Lindsay, who had been my first mentor as Province Judge in the Blue Nile when I was an inexperienced magistrate.

All the British and Sudanese involved were devoted to the principle of the independence of the Judiciary and strove hard to make it work. Sadly it became impossible for this grand design to take shape without being affected by the politics of the time. These ultimately destroyed British participation and, some while after Independence, the whole concept and practice of true judicial impartiality was further attenuated though happily did not die. The pace of events became even more feverish and attempts made to ensure that the Sudanese should enjoy true self-determination were directly affected by Egyptian self-interest in working openly for a Sudanese Government with very close legal ties with Egypt. Though it had earlier been envisaged that the Sudanese would be able to opt to join the British Commonwealth, the Anglo-Egyptian Agreement of 1953 only gave the Sudanese the choice of complete independence or a link with Egypt. The British Government was so eager to sign a treaty with Egypt for wider strategic reasons that many British officials felt the Sudan's interests were not pressed as hard as they, and some Sudanese, would have wished.

Although formal elections in rural areas of North and South were an entirely new phenomenon, the general Parliamentary elections in 1953 under the Self-Government Statute, supervised by an international commission presided over by an Indian, Dr Sukumar Sen, were generally regarded as fair in themselves. The Egyptians, however, had spent very considerable sums to achieve the resulting majority in favour of the Unionist Party, the NUP – a coalition of broadly pro-Egyptian parties. Ismail el Azhari became the Prime Minister and began at once, at the insistence of extremist Sudanisation Committee set up under the Anglo-Egyptian Agreement, to draw up something closely akin to proscription lists of British officials who might 'affect the freedom of choice of the Sudanese at self-determination' and consequently be required to leave the country with compensation. This unfortunately led to a far more precipitate exodus of British officials than occurred in India, former Colonies and indeed Egypt itself.

There was particular concern about the South at this time, especially among the British who had served there and come to love the people, whose way of life remained largely tribal and simple. Missionaries of various denominations had brought Christianity and increased sophistication in many areas as well as providing education, but the three southern provinces were, despite government efforts after the Second World War, well behind the largely Muslim provinces of the North in education, cohesion and experience of the modern world. It was not until 1952, for instance, that a Judge of the High Court was posted to Juba. Southern political groups pleaded that British rule should continue for a further five years in the South in order to enable the Southerners to catch up with the North, but their pleas were swept aside in the turmoil of northern Sudanese and Egyptian politics.

Although Sudanese administrators of very high calibre – invariably Northerners at that stage – were appointed as Governors of the southern provinces, the Southern Sudanese were unhappy and, with the memory of slave trading before the Condominium still unfortunately alive, feared increasing and unsympathetic Muslim influence. In August

1955, shortly after the British officials had left and before Independence, there was trouble in Equatoria and Bahr el Ghazal and the Equatorial Corps of the Sudan Defence Force mutinied at Torit, their headquarters. It was particularly poignant that the Southerners had total faith that the British would come back to sort things out, not realising that the curtain had dropped on British rule. Tragically there has been almost continuous turbulence ever since – a complex pattern of South against North, intertribal and interfactional feuding, and fighting amongst the Southerners themselves. The fears of concerned people in 1955 were amply justified and the continuing plight of the people of the Sudan is particularly distressing to former British officials of the Sudan Administration who loved those people.

The Sudanisation Committee in 1954 turned its attention to the Judiciary, over which their jurisdiction was questionable. Riots had taken place when the first Sudanese Parliament was opened in March 1954, to which Ismail el Azhari had invited General Neguib, the President of Egypt. The Ansar and those opposed to union with Egypt demonstrated against him on arrival and very serious violence followed, resulting in the death of several people including the British Commandant of Police, Hugh McCuigan. A number of cases ensued and in *obiter dicta* the Chief Justice, Wob Lindsay, sitting with the two most senior Sudanese judges, criticised the Government's role in the tragedy. There were two consequences. The Sudanisation Committee recommended the Sudanisation of all the British posts in the Judiciary and the Government responded by issuing a statement criticising the British judges as a body. This criticism was in general terms but so forcible that all the British judges felt it both necessary and desirable to submit their resignations to the Governor-General.

It was hoped that, as a result, the Sudanese could continue to enjoy an independent Judiciary with Sudanese judges free from political interference as envisaged in the Self-Government Statute. I submitted my resignation with my British colleagues, although the Sudanese judges and many others including the Sudanese Bar unanimously wished at least three or four British judges, including me, to stay and serve under Abu Rennat as Chief Justice. Despite pleas, notably from the Sudanese judges and the whole of the Sudanese Bar, Azhari remained adamant, claiming that any reversal of the Sudanisation Committee would cause problems with the Egyptians. We all prepared to leave as our friends and colleagues in the Political Service, Police, Sudan Defence Force and other departments had already done.

Sad farewells were said and the mutual affection between Sudanese and British which survived the political turmoil shone through. When I called on Sayyid Abdel Rahman el Mahdi to say goodbye, he embraced me and said, 'Farewell my son.' Perhaps the hardest parting was from the loyal and ever-cheerful Mustapha. Ironically, however, it was Azhari himself, elected on a pro-Egyptian ticket, who proclaimed the Sudan's complete independence in November 1955 after the withdrawal of most of the British officials. The Sudan was immediately recognised by Britain and Egypt as the first African country to become totally independent on 1 January 1956.

An era had come to an end, but it had been a good one even though the final phase was sadly rushed. For my own part, in addition to the joy and deep satisfaction of working in the Sudan, I redeemed my lack of a Blue by becoming runner-up in the Sudan Open Squash Tournament and reaching respectably late stages of the Open Tennis competitions. I sailed and rode. I sang in the choir in the cathedral and was Honorary Secretary of the Sudan Football Association, in which capacity disputes between clubs caused me more headaches than cases in court ever did. The intensity of passions aroused may be glimpsed from a letter addressed to me marked 'top urgent and rush'! I acted as Honorary Secretary of the Sudan Club and as legal adviser to the Sudan British Officials' Association. I played Napoleon in Shaw's *Man of Destiny* in the Khartoum Repertory and a Sultan in the annual pantomime. I visited Sudanese clubs and played bridge with young Government officials. In the winter delightful girls came out to visit their families and friends and there were many dances. A full, satisfying and enjoyable mode of life had ended and, like all the other British, I had to seek a new career.[9]

9 A fuller account of the author's life in the Sudan is to be found in his book *Sandtracks in the Sudan*.

3
The Foreign Office

The parting from the Sudan and my first chosen career was as painful as the end of a love affair. On leaving I travelled with Jim Treadwell, who had also joined the Judiciary from the Political Service, on a Japanese ship from Port Sudan to Istanbul. The captain was at first disbelieving that we could actually have booked a passage on his cargo ship, the *Asu Maru* of the Nippon Yusen Kaisha Line – NYK. After a while, however, he and his officers warmed to us.

The handful of other passengers also seemed pleased to see us, in particular Mr Quasti, a gnome-like German from the Black Forest. He had lived for many years in Singapore travelling, as he told us in his thick German accent, 'in the musical line' and much enjoying the company of 'taxi girl' dancers in the local bars. The arrival of 'two British gentlemen' on board had, he said, changed the mien of the crew – the Germans' former allies – beyond measure. Before we joined the ship, the food had been 'uneatable' but suddenly there 'was cleaning and sweeping, menus and uniforms'. The British then still clearly carried some clout in the world. The captain even carried out a small act of market research on us, asking how his Japanese whisky compared with the Scotch 'Queen Anna' which the ship also carried.

The *Asu Maru* called at many ports on its fortnight's journey to Turkey. In Jeddah we were met and entertained by an old friend, the Sudanese Liaison Officer Hamed el Sayed, who was to become Ambassador in Saudi Arabia on the Sudan's Independence in January 1956. It would have been a long and complicated process to obtain visas in advance, but Hamed said the Saudi officials were his friends and there would be no difficulty. In the event the procedure to which we were subjected was unusual – perhaps unique. The Customs officer, who did not believe that any Englishmen spoke Arabic, examined us in that language and, pronouncing himself satisfied, courteously admitted us to the country! Thus we saw the old Arab city with its narrow streets, tall houses and beautiful *mashribya* windows, on to which a modern city with entirely different proportions, style of life and architecture was rapidly being grafted.

We jettisoned our 'Bombay Bowlers' in the Red Sea thinking we would never serve in tropical countries again. In fact Jim Treadwell and I followed each other round the world in various hot places for another quarter of a century. We were right in that old 'topees' went entirely out of fashion. When we reached Alexandria we made a nostalgic visit to Cairo and at Latakia in Syria were allowed ashore by a suave young immigration officer, who had initially expressed some fear we might have red diplomatic passports. He need not have worried as the one country in the world not to give its diplomats special red passports was the United Kingdom. However, noting that our ordinary blue British passports stated that we were Sudan Government officials, he welcomed us to Syria as representatives of 'a sister Arab country'. We had time to take seats in a *dolma*[1] to Aleppo, where we stayed, seeing the Id festival at the end of Ramadan and visiting the fortress at Aleppo before rejoining the ship. We were quite sad to leave the *Asu Maru* in Istanbul where I spent a happy two weeks staying with Jim and Philippa Treadwell and met many of her numerous relations – the Whittalls were an English 'dynasty' established for many decades in Istanbul and the Levant – before leaving by the Orient Express for England.

At the age of fifteen I had entertained the remote hope of a career in 'The Diplomatic'. Circumstances had caused me to forget this but a new opportunity now arose. The Foreign Office offered a number of appointments in a competition, as they had earlier to the Indian Service, to members of the Sudan Service – not least perhaps for their knowledge of Arabic. I appeared before intimidating selection committees and was offered a place, but, requiring time to think and considering also the possibility of practising at the Bar or going into the oil industry, I delayed acceptance and travelled. My father received a telegram reading, 'Can you please tell me the whereabouts of your son Donald? Signed Cakebread (Miss).' He furnished my address and telephone number and asked me sternly on the telephone what I had been up to. I then visited the office of the Civil Service Commissioners where an agreeable middle-aged lady official, apprised of my hesitations, said, 'Mr Hawley, you must know what you really want when you wake up in the middle of the night.' I could not tell her.

---

1 A taxi, running as in Turkey between two places, in which you could buy a seat rather than hiring the whole vehicle. In this tightly packed taxi a Syrian fellow passenger inquired very tenderly about a Captain Jones who had been his commanding officer in a locally raised unit during the war. It was a tribute to this officer that the Syrian was certain that we must know him!

On 1 January 1956, however, I joined the Levant Department with responsibility for Jordan sitting by a strange irony in the 'Third Room' at a desk opposite my school friend, Peter Laurence, who was dealing with Israel. Michael Rose was Head of Department and Michael Hadow his Assistant. It was perhaps a parable of modern Middle Eastern politics that an Israeli diplomat asked me out to lunch well ahead of the Jordanian Embassy.

On this same 1 January, the Sudan became the first state in Africa administered by a European power to become independent. The British and the Egyptian flags were ceremonially pulled down at midnight and the flag of the new Sudan – yellow for the desert, blue for the Nile and green for Islam and cultivation – was raised. The first gentle breeze of the 'winds of change' was stirring. This even had some effect in Jordan, my new concern, and in Egypt the revolutionary officers, led by Gemal Abdul Nasser who had expelled King Farouk in 1952, were beginning to show their muscle. Words from Nasser's book *Egypt's Liberation*, published in 1955, did not inspire confidence either in Britain and the West or other Middle Eastern monarchies in view of its tone: 'We removed the former King without consulting anyone because he was an obstacle in the clear path of our caravan. We began our plans for expelling the English from Egypt because their presence here weighs upon us and our progress ...' This Egyptian stirring directly affected Jordan and future Anglo-Egyptian relations.

Central to Nasser's philosophy was the belief that the Arab States had emerged from the Palestinian struggle in 1948 with common bitterness and disappointment that 'imperialism' was imposing a 'murderous invisible siege upon the whole region'. Israel itself had been created by 'imperialism' and all the Arab States had been affected. He had been influenced – perhaps unwittingly – by Soviet propaganda but his proclaimed belief in a common struggle was very popular with the people of the region, if not the rulers, and his portrait was displayed everywhere between the Persian Gulf and the Atlantic. One of the principal vehicles for the spread of Nasser's ideology was the Young Officers' Movement, which became established in many Arab countries.

One of the most prominent in the Young Officers' Movement in Jordan was Colonel Abu Nuwar, the ADC to King Hussein who had succeeded to the throne in May 1953. He was an officer in the Arab Legion, still commanded by Glubb Pasha, a British Arabophile and scholar whose name was a legend. But pro-Nasser nationalist sentiment was not confined to a handful of officers. It was widespread in Jordan, where anti-Israel feeling was stronger than elsewhere on account of the very large influx of Palestinian refugees dispossessed from the new State of Israel. Moreover the State of Jordan at that stage effectively included parts of the former Palestine – the West Bank and the Arab part of Jerusalem, which were held in trust by Jordan 'until the Palestinian case [was] finally solved in the interests of its inhabitants'.

To the Palestinians, and young Jordanians, Nasser appeared to be a possible saviour and his prestige was enhanced when in September 1955 he announced an arms deal with Czechoslovakia which marked the beginning of a process of removing the peoples of the Middle East from the Western orbit. Much jubilation in Jordan followed this announcement and intellectuals – a category much cultivated by Socialist regimes – deputies and young people's organisations of Nablus displayed a banner reading, 'The strength of Egypt is the strength of all Arab peoples who should not expect to acquire strength from the creators and protectors of Israel'.

On the other hand Jordan was still within the British, and hence Western sphere of influence. At the end of the First World War the League of Nations had awarded the mandate to Britain not only for Jordan and Palestine but also for Iraq. Jordan's relations with Britain were governed by the Anglo-Jordan Treaty of 1950. The spirit of the times was changing, however, particularly in view of the perceived threat of Communist USSR to the north. A Turko-Iraqi defence pact was signed on 24 February 1955 in Baghdad and in April Britain terminated the Anglo-Iraqi Treaty to join the Baghdad Pact, thus substituting a multilateral commitment for a bilateral one. This organisation became CENTO, the Central Treaty Organisation, and was joined by Iran and Pakistan as Regional Powers as well as the US.

The Hashemite ruling family of Iraq, very closely related to the Hashemites of Jordan, and the Prime Minister of Iraq, Nuri al Said Pasha, were as friendly towards Britain as Nasser appeared to be opposed. Thus Jordan was at the centre of a tug of war between opposing forces and British and Western policy was to keep Jordan and its young Hashemite King within the 'friendly' camp. For all that, the frequent reference in Whitehall to 'our friends in the Middle East' sometimes made me uneasy as it tended to imply opposition and unwillingness to find a way of coming to terms with the popular tide of Arab nationalism which was rising inexorably and with which I had some sympathy. In the event it was King Faisal of Iraq who was to lose his throne and his head while King Hussein, despite many predictions about his imminent demise, survived by his statesmanship and political acumen. The path to survival was long and thorny.

The Turkish President flew to Amman in 1955 to woo Jordan away from Nasser's alarming policies. Shortly afterwards, in September of that year, General Sir Gerald Templer, the Chief of the Imperial General Staff, headed a delegation for talks in Jordan to amend the 1950 treaty and cover 'the defence of Jordan and the Arab Legion'. Discussions on Jordan joining the Baghdad Pact, however, led to the resignation of Palestinian members of the Jordanian cabinet and intensified political activity by Egypt. Four days of rioting followed in which many elements, including Communist and left-wing groups, collaborated. The Prime Minister Hazza Majali resigned and the Lower House of Parliament was dissolved in December, the King promising new elections. Some argued that Templer's role should have been undertaken by a diplomat but it was certainly the situation rather than Templer's style which affected events.

Jordan was in this turmoil when I joined the Levant Department. Samir Rifai had just become Prime Minister and, on 14 January, the High Court in Amman ruled that the decree dissolving Parliament was unconstitutional. A new bout of serious rioting broke out and order was only restored when Samir Rifai called on the Arab Legion, in which a considerable number of British as well as Arab officers were serving. King Hussein, faced with a thorny dilemma, decided to forestall the sentiments which were taking root amongst his officers and troops by putting himself at the head of the Nationalist movement. He peremptorily and dramatically dismissed Glubb Pasha and the other British officers. It was a very hectic day in the Foreign Office as the reports came in. My Head of Department was impatient when I could not provide the precise number of officers dismissed. No one knew the figure at any particular moment but a Ministerial Statement had to be made in Parliament in the afternoon. I therefore picked the best available guess, stuck stubbornly by it and in the event faced no recriminations.

When Glubb returned to London I took him over to the Houses of Parliament to see the Prime Minister Anthony Eden with Sir Alec Kirkbride, who had been on the panel for my final interview for the Foreign Office. Sir Alec had long been associated with Jordan since serving with Lawrence in the Arab Revolt and was an authority on the country. Similarly Glubb's name had been associated with Jordan for two decades and the British Government, the Foreign Office and the British people were all shocked by his dismissal after his years of faithful service to

Jordan. He himself bore the trauma with dignity and tolerance and was immediately knighted and invested with the insignia of the KCB by the Queen. His advice was naturally much in demand.

Kirkbride asked me how I found the Foreign Office after my Sudan experience. I said it was tough and he told me of his own experience. Having served under the Colonial Office and the Foreign Office, he had concluded that the Colonial Office virtually always said 'No' to every case put up but, if eventually persuaded, followed it through; the Foreign Office, on the other hand, tended to say 'Yes' more readily, but were less reliable in execution. Happily that was not my own subsequent experience in the Diplomatic Service.

Nevertheless I did not enjoy my first few months as much as I might have. It was not because of the people, who were uniformly friendly and helpful, but because in trying to deal with substance I had little time to learn the niceties of procedure in an exceptionally busy department. Simple though important things, such as the difference between blue and white minutes and whether a formal despatch, a Chancery letter or a personal one was appropriate, were initially very confusing if essential to good administration. But I admired the manner in which the ex-Sudan Government entrants were accepted and welcomed, as the ICS[2] recruits had been earlier, without any sign of intolerance.

As for the 'third room' in which I worked, it was Bedlam compared with my large quiet office in the Law Courts in Khartoum, with four of us in a small room interviewing visitors, feverishly making telephone calls, and dictating to a secretary or a machine. Life was doubly busy as Anthony Eden, who had succeeded Winston Churchill as Prime Minister in 1955, annotated as many telegrams as Selwyn Lloyd, the Foreign Secretary, did himself. Each query or comment had to be answered formally. In brief tea or coffee breaks the Arab-Israel question was discussed eagerly amongst the whole department with Michael Hadow, later our Ambassador in Israel, arguing the Israeli case strongly. I learned a great deal and also admired the succinct and clear writing which was the norm, but the learning curve was steep.

Hugh Thomas, now a distinguished historian, was in a neighbouring 'third room' and wrote wittily of his experiences, which matched my own, in *The World's Game*. It was his debut into the literary and historical world but some old 'Office' hands were not amused and

2 Indian Civil Service.

wrote it off loftily – 'Rather a bad book, I hear.' For myself, I was beginning to contemplate trying my hand in practice at the Bar and might well
have resigned if, as the Suez crisis was breaking in August, I had not
moved to the Permanent Undersecretary's Department. There I quickly
carved a more comfortable, if equally onerous, niche for myself.

There were social compensations in Levant Department. When our
Undersecretary Evelyn Shuckburgh's daughter had her coming out
party at the House of Lords, the bachelors in departments he supervised
were all invited. Falling into conversation with a delightful debutante, I
became all too conscious at the age of thirty-five of being what was
charmingly termed an 'Overage Entrant' to the Foreign Office. We discussed Italy and art, especially Florence, Siena, and Venice, and I then
mentioned Rome adding, 'Come to think of it, the last time I was there
they were putting up the decorations for Hitler's visit to Mussolini.'
'Mussolini! My dear,' she retorted brutally, 'we did him in history at
school.'

The new job in PUSD involved liaison with the Joint Planning Staff
(JPS), which had Directors from each of the three Armed Forces. We
wrote numerous papers on NATO, CENTO, SEATO and other subjects such as Aden, the bases for British troops after the withdrawal
from the Suez Canal Zone in 1954, closer integration of the Services
and plans for the evacuation of British communities in virtually every
country in the world in case of emergency. There I represented the Foreign Office at Director and Deputy Director level and so met Mike
Carver, who was Director of Plans for the Army, Denis Spotswood,
Deputy Director of Plans for the RAF, and Roly Gibbs, Deputy Director
Plans for the Army.[3] All three were in very senior positions when later I
became Ambassador to the Sultanate of Oman and my task then was
made easier by my knowing them well. The writing and consideration
of important papers was taken very seriously but a sense of fun and a
very good spirit pervaded the meetings. My role carried the additional
advantage of membership of the Cabinet and Defence Staff mess, where
not only was the food good as well as reasonable in price but there was
a constant coming and going of people at the centre of things.

In August 1956 Nasser nationalised the Suez Canal in response to
the US and Britain withdrawing their financial support for the High

3 All three reached the peak of their professions, Field Marshal Lord Carver becoming
Chief of the Defence Staff, Marshal of the Royal Air Force Sir Denis Spotswood Chief of
the Air Staff, and Field Marshal Sir Roland Gibbs Chief of the General Staff.

Dam at Assuan on which Nasser had set his heart. Planning of the Suez Campaign was entrusted to a special team and not the JPS, though we were cleared to receive top secret information, bizarrely not even available to the Undersecretary in charge of the Middle East. A general air of expectation prevailed. The military build up in Britain and France was impressive, but by October it began to look as if other means of placing pressure on Egypt over international rights of navigation in the Suez Canal, such as SCUA, the Suez Canal Users Association, might succeed.

The US, hawks in August with John Foster Dulles as Secretary of State, changed their tune in the autumn and their inconsistent diplomacy acting like the Eumenides drove Anthony Eden and Pierre Mendès-France, the French Prime Minister, into their tragic and ineffectual course of 'stopping the rot'. A week or two before the Anglo-French strike on Egypt it was clear that something strange was happening, for the Chiefs of Staff went into conclave without the usual support staff. Even John Worsley, Secretary of the Chiefs of Staff Committee and my main contact, was excluded and he, looking through the keyhole, and I with what knowledge I could glean, put our heads together. We pieced together part of the jigsaw but the eventual decision to strike against Egypt to 'separate the combatants' came as a surprise. It was after all Israel which attacked the Egyptians who were on the defensive, but collusion by Britain and France with Israel had not occurred to me. Despite all my security clearances and knowledge of operation 'Musketeer',[4] the first I knew of Britain and France's action was when I bought an *Evening Standard* at lunch time on 31 October.

Earlier, the Directors of Plans had written a paper enumerating the domestic, international and Middle Eastern difficulties which might result from an attack on Egypt – the uncertainty of the Home Front, the possible stance of the US and the USSR and the reaction of Arab nationalists all over the Middle East. The Prime Minister, Anthony Eden, was said to have thrown this paper into the fire. A joint minute written by Derick Ashe and me about likely Arab reaction received similarly short shrift. These papers were, however, sadly prescient and Nasser, despite military defeat, came out the real winner. The Prime Minister ended up in Cato's situation: 'Victrix causa Deis placuit sed victa Catoni',[5] and

4 The plan for the invasion of Egypt in earlier circumstances.
5 'The victorious cause pleased the gods, but the lost cause pleased Cato.'

1956 may be seen by future historians as the determining date to mark the end of the British Empire.

I shared a room first with Philip Mallet, then John Snodgrass and finally Robin Andrew, with whom I had been at New College. Philip Broadbent, who had been my first DC in the Sudan, and his wife Mary were living in London and often invited me to dinner. On one occasion Mary rang me in the office and a voice she took for mine answered, 'Hawley's telephone; Snodgrass here,' to which Mary Broadbent replied, 'If you are Snodgrass, I am the Queen of Sheba!' It says much for Foreign Office *sang froid* that it was not John Snodgrass who revealed this to me.

The Foreign Office dealt with all foreign countries. There was still a separate Colonial Office for the colonies and a Commonwealth Office to deal with the old Dominions and India and Pakistan. The Foreign Office was then entered from Downing Street through a small door under the arch, now shut for a degree of security unnecessary in the 1950s. The lifts, even then not in the first flush of their youth, were the same as today's and bore us creakingly up and down. The main staircase stood in its full grandeur with the broad murals on the first floor outside the Secretary of State's office of Britannia in several guises: Bellatrix, Pacificatrix, Nutrix etc. Ministers' rooms and those of the most senior officials too were still splendid, but much of the office accommodation was cramped, dowdy and even squalid. The Locarno Room – now happily restored – was the abode of hard-working officials (including Douglas Hurd) in small, temporary, partitioned cubicles and the splendid Durbar Court of the old India Office was totally neglected.

Nonetheless it was possible to have a real affection for the FO of those days with its old leather chairs, substantial desks and the odd good or interesting picture on the wall. I formed quite an attachment to the draughty corridors and bare staircases; the lonely-looking statues of kings and queens and of a solitary Gurkha with bayonet fixed; the 'hole in the wall' between the old Foreign Office and the old India Office, into which it had spread; the Ministerial office in the old India Office with its twin doors designed to enable two Indian princes of equal rank to call formally on the Secretary of State for India at the same time; and the messengers in long blue frock coats. My job entailed extensive internal consultations and I moved through the building from department to department with drafts of papers produced by the Joint Planning Staff to collect their views.

A splendid character called Archie – who would have been anathema in less tolerant 'politically correct' days – was not only a wholesale purveyor of unsolicited information about when Chelsea would play at home and other sporting events but also apt to reduce girls momentarily to tears by a bizarre proposal of marriage out of the blue. However, the Foreign Office probably employed more messengers who were incapacitated in one way or another than most Whitehall Ministries and Archie's idiosyncrasies were generally regarded by everyone, girls included, as mere aberrations. Dress was formal and the majority of men wore pinstripe trousers and black jackets rather than dark suits, though both were permissible. Everyone wore a stiff collar and outdoors a bowler or Homburg hat and rolled umbrella were *de rigueur*. I always wore a bowler until 1975 when an American in St James's Park asked me as a 'real Englishman' to pose for a photograph. Balking at becoming a tourist attraction I gave it up. Half the staff of every department worked on Saturday mornings but everyone wore a country suit on that day of the week. Wearing this and a bowler hat we looked like Army officers and were often saluted smartly by confused sentries if we happened to walk through the Horse Guards Arch.

The secretaries attached to a department were known as 'the departmental ladies' and there was also a typing pool, out of which it was possible to extract a secretary from time to time. I gained the impression - and this was confirmed later by a girl friend of mine – that the men requesting a secretary were, as it were, put up for auction. If you had acquired a bad reputation, your chances of getting a good bidder among the girls were slight! One of the pleasures of working in PUSD was that we were privileged to have tea with the exceptionally agreeable and good-looking girls who worked for the PUS and the Deputy PUS, Pat Dean. We still had open fires in winter and from time to time a messenger would come in and throw on more coal. These messengers were also constantly depositing or removing locked red document boxes with the royal coat of arms, in which papers were moved securely from office to office. Officials in the 'third room' kept the keys.

I enjoyed living in London and entertaining in my flat opposite Harrods. A good life for a bachelor, it came to an end all too soon. Personnel Department had plans for me – a posting to the Persian Gulf as HM Political Agent Trucial States with Headquarters in Dubai.

4
The Trucial States

Modernity had barely touched the Trucial States in 1958. The people still pursued an ancient way of life, and I was fortunate to witness this before it all disappeared – with astonishing speed. The seven States now forming the United Arab Emirates (UAE) took their earlier name from the Perpetual Maritime Truce of 1853, a paternal provision designed by Britain to preserve peace at sea during the annual pearl fishery on which local livelihoods then depended. Greek and Roman maps showed the area as the home of the Ikthyophagoi, or fish eaters, and mounds of stinking fish laid out to dry along the beaches were a reminder of this. Eighteenth- and nineteenth-century cartographers marked the area as the 'Pirate Coast' or 'Côte des Pirates' but I was nonetheless surprised to receive a letter in 1959 addressed to 'HM Piratical Agent'. The true title, Political Agent, stemmed from the Indian Political Service, whose officers staffed the British Protected States of the Persian Gulf until 1948, when the Foreign Office assumed responsibility.

The States lie between latitudes 22° and 26° in South-East Arabia and, shaped like a full water skin with internal boundaries resembling a jigsaw puzzle, have an area of 32,000 square miles. The climate is very humid in summer but usually delightful between November and April. In 1958 the total population was only around 180,000 compared with 2.443 million now. There are two distinct regions: an eastern mountain zone and a western desert zone. The mountain zone is roughly fifty miles from north to south and twenty miles from east to west; it forms part of the Hajar range with its high peaks sweeping down in a curve for nearly 400 miles from Ras Musandam in the North to Ras al Hadd in the South – cutting a sort of swathe through the North of the Sultanate of Oman. In places the range falls precipitously into the sea, and some peaks rise to 7,000 or 8,000 feet. The desert area consists of dunes, flat gravel plains and salt flats. Their neighbours are Saudi Arabia to the south, Qatar to the west and the Sultanate of Oman to the east.

Nomadic Bedu tribes lived in the desert interior but throughout history the coast was occupied by seafaring people who, with sailing ships of up to 500 tons, could in the eighteenth century outsail the Royal

Navy. Historically the people shared much common culture with Oman and the area was sometimes known as *Sahl Oman* – the coast of Oman – or 'Trucial Oman'. However, though there was always great respect for the Imam or Sultan of Oman, the Trucial States long had an identity of their own.

Umm al Nar near Abu Dhabi gave its name[1] to an advanced early culture widespread over Oman and the Trucial States. It dated from the fourth millenium BC and its people traded with Mesopotamia, Iran and the Indian sub-continent. They were skilful craftsmen, constructing rounded graves of very fine *ashlar* masonry.[2] They also carved sophisticated images of humped bulls, gazelle and camels suggesting that the camel might already have been domesticated by this early date. Other excavations in the area have revealed that, much later but before the advent of Islam in the seventh century AD, there were churches and monasteries practising the Nestorian[3] rite.

In July 1958 I flew out to the Trucial States via Bahrain, where the Political Resident (PR)[4] had his headquarters, to meet Residency staff, senior Naval and Army officers and businessmen. Charles Gault, a tall soft-spoken man who had started his career in the Levant Consular Service, was Political Agent in Bahrain and Acting PR. He and his lively wife Madge, who had a penchant and talent for amateur dramatics, welcomed me very hospitably in the new Agency, built to replace the building which had startled his predecessor, John Wall, by collapsing as he was quietly having his breakfast.

My predecessor in the Trucial States, Peter Tripp, a friend from Sudan days, had written, 'Bring a hat, as you will be met by a Scouts Guard at Sharjah.' Visions of Arab Boy Scouts flitted briefly across my mind until I recalled that the British-officered Trucial Oman 'Levies' had recently become 'Scouts'. I flew from Bahrain in an old Gulf Aviation Dakota. The heat and discomfort of the journey exceeded anything for which the Persian Gulf's ill reputation had prepared me. A haze hung over the sea like a pall and it looked as hot as it felt. Flying over Das Island and the drilling rig *ADMA Enterprise* I had a first glimpse of the oil operations, which were to change the face of Abu Dhabi and the whole area.

1 Following excavations there in the mid 1950s.
2 There were also elegant houses perhaps closely resembling Gulf homes of much more recent date.
3 A sect named after Nestorius, patriarch of Constantinople in AD 428. He believed that Jesus was two persons: the son of man born of Mary whose human body was the dwelling place of the Logos, the Word, the Son of God.
4 The senior British Representative in the Persian Gulf.

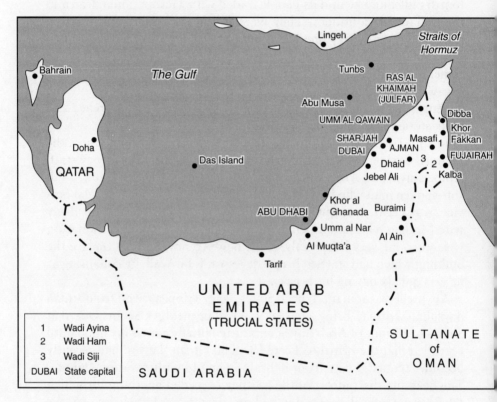

Trucial States, now United Arab Emirates

Shaikh Saif bin Abdul Rahman, Acting Ruler of Sharjah, was waiting on the stark airfield. Slim and genial, with tortoiseshell glasses, he wore customary Arab dress, rifle slung over shoulder and bandolier across chest. The welcoming party also included Peter Tripp,[5] 'Hooky' Walker the Assistant Political Agent, Desmond Bannister the Acting Commander of the Scouts, Alec Kelham who commanded the RAF station and Desmond McCaully, Senior Medical Officer Trucial States. Nearby stood the fort, built in the 1930s to protect air travellers between Britain and India from unwelcome attention by marauding Bedu. There, drawn up for my inspection in front of rusting cannon, was a TOS Guard of Honour, smart and colourful in mottled red and white Arab head-dresses.

Then, after paying a return call on Shaikh Saif, Peter Tripp and I drove in the silver Humber car, with flag flying, over the desert road to Dubai skirting sand dunes and palm plantations. A skyline of tall square wind towers, cunningly devised to catch breezes from every quarter, began to emerge from the haze like a maritime San Gimignano. We crossed the creek dividing Deira from Dubai itself in a graceful *abra*,[6] and I was installed in the Agency, an unimpressively low modern building overshadowed by a huge flagstaff with Union Jack fluttering – slaves still occasionally came to clasp the flag and claim their freedom.

In Dubai itself the *suq* teemed with life. Merchants sat cross-legged in small square shops with goods stacked high around them, occasionally murmuring dictations to a scribe. In the crowded streets Arabs mingled with Persians in gold-brocaded turbans, smooth-faced Indians in *dhotis* and round caps, and Pakistanis in astrakhan caps. Sweating porters man-handled barrows, and donkeys laden with water-tins trotted, bells jingling, ahead of the water-sellers. In the camel park, camels temporarily abandoned by their masters sat hobbled, ruminating and casting disdainful glances around. In some years there were piles of locusts, looking remarkably like mounds of prawns. Much prized by the Bedu who regarded locust swarms as God's blessing, they were a curse to cultivators, whose whole crop could be destroyed in a few hours.

I had to represent British views to the Rulers and the Rulers' views to the Political Resident and the Foreign Office. Although the British Government's main responsibility, stemming in particular from the so-

5 Unusually we were to have a few days' handover together.
6 A small ferry boat, then propelled by oars but now by motors.

called Exclusive Treaty of 1892, was for the States' foreign relations and defence, the Rulers also expected the Political Agent to give general advice and settle disputes between them. There was normally no interference in internal affairs but practices repugnant in a State under formal British Protection were discouraged. For instance a rumour might occasionally be picked up that a convicted prisoner would have his hand cut off or be publicly tied to the cannon outside the Ruler's Palace in Sharjah or in another State, and lashed after Friday prayers. Then the Assistant Political Agent or the Arab Assistant would hasten to see the Ruler or his representative and mention that the Political Agent was certain there could be no truth in what he had heard. The severe sentence was virtually always commuted.

I had a very independent 'command', though subordinate to the Political Resident, with direct responsibility for all seven Trucial States – Abu Dhabi, Dubai, Sharjah, Ajman, Umm al Qawain, Ras al Khaimah and Fujairah. The Political Agent (PA) was known locally as 'Mu'tamad', 'Consul' or curiously 'Balioz'.[7] The British Government was known as the 'Daula' – paramount power – or 'Hukumat Sahib al Gelala' – Her Majesty's Government. The honorific 'Tawal Umrak' – May your life be prolonged[8] – was also sometimes used as a prelude to speaking to the Political Agent or the Political Resident, who was generally referred to as 'Rais al Khalij', the Head of the Gulf, or just 'Fakhamat ar Rais' – His High Presence the Chief. The legacy of the Indian Political Service still remained in other matters such as time, of which three sorts were recognised: Arabic time – 'Tawkit Arabi' - reckoned from sunset; 'Tawkit Ingelesi', local time as reckoned by Europeans; and 'Taim', which implied an obligation to arrive exactly on the dot for an appointment, as the Indian Politicals had required and themselves practised.

As late as 1945, Britain did not intervene directly in wars between the States, unless the Truce was breached in a sea campaign, but in that year Shaikh Rashid bin Said of Dubai, son of the Ruler at the time, led a sea raid against Abu Dhabi, landing at Khor Ghanadha. He was immediately required by the British who adjudged it a 'foul' in breach of the Perpetual Maritime Truce, to withdraw his expedition. This he did, though fighting between the two 'cousinly' States broke out again, this time on land. Similarly Britain did not intervene in the war between

---

7 A term used throughout the whole area perhaps deriving from the Byzantines.
8 Often used in addressing a Ruler or senior member of a Ruling Family.

Dubai and Deira earlier in the 1940s, when solid cannonballs were lobbed from one side of the creek to the other.

It was not considered safe until 1946 for a resident British Political Officer to live on the Trucial Coast though a 'Residency Agent' of local origin had been based in Sharjah since the early nineteenth century. General peace had been maintained by the diplomacy of visiting British political officers and the Royal Navy. Three frigates of the Loch Class were still based in Bahrain in 1958 under a commodore and paid frequent visits.

The pattern of such visits varied little. The Captain called on the Ruler and PA, and the Ruler gave a traditional Arab lunch for the crew. With British respect for tradition, the visitors enjoyed eating on the carpeted floor and many felt disappointed when tables and chairs appeared for the first time. Football matches between ships' crews and local teams were followed by a cocktail party on board. When the one US ship based in Bahrain came from time to time there was always an admiral on board. As the US Navy is 'dry', he could not throw a party with alcoholic drink on board, but we allocated special beach areas in consultation with the Rulers for American crews to enjoy drinks parties ashore.

The formation in 1951 of the British-officered Trucial Oman Levies – later Scouts – revolutionised security on land. Warfare between States virtually ceased. This force, constituted under the Political Resident's authority, was under my local political direction and my relationship with the Commander, Stewart Carter, was close and friendly. A tall Sherwood Forester with bristling moustache and aquiline nose he looked, under his red and white Arab headdress, like his own men and even kept hawks as the local Shaikhs did. The Scouts patrolled everywhere and were also involved in supporting the Sultan's Armed Forces in Oman. They did not, however, operate in the capital towns without the Ruler's agreement, though Stewart Carter himself and other senior TOS officers like Tim Budd and Peter Chubb often frequented Rulers' *majlises* to cultivate good relations. These two were former bimbashis in the SDF and their knowledge of Arabic was a special asset.[9] Otherwise British military involvement locally remained light and, though the RAF Station at Sharjah housed a small detachment from a cavalry regiment based in Aden, no further deployment of troops was necessary.

9 Roy Watson, who later commanded the force, had also been in the Eastern Arab Corps of the SDF when I was in Gedaref, and John Pott too had served in the SDF.

The Brigadier in Bahrain had only a very tiny staff and overall command of British Forces and operations was exercised by the Air Officer Commanding in far-away Aden, Air Vice-Marshal Maurice Heath.[10]

Every Ruler seemed convinced that there was a sea of oil under his State and a close relationship with the oil companies was therefore also essential. Oil exploration by Petroleum Development Trucial Coast (PDTC), a company with the same structure as the Iraq Petroleum Company, as well as Abu Dhabi Marine Areas (ADMA) largely owned by BP, was already arousing hopes of a future bonanza.

Such was the local scene. 1958 was, however, still a period of ferment in the Middle East. Two years after the Suez debacle, Gemal Abdel Nasser's star was at its apex and his picture hung in shops in every local market. Describing the Arab world as stretching from the 'Persian Gulf to the Atlantic Ocean', his call to Arab nationalism was spread by the new but ubiquitous transistor radio; Cairo Radio and 'Sawt al Arab', with their strong 'anti-colonialist' bias, could be heard everywhere. A small Arab girl on the beach at Khor Fakkan even advised me to 'watch out or Abdel Nasser will get you'!

In Lebanon there was civil war, caused by internal rivalries and differences of opinion about Nasser, and in February 1958 Syria joined with Egypt to form the United Arab Republic. Nasser and the UAR remained hostile to King Hussein in Jordan and to Iraq's participation in the Baghdad Pact Treaty and CENTO.[11] Britain's paramount influence in the Middle East generally had been undermined by growing USSR and US involvement after Suez, and French influence over the three Maghrab countries – Morocco, Tunis and Algeria – was likewise weakened. In Algeria the last battle was being fought out between Algerian nationalists and the French, who stubbornly maintained that Algeria was a *Département* of metropolitan France.

Arab nationalism not only mesmerised the Arab world but also liberal opinion in the West. The 'serious press' in London were convinced that the conservative Arab regimes of Saudi Arabia and the Gulf could not long survive the force of Arab nationalism and, like the monarchies

---

10 Later Duncan Sandys, the British Defence Secretary, increased the status of the Commander by two ranks – and the consequent size of the military establishment – by appointing an Air Chief Marshal, Sir Sam Patch, who personally thought that the appointment was extraordinary, as overall Commander in Aden.

11 Iraq, Iran, Turkey, Pakistan, the US and Britain were by then members. The alliance became the Central Treaty Organisation in 1960, the headquarters having been transferred from Baghdad to Ankara in 1958 after the Iraqi Revolution.

of Jordan and Iraq, were ripe for a fall. In one respect only was this view proven correct. On 14 July, four days after my arrival in the Trucial States, news of the Iraqi revolution reached me when I was sitting with a group of local people. There was some initial elation, but quick realisation that the tragic murder of King Faisal II, who had paid a State Visit to Britain earlier in the year, and the Prime Minister Nuri al Said, a towering figure in Middle East politics for forty years, had very dangerous implications.[12]

I felt after only a few days in the Trucial States that the prophets of doom were wrong in their analysis. These small traditional Shaikhdoms seemed to possess an unusual stability rooted in the Rulers' open *majlis* and a general tolerance in society. Nasser's message moreover had less practical effect than emotional appeal among people principally concerned with their immediate affairs – agriculture, animals, seafaring, fishing and trade. Thirty-five years later, it is the traditional Arab societies and States which have remained the most stable, perhaps because, like bamboo scaffolding in Asia, a seemingly rickety structure has been able to sway with the wind and so maintain its strength.

The fortunes of Britain and the Rulers were closely bound together. This had some complications. Anti-British manifestations in Bahrain earlier in the year had led to the Foreign Secretary, Selwyn Lloyd, being stoned. A number of Bahraini nationalists, whose activities had got out of hand, had with the approval of the British Government been exiled to St Helena by order of Shaikh Sulman bin Khalifa, the Ruler. In circumstances not unlike those in Jordan when Glubb was dismissed, the Ruler's British Adviser since 1926, Sir Charles Belgrave, had to withdraw, a sad blow for the man chiefly responsible for establishing a good educational system and a sound government structure there. Nonetheless the personal friendliness of the Shaikhs and people in the Trucial States, as well as their apparently willing adherence to the long-standing official relationship based on the treaties, made a deep impression on me. It seemed to augur well for the future.

Hooky Walker and Julian Walker, both destined to become Ambassadors, worked with me.[13] The former was Assistant Political Agent and a first rate right hand man. The latter was known as 'Walker of the Boundaries', because his job was to determine the borders of the various States, a role in which Martin Buckmaster also played his part. It

12 The British Embassy was burnt down and the Military Attaché shot.
13 Ian Winchester and his wife Shirley came to replace Hooky Walker in 1960.

was a vital task as oil companies could have no confidence in concessions without the certainty of fixed boundaries. It was also exacting as it involved much desert travel and negotiation with local Shaikhs and tribesmen. The result was inevitably a 'squiggly' cartographer's nightmare, but a fair degree of certainty and consequent stability was nevertheless achieved.

The British Community in 1958 and 1959 was tiny. My small dining table could accommodate either all the British in Dubai or the heads of every British institution in the Trucial States. There were only about five or six wives including Jill Huntingdon, who arrived aged seventeen as Robin Huntingdon's bride. Their first home was a palm frond hut, a '*barasti*', on the British-funded Agricultural Trials Station near Ras al Khaimah, from which Robin kindly brought me vegetables from time to time. For meat I depended on supplies from the weekly BI[14] steamer. Another bride was Margaret Worsnop, whose husband Edric set up the Agency's Commercial Office in Dubai after a spell in Abu Dhabi. There were no single girls but all the girls in the Bahrain Residency were permitted to come down for a Ball given by the TOS officers on 27 March 1959. This resulted in two marriages and I conducted the Consular ceremony for Glynne Jones, the BP Representative, and his wife Vivienne.[15] Peter Chubb also met his wife Gilly on that occasion.

Before oil began to flow, the States had only very small revenues and these had been adversely affected by pearling's decline. Britain, therefore, financed a Trucial States Development Scheme and this involved preparation of annual estimates and administration of the funds under the general direction of the 'Trucial Council'.[16] Founded in 1952, this brought the seven Rulers together twice a year. I usually presided but the Political Resident sometimes opened the session with a policy speech. Mutual courtesies were impeccable but at first the Rulers were rather reticent in speaking, preferring to deal with the Agency bilaterally. Nonetheless a formal agenda did lead to general debate about hospital and medical services, technical training, locust control and agriculture.

There were other concrete results. The postal service in the Gulf, run by the British Post Office, issued British stamps overprinted with Indian rupee denominations, but the Rulers were offered – and approved – a special Trucial States issue featuring their sources of wealth: *dhows*,

14 British India Line.
15 Vivienne Avery.
16 Later called 'Trucial States Council'.

date palms and pearls. In the event these stamps were not in circulation for long as the States began to issue their own, and they have now become collectors' items. Thus the Trucial Council for all its limitations was the embryo of the United Arab Emirates federation formed in 1971.

Medical services were provided by a handful of Indian and Pakistani doctors under a very colourful character, Lieutenant Colonel D. G. McCaully OBE, IMS (Rtd) – to give him his full title. He would go anywhere at any time of any day or night and was well known and almost revered by the Shaikhs and their families. A man of immense size, generosity and kindness, he had his foibles, was as conscious of protocol as any Indian official could be, and regarded himself as second only to the Political Agent in precedence. All newcomers had to call on him formally before he even recognised them and a letter addressed without his full title and decorations might be returned! His parties were memorable, however, and expected to last well into the next day. Once in the small hours he tried to tempt me to stay longer by saying, 'Let's have one more record. Er, shall I play *The Ring*?' To ensure that other guests did not leave as he saw me off, he locked them into his house.

The larger budget I obtained in 1960 for the Trucial States Development Fund included a touring doctor's post. Shortly afterwards, an Omani doctor with a sad tale came to see me. Dr Asem Jamali was the first qualified Arab doctor in the whole area, but on returning to Muscat he had found no job in his own country. He wondered if he might fare better in the Trucial States. His unexpected appearance was the answer to prayer and he was immediately engaged to fill the new post. He remained in the Trucial States until Qaboos became Sultan in Oman in 1970 and thereupon became the first Minister of Health there.

An era came to an end on 10 September 1958 when the Ruler of Dubai, Shaikh Said bin Maktum, CBE, died. He had been Ruler since 1912, though his eldest son Shaikh Rashid had been Regent for some years. That morning was grey and sticky and the condensation ran down the windows in slow trickles. Shortly after 7 a.m., the burly figure of Desmond McCaully appeared at my house – a little dishevelled, his usually impeccable white 'Gulf Rig' creased and dirty. He announced he had been up all night with Shaikh Said who had just died.

Not long afterwards Ali Bustani, the Arab Assistant, arrived to say the funeral would be at 9 o'clock that very morning, it being a sign of respect that the burial be rapid. With others from the Agency I drove to Shaikh Said's house on the creek side, outside which silent crowds of white-clothed people sat quietly on rough wooden benches or stood in the shade. All exchanged the greeting 'May God give you consolation' as the Ruler's death was regarded as a personal family loss. On the creek *dhows* swayed gently with the tide. Suddenly the crowd stood. A woman set up a high-pitched wail and white-robed men carried the body, swathed in red chequered cloth, out on a rough bier. The mourners set off on foot and Shaikh Rashid and his brother, Shaikh Khalifa, in simple white robes and no cloaks, walked amongst the crowd. Women in black clothes standing at each street corner set up fresh waves of wailing and from time to time the cortège stopped while passages from the Koran were read. It was incredibly hot and sticky on the long dusty walk to the cemetery, where mourners threaded their way through graves and little tufty bushes, before halting near the simple family grave. After the burial the local people took leave of Shaikh Rashid kissing him in customary fashion on the nose. It was a ceremony made the more moving by its simplicity.

Next day I called on Shaikh Rashid to convey official condolences on behalf of the Secretary of State for Foreign Affairs, the Political Resident and myself. He was alone except for his eldest son, Shaikh Maktum who, then about eighteen, was making his first formal appearance. Coffee was served in small round cups but little said, almost complete silence being usual on such occasions. Shaikh Rashid handed me a letter as I took my leave and as the car headed homeward I opened the crinkly envelope. It contained a letter neatly typed in Arabic on white paper, headed 'Government of Dubai' in red letters. Signed by Shaikh Rashid it simply read: 'After greetings, I have the honour to inform you that on the death of my father I have assumed the Rulership of Dubai. Please accept my highest respects.'

On 4 October Bernard Burrows, the Political Resident, arrived in Dubai on HMS *Loch Insh* to convey the British Government's official recognition – his last act before leaving the Gulf. In white tropical uniform and white Wolseley helmet, I went out on my launch to meet him and we left for the shore with the Captain, Nigel Matthews. The sea was exceptionally calm which augured well for the forthcoming ceremony, and the Agency *jalbut* with the Political Resident's flag flying came slowly up the creek with its sweeping curve like the Grand Canal in Venice in reverse. The air was bright, and the blue and green of the water particularly lovely.

At the Ruler's Palace a guard of honour of Dubai Police was drawn up and Shaikh Rashid, his grey-bearded uncle Shaikh Guma'a and other close relations came forward to shake hands. We passed the double wooden gates and climbed the winding stairs to the broad verandah overlooking the creek. It had been transformed with green canopies overhead, fine rugs covering the floor and balustrade and red and white Dubai flags. A life-size photograph of the new Ruler adorned the wall above the seats of honour, where the Rulers of the other Trucial States were already seated. The concourse of notables sitting expectantly in Arab and national dress was such that it seemed the verandah might not bear the strain. As the Ruler entered, all stood and we took our seats in the middle. Orange squash and coffee were served and we all stood again to observe a minute's silence in Shaikh Said's memory.

Bernard Burrows made a speech of congratulation to Shaikh Rashid in Arabic and handed him a formal letter of recognition, at which moment HMS *Loch Insh* fired a five-gun salute. Unfortunately only those with exceptionally acute hearing heard it as the ship was a mile off shore and the wind adverse! Shaikh Rashid, shy on ceremonial occasions, rose and handed a formal a letter of reply to the Political Resident after which Shaikh Maktum delivered a short but sincere speech on his father's behalf. It invited the people's co-operation and assured them that he would always work in their interests. Saif bin Ghurair, a young member of the Bani Yas tribe, rose to express the people's loyalty – a specially significant contribution as his father had only recently returned from exile. The Jordanian Supervisor of Education acting as Master of Ceremonies followed him and, holding the microphone like a modern pop star, spoke with considerable hyperbole of the Ruler's 'coronation'. It was the genuine affection of the people for Shaikh Rashid, however, that was the most significant impression of this happy occasion.

Amongst the States, Dubai was readiest for change and Shaikh Rashid set out to develop it rapidly, using funds largely gained from successful merchant ventures including gold exports. He took advice, placed implicit trust in those chosen to execute his plans and, rising every morning at 5 a.m., followed every detail of progress on each successive scheme. I had a sincere regard for this remarkable man and our relations were very close. He was the most intelligent man without formal education I have ever met. On 11 October 1958 Shaikh Rashid told me, spontaneously and much to my surprise, that he 'always wanted to consult me about everything' and, putting this into practice, he would sometimes arrive at the Agency unannounced if some new idea had occurred to him. On these occasions a little ritual with his tiny pipe, '*midwakh*', had to be gone through. Sitting down, he reached into the fold of his garments for an old aspirin bottle, from which he took a plug of strong tobacco grown in his own garden near Ras al Khaimah. After a pull or two, the pipe was empty, the room full of smoke and general conversation could begin. There was plenty of humour in our relations and Shaikh Rashid, a merry man with twinkling eye and impish sense of humour, chided me constantly for not being married. I retorted by asking why as a Muslim he only had one wife, to which he replied with a laugh that one was 'quite enough'.

In January 1959 Cairo's *Ahram* strongly criticised the Trucial States Rulers and the Agency, claiming that I and the other Political officers talked to them 'daily'. I was indignant, though my diary does confirm that contacts were indeed very frequent. My service in the Sudan seemed to have given me itchy fingers to help modernise the area and in this I was encouraged by some younger local people. It was a heady time and a girl friend with whom I corresponded accused me of becoming pompous. My diary noted, 'She is dead right.'

Shaikh Rashid was a true Merchant Prince and from his Palace he looked out over his customs area and the beautiful creek. Beauty was not enough; Dubai's commerce depended on its creek. Its mouth was by 1958 nearly silted up and there was danger of sand closing it for ever like other creeks along the coast, on which prosperous towns had once stood. To prevent this the civil engineering consultants, Sir William Halcrow, were appointed by HMG to solve the problem.[17] The contractors appointed to implement Halcrows' report were the Austrian Kuwaiti Company, whose task was to increase the scouring effect by dredging and erecting piling along both banks. One night when work was well under way an exceptionally heavy 'hundred year' storm silted the mouth of the creek again. It was a very nasty moment and at a midnight meeting in my house with Harry Ridehalgh, Halcrows' senior partner, Shaikh Rashid demanded a foolproof solution. Ridehalgh said no engineer could guarantee one, but he recommended extension of the planned piling seawards, pledging his belief that this would work successfully. Shaikh Rashid accepted his assurance. The plan worked and much of Dubai's subsequent prosperity stemmed from this crucial decision.

The British Bank of the Middle East, BBME, had a monopoly of banking in Dubai. It had a predominant position both in the Trucial States and Oman and became the 'university of its time' as the training

17 And curiously I signed the contract on behalf of the Ruler.

ground for many young men, later to reach positions of influence in governments and the private sector. It had one British rival, the Eastern Bank, later absorbed into the Standard Chartered, with a branch in Sharjah. Neville Green[18] was Manager and every three months, regular as clockwork, he came to request permission to open up in Dubai. This I could not grant, having no power to break the monopoly. Nonetheless the constant dripping of water on stone with the Ruler as well as the Agency, combined with general expansion of commercial activity, later led Shaikh Rashid to permit the Eastern and other banks to open their doors as Dubai's economy expanded.

I often walked round the *suq*s chatting to the merchants in Arabic, and taking tea, coffee or Coca-Cola with them. In this way I heard people's views at first hand and enjoyed observing a mercantile community trading as their forebears had for hundreds, if not thousands, of years; and savouring the delicious smells of the ubiquitous spices. Even the most prominent merchants, Ghurairs, Futtaims, Awais and Awazis, did their business from shops only a few yards square. They were frequently accompanied by their sons, the very people who have since developed the distinguished modern buildings of modern Dubai. Few except the genial gold-toothed Hassan Abdul Latif, Abdul Rahman Arif, Ghaffour Awazi and Hussain Abdul Rahman[19] spoke English.

I kept an open door and many local people called informally, including merchants and leading members of the Bani Yas constantly in Shaikh Rashid's *majlis*. Visitors included a member of the ruling family, Ebeid bin Guma, who often pressed me for a full British passport instead of the British Protected Person's passport, to which he was entitled as a Trucial States subject. An unusual number came spontaneously to offer congratulations and thanks to HMG in 1961 when Iraq's threat to invade Kuwait was averted by British troops. For the most part, however, conversation was merely about local affairs. One prominent citizen, Khansahib Hussain, who had himself served the British Government in the past, came frequently, dressed in a long brown robe with an impressive white and gold patterned turban, to discuss the local scene, often bringing his nephew Hussain. An old man, he had clear recollections of his younger days and loved to recount how he had originally come to the Trucial States. When working as a pilot on the Shatt

18 Neville Green was also Chief Executive of the Chartered Bank in Malaysia during my time there in the 1970s.
19 Now the head of the large construction concern founded by his uncle Khansahib Hussain.

al Arab, no less a personality than Sir Percy Cox, then High Commissioner in Iraq, had 'sent' him to work with his uncle in the British Residency in Sharjah. He had said, 'Sir Percy Cox,' – which he pronounced as a single word – 'I will go.'

Apart from the Shaikhs and merchants, there were three influential people. They all spoke fluent English – then an extremely rare skill. Ali Bustani, the Agency's own Bahraini Arab Assistant, gave me much good advice and was a very useful go-between with the Rulers and other people of consequence. Mahdi Tajir, also a Bahraini, became Director of Customs in 1956. Though not a local man he was very clever and persuasive and became influential in Shaikh Rashid's counsels, though his dealings were disapproved of by some prominent people. Later, numbered amongst the world's richest men, he was a very big investor in Britain, owning *inter alia* the Highland Spring mineral water business. At the same time he became the UAE's first Ambassador in London, a function he exercised in rather unorthodox style, having only minimal contact with his diplomatic colleagues.

Easa Gurg, the senior local executive of the BBME, was a Dubai man and also destined for fame. In Shaikh Rashid's inner counsels, he sometimes conveyed informal messages emanating from the Ruler. Something too of a 'Young Turk' or 'Angry Young Man' he waxed eloquent on his own ideas and constantly urged swifter development and governmental progress, always putting his case very politely. I did not then foresee that Easa would become a very successful Ambassador to the Court of St James's, the owner of highly successful and well-managed businesses, a major investor in international companies and a prize-winning farmer in Essex. Already, however, he was demonstrating in fluency of speech and strong conviction a remarkable personality, and his enthusiasm for change fully justified his later appointment as Director of Development in the Trucial States.

Easa, like other English speakers, was a frequent guest at my house – particularly when there were non-Arabic speaking visitors - and his future wife, Soraya, was another. Soraya promised, if and when I married, to give my wife a sari but it was many years before she met Ruth. Then, immediately recalling her earlier promise, she redeemed it by presenting a length of beautiful silk cloth.

Despite what Mahdi Tajir had achieved as Director of Customs, the administration of the Port of Dubai was not satisfactory and Shaikh Rashid established a strong Port Committee, to co-ordinate administration. I drafted the constitution. As there were no maps of Dubai,

Shaikh Rashid authorised an aerial survey by Hunting Air Services, who produced maps enabling John Harris, a talented architect and planner who walked every inch of Dubai, to draw up the development plan – the basis for all future town planning. This done, a Lands Department was founded under Shaikh Maktum bin Rashid to settle the ownership of land and establish a registry of title to specific plots tied accurately to the maps and plan.

Before this, banks were inhibited from making loans on freehold property as title deeds were vague and not adequately defined. When title became certain and secure, immediate impetus was given to economic activity. The expert input came from Ahmed Adam, a Sudanese who had worked with me in the Legal Department. He came to Dubai after I visited Khartoum, with Shaikh Rashid's blessing, to obtain agreement from my old friend Mohamed Ahmed Abu Rennat, the Chief Justice, to second him. Shaikh Rashid was delighted with his vigour and told me admiringly that Ahmed 'worked like a *shaitan*'![20]

The Municipality, of which Ali Bustani was part-time Executive, needed to be formalised. My Khartoum visit was therefore also an opportunity to seek the Sudan's help over this. I called on the Minister of the Interior, Bimbashi Mohamed Ahmed al Bahari, who was in my battery in the war, and Ali Hassan Abdulla, the Permanent Undersecretary, a former colleague in the Administration. They responded immediately and a Sudanese Inspector of Local Government visited Dubai to make a report, which Shaikh Rashid accepted. I then helped draft a new Municipal constitution[21] and a formally constituted Dubai Town Council was set up under the respected chairmanship of a leading merchant, Ali bin Awais. To serve this the Sudan Government also seconded Kemal Hamza[22] as town clerk to set the ball rolling for a year. *Rien n'endure que le provisoire* and in 1999 he was still in Dubai having served the Municipality as Director for over twenty-five years. He was succeeded by Abdul Ghuffar Hussain, a local man who also served the Municipality from its earliest years.

It was an odd, but for me very satisfying, situation that in all these matters Shaikh Rashid had specifically made me 'plenipotentiary' to get

20 Devil.
21 I was building on work in the Municipality instituted earlier by my predecessor, Peter Tripp.
22 Previously town clerk in Wadi Halfa.

things done and, unlumbered by bureaucracy, he paid the modest associated costs without the Agency or me having to handle any monetary
transactions. The Residency and Foreign Office gave me invaluable
support in all this.

In 1958 Dubai had no electricity, apart from a few small private gen-
erators. The British Middle East Development office in Beirut recommended Kennedy and Donkin as consultants and Shaikh Rashid
appointed them to supervise the design and installation of a power
supply, which was in place by 1961. A limited company with State and
private capital seemed to be the best means of funding a general supply
and with Col Kelly, the Manager of the BBME, I drafted the memorandum and articles of the Dubai Electricity Company, in the form of a
Charter granted by the Ruler. This became the first company to be
incorporated in Dubai under local law and was chaired by Shaikh
Rashid personally. Similarly there was no telephone system in 1958 and
our letters had to be delivered by messenger. This old-fashioned and
peaceful era was, however, ended in the cause of progress. A British
company, IAL, under the inspiration of Sidney Hodge, took shares with
the Ruler and a number of merchants in the Dubai Telephone Company
and thus the first telephone system was established.

There was no piped water and the town was supplied by cans
brought in on donkeys. The first modern supply was provided by the
generosity of Shaikh Ahmed bin Ali Al Thani, the Ruler of Qatar who
married Shaikha Miriam, Shaikh Rashid's daughter. The Water Engineer brought in then, Eric Tulloch, was still in Dubai in 1999. I advised
Shaikh Rashid that the Municipality should from the start keep detailed
maps and records of where the major services, water, electricity and
telephone cables ran and this was made the responsibility of the Municipal Engineer's department.

Dubai had no airport in 1958 and Sharjah, twelve miles away, served
the whole area, combining facilities for the RAF and civilian aircraft.
Shaikh Rashid, pressed by his merchants who resented having to pay
tax on their gold imports at Sharjah, wanted an airport of his own –
only a small one, 'just large enough to take Doves and Herons'. Previously it had been suggested in a British report that there was nowhere
suitable very close to Dubai itself but, when I relayed this to Shaikh
Rashid, he said, 'May God prolong your life. What about the place
where the RAF used to land during the war?' This enabled me to persuade the Residency and the Foreign Office that we neither could nor
should stand in his way, and Shaikh Rashid and I signed a formal Civil

Air Agreement in 1959 on behalf of our respective Governments. Shaikh Rashid then pleaded successfully for the airport to be large enough to take Viscounts. Costains were awarded a design and construct contract for both airport and terminal and it was opened in 1960. I remain proud to have been associated in these ways with the early development of a place which has grown and prospered so remarkably.

In one aspect, however, I failed. In the late 1950s Kuwait, Qatar and Egypt financed modern education in Trucial States schools and most teachers came from Egypt, though there were also Syrians, Palestinians and Jordanians. Apart from teaching the 'Three Rs', they quickly effected one particular change in local usage. On first arrival they were horrified to find that the ordinary local word for a donkey was *Misri*, which means Egyptian, and to see men and boys driving them with the cries of '*Heh, Ya Misri!*' This usage may have derived from a particular type of donkey, perhaps Egyptian donkeys introduced into Arabia by Ibrahim Pasha during his invasion of Arabia in the nineteenth century. Whatever the explanation, schoolchildren were authoritatively taught not to use this word and that the correct word for an ass was '*Humar*'!

The teachers needed visas from the Agency. These were unhesitatingly given but, when the heads of the teachers' delegations paid me a courtesy call every year, I did urge them to stick to teaching and not to involve themselves in political propaganda. They always assented politely but, nonetheless, were unable to prevent an element of political indoctrination creeping into both the syllabus and other activities. For instance the school Boy Scouts, drilled by the teachers for the annual sports day, which was more of a parade than sporting occasion, would march round chanting slogans behind a large painted figure of a 'struggling Algerian'.

Leading local people told me they wished their children to be given a sound education rather than be indoctrinated. This led me to suggest that the Rulers should engage their own Trucial States Director of Education to co-ordinate the various educational missions' work and Shaikh Rashid was persuaded to appoint one for Dubai as a first step. After I had approached the Sudan Government yet again, an educationalist of high calibre, Banaga el Amin, was seconded. Though he made a very good impression with the local Arab families, his appointment was seen as a threat and was strongly resisted by the non-local teachers. Shaikh Rashid was thus placed in an awkward predicament, heightened when the Egyptian Government sent a special delegation to persuade him to annul the arrangement. Banaga was therefore unable to function properly and returned to the Sudan. Politics is the art of the possible and in this case my advice to Shaikh Rashid, intended in the public interest, proved a step too far.

Meantime the prospects for oil wealth in Abu Dhabi, the largest State, grew increasingly good and by 1959 it was clear that oil would be produced commercially on land and sea. In 1958, however, Abu Dhabi was still a very poor place, having been in decline since the end of the pearling trade a few years earlier. Many houses were simply *barastis* built of palm fronds, and people suffered considerable hardship when in 1960 a combination of very heavy rain, high tides and north winds left the town flooded. Shaikh Shakhbut, the Ruler, appealed for help and the Royal Navy came to the rescue, pitching tents on the shore to give the people shelter.

Though there was a Political Officer in Abu Dhabi, the Political Agent had overall responsibility and I used to visit this then rather moribund town for several days every month. Martin Buckmaster was succeeded by Edward Henderson as PO and both were legendary figures in the area, Buckmaster being known to the tribesmen as 'Hamad' and Henderson as 'Bin Hender'.[23] On one typical visit to Abu Dhabi, I set off from Dubai early in the morning when it was pleasantly cool and crisp even in summer. When the tide was out we drove along the firm sand of the beach for several miles before striking inland. The tiniest of waves edged the shore with a silvery thread, contrasting with the deep, fresh blues and greens further out. Small graceful wooden boats, in which fishermen were tidying their nets, lay off shore every few hundred yards, their shape – with high tapered sterns like large immovable rudders – suggesting great antiquity of design. The brown naked bodies of the fishermen and little groups of children playing in the shallows brought life to the stillness and the early morning sun gave the scene an ageless, timeless quality.

Above the beach there was a sandy plateau in which there were innumerable broken shells, indicating that in past ages it had been under the sea. The square *barastis* of the fisherfolk stretched out along the coast and behind these there were rows of date palms. Leaving the beach, we drove over rolling dunes of clean, white sand to reach the main road – a dull highway, crossing gravel plains, sandy wastes studded with camel

23 He would have become Political Agent when later the Agency was separated from Dubai had he not developed trachoma. Edric Worsnop and Oliver Miles also held the post during my time for short periods.

thorn and scrub, passing an unimpressive elevation grandiosely called 'Jebel Ali'. Here and there strange shapes left by wind erosion stirred the imagination.

The approach to Abu Dhabi was difficult. In winter, the *shemal* – a strong north wind – brought the sea in over the low salt flats and, especially after rain, water stretched for miles, as far as the eye could see. The track suddenly disappeared into the water. My driver Muhamad Mahmoud got out, hitched up his *dishdasha* and waded into the water. I then drove the Land-Rover on, following in his footsteps, for, if the car came off the compounded track made by vehicles before the flooding, it would stick in the *sabkha*. It then became very hard or impossible to rescue.

A white tower shimmering in the distance indicated that Abu Dhabi was near. It emerged as a square cut fort guarding the causeway, known as Al Muqta'a, connecting Abu Dhabi island with the main land. There an Abu Dhabi policeman, seeing the Land-Rover with its official flag, presented arms and leaped on to the car to escort us to a barrier a hundred yards or so further on. Other policemen emerged and shook hands before raising the barrier. Earlier travellers drove or rode through the shallows of the sea past a round tower in the water.

Sand dunes – long since dispersed – lay between the Muqta'a and the town itself. In summer the sand was so soft that a Land-Rover could not cross, unless tyre pressures were much reduced. Tyres had to be pumped up again after crossing when the flat ground was reached again. The red and white Abu Dhabi flag flew over the Ruler's white palace fortress which dominated Abu Dhabi and the mosque stood nearby. The British Political Agency was on the sea shore set among palm trees. The short journey from the Agency to the Palace for calls on the Ruler was difficult and, bringing the car to maximum speed along the thirty-yard strip of concrete road inside the Agency walls, one guided it complaining and lurching horribly through the sand to the Palace gates.

There a bearded policeman, after peering out of the wicket gate, would fling the double gates wide open. Shaikh Shakhbut bin Sultan would have been apprised earlier by messenger of the visit and stood ready, with members of his family to offer greetings. The police guard would present arms noisily and Shaikh Shakhbut accompanied us into the *majlis* where coffee, poured with a ceremonial sweep from a brass or silver coffee pot or even a thermos, was served in small round cups. Conversation could then begin, though it was unthinkable to do any business on the first call.

Shaikh Shakhbut did not welcome the prospect of oil wealth. A Bedu Shaikh of some nobility, he hated the idea of a development which would 'destroy the centuries old way of life of his people and pollute the clean freshness of the desert'. He would sit in his *majlis* clasping a thin camel stick in his small delicately shaped hand, sometimes tapping the carpet impatiently. He looked like an Arab version of King Charles I of England and, like him, was to lose his throne – though not his head. His brow puckered, he spoke with animation. 'Such a scheme', he would say with a smile, 'may be very good and appropriate elsewhere. But Abu Dhabi has special needs.' There was no Governmental machinery in any modern sense and Shakhbut was in no hurry for change 'until the company turned the tap on'. This dilatoriness and unpredictability led his family to depose him in 1966 with British connivance, but he bore further witness to his noble spirit by continuing to attend the Queen's Birthday Party every year until his death. Asked why he did so, he replied that he bore no animosity towards his old British friends. He suggested that they might not have considered him 'the most suitable man for the job'!

Shaikh Shakhbut had some reputation for meanness but nevertheless could often be the most delightful of men. The excavations at Umm al Nar which had begun a year or two before my arrival interested him deeply, and he took pride in the site's very long history. An avid listener to the BBC, he was interested in foreign affairs, science, astronomy and many other surprising subjects. Knowing the answer himself, he would casually ask a visitor questions such as the distance of the sun from the earth and write off anyone who tried to fob him off with a confident but wrong reply. On bad days he was the reverse of easy.

Britain at that time exercised extra-territorial jurisdiction over almost everyone except inhabitants of the Gulf States, but provision was made in British legislation for joint jurisdiction in 'mixed' cases – litigation between a local citizen and someone subject to the British jurisdiction. The British Judge of the Chief Court for the Persian Gulf, however, generally insisted that if the accused in a criminal case were subject to the British jurisdiction he must be tried in the British court alone. When an Indian killed a local man in a car accident on Das Island, Shaikh Shakhbut thought otherwise and, though there was then no developed system of justice there, insisted on his trial being held in an Abu Dhabi court.

Despite my attempts to find a solution acceptable to Shakhbut and the Judge, neither would change his position and there was impasse.

Though obstinate himself, Shakhbut felt - not totally without reason – that the British authorities were also unduly stubborn. I had some sympathy with him but an important issue of principle could not be settled at a stroke and Shakhbut retreated to the Buraimi region in protest. A year later my recommendations about a Mixed Court were accepted and the matter was settled to the satisfaction of both sides. My wider hope was that a similar body of law could be gradually introduced into both the British and the local courts as a means of reconciling the two jurisdictions, and thus facilitating Britain's handing over all its jurisdiction to the local authorities. Meantime, more categories of foreign nationals were gradually brought within the local jurisdictions.

Despite his reluctance, Shaikh Shakhbut did take a modicum of advice about the future and he engaged a British police officer, though he failed to pay him for seven months. He also took on an Adviser, a British academic Peter Lienhardt, who had earlier won his confidence when conducting a sociological survey. Lienhardt recommended some modest expenditure on development but this created a sudden and final breach with the Shaikh and he returned, no doubt with relief, to his academic post at Oxford. His successor, Bill Clark, who had served in the Political Service in the Sudan, was more successful, remained longer and became Shakhbut's lifelong friend.

My Machiavellian thought was that development in Dubai would lead Shakhbut to emulate it, but he seemed unable to rid himself of suspicions of new ways, complaining to me once that the British Bank of the Middle East had stolen ten lakhs of rupees from him. They had been unable to produce the actual money deposited when he unexpectedly visited the bank to see that his money was safe. Nonetheless, I believe that the popular story alleging he kept all his money under his bed is not correct. After his deposition I had lunch with him in Al Ain more than once in the 1980s, when, without the burden of office, he was a much happier man and we enjoyed much hilarity about the past.

Shaikh Zaid bin Sultan, Shakhbut's brother, who succeeded him as Ruler in 1966, was the Governor of the Buraimi region, living in Al Ain. He was the most powerful personality throughout that desert region and was widely respected and loved. Possessed of a robust sense of humour, he was a delightful gentleman to deal with and always very helpful over matters affecting relations between HMG and Abu Dhabi.[24] He had the same pride in Abu Dhabi and love of Bedu life as

24 Shaikh Shakhbut's two sons, Said and Sultan, were also helpful.

Shakhbut, but was much more realistic. I asked him more than once what HMG should do about Shaikh Shakhbut's obstinate refusal to move with the times. Zaid said we should be 'very very patient' as he and his brothers had been, counting ourselves lucky if Shakhbut conceded one tenth of what was desirable!

I often met Zaid and enjoyed his hospitality in Al Ain, where I stayed in the Murabba. This was a fort-like guest house with no modern amenities but plenty of ancient charm. On arrival after a long dusty journey I used to bathe in the cool running water of the nearby *falaj*[25] with voracious little fish nibbling the toes, after which, later in the evening, Zaid and I would dine together and chat well into the night.

In winter, hunting expeditions in the desert occupied much of Zaid's time, but he frequently accompanied Shaikh Shakhbut on visits to Abu Dhabi or Dubai. The Ruler was also invariably accompanied by his cousin Shaikh Muhamad bin Khalifa[26] and his agreeable but slightly hypochondriac brother Shaikh Khalid. It was impossible then to envisage just how significant the changes would be with oil wealth and what an influence Zaid and Abu Dhabi would become in the world. Wilfred Thesiger, however, in *Arabian Sands* quotes one of the Rashid tribe from south of the Empty Quarter (Rub' al Khali) as saying of the Abu Dhabi ruling family, 'The Al bu Falah are different; if one of that family, even a child, gave me an order, it would be awkward to refuse.' Zaid with the aid of oil wealth has raised a local reputation into a global one.

The two States of Sharjah and Ras al Khaimah were ruled by members of the Qawasim family, both bearing the name of Saqr, which means 'hawk' – Shaikh Saqr bin Sultan of Sharjah and Shaikh Saqr bin Muhamad of Ras al Khaimah. In the eighteenth and nineteenth centuries the Qawasim were notable seamen on both shores of the Gulf, and it was their activities, impinging on British trade, shipping and interests, which prompted British military actions against Ras al Khaimah in 1809 and 1819. This led to the first treaty with the States in 1820.

Shaikh Saqr bin Sultan's State was poor, as was Ras al Khaimah. Both Rulers were sensitive about this in view of their family's illustrious history. Qawasim prosperity had, however, begun to decline somewhat since 1866 when Shaikh Sultan bin Saqr, then Ruler of both States, was killed by Shaikh Zaid bin Khalifa of Abu Dhabi in single

25 A man-made water channel leading water from a tapped water source.
26 The father of Shaikhs Hamdan, Mubarak, Tahnun and Suroor and grandfather of Shaikh Nahayan.

combat. Sharjah had been the headquarters of British representation on the Coast from early in the nineteenth century until the early 1950s, when the Agency was moved to Dubai, but the headquarters of the Trucial Oman Scouts remained there. Both States produced some officers and men for the TOS.

Shaikh Saqr bin Sultan, a poet who liked to keep in the mainstream of Arab nationalist thought, was a hospitable man and we frequently lunched or dined together. A modern man as well, he would take out a packet of cigarettes, though tobacco is forbidden by some strict Muslims, and offer me one. Not being a smoker I always refused. 'Tell me,' he said, 'who is the Wahhabi here, me or you?' There were three parts of Sharjah – Kalba, Khor Fakkan and Dibbah – situated on the Gulf of Oman, totally separated from the rest of the State. This had led a former Ruler to describe himself quaintly on his English letterhead as 'Ruler of Sharjah and its Independencies'. Shaikh Saqr's English was, however, better than his predecessor's and he changed that charming and descriptive last word to 'Dependencies'. Sharjah had the distinction of being the only State with a Prime Minister, Ibrahim al Midfa.

A relation of his, Shaikh Muhamad al Midfa, was the Qadhi of Sharjah – a humorous man. I called on him following the fast of Ramadan one year and we discussed the anomaly of the Id festival often being celebrated on three different days in the Trucial States. The declaration of Id in each State depended on its own Mufti being satisfied that two good local witnesses had observed the crescent moon. I asked whether dates could not somehow be reconciled or the lead of a larger Muslim country followed. Shaikh Muhamad demurred at any thought of following Saudi Arabia, the principal Wahhabi state. He could not, he said, trust the Ulema of Bireida where the declaration was always made. They were old and venerable but might easily mistake an eyelash caught on a lens of their glasses for the crescent moon itself!

At Id, calls were made on all the Rulers and the principal merchants of the various different communities living in Dubai and Sharjah. There were also public celebrations and festivities around the large banyan tree in Sharjah which were highly popular. It was an animated scene. Small girls in brightly coloured blue, green, purple, red or orange dresses enjoyed themselves on the swings suspended from the tree while Arab men in a line, with camel sticks in hand, performed the *arda*, swaying gently and moving forwards and backwards. Brightly clad women dancers also appeared and other communities presented indigenous

dances with young Pakistani men whirling and flourishing handker-
chiefs. On the *maidan* in front of the Palace there were displays of
horsemanship, in which Shaikh Saqr himself took part, with men
demonstrating their skills and the speed of their mounts.

Shaikh Saqr bin Muhamad of Ras al Khaimah became Ruler in 1948
and was still ruling in 1998. He was a man with his own special charm
who, like the other Shaikh Saqr, made contributions to debate in the
Trucial Council. The capital of his State, located on a creek, was the site
of ancient Julfar and archaeological excavation has confirmed the
impression given by the plethora of pottery and other signs of civilisation lying near the shore that the area has been inhabited for more than
5,000 years. Its situation was particularly beautiful, surrounded by
palm trees – the soaring red mountains of the Hajar range rising above
it. Shaikh Saqr was always keen to find ways of developing his State
with limited resources, but oil wealth eluded him and he had to concentrate most of his immediate efforts on the increasingly thriving agricultural areas.

The three other Trucial States were Ajman, Umm al Qawain and
Fujairah, which was only recognised as a separate State in 1952 and
regarded by the six others as somewhat parvenu. All were, as they have
remained, relatively poor. Shaikh Rashid bin Humaid, the Ruler of the
smallest state of Ajman, was tall, lean, remarkably fit and boastful of
his prowess as a marksman. He had a large grey beard and a twinkling
eye. When my parents visited me, he insisted on calling on my father at
the Agency and greeted him by saying directly, 'Peace be on you. How
old are you?'

Shaikh Ahmad bin Rashid, the Ruler of Umm al Qawain, was a man
of quiet dignity and presence who kept a good table and was renowned
for his wisdom. When in 1959 a small war broke out between Ras al
Khaimah and Fujairah, he helped me work out a settlement on a customary basis, after the Trucial Oman Scouts had separated the parties.
I had first asked the two Rulers to produce their own settlement with
the help of Shaikh Ahmad. When word was sent that they had reached
agreement, I laid on a celebratory lunch in Arab style for the three
Rulers. Caution, however, made me first ask what the basis of their
agreement was. A somewhat awkward silence ensued. Then Shaikh
Ahmad coughed and with slow deliberation said, 'We are all agreed.' I
pressed him further. 'We are all agreed,' he said, 'that you should pre-
scribe the terms of the settlement!' I examined the facts and was advised
on local custom about compensation and punishment by Shaikh

Ahmad. After considering the deaths and damage to property on both sides, as well as the breach of a state of amity between two States, I concluded that Fujairah was due to pay a heavy sum in net compensation to Ras al Khaimah. When I announced the award, the Ruler of Fujairah whistled through his few remaining teeth but promptly paid the sums due.

Shaikh Muhamad of Fujairah was an engaging man with a pronounced penchant for hypochondria, enduring traditional remedies such as branding with fearful regularity and stoicism. He was also an activist in local development and with the help of a few sticks of dynamite from the TOS, he personally supervised the making of the first road in 1960 through the Hajar mountains between Dibbah and Masafi. It was rough and went over bed rock in places but for the first time even 3–ton lorries could take a short route, formerly fit only for donkeys. He was hospitable and lived a traditional and simple life on the Batinah Coast, entertaining in the summer months in the *barasti* which gave shade and coolness as the sea breezes blew through the walls.

George Middleton was Political Resident for most of my time and he visited every few months. On one visit he made a very popular presentation of 25–pounder saluting guns to the Rulers of Ajman and Umm al Qawain. They had requested this gift, as firing their old muzzle-loading cannon was dangerous to life and limb. Bill Luce succeeded Middleton as Political Resident in 1961 and it was my particular pleasure, having known him well in the Sudan, to take him on his inaugural tour, as in 1958 I had taken George Middleton. We called on all the Rulers, visited the oil operations in Abu Dhabi at Tarif and Das Island, flew to Al Ain to lunch with Shaikh Zaid and visited various TOS units. The programme I arranged was so complicated on one day that Luce said it would be a miracle if we pulled it off. We did, however. Driving from Dubai to a TOS squadron at Idhn on the western edge of the Hajar range, we then flew over the mountains by RAF Twin Pioneer to Kalba on the Indian Ocean, and drove on to Khor Fakkan. From there we went by launch to Dibbah, the bay of which was described by the nineteenth-century traveller W. G. Palgrave as 'in no whit inferior to that of Naples'. There we had a light lunch with Shaikh Muhamad of Fujairah before driving on by Land-Rover up Shaikh Muhamad's road, through the very rough Wadi Ayyina, to Masafi. A Twin Pioneer flew us from there back to Dubai's new airport. They were exhilarating days.

Events across the border in the neighbouring State of Muscat and Oman, as it then was, impinged on the Trucial States. The authority of

Sultan Said bin Taimur was challenged in the mid 1950s by the Imam Ghalib, his brother Talib, Shaikh Salih bin Isa of the Sharqiya and Shaikh Sulaiman bin Himyar of the Bani Ghafir – who styled himself 'Lord of the Green Mountain'. The struggle was essentially about control of the oil-bearing parts of Oman and together these leaders of the Interior made some attempt at secession with the support of Saudi Arabia. The TOS, who had many recruits from the Bani Kaab tribe living near the borders, joined the Sultan's Armed Forces in the military campaign which culminated in the SAS successfully dislodging the rebels from their mountain fastness in the Jebel Akhdar in 1959. They fled to Saudi Arabia.

The officers and men of the TOS enjoyed this involvement but sympathy in the Trucial States for the rebels made it sensitive and the TOS were consequently withdrawn at the end of the campaign. Support for the rebel Omanis, however, evaporated rapidly when they continued a dangerous campaign of mining and the British India ship MV *Dara* was sunk off Dubai in 1961 by an Omani bomb, with considerable loss of life. They had earlier made an unsuccessful attempt to assassinate Sayyed Ahmad bin Ibrahim, the Sultan's Minister of the Interior, on another BI ship. All Dubai's rescue and emergency resources were put to the test and, thereafter, Shaikh Rashid and other Rulers willingly handed over Omani mine layers to the Sultan's jurisdiction when they were caught in the Emirates.

Apart from official contacts with Shaikhs and local people there were many less formal ones. Sometimes I joined Shaikhs' hawking parties in the desert, when falcons were flown against McQueen's bustard – a delicious and popular dinner dish for the Shaikhs. Hawking was so important in the lives of the Shaikhs that, when travelling on Gulf Aviation in those days, it was commonplace to have hooded hawks belonging to one or other of them hopping around at one's feet.

Ted Heath, then Lord Privy Seal and a Foreign Office minister, paid the very first British ministerial visit to the Trucial States in January 1961. There had been nothing comparable since Lord Curzon, then Viceroy of India, visited and held a Durbar at Sharjah in 1903, and it had its complications as the title Lord Privy Seal perplexed people and was not easy to translate meaningfully into Arabic. George Middleton came down from Bahrain and together we accompanied Ted Heath in calling on Rulers, visiting the TOS and oil companies and sampling the delights of the desert by driving over steep dunes. The visit was highly successful except in one way.

After a reception and small dinner party at my house, the Minister was asked by my Pakistani steward, Ghulam Nabi, what he would like for breakfast and where he would have it. It was a regular drill which always worked like clockwork with Ghulam providing breakfast exactly as prescribed. Ted Heath chose to have it in his room, but George Middleton and I breakfasted together in the dining room. (George had brought his Indian bearer, Sam, with him.) When further time passed and Ted Heath did not appear to begin the morning programme, George Middleton became anxious and went to see why. He returned very rapidly and said Ted Heath was 'fuming' as he had received no breakfast. I was astonished but ordered it to be sent at once. When I later held a post mortem it appeared that Ghulam and Sam had differed as to whose privilege it was to take breakfast to the distinguished guest. Sam argued that his employer was more important than Ghulam's. Ghulam defended the claims of the host. As they could not agree, there was impasse. Subsequently, whenever we have met, Ted Heath has pointed at me, roared with laughter and, with shoulders heaving typically, exclaimed, 'Breakfast!'

British influence remained strong in the Trucial States and, when attending the Indian Association's Indian National Day celebrations, I was requested by the President, Mr Padiyath, without any forewarning, to address the large crowd because 'Honourable Political Agent is not only representative of Her Majesty's Government but also Government of India'. It mattered not that this was not quite true. The Indian Consul-General in Muscat had that privilege. But, garlanded with orange flowers by a young girl, I stood on the stage and gave an impromptu speech, congratulating the assembled Indians on their Independence. The twilight of the British Empire was still not ended in Dubai.

It was impossible even in 1961 to envisage the later riches and consequent world influence of Abu Dhabi; the broad areas of finely designed high-rise blocks in Dubai and Abu Dhabi; the number of magnificent Arab horses in Abu Dhabi or the predominating influence and success of the Maktums, sons of Shaikh Rashid, on the British Turf. The building of numerous luxury hotels, massive 'centres' and shopping malls, Dubai's international fame as entrepot and financial centre, its airport and the worldwide routes of Emirates Airlines were all very much in the future. The later acquisition of much valuable London property by UAE citizens was not even contemplated. The beauty of Abu Dhabi as a green city, the development of Sharjah, the existence of several universities, Dubai's Port Rashid, Jebel Ali port and dry dock, and Fujairah's position as the world's third largest bunkering port could not even have been dreamt of. As for the future arrival of large numbers of Russians and citizens of the Central Asia Republics, this would have been dismissed as totally impossible. Yet all these things have come about in recent years.

In August 1961, my tour came to an end. James Craig followed me in Dubai, with responsibility for the six northern States. Hugh Boustead, an elderly and very colourful figure who had served in the Sudan and the Eastern Aden Protectorate both as soldier and administrator, became the first Political Agent in Abu Dhabi with a separate Agency. Having had seven months' notice of a posting to Washington I came home on leave to prepare for this. One morning Personnel Department rang to say they did not know how to face me but the Washington posting was off. The 10% cut imposed on all Government Departments had led to the post there being pruned and as a bachelor I was a 'sitting duck'. I then worked in Western European Department – involved in the preparations for de Gaulle's State Visit – before being sent to Cairo after Christmas in 1961. There I was to meet my wife Ruth.

5
Egypt

Egypt, situated at the crossroads between Asia and Africa, has been called 'The Most Important Country'. It is certainly one of the most fascinating, and the Nile civilisations captured my imagination from an early age. It has a palpable sense of continuous history with its magnificent Pharaonic monuments; early Islamic, Mameluke and Ottoman mosques, schools and hospitals; and Coptic churches and desert monasteries. In 1962, the population of some twenty-eight million people, of whom four million were concentrated in Cairo, formed an essentially homogeneous society despite Egypt's many invasions throughout history. Of the country's total area of 387,000 square miles much is desert but the vivid green fertility of the Nile's banks and delta, irrigated for 5,000 years by the annual flood, combine with marvellous light to provide especially beautiful contrasts.

The Egyptians are a kindly, hospitable people with a highly developed sense of humour, despite or perhaps because of the hard conditions in which the majority live. An Egyptian friend, asked why they joked so much, replied that, if they did not laugh, they could only cry at their constant plight. This was one reason why I enjoyed my three years among them so much; besides, Cairo's international society was sophisticated and amusing.

From Egypt's occupation in 1882 until 1956, British influence had been dominant and, despite the clash between Egyptian aspirations and British interests, relations were generally warm – always close. The unsuccessful Suez venture marked the nadir, with diplomatic relations broken off from December 1956 until a Property Mission was opened in the spring of 1959 under Colin Crowe. He personally did much to restore personal and diplomatic relations and opened the way for Harold Beeley in 1961 to resume Ambassadorial contact for the first time since Humphrey Trevelyan had been forced to leave five years earlier. The health of political relations with Egypt, however, depended on Britain's attitude to a number of Middle East and world issues dear to Nasser's heart and aspirations. In Cairo I became a 'Kremlinologist' of his Arab Socialism.

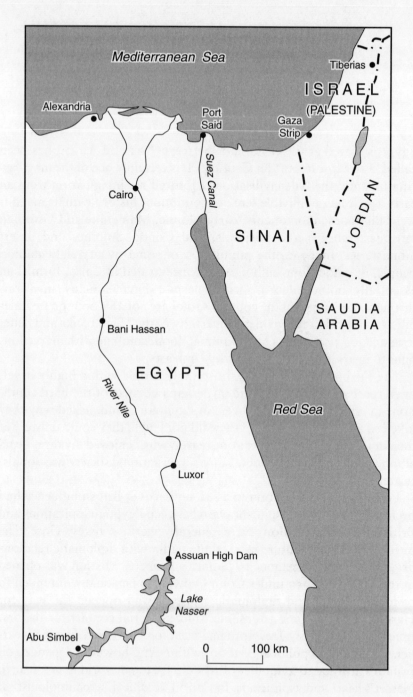

Egypt

Geoffrey Arthur was the Counsellor and he and Harold Beeley expected me as Head of Chancery to run the Embassy, subject only to their political direction. He made his point by citing a pre-war Ambassador who, dissatisfied with papers put forward by the registry, entered within the grilled sanctum. The Head of Chancery, finding him there unexpectedly, accepted the justness of the Ambassador's complaint but expostulated, 'However, sir, you have no right to be in my registry!'

Harold Beeley and Geoffrey Arthur formed an ideal and much-respected pair to lead the campaign to restore relations with the Egyptians. Harold Beeley spoke no Arabic but had a sure and intellectual touch in his meetings with Nasser and other senior revolutionary officers. Geoffrey Arthur, more mercurial, was a master of quotation in Arabic, Persian and Latin, and this, coupled with his quick sense of humour, made him very popular with the Egyptians. His successor Donald Maitland also had notable but different talents which later led to his appointments as British Representative at the UN in New York and Permanent Undersecretary in the Ministry of Energy.

Generally it was a large and strong Embassy. The Commercial Counsellor was first John Wraight and then Ralph Daniell and there were ten First Secretaries, Military and Air Attachés – joined later by a Naval Attaché – and a big supporting staff, local and UK-based. Paddy Doyle, a former RSM in the Irish Guards, was the much-loved Head Security Guard who with the steel of Toledo and Irish blarney could fix absolutely anything – a very useful attribute in Egypt. Michael Weir, First Secretary (Information) later himself became Ambassador in Cairo and it was in his office that for the first and last time I met Kim Philby, then a Beirut-based correspondent for the *Economist*. He appeared a trifle dishevelled and drunk, though lucid on Middle Eastern topics, but not long afterwards staged his dramatic disappearance from Beirut and reappearance in Moscow. It was no doubt coincidence that Donald Maclean, who had defected to the USSR ten years earlier, also had a Cairo connection, having been a predecessor of mine, as Head of Chancery. Of the other First Secretaries, Hooky Walker became Ambassador to the UAE, Ethiopia and Iraq and Colin Brant Ambassador to Qatar.

The competence and loyalty of the local Embassy staff was notable. Many of them had a number of years' service and had looked after our interests under the Swiss during the break in diplomatic relations at the time of Suez. The telephone operators had been with the Embassy from the time of Lord Killearn, who served first as British High Commissioner and from 1936 as Ambassador. When answering the telephone they sometimes replied simply, perhaps out of long habit or mere elision, 'Embassy here.' One or two foreign colleagues complained but, perhaps too fond of anomaly and tradition, I did not go out of my way to reprove these robust and loyal Egyptian men and women. Alf Dutton, who was one of our gate guards, was another link with the past, having lived in Cairo since the time when Sir Lee Stack, Sirdar of the Egyptian Army and Governor-General of the Sudan, was shot and murdered there in 1924.

There were no women diplomats in our Embassy in those days but the secretaries played their part fully in social life, helping at diplomatic parties and making many Egyptian friends. They had various social talents. One girl did the Can-Can and another – who was asked to appear on Egyptian TV as a model (of which we did not approve!) – was a good modern dancer and taught me the Twist, then in high vogue. One girl was particularly friendly with a young Egyptian, and I received instructions to tell her to stop seeing him. Whereupon she burst into floods of tears and said she loved him. I had expected this but she went on to say that she was going to marry him, which she duly did, living happily with him and their children ever since.

Domestically I was well served. Hassan the cook I had 'inherited' from the Coptic owner of my flat, was a very hard worker and, not having previously worked for anyone British, had a low opinion of those who did. He believed them to be spoilt. He had a fine head – a living Nubian Pharoah hewn out of granite – and was an excellent cook. Arranging parties, however, could become difficult when he was joined by a new Nubian *suffragi*, Osman, who was tall, good-looking and untainted by having worked for anyone British. He spoke virtually no English and when I returned from the office he would announce in Arabic, 'One lady rang for you this morning.' To my eager inquiry, 'Who was it?' he would reply he did not know. So I charged him strictly to inquire the names and telephone numbers of callers and he promised to obey. Shortly afterwards, friends told me they had been alarmed on ringing my number to be greeted by a deep voice with the words, 'Mr Hawley's flat. What you?'

My own posting to Cairo had been unexpected but proved momentous. In 1963 it was agreed that a new girl should work for me as personal assistant as well as doing work of a more sensitive kind. I was asked what qualifications were needed. Tongue firmly in cheek, I asked for 'the most beautiful, the most talented, the most agreeable and the most cheerful girl they could find'. Seldom has a light-hearted request been so effectively answered, for Ruth Howes appeared.

Our engagement took place in May 1964 when I was on leave. We arranged a meeting in Athens. My flight from London was due in before hers from Cairo, but to this day our accounts differ on what happened then. We agree, however, that we looked vainly for each other for a while until suddenly and to my enormous relief I saw her, in a smart lime green suit, moving purposefully through a channel marked 'Air Crew Only'. I had brought a ring – exported, owing to regulations then in force, in an enormous plastic bag. Having considered my question whether she could put up with me for life she became engaged to me and we were married just over a month later in Dorset. The affair caused great excitement in the Cairo Embassy and when we returned from honeymoon Donald Maitland, then Chargé d'Affaires, and his wife Jean generously held another wedding reception for us and a series of celebratory parties followed.

Up to 1956 British investment in Egypt had been immense and, apart from the normal political and administrative tasks of a Head of Chancery, much of my time was taken up with problems caused by the Suez debacle to British commercial and property interests.[1] Solutions were obviously needed to restore normal British-Egyptian relations, though both sides knew it would take time.

Although Harold Beeley, who met Nasser often, had as good a rapport with him as circumstances allowed, my own first-hand impressions depended on a single meeting. When George Middleton, Harold Beeley's successor, presented his credentials on 22 September 1964 I was presented as a member of his staff. I was disappointed, noting that his speech in reply to George Middleton's was 'delivered in a flat monotone not unlike a priest saying Mass'. I also wrote in my diary, 'Nasser has a strong handshake but I did not feel he was very friendly.' George Middleton, who had half an hour with him, commented that he was a man obviously aggrieved against Britain – and it is true that there were then policy differences between the two countries over South Arabia. Nasser's manner contrasted starkly with that of Adel Murad, Chamberlain at the Presidential Palace and a former paratroop officer and frogman. Large, jolly and amusing, he commented favourably on the Service Attachés' uniform, adding 'I admire English officers very much.' It epitomised the complication and paradox of Anglo-Egyptian relations.

A good litmus test of the state of these relations and of Nasser's thinking was the periodic article written by the editor of *El Ahram*,

1 Particularly after Arthur Watts, the Legal Adviser, was withdrawn.

Mohamed Hassanein Heikal, who was a close confidant of Nasser – so close indeed that he was sometimes used as an unofficial channel of communication with the President. A highly educated, intelligent and civilised man, he would express his own views at private parties fairly freely and with objectivity and was thus a valuable intermediary.

Small things may affect a country's view of another and misunderstanding may arise from something trivial. The Egyptians were at this sensitive time as prone as we were to examine every nuance of our dealings together. In 1964 Egyptian friends mentioned that our policy towards Egypt seemed to be becoming more brittle. This surprised me but they cited unfamiliar difficulties in obtaining a visa for the UK. With this lead I visited the Consulate to see how this part of the Mission was working. A new man had arrived in the visa section. I asked him how he dealt with a typical visa applicant and he replied, 'Well I don't exactly treat them with hostility!' This response was enough to identify the source of the 'change of policy' and we took corrective measures.

We strove to put warmth back into Anglo-Egyptian relations. In April 1962 Roger Stevens,[2] paid the first high-level visit to Cairo after the exchange of ambassadors – a warm and well-conducted ice-breaking visit by a man of great charm, distinction and intellectual ability. Meeting Nasser and very senior Egyptians, he stressed that Britain's policy was not to interfere in the internal affairs of Arab countries. Although ministerial visits were then very much rarer than nowadays, Frederick Erroll, the President of the Board of Trade, came in April 1963 – the first British Minister to visit since Suez. Similarly well received, he struck the right note with Nasser by admitting that Egyptians were usually misjudged and underestimated in Britain. In June of the same year a group of Labour MPs – including Denis Healey, Chris Mayhew and Peter Shore – also came as guests of the Arab Socialist Union. They received a specially warm welcome from the Egyptians who reckoned that a Labour administration might, in view of the Labour Party's opposition to the Suez venture, be better disposed than the Conservatives. Denis Healey borrowed a fiver off me, which he repaid with commendable speed!

The French, Britain's associates in the Suez misadventure, were in some ways less well placed than we. A number of their diplomats, who had returned to Egypt in a Property Mission similar to ours without

2 Deputy Undersecretary of State at the Foreign Office who later became Vice-Chancellor of Leeds University.

formal diplomatic status, had been imprisoned with some Egyptians on charges of spying. Before I left for Cairo, M. Chauvel, the French Ambassador in London, clearly crediting me with higher rank and more influence than I had, charged me at a reception, 'Please do your best to get our diplomats released.' The trial of the Frenchmen, meanwhile, continued on a desultory basis until they were suddenly released on 7 April 1962[3] much to the relief of a diplomatic community highly concerned at the detention of fellow diplomats. The cease-fire agreement signed at Evian on 18 March 1962 ended the war in Algeria, which had caused 17,250 French and 141,000 Algerian deaths, and it was this which occasioned the Egyptian change of heart and restoration of full diplomatic relations with France.

The first Chargé d'Affaires, Henri Froment-Meurice, was extremely bright and we had a close relationship, especially as we faced similar problems over our nationals' property. We invited him once to stay with us at Agame near Alexandria in the house we had taken for the summer, and Ruth purchased a treat for him in Alexandria – a large piece of Roquefort, which unfortunately proved to be better endowed with maggots than cheese mites. The thought, however, evidently contributed to the local *entente cordiale*.

The European Diplomatic Corps was especially close knit because of the nature of Nasser's regime and ambassadorial entertaining was still in the grand style of earlier times. When still a bachelor I had found myself in demand as a gap filler for dinner tables, especially at the Italian Embassy where Count Magistrati, an old career diplomat closely related to Count Ciano,[4] presided with old-fashioned grace and style. Wolf von Arnim and Rudi Pachelbel, both First Secretaries in the German Embassy, were sociable and agreeable colleagues, whose family names are perhaps best known for musical connections – Elizabeth von Arnim, the patron and friend of Beethoven, and Pachelbel the seventeenth-century composer.

The Olympic Shooting Championship was held in Cairo in 1963 and I asked the British team to a reception in my flat at 7 p.m. It so happened that the German Counsellor, Gunther Gnodtke, later Ambassador in Lagos, lived on the same floor and was giving a reception for the German team at 7.30 p.m. The British team arrived punctually at 7 p.m. and, seeing the red carpet, assumed it was for them. They rang the

3 The legal device was an adjournment *sine die*.
4 The former Italian Foreign Minister.

bell of the German's flat and a *suffragi* admitted them requesting them to sign the visitors' book, which they all did. Moving into the drawing room, they were surprised to see a man hastily donning his jacket. 'Guten Abend,' he said. After a few pleasantries about the confusion, they retired and came on to my flat for the right party.

It was in Cairo that I first became involved with Malaysia, though having no inkling then that I would later serve there. When the Malaysian Government first established diplomatic relations with Egypt in 1962 the first Chargé d'Affaires, Jamaluddin bin Haji Abubakr, made contact and I was able to show him and his wife Rahmah some of the ropes as he opened up the Embassy. Some while afterwards the first Ambassador, Tunku Jaafar Ibni Al-Marhum Tuanku Abdul Rahman, arrived – a keen sportsman with a delightful wife and family. Fate decreed, though he was not expecting it, that he was later to become Yang di Pertuan Negara[5] of the Malaysian State of Negri Sembilan and in 1994 Agong of Malaysia. Members of two other royal families, both displaced, were also prominent socially in Cairo: Queen Dina, the first wife of King Hussein of Jordan, who though related to him had been brought up in Cairo; and Leila Rishtya, the daughter of the Afghan Ambassador, who in other circumstances would have been King of Afghanistan. Other diplomatic friends included Abdul Husain Jamali, the Counsellor in the Iraqi Embassy with whom I later frequently dealt in the Ministry of Foreign Affairs in Baghdad, where he was Undersecretary, and George Dove-Edwin who later became Nigeria's High Commissioner in London for many years. We enjoyed the company of them both and their wives.

Cairo was then an exciting place and Nasser a towering figure at home and abroad. A diplomat's perspective in Cairo was consequently a wide one. In his *Philosophy of the Revolution*, conceived in 1948 when fighting in Palestine against the Israelis, he foresaw a 'role in search of a hero' and concluded that only he and Egypt matched the challenge. Cairo became the centre of intersecting Arab, African and Islamic circles of influence and Nasser's prestige was enhanced by being a founding member – with Mr Nehru of India, President Sukarno of Indonesia and President Tito of Yugoslavia – of the Non-Alignment Movement.[6] In tune with Nasser's aims the Arab African People's Solidarity Organisation was also established in Cairo with Mursi Saad el

5 Ruler of a State. The Agong is King of Malaysia for five years, and each Yang di Pertuan Negara takes his turn.
6 At the Bandung Conference in Indonesia in 1955.

Din as Secretary-General – an Egyptian celebrated on the diplomatic circuit for his bedroom eyes. Nasser's was an authoritarian regime but as one of the Big Four Non-Aligned leaders he tried to tread a sort of middle path in international affairs. This prompted him to have periodic meetings with Tito and, when I arrived in Alexandria on the *Esperia*[7] in January 1962, we were held up to allow President Tito's ship to enter harbour first. Such visits usually portended further socialist measures and were, therefore, anathema to many Egyptians.

Britain and the West aimed from the beginning of the Cold War to keep the Soviet Union out of the Middle East. The door was, however, inevitably opened to them by the withdrawal of US and British support for the Assuan High Dam in 1956. It was this which led to Nasser's nationalisation of the Suez Canal and the Suez episode. When Soviet engineers started work on the dam, Egypt also began to rely on Soviet and Eastern Bloc arms supplies and general support, and this Soviet connection, reinforced by a lavishly staffed Soviet Embassy, obviously influenced Egyptian policies. Britain, the US and the West were adversely affected, but paradoxically Soviet involvement with the High Dam was very unpopular with the Egyptian people, and Nasser's regime, which strongly rejected Communism, took firm action against Communists at home and abroad.

Nasser instigated his Young Officers group to depose King Farouk on 23 July 1952. The King, unlike the unhappy King Faisal II of Iraq, was seen off from Alexandria with gun salutes and full military honours. General Mohamed Neguib, intended originally as an older figurehead, was installed as first President. Like his brother, Ali Bey Neguib, Egyptian ADC to the Governor-General of the Sudan, with whom I frequently played tennis at the Palace, he had been educated at the Gordon College in Khartoum and had an easy manner, which made him popular. He became too personally popular for the revolutionary officers and it was Nasser who, brushing him aside in November 1954, assumed the Presidency. Yet even after this Egyptian life went on much as before and the Egyptian upper classes were relatively unaffected. In 1961 the true socialist revolution took place and the cause was Syria.

In 1958 the United Arab Republic was formed. It was a Union of Egypt and Syria, though largely dominated by Nasser, his Army and his Intelligence officers. Syrian political groups, including the Baath Party who originally supported union, felt excluded from government in their

7 Of the Adriatica Line.

own country, and resulting tension led to a coup in 1961 by Syrian armed forces who took Damascus. Efforts to preserve the Union failed as Nasser would not agree the terms on which Syrian officers insisted. The dissolution had a profound effect on Nasser. Attributing it to wealthy Syrians, who feared Egyptian style agrarian reform, he immediately turned his attention to wealthy Egyptians and foreign residents who might be tempted to finance opposition to his regime. By Proclamation 138 of 1961 he drew up a list of such rich people, some of whom were British, and summarily sequestrated their assets.

Despite the setback with Syria, Egypt continued to style itself the UAR,[8] though many Egyptians, conscious of their own long history, were never fully convinced about their role as prime leader of Arab unity. There was therefore relief among some, though by no means all, at the break with Syria. There was also an ambivalence about the very term 'Arab' which, when I first went there – strange as it may now seem – was sometimes used in the 1940s in Egypt and the Sudan to mean wild and uncivilised. I have to declare that my own perspective of Arabs from Bedu to intellectuals has never been that.

Like the nineteenth-century Egyptian nationalist Arabi Pasha, Nasser was of Fellahin stock, his father a modest district postmaster. A clever boy, he was admitted in 1936 to the Military College, thus joining the officer corps, hitherto the prerogative of aristocratic and rich families. His political perspective was nevertheless formed by his original background, leading him to preach against the iniquity of wealthy landowners, bankers and others who had been in 'unholy alliance with the forces of external capitalism'. His socialist and confiscatory policies after 1961 changed the fabric of Egyptian society and few families amongst the former ruling hierarchy were unaffected. Some lost land through agrarian reform introduced in the 1950s which reduced the maximum individual and family holding of land to 200 *feddans*,[9] though this was regarded by agriculturists as an uneconomic unit. The companies of others were nationalised and a plethora of state companies and organisations appeared, in which Army officers held plum jobs. Other members of the *ancien régime* left the country while the wealthiest, even if they stayed, were neutered by sequestration. Many had relations in gaol – in the notorious Wadi al Gadid Detention Camp – accused of being Communists.

8 United Arab Republic.
9 A *feddan* is roughly an acre.

Nasser convened the National Congress of Popular Powers, the assembly of the Arab Socialist Union, on 21 May 1962 to introduce the new National Charter. After that, it became the forum for his 'State of the Union' messages designed to rally faithful followers and the nation at large. The Congress had 1,750 deputies from many walks of life – farmers, workers, students, intellectuals and other groups. Searching for innuendo and clues on policy changes I listened to these long speeches, which started in formal classical Arabic. Nasser usually departed from his set script and, lapsing into the Egyptian vernacular, displayed that magnetism which gave him so powerful a hold over people's emotions. Then the occasion became charged with the excitement of a good football game spiced by heady politics.

Surprisingly Nasser's popular and populist messages were accepted by many wealthy Egyptians who agreed that greater social justice had been achieved by agrarian reform, even where they were personally affected. Nasser epitomised solid, decent Egyptian values and this also gave him the courage in the face of the population explosion to advocate the need for birth control – then an almost unknown and controversial concept in the Islamic world. The sceptical Egyptians, however, had their credulity stretched when Nasser received over 99% of the vote in elections.

The wonderful Egyptian sense of humour could still assert itself even in the face of the rather forbidding title of National Congress of Popular Powers. A charming girl called Lulu[10] used to come to my parties with her brother as chaperon. The daughter of a professor, she was dark-eyed, beautiful and intelligent – the stone statue of a Pharaoh's wife come to life. Elected a deputy for the Students Sector in the Congress, she gave an account of electioneering which showed that Arab Socialism had not killed private enterprise. She had been 'Miss University' and 'Miss Sport' in the previous year but kept out of the limelight for her final year at Cairo University. She then realised that another girl's star was rising and desperate measures were necessary for success in her election campaign.

Lulu contrived to have her name put at the head of the candidates' list. She announced that she could influence professors to pass students in three subjects and not merely two – and no male student was likely to disbelieve her. Her glamorous girl friends distributed pamphlets urging students to vote for the former 'Miss University and Sport' and picketed the male students on election day; then a group of presentable

10 The name means Pearl.

young men, led by her brother Hassan, escorted the girl students towards the polling booth, where a policeman sat to ensure fair play. Duly elected she went for a tutorial with her professor, who had been elected a deputy for the University Teachers' Sector. He pointed out some errors in her work but she retorted, 'You can't talk to me like that, old boy; we're colleagues now!'

The reverse in Syria did not discourage Nasser from further essays in Arab political unity. 1963 was a crucial year and coups d'état in Arab States gave impetus to the movement. General Qasim, who assumed power in Iraq after the monarchy was overthrown, fell in a successful coup on 8 February 1963. He was perceived as being a Communist and his downfall was welcomed in official Cairo, enhanced by a further coup in Syria on 9 March. Both coups were predominantly Baathist – then the most anti-Communist party in the Middle East – though Unionist, pro-Nasser involvement caused Cairo to think things were going their way. On 10 April Ali Sabri, the Prime Minister – who was incidentally a member of an *ancien régime* family who disapproved of his involvement in Nasser's regime – announced the creation of a Single Federal State with a joint flag on which three stars represented Egypt, Iraq and Syria. A fourth member came in when on 25 June the revolutionary government of Abdulla Sallal in Yemen, having overthrown the Imam Badr bin Ahmed on 27 September 1962, proclaimed the United Yemen Republic. The new regime, allying itself with the Egyptians, joined this new Arab Federation, despite the royalist-revolutionary civil war which was by then raging in Yemen.

This, however, was the high tide of Arab unity and the Federation began to fall apart, largely because of deep differences about philosophy and competition for influence within the Arab Union. Egypt and their allies, the Unionists, ranged themselves on one side and the Baathists, who dominated the governments in Iraq and Syria, on the other, though centrifugal tendencies further increased when Baghdad and Damascus became increasingly bitterly divided against each other.

The breakneck drive towards unity was always very much Nasser's personal initiative and, when on 20 March 1963 Harold Beeley asked the Permanent Undersecretary about the course of the unity negotiations, Hafiz Ismail knew nothing – 'Such high-level negotiations are outside the province of the Ministry of Foreign Affairs.' Similarly the Head of the Arab Department, Hassan Fahmy Abdel Maguid, told me the matter was being dealt with 'at a very high level'. This illustrated the strange dichotomy between the revolutionary leaders and the professionals, with which Egypt was very well endowed and among whom Dr Mahmoud Fawzi, a very experienced Foreign Minister, and Dr Kaissouni, a brilliant Minister of Finance, were pre-eminent.

By 14 May 1963 the UAR radio, disillusioned over unity, was attacking the Baath and condemning it along with the 'secessionist revisionist' government of Syria. An optimistic cartoon in the newspaper *Musawwar* depicted an Arab driving a steamroller with a stone ahead of him and saying, 'This little stone will not stay in my way.' I noted in my diary, 'Certainly there is a will towards unity, but the little stone may be quite a big rock', and publication of the proceedings of unity meetings held in June 1963 revealed Nasser on this occasion as petulant, self-centred and obsessed with personal grievance against the Baath. When Amin el Hafiz took over the government in Damascus on 19 July, the Cairo press resorted to hyperbole, calling him a 'Fascist blood shedder' while Nasser personally launched an all-out attack on the Baath Party.

Arab governments wanted a common Arab strategy towards Israel and Nasser took the main responsibility for this on himself, even though Egyptians felt the loss of Palestine less acutely than the Jordanians and Syrians, who were relatively critical of Cairo's words instead of deeds. There was certainly no lack of rhetoric. Egyptian radio stations poured forth a constant stream of abuse against Israel, and general sentiment against the implanted State ran high. But Nasser, even though Egypt had the strongest forces in the area, would not be pushed to military action until Arab unity was achieved. The problem of Palestine and the ever-present possibility of war with Israel was nevertheless in everyone's thoughts. Israel's diversion of the Tiberias, Yarmuk and Jordan rivers concentrated minds and in January 1964 the first 'summit' of Arab Kings and Presidents was held in Cairo to address the whole problem.

Since 1948 the Arab case had suffered from the lack of anybody to represent the Palestinians. The Arab-Israel war of 1948/9 had, however, left the Egyptians in control of part of Palestinian territory – the Gaza strip, which remained under Egyptian military administration – and Nasser had instituted a Cairo radio station called 'The Voice of Palestine'. Marking a new phase in the Arab-Israel dispute, a Palestine Entity was set up in Gaza in 1963, which was formally recognised at the Kings and Presidents Cairo Summit of January 1964. This move was not opposed by Britain, who later earned respect in the Middle East by sponsoring Security Council Resolution 242 in 1967 following the war of that year and still later Resolution 338. The double standard displayed by the US and Western Governments in enforcing UN resolutions, so much resented by Arabs everywhere, was not then so apparent as now, nor had Israel flouted so many.

Although the grand plan for Arab unity fell apart, Nasser's personal influence in the Arab world remained formidable and Cairo continued also to be a magnet for leaders of African, Non-Aligned and Islamic states. African Heads of State such as President Houphouet-Boigny of the Ivory Coast, President Ahmed Ahidjo of Cameroon and other personalities from countries newly, or about to be, independent were made welcome. Leaders from parts of the former British Empire also came, including Kenneth Kaunda of Zambia and Dr Hastings Banda of Malawi, who were entertained by Harold and Karen Beeley at the Embassy. Both made graceful lunch-time speeches about the smoothness of the handover from the British on Independence and Lee Kuan Yew, returning in 1963 from London through Cairo at the time of Singapore's incorporation into Malaysia, startled the Beeleys' Egyptian dinner guests – who heard little public pro-British sentiment – by complimenting former British Administrations and calling Britain's governance of India by only 1,100 British administrators 'a remarkable achievement by any standard'. British tolerance too was indirectly praised when Oginga Odinga, who had been associated with Mau-Mau and looked very sinister with a fly whisk and round straw cap, brought a delegation of prominent KANU[11] politicians to Cairo, including Koinanga and Murumbi. When I asked the latter what he had been doing during his seven years in London, he replied gaily, 'Oh, agitating, you know!'

Shaikh Mohamed Shamte, the Chief Minister of Zanzibar, was another visitor and, as Zanzibar was still a British Protectorate, I went to the airport early in the morning to represent Harold Beeley. On the Egyptian side Mohamed Faiq, one of Nasser's advisers, had been deputed to meet him but had not arrived at the bottom of the steps when Mohamed Shamte descended, inquiring as he shook my hand, 'Mr Mohamed Faiq?' At this moment the Egyptian, who was about my height and colouring, came rushing up, flustered and tightening his tie. Despite this hitch the official Egyptian welcome then took its normal course.

My flat, which belonged to a wealthy Copt who was out of the country, looked over the Libyan Embassy – King Idris was still on the throne

11 Kenyan National Union Party.

before Gaddafi appeared – and also down on the North Korean Embassy. No Koreans ever seemed to emerge, but oppressively boring revolutionary films were shown in the garden. Nasser's non-aligned policy had led to Egyptian recognition of both North Korea and North Vietnam, much to the annoyance of the Western powers. He also lionised and gave strong support to leaders of the Algerian 'struggle' against France at a time when Algeria, still a metropolitan *Département*, inspired the French patriotic slogan '*L'Algérie Française*'. For example, Ben Bella, who was brought up a French speaker but learned his Arabic in Cairo, was seen off to Algiers with honours usually accorded to a Head of State, even before he became the first President of independent Algeria. The Egyptian regime was on the other hand very cavalier in its dealings with conservative Arab States and, highly improperly, gave the sequestrated palace of Prince Faisal of Saudi Arabia to Algeria as an Embassy. Nasser honoured the first Algerian National Day party there, which I attended, by a Presidential appearance without precedent and in April 1963 himself went to Algiers, where he was rewarded by facing a crowd so great and rapturous that he had to be rescued by a fire engine!

Arab Socialism and the call for unity were, even if unrealised, heady doctrines to the people of the Arab world. The monarchical and traditional regimes were naturally less enthusiastic, though Nasser's attitude towards them was equivocal, opportunist and variable. Nasser's generally anti-colonial and anti-imperialist stance caused few problems for Britain in Africa. Harold Macmillan had made his controversial 'Wind of Change' speech and Britain was busy withdrawing from its African possessions. The Arabian peninsula was a different case and dissidents from Aden and the Protectorates, Muscat and Oman and the Gulf States found their way to Cairo. Some younger ones were educated there.

Egypt's immediate support for the revolutionary Sallal regime in the Yemen drew them quickly into giving military support to the republicans in the civil war which ensued when the Imam Badr was toppled. The Saudis out of principle and self-interest supported the royalists who were strong amongst the tribes. The Egyptians had probably not intended to be locked into the Yemen as long or as deeply as they became, and fighting in the unfamiliar mountainous terrain proved a formidable military challenge to the Egyptian troops. Field Marshal Abdel Hakim Amer and Anwar Sadat were therefore constantly paying prolonged visits to assess the situation and urging the traditional

Shaikhs by political persuasion to support the revolutionary government. This war was unpopular in Egypt, however, and on 3 March
1963 there were Army demonstrations against it in Cairo.

Egyptian action in Yemen inevitably impinged on the British position
in Aden and the Eastern and Western Protectorates, and consequently
coloured our relations with Cairo. The Egyptians desperately wanted
British recognition of the new revolutionary regime but British criteria
for recognition were not met. A serious civil war was raging, opinion
differed on how much of the country the new regime controlled effectively, and increasing Egyptian military involvement – eventually up to
70,000 troops – distorted the pattern.

The Egyptians did not want to see a strong Federation of traditional
elements in the States of the British South Arabian Protectorates.
Nonetheless they made little comment when in 1963 Aden itself, long
administered as a Crown Colony, joined the British-inspired South Arabian Federation. Border clashes, however, caused trouble and were
always hot news – the border between the Yemen and the Western Aden
Protectorate in Beihan causing the most difficulty. I suppose that the
Military Attaché, Brigadier Trevor Mossman, must have been on leave
but I was personally drawn into negotiations with General Hadidi, the
Egyptian Director of Military Intelligence, and on 26 November 1962
he asked me to arrange the repatriation of two wounded Egyptian soldiers, said to be in the hands of the Sherif of Beihan. The Egyptians also
sought our help when an Egyptian IL14 came down at Lodar in South
Arabia on 5 December. On the other hand an incident on the Beihan
border on 1 February 1963, when the Yemenis attacked Beihan forces,
was described by *Akhbar* as a British plot.

The boot was on the other foot when twenty-one British men and
women soldiers on a recreational exercise, crossing the border with
astonishing carelessness on 25 June 1963, fell into Yemeni hands. This
time I had to request Egyptian help over the return of our troops and I
became busy again with the Ministry of Foreign Affairs and General
Hadidi, who was helpful. When the Egyptians were accused of using
poison gas in the Yemen campaigns, however, their response was fierce
criticism of Britain's role in South Arabia and elsewhere. This chimed in
with Nasser's strong and specific charges against Britain on 22 February 1964 on account of our bases in Libya and Cyprus, while our
attitude to the very existence of Israel kept cropping up as a grievance.

There was no single way of responding to such attacks but on one
occasion Geoffrey Arthur, adopting a light touch, countered Egyptian

criticism of our position in South Arabia by showing Nasser's adviser Mohamed Faiq an old picture, fortuitously found in the Embassy. It portrayed Aden in the early 1920s bedecked for the Prince of Wales's visit with a great banner displayed by local people bearing the caption, 'Tell Daddy we are all happy under British rule'! But when the Sultan of Fadhli defected and arrived in Cairo 6 July 1964, this was a blow to the Federation, even though the Egyptians, abandoning consistency for pragmatism, hailed the man they had earlier branded a 'feudal ruler' as a nationalist hero. We were not involved in Cairo in any political negotiations about the future of South Arabia but we did have some very informal talks with Abdulla Asnaj, a leading pro-Yemeni and pro-Nasser Adeni politician, and, though we had no diplomatic relations, I was introduced to the Yemeni Ambassador by the Ethiopian Ambassador.

Sawt al Arab was beamed from Cairo to the whole Arab world and, even though men in the street knew the broadcasts were packed with inaccuracy, they found the tone and sentiment seductive. Sometimes, however, exaggeration reached laughable proportions. For instance on 8 April 1963 Akhbar reported quite inaccurately that the UK was bitterly opposed to Arab unity because of our position in the Gulf and Arabian Peninsula. Sawt al Arab warned Trucial States people to beware a British agent called General Huntingdon masquerading under the name of Mansur. Robin Huntingdon, who had never risen beyond captain in his Army days, now ran the Agricultural Trials Station at Ras al Khaimah where all the local people, who knew him well, saw him as a benefactor and called him Mansur out of affection. Even more absurdly the Voice of the Arab Nation on 23 April 1963 urged the people of Jordan to cut King Hussein into small pieces and leave half of them at the British Embassy.

Despite Nasser's vehement rhetoric and media antagonism, it never resulted in direct personal or physical attacks on our Embassy. In this we were more fortunate than the Americans, whose Embassy was burned by a mob on 20 November 1964. Perhaps it was taken for grace in us that the ballroom of the Embassy had been turned into the British Council library, which was much used by students. Moreover the Egyptians are a hospitable people and the warmth displayed towards us in personal relations contrasted starkly with the stream of disobliging remarks about the British on Sawt el Arab. One Egyptian friend emphasised this by remarking that the Egyptians are a good and easy-going people, who did not deserve their present Government.

The Egyptians certainly showed their basic friendliness and goodwill towards us in many ways. For instance when Brigadier Green, the Deputy Director of Military Intelligence, came in July 1962, some senior members of the Embassy, including me, were entertained at the Officers' Club – the first Anglo-Egyptian military event since Suez – and I was a guest at the Police Officers' Club early in my stay in Egypt. I also fell into chance conversation on the water front at Port Tewfik with someone who might have been expected to hold anti-British feelings – an Egyptian Suez Canal pilot. We talked about the Canal in a very friendly way and he revealed that he had had a very tough time when the British and French pilots were withdrawn in 1956 just before Suez, not because of the inherent difficulty of the task but simply owing to the shortage of hands.

This reminded me that in 1956 guidance had been circulated to British diplomatic posts, predicting that the withdrawal of the European pilots would halt the operation of the Suez Canal. I laughed on reading this, much to the astonishment of my room mate in the Foreign Office, who asked the cause of my mirth. I said that, from what I had seen of Egyptians running railways and ports, they were completely capable of managing on their own, although the British and French Canal pilots had an interest in emphasing the difficulty of their task. A retired British naval commander endorsed this view in a letter to *The Times*, explaining that during the 1939–45 War he had taken his destroyer straight through the Canal without difficulty, when no pilots were available.

A very special old family friend was Dr Kawkab Hefni Nassef, the first Egyptian lady doctor, who had been in my aunt's guardianship in England in the early 1920s and at times had felt so passionately about the Anglo-Egyptian politics of the time that she had barely spoken for days. Despite this she kept up a warm correspondence with my aunt until her death. By the 1960s she was a large lady with a proportionate sense of humour – sometimes Rabelaisian – and her humour was matched by her humanity. Although she came from a wealthy family – her father was a famous poet and liberal – she worked in Shubra, a very poor part of Cairo, becoming the first Egyptian Director of the Kitchener Hospital there. Her sense of fun showed when she announced that my grandfather Tom – who nicknamed her 'Corky' and whom she adored – was the best of the males in the family. My father was next best and I was way behind!

Dr Kawkab's brother-in-law Moukhtar Madkur and his beautiful wife Malak, who was deeply involved in various Egyptian charities, also became close friends. Another Egyptian lady doctor, Dr Tawhida who had been my aunt's pupil and charge, also came again into my ken, but I was to disappoint her being unable to find a suitable slot for her delightful daughter in the Embassy.

Like Harold Beeley, the President of the Egyptian Football Association, who was also a member of FIFA believed in the value of sportsmanship to foster good relations. He was a Cambridge-educated former Minister of Agriculture, Abdulla Salim – the father of Malak Madkur, and a great admirer of Stanley Matthews. Thus, in 1962, a very strong Tottenham Hotspur team led by Danny Blanchflower came to play a Selected Egyptian Xl. Many Egyptians followed English league football with all the passion of English supporters and the stadium was crammed, the excitement intense. In the first minute the Egyptian team scored a breakaway goal and the crowd rose to their feet, wild with joy, but the Spurs settled down, winning comfortably, and the Egyptians very sportingly acknowledged Spurs' superiority, commenting philosophically on the pleasure of watching good football.

This was a good curtain-raiser and a number of cultural events followed – another route to the hearts of educated Egyptians, starved for years of European culture. The highlight was a uniquely beautiful and unforgettable performance of *Romeo and Juliet* by the Old Vic with Judi Dench as Juliet; for this, we made up parties and Queen Dina was one of my guests. Other much appreciated manifestations were performances by the Ballet Rambert and the pianist Denis Matthews. A public lecture at Cairo University by Colonel Draper, the distinguished international lawyer and one of the prosecutors at the Nuremberg trials, was the result of an invitation from Professor Hamid Sultan, the Dean of the Law School – the first lecture there by an Englishman for twenty-five years!

Harold Beeley believed strongly that culture was an important element of diplomacy and he objected strongly – with success – when visiting Foreign Office Inspectors sought to suppress an Embassy post, held by a local Armenian who sang in the chorus of the Cairo Opera. Equally persuasively, perhaps, he was the only man in the Embassy who could obtain new telephones and guarantee repairs. His brother worked in the Telecoms Department. Cairo Opera House, a nineteenth-century gem – for which *Aïda* was written at the time of the opening of the Suez Canal – had not then been destroyed by fire and members of the British and American Embassy put on a joint production of *The Mikado* there. Hywel Duck our Second Secretary, an accomplished musician and organist, was to conduct it, but at this moment the Foreign Office wished to send him on a temporary assignment to Syria. Harold Beeley objected because he 'attached importance' to Hywel

Duck conducting the public performances in Opera House – and anyway could not be spared. Such is the magic of music. He was not removed.

Cairo happily also gave me opportunity to renew acquaintance with old Sudanese friends. Dardiri Ahmed Ismail, a leading member of the Sudanese Bar – who once protested in my court in Khartoum that his opponent's tactics were 'not cricket' – had become Assistant Secretary-General of the Arab League. My Khartoum colleague Judge Abdel Rahman el Nur and his wife came to visit me in the flat, as did Nazir Abdulla Bakr from Gedaref District. The Sudanese Chargé d'Affaires, Abbas el Dabi, was always very friendly and in a curious manner we still regarded each other as close colleagues. He shared the general sense of Sudanese humour and once when I called on him I found Bimbashi Biheiri – the father of Mamoun el Biheiri, at one time Finance Minister in Khartoum – who indulged in a great deal of nostalgia about the British period. He branded Abbas 'modern rubbish' to the latter's huge delight and claimed the only people for whom he had any time were the old British administrators! Abbas believed strongly in the British connection and indignantly warned that the Americans were working against our interests in the Middle East. However this may be, we had very close ties with the US Embassy in Cairo and compared notes very frankly on Middle Eastern issues in particular with Don Bergus, the Counsellor who spent many years there.

Another curious reminder of my Sudan days came from an encounter with a tram driver in Alexandria, a typical old school Egyptian still wearing a red *tarbush* – though these had gone out of fashion with the revolution – and thick glasses. My car had run out of petrol and I was taking a tram to find a source of fuel. He recognised me as having tried him in Khartoum for causing what he was proud to call 'a very big disturbance in Omdurman' when the political campaign for 'Unity of the Nile Valley' was in full swing. Instead of showing any resentment he welcomed me as an old friend, address me as 'Excellency' and bowed me off his tram.

The complex property problems arising from Suez and its aftermath occupied the time of six British staff in the Embassy. They answered to Claims Department in the Foreign Office and the Foreign Compensation Commission, and also had to deal with the loss adjusters Toplis and Harding and local lawyers. In the worst cases, a particular British property might have been affected by several measures – Egyptianisation, nationalisation, sequestration of 'enemy' assets as well as political sequestration under Proclamation No. 138 of 1961. Inevitably many parts of the Egyptian bureaucracy were involved – Ministry of Finance, Ministry of Commerce, two Sequestrators-General, Exchange Control, and nationalised British banks like Barclays DC and O. Thus we had to deal with a nightmare of red tape, often as frustrating to the Egyptians as to us. As an example of Egyptian procedure, it took no less than twenty signatures and nineteen countersignatures to get my car released from the Customs in Alexandria. Nonetheless the Sequestrator-General of British Property, Hafiz Abdel Hamid, and the Sequestrator-General of Property sequestrated under Proclamation No 138, Abdel Latif Ezzat and his successor Anwar el Shellabi, were agreeable, came frequently to my flat on social occasions and did their best to help. I had known Dr Ezzat earlier as Egyptian Trade Commissioner in Khartoum. Cairenes joked that, since the property of so many rich Egyptians had been sequestrated under the 1961 Proclamation, he could not lose a race at the Gezira race meetings as he owned all the horses!

The agreement signed in August 1962 by Dr Kaissouni for Egypt and Geoffrey Arthur, then Chargé d'Affaires, for Britain demonstrated inventiveness. Egypt was desperately short of foreign currency to make compensation payments to British citizens who had left Egypt, and it was agreed that the Egyptians would provide monthly drafts in Egyptian pounds to cover the Embassy's local expenses to enable the Foreign Compensation Commission in London to make sterling payments to individuals by way of set-off.

This agreement also included Egyptian undertakings to release many items of property from sequestration immediately. When nothing happened, I called on Dr Hamed el Sayeh,[12] to protest. He listened carefully and then said, 'Cut the cackle. Tell me, Mr Hawley, what per cent efficiency do you think that this agreement is working at?' I replied, 'If one is generous, possibly 60%.' '60% efficiency in Egypt,' he exclaimed. 'You do not know how lucky you are!' He explained that, if Dr Kaissouni had not judiciously entered into an international commitment, there would have been no hope of persuading the Egyptian ministries concerned to agree the detailed measures. As it was, they were gradually brought round and progress, though slow, increasingly became effective.

There were other unusual problems. The Governor of Cairo wanted to move the Anglican Cathedral – which I attended regularly being Honorary Secretary of the Cathedral Council – to build a new bridge across the Nile. This eventually came about and the Egyptians provided

12 The Undersecretary in charge of the problem.

funds for a new cathedral in Zamalek. A plan to move the war cemetery at Hadra in Alexandria was an equally knotty and emotive issue, which also concerned all the other Commonwealth countries, but fortunately this scheme was dropped.

Hadra was only one of the Commonwealth War Graves war cemeteries in Egypt resulting from the two World Wars, the largest being at Alamein – a particularly beautiful and haunting place, especially poignant for those who served in the desert war in the 1940s. An annual wreath laying ceremony took place there on Remembrance Day, attended by Egyptian officers, including the Governor of the Region, as well as the Ambassadors of all the Commonwealth countries. The greater number of graves there are British, including those of some of my personal friends. On these occasion we always also visited the German and Italian cemeteries, remarking how each cemetery somehow displayed its own national character and aura.

Apart from this I had several reasons for going to Alexandria. Raymond Flower, who had been brought up in Egypt, lived part of the year there. He was a congenial man of my own age and a sportsman, and we often played squash and tennis together. He and his mother invited me not only to Badr el Shin on the Nile near Cairo but also to their house at Agame near Alexandria – on the beach on which Napoleon's forces landed in 1798. Raymond subsequently wrote a number of books, of which the first was *From Napoleon to Nasser*, and both he and I started our writing in adjoining rooms in that Agame house. In subsequent summers, when the Flowers were away, I took the house and enjoyed relaxing weekends there with friends. Agame was then an especially quiet place as many houses there belonged to people whose property had been sequestrated.

During the King's time the Embassy moved with the King's court to Alexandria in the summer, and on two occasions I stayed at the old Residence at Ramleh, which had been kept on a care and maintenance basis since those days. Visions of Mountolive, said to have been modelled by Laurence Durrell on Sir Laurence Grafftey-Smith,[13] came to mind as I sat at the Ambassadors' desk to write. Much of the life of Alexandria described by Laurence Durrell in his *Alexandria Quartet* had disappeared with the revolution, however, and opinion differed

13 Author of *Bright Levant* and *Hands to Play*, he had served in Cairo. He was a distinguished member of the Levant Consular Service though he was never Ambassador in Egypt, and his style earned him the sobriquet of 'Le Boulevardier'.

between old-time residents on Durrell's descriptions of it. A distinguished American former judge of the Mixed Courts,[14] Jasper Brinton, and his genial and matronly wife, Geneva, said Durrell did not reflect the Alexandria they had known. Others, perhaps more worldly, claimed he had not told the half!

The atmosphere in Cairo was a slightly strange mix of normality and awareness that Egypt was a police state, although not as harsh as some others. Egyptians were not unduly inhibited from contacts with us and other diplomats, but surveillance was both palpable and overt. A secret policeman noted the names of everyone attending diplomatic parties and the tall Nubian 'Boabs', custodians of blocks of flats, were no doubt on the Intelligence pay roll. A friendly *ancien régime* Protocol officer kindly warned me how the system worked.

Security men were anyway often crude in their methods. Mohamed Ahmed Mahgoub, a distinguished Sudanese Advocate, Head of the Bar and later Prime Minister, was an old friend from Khartoum and he came to lunch one day, arousing the curiosity of Intelligence officers. I was after all only a First Secretary. Shortly after his arrival, a furious knocking at the front door was followed by sounds of altercation and Hassan the cook appeared to announce that a man was demanding to see me instantly about becoming my *suffragi*. I had recently filled the vacancy, but the visitor continued to make loud demands for entry until Hassan, obdurate in my defence, got rid of him. Mahgoub, much amused, said he would tease his friend Zakariah Mohieddin, the Minister of the Interior, about his Intelligence officers' lack of finesse!

I just wondered whether the Egyptians had subjected me, in view of my earlier service in the Sudan and Trucial States, to special surveillance. Certainly a *suffragi* I took on stayed only a few months and then inexplicably said he must leave. A smart Nubian with perhaps more of the cut of a police or Intelligence officer than a servant, he did not seem entirely at home with the *suffragi*'s life, and more than once on returning unexpectedly to my flat I found him in my sitting room reading the newspapers – something very unusual for one in his position. His precipitate departure could have been due to conclusion that I was not

14 Mixed Courts were a relic of the Capitulations system in the Ottoman Empire, by which foreign nationals were subject to the jurisdiction of their own communities' courts rather than the local Islamic law. The Mixed Courts in Egypt were a sophisticated example and they dealt in particular with cases which involved both an Egyptian and a foreigner. They were only abolished in 1949, when their jurisdiction was assumed by the National Courts in Egypt.

involved in any clandestine activities. However this may be, he was not as blatant as the man who lined up at the end of the queue one Christmas Day, when Colin Crowe was distributing envelopes of tips to his servants. Asked who he was, he replied, 'Don't you know me, sir? I am your Secret Security man.'

I once came literally face to face with a uniformed Egyptian Intelligence officer when Shaikh Rashid, the Ruler of Dubai, passed through Cairo Airport on his way to the Sudan on a hunting trip for the greater bustard. I met him in the VIP room, but an Egyptian Intelligence captain insisted on sitting very close to us and listening to our conversation. Shaikh Rashid spoke his customary Gulf Arabic – which is very different from the Egyptian both in usage and pronunciation – with the velocity of a Frenchman and it was mildly satisfying to see the look of puzzlement on the young officer's brow as he sought to follow the thread!

Egyptian Intelligence overstepped the mark in 1964 when they kidnapped a wanted man in Italy, drugged him and took him to the airport in Rome for consignment to Cairo in a large box by air freight. Their plans were discovered when the victim woke and his cries alerted astonished airport staff. The incident produced a great deal of mirth as well as embarrassment in Cairo and relations between Egypt and Italy became the source of a number of typical Egyptian stories. One told of an Egyptian visitor to Rome, who came back to tell his friends that he had seen the Nasser car everywhere in Italy. The Italians must have copied it! This was a typical Egyptian joke against themselves, as the Nasser car assembled in Egypt was, as everyone knew, entirely made under licence from Fiat parts.

The Egyptian sense of humour, so widespread, often has a cockney cheekiness. In Zamalek where I lived, cars were always parked locked but with the brake off. This enabled a 'shunter' to push them to and fro to fit more into a given stretch. Our shunter, almost certainly an agent of the Egyptian secret police, proffered his hand for the expected tip one evening shortly after my arrival and I gave him ten piastres, the normal rate being only one. He looked at it aghast and exclaimed, 'What is this?' 'More than you usually get,' I replied. 'No,' he said. 'Every Excellency gives me £E1.' I retorted that I was not an Excellency. 'Never mind,' he said. 'You will become a lord!'

It was a facet of Gemal Abdel Nasser's humanity as well as vanity that he apparently collected the many stories which the Egyptians manufactured about him. God, according to one, had a reception in heaven for all past and present Kings, Queens and Presidents. St Peter announced them and God stood up to receive them in turn. However, when Nasser was announced, God remained seated. After the reception St Peter asked God why he had not stood for him. 'I thought that fellow might sit down in my place,' came God's answer.

Despite the irritations of Intelligence supervision, social contact was still surprisingly easy with some Egyptians. Many senior officials, including agreeable Army officers given civilian posts and members of the Ministry of External Affairs, had received official clearance to attend parties and some Egyptians also entertained us in their homes. I established good rapport with the Chief of Protocol, Hassan Kamil, a former Gunner officer like me, and with the Head of the Cultural Department – and later Arab Department – in the Ministry of Foreign Affairs, Abdel Meguid Fahmy. A former Parachute colonel with blue eyes, fair hair and moustache, he looked very like a British counterpart and I often played squash with him, though in introducing me to his friends he emphasised that I spoke Arabic – lest no doubt their tongues should wag too much. He and his elegant and charming wife became close friends and frequent visitors.

The Gezira Club, still a wonderful sports club, was no longer an exclusive institution and by the 1960s there were thousands of Egyptian members. Large areas had been turned into football pitches and golf, not deemed a revolutionary game, was confined to nine of the previous eighteen holes. Similar revolutionary 'political correctness' in regard to polo led to its abolition by Nasser, but this was too much for the influential cavalry officers in the regime who secured its reinstatement in 1963. The excellent tennis and squash courts were unaffected and I played there nearly every day, sometimes taking on the squash professional at the Club, even though he had to give me two or three points!

The British community included some elderly people who had been in Egypt for many years. The most eminent was Professor Cresswell, the authority on Muslim architecture, whose *magnum opus*, the meticulous recording of Islamic monuments in Egypt and elsewhere, cannot ever be surpassed. He was by then in his eighties and still dressed like an Edwardian gentleman with a stiff rounded collar, a prominent tie-pin and an old Homburg hat. Straight as a ramrod, he would walk with his stick through old Cairo visiting the Islamic monuments. Small boys would run before him, adoring his eccentricity for he would knock them gently aside with his stick with the words, 'Out of the way, dung!'

– a mild form of opprobrium in Egypt. He kindly agreed to take Ruth and me to Cairo's mosques on condition that we viewed them chronologically, beginning with the seventh century mosque of Amr ibn el As. His scholarly achievements were later rewarded by the conferment of a knighthood when he was ninety, and we happened to be at the same investiture, when I received my CMG. His work was far removed from the political arena but he spoke his mind bluntly about contemporary Egypt, calling Nasser and his associates 'masters of perfidy and evasion' and branding it a 'beastly regime all based on hate'.

Before our privileged 'tutorial' with Professor Cresswell I was already interested in Cairo's wonderful mosques and had visited some so often that the doorkeepers, taking me for an academic, addressed me as 'Doctor'. Among my favourites were the ninth century Ibn Tulun – the only one in Egypt with a staircase on the outside of the minaret, like those in Samarra in Iraq – the Mameluke Sultan Hassan, with its open and gigantic 'Gothic' arches, and Sultan Barquq and Qaitbai with their elaborate decoration.

The British old guard also included Squadron Leader Hindle-James, a still spry member of the community who had served as a Special Services Officer in Iraq at the end of the Great War with Glubb Pasha – later to command Jordan's Arab Legion. He proudly displayed his fine array of photographs of well-known Middle Eastern personalities and loved to discuss the detailed recent history of the region. Another character was Shirley Stiven, who had been married to a well-known British doctor, to whom she referred as 'Stiven' like a character in Jane Austen novel. Hers had been a full life as her first husband, whom she had accompanied *en poste*, was Hassan al Khalousi, the first Egyptian Ambassador to Rome in the 1920s. A close friend of Dr Kawkab and the Madkurs, she lived in a flat overlooking the Embassy, which enabled her to form strong opinions – probably on very inadequate evidence – on members of the Embassy staff whose comings and goings she could observe. Happily she approved of Ruth and me.

Despite our best efforts I had come to conclude that it would always be difficult for Britain to do business with Nasser on a fully normal basis. There was insufficient meeting of minds and his doctrine clashed with our pragmatic policies. A former Minister in Nasser's own government confirmed this view when he asked me why HMG seemed to want a dialogue with 'these people' when the country was bankrupt and clutching at every straw. Nasser was, he said, a man who trusted neither himself nor anyone else. His advice was succinct:

Don't believe
Don't trust
Don't lend
Don't commend him

I heard a similar assessment eighteen years later from Egyptians, who had held high office in his regime and worked closely with him. British relations with Egypt certainly became easier after his death. Whether relations could have been better from the start if a different approach had been made when the young officers first took over; or if some means had been found of going ahead with US and British financing of the High Dam, or if the Suez attack had not taken place, must be moot questions. However, no one embodied the Pan-Arab ideal more than Nasser and he was idolised for this. When he died on 28 September 1970, the mourning crowds of Egyptians and Arabs in many parts of the Middle East testified to the very deep affection he was capable of inspiring and the genuine sorrow at the loss of a man perceived as the greatest and most successful of the modern Rulers of Egypt, who like Arabi Pasha and Saad Zaghlul Pasha had risen from the ranks of the Fellahin.

As for me, marriage resulted in almost immediate promotion to Head of Chancery and Senior Counsellor in the British High Commission in Lagos. Immediately inviting the Nigerian Chargé d'Affaires, George Dove-Edwin, to dinner, I asked him for one very special tip about diplomatic life in Nigeria. 'Nigerians', he said, 'should never be asked to small sit-down dinners; their attendance is not guaranteed.' And he was proven all too right when we got to Lagos.

Ruth and I left Cairo on transfer in December 1964 for a short spell of home leave over Christmas. We left with very great regret, and we retain special memories of our time there. It was particularly touching when Mr Jamali, the senior member of the local staff and incidentally the brother-in-law of the Sultan of Zanzibar, made a speech at our farewell party. He said we would both be missed and I had been an exceptional Head of Chancery with 'the acumen of a diplomat, the fairness of a judge and the humanity of an author'. The Egyptians, who always address people by a higher rank than they possess, can be guilty of wild hyperbole but the flattery rang sweetly in our ears as we departed.

6

Nigeria

In 1965 Nigeria, the largest, most populous and perhaps most promising Commonwealth country in Africa, was divided into four Regions lying in the tropics between 4° 20 and 14° latitude. With an area of 357,000 square miles, it had over fifty-five million people, speaking several hundred languages or dialects. The Northern Region consisted largely of traditional Muslim Sultanates; the Western Region was peopled largely by the Yoruba – some Christian and others Muslim – and the Eastern Region dominated by mainly Christian Ibos; a number of different tribes occupied the Mid-Western Region. Thus the map conjured up a vision of a large tray: the North resting on a tripod with three unequal legs, the three Southern Regions. The River Niger, running down in a broad sweep to the many-mouthed delta on the Gulf of Benin through Guinea, Malawi and Niger before entering Nigeria in the northwest, inspired the country's modern name. Nigeria was formed from the British Protectorates along the river, before which there were a number of important kingdoms. Bornu had a known history of a thousand years and the names of others were known throughout the world – the Fulani Empire, the Yoruba Empire of Oyo and the kingdoms of Ife and Benin.

Achieving Independence in 1960, Nigeria was a multi-faceted federal democracy with a representative Government at Federal and Regional level and a strong and independent Judiciary, bequeathed by the British Colonial Administration. The country's importance and potential was obvious but in 1965 there were two British views about its immediate future. Francis Cumming-Bruce, the High Commissioner, saw it as a young elephant gradually struggling to its feet. Senior officials like John Chadwick, Assistant Undersecretary of State in the Commonwealth Office, did not discount a bright future but thought it first faced a period of trauma. John Willie Robertson,[1] the last British Governor-General from 1955 to 1960, with his experience of both the Sudan and Nigeria, doubted if it would hold together as a democratic country and

---

1 Sir James Robertson, KT, GCMG, GCVO, MBE, formerly Civil Secretary in the Sudan Government.

he proved right sooner than expected. Only a year after our arrival, democracy was transformed overnight into military rule. Thus we witnessed Nigeria's rapid transition from a rich and fairly stable country still enjoying peace and many good aspects of the British Colonial administration to an area at war with itself.

West Africa began for Ruth and me at Euston as we caught the boat train. Platform 14 was thronged with black West Africans seeing relations off. We sailed from Liverpool on the last day of 1964 on the *Apapa*, a ship of the Elder Dempster line – a name famous throughout West Africa, as it featured in the Pidgin English Bible used by missionaries to describe Noah's Ark! Two passengers on the *Apapa* had been commended to us by John Willie Robertson – old Chief Ben Oluwole with his blue robes and round gold-embroidered cap and Brigadier 'Zak' Maimalari, fresh from the Staff College but sadly killed in the first military coup d'état a year later.

The *Apapa* was not prepossessing. Climbing the rickety gangway we saw she lacked the chic of the *Ausonia* on which we had crossed from Alexandria to Venice on leaving Egypt. Stern first we went out into a perturbed Mersey. It remained rough for the first day or two and many passengers did not show their heads. Captain McWilliam invited us to his table and we soon appreciated the *Apapa* for its friendly and informal spirit. As it became less wintry we joined in deck activities and I reached the final of the greasy pole fight. Ruth won first prize for fancy dress as 'In Vogue' and was taught the swaying West African 'High Life' by the octogenarian Chief Ben at evening dances.

Las Palmas in the Canary Islands, chiefly notable for Scandinavian 'sun worshippers', is engraved on our hearts. Not one of the twenty-five letters we posted there reached their addresses. Our next call was Bathurst in the minuscule Gambia, Britain's last and smallest colony in West Africa. Strung out along the river dividing Senegal into two halves, it was only the size of a District in the Sudan but still had the full panoply of Governor and Government House. Britain had established Bathurst[2] in 1816 but Fort James on James Island had stood there since 1661. All that remained of it was a small tower and a few short stretches of crenellated wall. We visited it on the *Lady Wright*, a slut of a boat which poured black soot not only over us but over the spotless robes of the Irish nuns who were our fellow passengers on the *Apapa*. The climate was beautiful, though remarkably cold, and

2 Named after Henry Earl Bathurst, Colonial Secretary 1812–28.

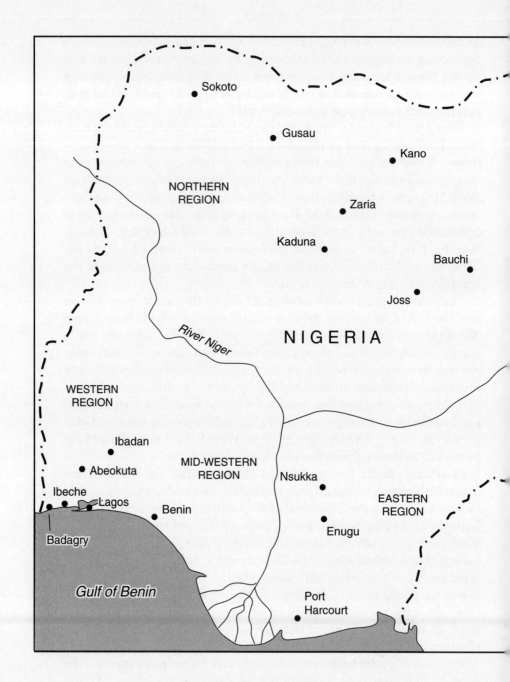

Nigeria 1965

Gambia seemed bound to become the tourist resort it subsequently has. The eye was struck by the bright blue clothes, dyed with local indigo and worn by most of the local people, but the Wolof tribeswomen, still wearing the beautiful clothes of Marie Antoinette's epoch, were equally stunning with their colour and anachronism.

From this old smuggling enclave we sailed for Freetown in Sierra Leone built on rolling green hills around a harbour, the town itself a curious mixture of English and African styles. Lord Mansfield's decision in Somerset's case in 1772, that every slave setting foot in Britain was a free person entitled to the benefit of Habeas Corpus, led to the creation of the colony with Freetown as its capital and the founding fathers were 351 freed black slaves sent out from England by Granville Sharp, a friend of Bishop Wilberforce, together with 60 'shanghaied' Plymouth prostitutes. Their descendants became the 'Creoles' of Freetown.

Music from a remarkable number of churches of different denominations filled the morning air on the Sunday of our arrival. People observed the Sabbath faithfully and appeared in their Sunday best, many men wearing frock coats and top hats. We visited the Parliament, where a lively old man in the Sergeant-at-Arms's office showed us the chamber and other parts of the buildings, adding conspiratorially that members spent little time in the library but much in the canteen where free food was provided. Outside, near the tree where slaves were sold before the British colony was established, stood a statue to the first Prime Minister of Sierra Leone, Sir Milton Margai, surrounded by sad but bright plastic flowers.

At Tema in Ghana we also visited Parliament, driving past splendid palms along the coast on the way. On entering, one was immediately struck by a large picture of the first Prime Minister and leader of independent Ghana, Kwame Nkrumah, trailing clouds of glory. An inscription on the Speaker's Chair revealed it as a gift from Parliament in Westminster, but over it Nkrumah appeared again in a 'Byzantine' icon of rich red and orange. Outside the building Ghana's Osagyefo, or 'Saviour', was commemorated on yet another memorial bearing the caption 'Seek Ye First the Political Kingdom'. Nemesis avenged his hubris some years later.

We arrived next day in Lagos, immediately more striking and significant than other ports on the West African coast. Ships lay alongside the quays on both sides of the harbour and others were anchored offshore, awaiting a berth. The horizon was outlined by skyscrapers, mainly built after Independence. Closer acquaintance raised doubts about first appearance. Pleasant suburbs, impressive buildings such as Parliament and the Supreme Court and the fine drive along the lagoon – the Marina – were one side of the coin but behind the façade it was often sordid. Lagos was mainly a place of narrow, poorly planned streets, open stinking drains, and of colourful but squalid native markets, where women predominated.

We were to live, however, in Ikoye in considerable comfort. No. 3 Queen's Drive was a pleasant modern house, looking out over Five Cowrie Creek, to Victoria Island and distant palms beyond. Fishermen cast their nets in the early morning and punted past in flat-bottomed boats for all the world as if they were on the Cherwell or the Cam. Ruth, having read a book on tropical gardening from A to Z, helped the gardener put theory into practice in our large garden. We were surrounded by people with biblical names: Titus the cook, David the head steward and Moses the 'small boy'. The gardener was named after Saint Francis and the nannies Comfort and Beatrice.

The High Commission was a large mission of more than a hundred members, with five Counsellors and over fifty-UK based staff and there were also sizeable Deputy High Commission Offices in Kaduna, Ibadan, Enugu and Benin. Francis Cumming-Bruce, later Lord Thurlow, was the High Commissioner. Angular, ascetic, academic and stimulating, he was delightful though sometimes rarefied in thought. The Deputy High Commissioner was Nick Larmour, a very good-natured and friendly Northern Irishman who was once startled to be taken by a senior Nigerian for the Irish Ambassador! He had started his career in the Indian Civil Service in Burma and had been in the room adjoining the Cabinet room when, on 19 July 1947, General Aung San and six other Ministers were murdered there by agents of U Saw. Ted Dymond, succeeded by Larry L'Estrange, was Commercial Counsellor, Arthur Peckham Aid Counsellor, David Condon Information Counsellor and Victor Rose Agricultural Counsellor. Several of the First Secretaries later became Heads of Mission including Peter McEntee and Mike Newington, and we also had a Defence Adviser and other diplomats with specialist functions. We all evolved a happy working relationship. The very large British Council offices in Lagos and the four Regions operated independently of the High Commission but were always in close touch.

The Plowden Report was accepted in 1964 by the Government. It resulted in the merger of the former Foreign and Commonwealth Services and establishment of 'The Diplomatic Service'. As Head of

Chancery and senior Counsellor, I was involved in implementing it locally and, as a diplomatic challenge, it was unenviable. The High Commission had to conform broadly with the pattern of an Embassy, newly prescribed regulations had to be introduced and some privileges enjoyed in the Commonwealth Services removed. The Senior Trade Commissioner and Director of Information lost their independent status, their staff were amalgamated into the High Commission's and senior officers' official cars had to be put into the pool (though with a 'wink' it would always be available to the former 'owner'). Duty rosters had to include people formerly exempt. I also became engaged in a pruning exercise in the High Commission and the Regional DHC's offices, but this caused very few problems as the existence of fat in the system was generally recognised.

On arriving I asked about the Emergency Scheme for the British community and was astonished to be told it did not exist as there had been 'no need for one in a friendly Commonwealth country'. I immediately put preliminary work in hand and with the coup of January 1966 it had to be quickly finalised. The Deputy High Commissioner in Enugu was reluctant to prepare his scheme, though in the event it was only in that Region that it had to be put into practice when the Biafran War started in 1967.

Nigeria, lying roughly on the same latitude, was often very reminiscent of the Sudan. Both countries had a Muslim north and a Christian or pagan south but Western traders, administrators, soldiers and missionaries had opened Nigeria up from the south. The Sudan on the other hand had been opened to the west from Egypt in the north by soldiers, only later followed by the administrators, traders and missionaries. Thus the people in the Sudan most exposed to European influence were northern Muslims whereas in Nigeria it was the Christian Ibos in the south-east and Yorubas in the south-west. The Yoruba tradition of having emigrated from the east and their tribal cheek markings bearing great similarity to the Shaiqia's in the Sudan suggested a former direct connection between the two countries.

Members of the Colonial Service in Nigeria enjoyed a considerable reputation and in 1965 – five years after Independence – there were still no fewer than 3,000 British serving in the Northern Region. My Sudan experience gave me an immediate affinity with those I met but a number of more direct and personal connections between the Sudan and Nigeria had been established. Not only had John Willie Robertson been Governor-General but Gawain Bell, who had also been in the

Sudan Political Service, was from 1957 until 1962 the last British Governor of Northern Nigeria, and there were a number of other 'Ful Sudanis', some of whom were still there in 1965. Sammy Richardson, the head of the School of Administration in Zaria University, was one of these. Some Kadis from the Sudan, including Bashir er Rayah, had also been seconded from the Sudan Judiciary as Islamic Judges in Northern Nigeria. In February 1965 John Willie Robertson with his wife Nancy returned on a visit and, touring widely in the country, received a very warm reception everywhere from Nigerians and British alike. Ruth and I were able to repay some of their hospitality to me as a young man in Khartoum in the 1940s and 1950s when we held a lunch party in their honour, inviting mutual Nigerian friends like Chief Ben Oluwole and George and Norma Dove-Edwin.

Another distinguished former colonial servant, who had been Chief Secretary in Nigeria, made a return visit in April 1965. This was Hugh Foot, Lord Caradon, the eldest of the three eminent Foot brothers. He was by then a Minister in Harold Wilson's Labour Government and, whilst retaining Ministerial office, had just been appointed Britain's Permanent Representative to the United Nations. The Nigerians, liking his easy, friendly and unpompous manner gave him a very warm reception and he found a happy rapport with Sir Abubakar, who held a large dinner party in his honour. Unorthodox in some ways, he later wrote to me personally from the UN about specific matters with which he knew I was dealing, even though correspondence from someone of his rank would normally have been with the High Commissioner. This pragmatic approach, combined with his intellect and grasp of affairs, greatly impressed me.

In early 1965 Nigeria was still well endowed with federal democratic institutions. The veteran Ibo politician Azikiwe ('Zik') occupied State House as President,[3] and the Federal Prime Minister was Sir Abubakar Tafewa Balewa, whose objectivity was enhanced by his not belonging to any of the main tribes of Nigeria. (His home was at Bauchi on the Niger in the south of Northern Nigeria.) The Federal institutions consisted of a cabinet with Federal Ministries, a Federal Parliament with two Chambers and an independent Judiciary. Each of the four States too was blessed with a State Governor, Premier, Executive Council and Legislature. Overall, therefore, there was such a plethora of Ministers and public servants that in March 1965 an article in *Foreign Affairs*

3 He had previously been Nigeria's first Nigerian Governor-General.

suggested that Nigeria could not afford so expensive a structure. Seen as external interference by the Americans in Nigerian internal affairs, this caused much resentment. Privately, however, senior Nigerian civil servants agreed whilst accepting that their politicians were not to be deprived of the fruits of office. The political atmosphere was also tainted with corruption, of which the Finance Minister, Chief Festus Okotie-Eboh, was reputedly an architect and practitioner. When negotiating a contract, it was said, he kept an open draw for the receipt of bribes, which he only closed when satisfied his 'cut' was sufficient.

The *Foreign Affairs* article proved prophetic of things to come but the reduction in the Government expenditure on Federal and Regional Ministers came about in a sudden and unexpected way. In his last days in 1965 Major-General Sir Christopher Welby-Everard, the last British Commander of the Nigerian Army, passionately urged Nigerian officers to overcome tribal loyalties and maintain their overall loyalty to the Army and the country. In 1966, however, Nigeria had two major coups d'état bringing the Army into politics and ruining the consensus and tribal co-operation hitherto prevailing in the Armed Forces. The democratic structures were swept away and civil servants took over the running of all the Ministries and Departments – rather more efficiently in fact without Ministers.

More immediately – and at the time of our arrival – Nigeria was recovering from the very deep political crisis which had arisen in December 1964. The causes included the conflicting ambitions for influence between the leaders of the North, East, West and Mid-West and their associated political parties as well as the personal ambition of Azikiwe to become an executive President. One central consideration was the ever-present need for Northern Nigeria to have a political alliance with one or more of the Southern States to ensure access to the sea. The first Federal election to be held since Independence that month brought things to a head and, despite the pleas of the Inspector-General of Police, L. O. Edet, the election itself was marred by every form of trickery and intimidation – boycotts, lack of voting papers, restraint, fraudulent prevention of putting in nominations, violence, riots and thuggery. The main political groupings were the NNA[4]

---

4 Nigerian National Alliance consisting of the NPC (Northern People's Congress), the NNDP (Nigerian National Democratic Party) essentially a Yoruba party and various splinter groups.

on the one hand and on the other UPGA.[5] The North's largest and most influential party, the NPC led by the Sardauna of Sokoto, was at this time associated with the Yoruba NNDP led by Chief Akintola and thus the influence of Chief Michael Okpara, leader of the Ibo NCNC Party in the Federal Government and the country, was reduced.

Realisation that UPGA were unlikely to win the election led their leaders to boycott it in the hope of having it declared invalid by the Ibo President Azikiwe. This would also have given Azikiwe the opportunity and excuse for assuming executive powers as President. However, the Chief Justice of the Supreme Court, Sir Adetokunbo Ademola, and other powerful and distinguished lawyers persuaded him that he had no power to form a Government except as provided in the Constitution and, bowing to this advice, he called on Sir Abubakar the previous Prime Minister, who had been re-elected, to form a Government. Abubakar promised to nominate a broadly based 'national' Cabinet and set about creating a strong interim Federal Government. His party, the Northern People's Front (NPF), became the largest in the ruling coalition. The main parties were electioneering in Western Nigeria and Lagos, where elections were still due, at a time when the Electoral Commission or the courts so ordained. Elections in the West later gave them a very bad, indeed frightening name. In the High Commission we were mere spectators of these political manoeuvrings, which continued in modified form throughout 1965, with the last election to the Regional Assembly in the West the most notorious when Chief Akintola was the Premier.

Internal politics did not prevent Nigeria having great influence in Africa and many visitors were attracted to Lagos including Julius Nyerere, President of Tanzania, who paid a State Visit in June 1965. Godfrey Eneli, the Chief of Protocol, confided that the Nigerians had been taken aback by Nyerere's asking for a 'platform' to make a major speech, but he nonetheless scheduled this for a reception at Parliament House. Nyerere spoke at length of pan-Africanism, continental government for Africa, and socialism, referring also to differences with Nigeria over the OAU (Organisation of African Unity). He succeeded in thoroughly boring the pragmatic Nigerians who, preferring to swig beer and chat, began to murmur embarrassingly. Applause when he finished was consequently lukewarm but the few political words spoken

5 The United Progressive Grand Alliance consisting of the largely Ibo NCNC (National Council of Nigerian Citizens), the AG (Action Group), the Northern Elements Progressive Union and the United Middle Belt Congress.

by Sir Abubakar, who was not doctrinaire, were delivered in beautifully enunciated and polished English and consequently greeted with considerable enthusiasm. There was no doubt whose style the Nigerians preferred.

Nigeria's importance was reflected in the size of the Diplomatic Corps and most major countries were represented, including Israel which had been very active both in establishing relations with many 'Black African' countries and funding aid programmes. Shortly after our arrival we met the Israeli Ambassador at dinner with the Cumming-Bruces. Such is the power of conditioning that, after three years' exposure to the Cairo media, it seemed almost impious to shake hands with him. There were other anomalies in the Diplomatic Corps and on one occasion Ruth and I were invited to a party of Ambassadors of West African States, at which we and the Turkish Ambassador and his wife were the only outsiders. We were also the only intermediaries between the French speakers from former French colonies and the English speakers. It highlighted the disadvantage of States which had been colonies of two peoples who could not (or would not) speak the other's language.

Nigeria's size and significance was also recognised when the British Labour Government decided that immigration from the Commonwealth could no longer be totally unrestricted. Lagos was therefore visited in May 1965 by a mission led by Lord Mountbatten to explain why in future entry certificates, comparable with visas, would be required. Mountbatten's meetings with Abubakar and senior Nigerian Ministers established that the British Government's proposals caused no difficulty for the Nigerians, as soon as it was made plain that young Nigerians would still to be able to come to Britain for training, even for prolonged periods. Nigeria made no claim to any right for her citizens to settle in the UK. More detailed talks followed with Nigerian officials; Sir Charles Cunningham, Permanent Undersecretary at the Home Office, and I as leader of the High Commission delegation participated in these talks and George Dove-Edwin was the chief negotiator from the Nigerian Ministry of External Affairs. A joint memorandum was fairly easily and quickly drafted and agreed, though at one point I had to rephrase a Home Office point in a form which the Nigerians could accept, thus showing that diplomacy as an art has its place. The visit was crowned by a large dinner hosted by Sir Abubakar.

Our first child was born in Nigeria on 31 May and Ruth stayed in Ibadan for a week or two immediately before Sara's birth enjoying the hospitality of both Godfrey Bass, the Deputy High Commissioner, and his wife Monica, and an old school friend of mine, Michael Barbour – Professor of Geography at Ibadan University – and his wife Jane. 1 June was the 'Glorious First' for me. In the early hours I heard news of Sara's birth. My journey to Ibadan to see the newborn child was an adventure. Owners of 'Mammy wagons', the ubiquitous Nigerian lorries which always bore captions like 'God Speed', 'Thy Will Be Done', 'Love Thy Neighbour' or 'Golden Rule', were aggrieved that Lagos City Council would not permit them to enter the capital. Taking the law into their own hands they blocked the access roads, preventing any traffic from leaving Lagos. Kind friends in the US Embassy, Clinton Olsen and Al Wellons, came to my rescue. A regional meeting in Lagos of American Ambassadors had just finished and an amphibious aircraft had been chartered to lift them from the creek near our house to Ikeja airport beyond the blockage. I went with them and was met there by a member of our staff at Ibadan who kindly drove me straight to the Catholic Mission Hospital at Oke Ofa. Sara, a lovely child, struck me as a cross between her Great Aunt May and Winston Churchill and I commented, 'Maybe she will be our bluestocking – her poses are very pensive!' She was christened in Lagos by the Revd Yinka Olumide, and her godfathers were two old friends – Michael Barbour and Jim Treadwell, who had come out to be Deputy High Commisioner in Enugu only a fortnight after our arrival.

Despite the electioneering and party political jockeying, relations with the Nigerians were easy – certainly in our first year – and members of the Nigerian Diplomatic Service were particularly friendly irrespective of their Region of origin; Godfrey Eneli was an Ibo from the East, Leslie Harriman from the West and Hamzat Ahmedu from the North. George Dove-Edwin, my former colleague in Cairo, who was later High Commissioner in London for many years, was a particular friend and I had many official dealings with him. We have him and his wife Norma to thank for saving Sara's life when she developed meningitis at the age of three months, for they had introduced us socially to Dr Ogbeide, one of Nigeria's leading paediatricians. A few days after this meeting, Sara's nurse Comfort was alarmed to notice a sudden swelling of the baby's fontanelle and rushed in alarm to tell Ruth, who took her immediately to Dr Ogbeide. Diagnosing meningitis he began treatment instantly and after a few worrying days Sara fortunately recovered completely.

My predecessor John Moreton had been invited to join a group of Nigerian Permanent Secretaries who played tennis once a week, and I was fortunate to be asked to replace him. We were the only two British to join this group,[6] and it was particularly useful as well as enjoyable, enabling me to build up strong personal friendships and also to learn informally much about Nigerian official thinking, particularly after the coups of 1966. The Permanent Undersecretary of Finance, Abdou Atta, did not play tennis and was not one of this group. We had, however, met briefly in Cairo and, told by some people – rather to my surprise – that he was anti-British, I decided to cultivate him. It always intrigued me to discover whether such allegations were true and if so, to discover the cause and assess whether the 'condition was remediable'. This policy served me very well in Atta's case. He and his bright and intelligent wife often came to our house and we developed a close friendship. When all the politicians disappeared from the scene after the first coup in January 1966 and the Permanent Undersecretaries ran their Ministries under the military regime, Atta without any disloyalty to his own people came round to the house on several occasions and told me frankly what was going on.

Apart from tennis and squash, our main relaxation was the 'Robinson Crusoe' house, a childhood's dream, which we had built next to our friends the Conyers on the splendid Golden Palm beach at Ibeche with its great Atlantic rollers. It was finished in July 1965 and cost £70 including the concrete floor. It was made of palm fronds and bamboo poles and stood among waving coconut palms with a fine open view of the golden beach and rolling sea. We went up there most weekends and our most exciting adventure was the first time we went up in our newly acquired boat. The boat looked like a swan with gleaming hull and black outboard engine and as we sped up the creek towards Ibeche it seemed that nothing could go wrong. It could and, when we came to leave, having had a long day negotiating details and watching the men thatching, it was late and the engine recalcitrant. Consequently we had to leave our boat with villagers, who offered to help us get home. We then all climbed into their dug out canoe, including the landlord.

Ganiyu, who later looked after our house for us and another youth, Timmy, placed the loads – picnic case and bathing bags – in the canoe and spread mats on the floor. We set off, Timmy punting, or 'pulling' as they called it. We glided peacefully past palms reflected in the dark water of the creek. Out of dreamy silence Timmy suddenly said, 'Master, this is a day you will remember and write about in your diary.'

6 On Freddy Coker's court.

I assured him I would. Again he chimed in, 'Master, this is like a day of war, like the Punic War.' I found this an astonishing remark from an ordinary village boy educated in a Mission school.

Timmy steered the boat into a little inlet, where we landed. The boys cheerfully picked up the loads and we set off along a forest path in the fast-dimming light. Figures loomed out of the darkness, muttering a gruff greeting of 'Akabo' as they passed. The sound of crickets and birds singing their last shrill songs before night set in was almost deafening. A distant church bell rang out, followed by loud singing from the West African church of 'The Cherubim and Seraphim'.

Fireflies flashed around us. Timmy stopped. Quick as lightning he bent down and seized a large land crab, which he gave to a girl friend in the little village at which we then arrived. A small group of men and women were sitting under a verandah lit by a single hurricane lamp. The boys shouted out a few Yoruba words, whereupon an enormous man stood up and without a word walked to the water's edge on the far side of the island we had crossed, where there were a few canoes waiting. Again mats were spread in a canoe and we set off bound we knew not where. Timmy said, 'Master, you will pay the puller ten shillings.' I held my peace awhile but when we reached the mainland an hour later it was clear he deserved every penny and more. The man of few words, evidently satisfied to receive his money, left his canoe and relieved himself *coram publico*.

By now it was a bright starlit night and we had landed near the Kerikera prison, the lights of which had been our beacon over the water for the past half hour. Walking towards the main road we saw the lights of an approaching car, an old and decrepit Austin taxi. The boys negotiated a price to take us to the 'boundary' between Western Region territory and the Federal territory of Lagos and we all piled in eagerly as if it had been a Rolls. A terrible clattering soon shattered our illusions as the exhaust pipe fell off. The Yoruba driver, who had cat's whisker face scars like the Shaigia of the Sudan, roared with laughter and fixed it with a handy piece of string. He could not go beyond the boundary, where the two boys who had been charming companions also left us. We paid him and them off and took a Federal taxi home to Ikoyi, arriving there some three hours after we had planned. Ruth was heavily pregnant with Sara.

I was lucky to be able to visit the capitals of the Regions and other parts of Nigeria to see something of the different areas with their varied peoples. There were significant developments taking place, including schemes under Britain's considerable aid programme and many projects in which Technical Assistance Officers were involved. British contractors were also involved with the Kainji Dam on the Niger and the work was held up at one stage when British welders went on strike. A senior and elderly union official arrived out to deal with this and I asked him what he was going to do. He said he would appeal to their patriotic sentiment and request them to 'work for Britain'. I admired his decent, old-fashioned union attitude but these 1960s welders were not persuaded. They then lost their jobs and were replaced by more willing foreign workers.

When I visited the Northern Region in June 1965 I found it reminiscent of the Sudan both in terrain and style of administration. I stayed with Bill Bates, our Deputy High Commissioner in Kaduna, and made a tour with him. At times I had to pinch myself to recall that it was five years after Independence, with the remaining 3,000 British officials serving in the Government of Northern Nigeria in one capacity or another, and senior Nigerian officials with whom they worked unanimous in praise of their continuing efforts for independent Nigeria. They were equally warm in the praise of Technical Assistance Officers and GVSOs,[7] most of whom were working in educational jobs, though some were virtually doing the job of an Assistant District Officer. Nigeria as a whole was in no hurry to get rid of its British officials. It was very different from our precipitate departure from the Sudan.

We stayed in Kano with one of the British Residents who had stayed on after Independence – St Elmo Nelson and his wife. They lived in a house built for the first Resident under Lugard's administration as Governor. It was distinguished by thick mud walls, high domed ceilings with simple fan tracery decoration, the cornices adorned with the little crenellations shaped like little rabbits' ears typical of the place. We found our common experiences in African administration a close bond.

We called on the Emir of Kano in his palace, a little reminiscent of some Rulers' palaces in the Persian Gulf. Passing through several outer portals, we were met by the Emir's Waziri and Mitwalli. Watched by numerous men in long robes we crossed a small court, the mud walls of which were decorated with striking patterns, and reached what in Arab countries would be called the *majlis*, just inside which the Emir was standing with ceremonial spear in hand. After greetings he led us to the throne room, elaborately decorated with designs of black and gold,

7 Graduate Voluntary Service Overseas.

where he sat on a low throne looking very impressive in a robe of blue lace and a red cap, round which a gleaming white turban was wound that also covered his chin – two cloth horns stuck out at the top. This rather wild dress and panoply concealed a man who had been Nigerian Ambassador to Senegal before being summoned back from Paris to become Emir, a very amiable and civilised man with perfect English. When he arrived back to take up the succession he only had European clothes with him and so suitable robes had to be rushed to the airport to enable him to don the traditional garb expected of him. We sat on plush chairs for the meeting.

Our conversation was enlivened by the interpolations of the Mitwalli, an enormous elderly man wearing a turban of monumental proportions and a finely embroidered robe. He spoke with a pronounced Oxford accent and commented shrewdly on the morning's BBC news. We were shown a picture of the Emir's grandfather who had been installed as Emir by Lugard, and we signed his book before taking our leave. The Emir then, to the sound of horns and silver trumpets, mounted his horse, which had been brought into the inner courtyard, and rode under the great archway of the palace to his daily court, surrounded by his Ministers. A woman cried with a shrill voice as she ran out in front of him. Kano, being not only the seat of tradition but also the epicentre of the modern ground nut industry, was notable for enormous pyramids of ground nuts covered with green protective covers awaiting onward shipment by rail to local and world markets.

At Ahmadu Bello University in Zaria, Sammy Richardson, with experience in the Sudan Political Service, was running the Institute of Administration. A formidable go-getter who persuaded large companies to make considerable contributions to his Business School, Sammy also had other talents. Having taken a course in embalming during one of his leaves, he had become 'Embalmer in Chief' to the US Embassy and had also made money in a successful dog meat business called 'Dog's Delight', using aniseed as an ingredient. Northern Nigeria also produced other surprises. At a cocktail party given for me, the Information Officer for the Northern Region, Dodo Mustafa, introduced me simultaneously to his two wives saying, 'Meet Mrs Dodo Mustafa I and Mrs Dodo Mustafa II.' Both delightful, one younger than the other, they seemed to be on terms of complete amity.

In April 1965 Ruth and I stayed in Enugu, the capital of the Eastern Region, with old friends, Jim and Philippa Treadwell, whom I had known since my Kosti days in the Sudan. There I met the very forth-coming and likeable Regional Premier, Michael Okpara. We also visited Port Harcourt,[8] which was rapidly becoming the most important place in the Region with flourishing general trade and development based on oil production and refining. There was still considerable poverty, however, and a Christian Mission Project to alleviate it was ably directed by the Revd Michael Mann, a former soldier and administrator. He was later to become Dean of Windsor, where our son Christopher, born in 1974, became a chorister.

The East seemed an attractive country with vistas reminiscent of different parts of Britain; here a spot in Buckinghamshire, there the Devil's Punch Bowl and beyond the rolling Downs of Sussex. We found the Regional University of Nsukka, the birthplace of Azikiwe ('Zik') a very lively place, where Professor H.G. Hanbury, the famous Equity lawyer, was Dean of the Faculty of Law. Nigeria was clever then at attracting distinguished academics who had just retired in their own countries. At the Golden Guinea Brewery we attended a riotous board meeting and drank strong ale with members of the board clothed in long flowing robes of many colours.

In the West we were frequent visitors to Ibadan, the capital, and also enjoyed visits to Badagry, sixty miles west of Lagos, with its fine beach and coconut palms by the sea and its rolling silvery surf. Badagry's name was famous in Nigerian history first for the slave trade and then as a centre of early missionary endeavour, which had deep and broadly beneficial influence on the West Coast of Africa, and British 'legitimate trade'. The importance of missionary activity was still obvious in our time and on one occasion Ruth and I were invited to a festival arranged by Ibo women from the East in Lagos. It consisted of numerous plays put on by women from different villages but the common theme was the missionary activity and in each of them a white missionary appeared in typical garb, as a sympathetic and mainly inspirational figure.

We also visited Benin in the Mid-Western Region, famous for its bronzes and splendid carving and called on the Oba.[9] We stayed with the Deputy High Commissioner, Dennis Pepper, who was a close friend of General Ironsi. His wife Joan wrote *Thy People My People* about an English woman who married a West African, and other books, under the *nom de plume* of Joan Alexander. She had lived for some time in

8 Named after Viscount (Lewis) Harcourt, Secretary of State for the Colonies 1910–15.
9 The King.

West Africa and her brother, General Alexander, the last British General to command the Armed Forces of Ghana, was later to hit the headlines during the so-called 'Biafran War'. The then Defence Adviser in the High Commission, Colonel Bob Scott, wrote an important report assessing the military situation. It was still the age of trust and, albeit technically improperly, he showed it to his friend General Alexander who, also relying on complete confidentiality, showed it to Jonathan Aitken, then a young journalist with political aspirations. Unfortunately both for the DA and the General, Aitken disclosed this to the *Daily Telegraph*, creating an unwelcome furore.

The overall political situation was still shaky. We were, as recorded in my diary of 23 October, 'between the Scylla of the Western Elections and the Charybdis of Rhodesia'. Democracy was collapsing in Western Nigeria with corruption, earlier rigged elections and increasing violence in electioneering for the Regional elections to the House of Assembly. Our direct concern was for the safety of our British population but the situation gave cause for anxiety about the whole future of the country, especially as important personalities from outside the Western Region became involved in the electioneering there. In September the Sardauna of Sokoto, the Premier of the North, announced his intention to tour the West in support of Chief Akintola and the Nigerian National Democratic Party, the ally of the Northern Nigerian Peoples Congress in the federal Nigerian National Alliance. The Sardauna, it was said, had received large sums of money from Nasser in the UAR with which he funded Chief Akintola.[10] Dr Michael Okpara, Premier of the Eastern Region and Chairman of the National Council of Nigerian Citizens, NCNC, a member of the United Progressive Grand Alliance, also announced his intention of campaigning personally.

The situation was tense and the Government of the West decided to ban all public meetings and processions. The Sardauna gracefully withdrew, saying he quite understood the decision of his 'brother Akintola', in view of the rather explosive situation. Okpara on the other hand refused to take the decision lying down and threatened to storm the West, unless certain conditions regarding nominations were met. The NNDP, taking a tribalistic line, appealed to Yoruba sentiment against 'Ibo domination' of the UPGA opposition. Yet, despite external hands,

---

10 Joe Harold, a long-term and acute British resident with a very wide circle of Nigerian friends, told me that Fani Kayode told him this and that this also accounted for his zeal in making widespread conversions to Islam in the North.

it was Yoruba who fell on Yoruba, and these people later came to fear future elections. This fear was still alive in 1980 when the Nigerian Postmaster-General from the West attended the Commonwealth Postal Union Conference in Kuala Lumpur. He confessed that, deeply worried about coming to Malaysia at election time, he himself had asked his family to pray for him in the danger he imagined he was facing. Relieved, surprised and impressed to find no violence in Malaysian elections, he compared them most favourably with those in Nigeria.

It was hoped that the Prime Minister, Sir Abubakar Tafawa Balewa, would shortly turn his personal attention to the Western Region and with his authority bring a return to sanity. However, before he could do this, the first Commonwealth Heads of Government Conference held outside Westminster took place in Lagos. This had engaged the attention of the Nigerian Government and a heavy load had also fallen on the High Commission.

The future of Southern Rhodesia, then a British colony with self-governing status enjoyed since 1923, was of emotive concern to the Commonwealth States and the Organisation for African Unity (OAU). When the Federation of Rhodesia and Nyasaland broke up in 1963, Northern Rhodesia became Zambia with Kenneth Kaunda as Prime Minister, and Nyasaland Malawi under Dr Hastings Banda; Southern Rhodesia with its 230,000 strong white minority was left on its own. The ruling Rhodesia Front party with Mr Ian Smith as Prime Minister had won the 1962 elections.

The white Rhodesians would have preferred to become a self-governing Dominion, like Canada, Australia and New Zealand, but realised that this was no longer realistic. Rhodesia was better governed, with more freedom of speech, and was much more economically successful than the African and Asian States criticising them, and they were determined that the 'wind of change' should not affect them. They therefore sought independence on the basis of the 1961 constitution, in whose formulation the British Government at home had played a leading role. The British Labour Government was under too much pressure, however, internationally and at home, to agree to this without adequate safeguards for the African majority.

There was a dangerous impasse. Africans in Rhodesia had been offered participation but failed to benefit from it, as the 1961 Constitution provided for fifteen members of the Legislative Assembly of sixty-five to be elected on a B – largely African – roll. Joshua Nkomo and the Revd Ndabiningi Sithole at first accepted this but under pressure from more extreme followers rejected it. This brought the African opposition into some confusion. However, the states of Black Africa wished to see a black majority Government installed and favoured pressure to bring Smith and his white Government to heel, by force if need be.

The British Government, facing a delicate situation emotive on both sides, sought to square the circle, though the issue stirred the realistic Nigerians less than some other African States. Arthur Bottomley, the Secretary of State for Commonwealth Relations, visited in August accompanied by the Permanent Undersecretary, Joe Garner. Bottomley had a less intellectual style than Hugh Caradon but he courageously explained the British stance at the Nigerian Institute of International Affairs on 11 August 1965, stressing that long established self-governing rights established since 1923 could not lightly be brushed aside. His frankness and honesty made a deep impression even though most Nigerians could not agree with HMG's policy. His wife Betty came to lunch with us. She was a friendly lady and Sara, then two months old, blew bubbles at her.

The Nigerians were sympathetic to our dilemma and spoke with moderation at the Organisation for African Unity, OAU, meetings held in Lagos and Accra, and at the meeting of Commonwealth Prime Ministers held in October 1965. These meetings and negotiations with the Rhodesians failed to produce any agreed solution as the Rhodesians were unwilling to agree to the requisite safeguards. The possibility of a unilateral declaration of independence (UDI) became greater. Harold Wilson, the British Prime Minister, flew to Salisbury to prevent this and returned to London via Lagos, where he had a very fruitful meeting with Sir Abubakar, despite the latter's reservations about a Labour Government. I passed Harold Wilson's statement in the House of Commons to George Dove-Edwin on 4 November. On 5 November a state of emergency was declared in Rhodesia and Ian Smith sought to put the blame for 'slamming the door' on HMG. On 11 November UDI was suddenly declared. My diary read 'The small-minded fools! Lunch at Federal Palace Hotel for CPA delegation (Kennet, Fletcher-Cooke and other MPs). One Nigerian said he sympathised with the white Rhodesians!' The Nigerians did not much admire Rhodesian Africans, whom they considered ineffective.

The British Government's measures to end the rebellion at first seemed to satisfy the Nigerians but on 26 November Leslie Harriman at the Ministry of External Affairs (MEA) told me Nigerian opinion was hardening in favour of HMG using force to 'neutralise the situation'.

In early December an OAU resolution advocated breaking diplomatic relations with Britain but, on 9 December, Sir Abubakar denied this would help. There was no question of Nigeria breaking relations and Sir Abubakar proposed a special Commonwealth Prime Ministers' conference in Lagos. After seeing Francis Cumming-Bruce off to London for consultations,[11] I was left as Acting High Commissioner, Nick Larmour being on leave. On 16 December I delivered an urgent message from Harold Wilson to Abubakar who replied positively saying he had given immediate instructions to Chief Adebo, the Nigerian Representative at the UN, to do his best to avert a threatened boycott of Harold Wilson's speech to the General Assembly. Nigerians were clearly not so punctilious as we in following instructions and in the event, much to Sir Abubakar's annoyance, Chief Adebo walked out with other members.

In the middle of all this Robert Maxwell turned up, then an MP; he was a bit imperious but pleasant on this occasion. He had a major quarrel with our Commercial First Secretary, Michael Wasilewski, however, and complained vigorously about him. Michael Wasilewski defended himself and I suggested that they did not meet again. It seemed that Czechoslovakia and Poland were in contention again!

On 17 December I again saw Abubakar to inform him that, since Tanzania and Ghana had broken diplomatic relations with Britain, HMG faced a problem over attending a conference on the very subject which had caused the breach. Harold Wilson would himself have to decide what to do. A flurry of diplomatic activity ensued including suggestions that the conference should be held in Lusaka. Nigeria's solidarity with us paid off, however, and the conference was held in Lagos from 10 to 13 January. It was a turning point in improving the situation. Harold Wilson flew home on the evening of 13 January and Francis Cumming-Bruce and I stood on either side of Sir Abubakar at Ikeja airport to see him off. Returning in the car we marvelled at the energy and dynamism which Harold Wilson had shown and at the success of the conference. At the end of it the Foreign Minister, Senator Bamali, had rushed across to me saying with a beaming smile, 'Congratulations.' Earlier he had bet Francis Cumming-Bruce 10 lb of sugar – later converted to £10 – that evidence would be produced to show British connivance with Smith over UDI, but he readily admitted that this was not so and our High Commissioner had won the bet.

---

11 I was accompanied by Prince William of Gloucester, who was by then serving in the High Commission as Third Secretary.

Our sense of tired euphoria after the conference did not last long. On 14 January 1966 we went to bed early unaware that by next morning Nigeria's democracy would be dead. In the night I became aware of an unusual stillness. The air-conditioning and the power had gone off. At 5.45 a.m. there was furious knocking on the front door and when I went down I heard an urgent voice saying, 'Open up, open up. It's Marsden!' Leslie Marsden was Assistant Commissioner of Police and the most senior British officer left in the Nigerian Police. There had, he said, been some sort of military coup d'état and the Prime Minister, Sir Abubakar, had been abducted by soldiers. The situation was unclear except that there were troops on the move in various parts of the capital, including State House – which stood on the Marina close to the High Commissioner's residence.

I dressed hurriedly and drove to the High Commission, not running into any troops on the way, and sent a telegram to the Commonwealth Office reporting on the situation. By happy chance Diplomatic Wireless had been installed for the Commonwealth Conference as, until then, cyphered messages had been sent through the Nigerian Telecommunications system, which the military rebels had closed. The *Sunday Times* reported next morning that 'for once' the diplomatic channel had beaten the journalists for speed in reporting and that Harold Wilson had learned of the coup over his breakfast bacon and eggs.

Ruth meanwhile, putting on a dressing gown over her nightie, climbed through the fence separating our house from the Defence Adviser's to inform Tom Hunt who came immediately to join me in the office. The telegram despatched, I drove, again fortunately running into no military obstacle, to the High Commissioner's residence and told him the news. He was shattered. The situation was confused for a while though life went on entirely as normal and ordinary people in Lagos had no idea of what had happened; even our own staff in the High Commission were initially disbelieving when told on coming into the office of what had occurred in the night.

The facts began to emerge. There had been an attempted coup by young officers. Ibo officers of major or lower rank had been the main plotters and no Ibo leader of importance had been killed. The plot had been kept a complete secret and its execution was said to have shown signs of the main players' Sandhurst training. Major Ifeajuna, with the cunning of Mohamed Ali Pasha luring the Mamelukes of Egypt to a banquet to massacre them, had engineered a party at the house of Brigadier Zak Maimalari. Chief Festus, the notoriously corrupt

Finance Minister and seven senior officers, including Maimalari, had been murdered. Ifeajuna escaped to Ghana. The plotters' motives were unclear, though they claimed a desire for a better Nigerian society and an end to the intolerable situation in Western Nigeria and to corruption. Simultaneous action had been taken in Lagos, Kaduna, Kano and Ibadan. The Premiers of the Northern and Western Regions had been murdered – the Sardauna of Sokoto in Kaduna and Chief Akintola in Ibadan. In Lagos the Prime Minister, Sir Abubakar, had been abducted and it later transpired that he too had been murdered – after his request to say his final prayers had been granted.

The attempted coup, however, was only partially successful. General Ironsi, the Commander of the Army, had managed to gain control of the Army and the officers involved in the plot were arrested. Although himself an Ibo, he was almost certainly not a party to the coup and indeed had been warned by Colonel Pam, one of the victims, that his life was in danger. Colonel Gowon, the Chief of Staff to Ironsi, and Colonel Njoku, who were also on the death list, likewise escaped assassination. The battalion in Kano was commanded by another Ibo, Colonel Emeka Ojukwu who, though almost certainly a party to the coup, sat on the fence for a while before acknowledging Ironsi.

I wondered, though it was largely speculation, whether there might have been a plot by Northerners as well as other plots brewing at the time. If so, it is just possible that Sir Abubakar might have been aware of such a move, or even party to it. This would have provided a motive for killing him. It is more likely, however, that, bundled into the front of a military vehicle, he had simply seen too much of what the young plotters actually did that night, making him a dangerous witness after the coup had failed. This murder of an outstanding and honest man, who enjoyed the respect of people all over Nigeria, including Ibo officials and politicians, was a real tragedy.

The rump of the Cabinet met on 16 January and, when Al Haji Zanna Dipcharima the senior surviving Minister, refusing to assume office as Acting Prime Minister, concluded that law and order could only be preserved by handing power over to the Army under Ironsi. Leslie Marsden and another policeman, George Duckett, British officials who still had important roles to play, were sent to persuade Ironsi to come into Lagos from Ikeja, where he was with the 2nd Battalion of the Army. This was in view of the degree of control which Ironsi had established, though Ironsi had, I believe, not pushed for this himself. The Nigerian Broadcasting Service kept listeners in suspense playing religious music, including 'Jesu, Joy of Man's Desiring', until the Acting President in Dr Azikiwe's absence, Dr Nwafu Orizu, broadcast a short message announcing the Council of Ministers' unanimous decision.

On 17 January Leslie Marsden telephoned me suggesting that the High Commissioner should call on Ironsi. I advised Francis Cumming-Bruce that no official recognition could be given to the new regime at that stage. However we could legitimately ask Ironsi about the extent of his control of the country and seek assurances about the safety of the 18,000 strong British community and other expatriates. We therefore went together to Police Headquarters, where he had set up his own temporary headquarters, and waited briefly in the room of the Deputy Inspector-General of the Nigerian Police. Ironsi, whom we already knew well,[12] then entered in dark green uniform resplendent with red tabs. He was most informal, though on entering – I thought wickedly – he had something of the air of a boy appearing before his headmaster.

'I had to do it,' were his first words. There was a silence; then Francis congratulated him on restoring law and order. Ironsi said he was gratified that power had been handed to him by the unanimous decision of the Council of Ministers including Northern members. It would be temporary and he intended to hand it back as soon as he possibly could, reverting to his own job as Army Commander. A Constitutional Review Commission would be necessary but in the meantime Stanley Wey, the Secretary of the Cabinet, was coordinating the functions of government with the Permanent Secretaries in the Ministries. Expatriates were safe and he hoped that they would carry on exactly as they had before.

The troubles in the West continued with continued arson and hooliganism, and Michael Okpara, the Ibo leader of the UPGA (United People's General Alliance), was believed to be behind much of this. There were still dissidents in the Army and it was some days before the military were brought under full control all over the country. Nevertheless a mood of jubilation and hope for the future prevailed in Lagos. Military Governors for the Regions were appointed and the new structure of government was announced consisting of a Supreme Council and an Executive Council with Ironsi presiding over both. The members were all Armed Service or Police officers.

The house next to ours on Queen's Drive was occupied by Sir Kofo, and Lady, Abayomi – a distinguished Nigerian eye surgeon who was also Chairman of the Lagos Economic Development Board.

12 He had been to our houses on several occasions.

They were interesting and good neighbours but they had to move out in accordance with the Government policy of turning chairmen of boards as well as Ministers out of official houses. Brigadier Ogundipe the most senior officer in the Nigerian Army after Ironsi, came to occupy it and armed guards were posted.

I flew home on 23 January for consultations with Joe Garner[13] (the PUS of the Commonwealth Office) and John Chadwick, the Assistant Undersecretary. On the following day I gave a report to the Chiefs of Staff Committee presided over by Dick Hull[14] the CDS, commenting that the future largely depended on whether Ironsi would be able to rise to the occasion. On 28 January Ironsi announced plans for the future in a national broadcast. Regionalism and tribal loyalties were to give way to national reconstruction and the Government would preserve Nigeria as one strong nation. Corruption was to be stamped out and integrity and self-respect in public affairs restored. There would be no place for the few unscrupulous Nigerian and foreign businessmen, but honest businessmen and investors were welcome. The number of Federal Ministries was reduced and the offices of the Agents General in London for the Regions were abolished. All political appointees were removed from boards. Foreign investment and technical knowledge was necessary and would be encouraged.

The Government intended to succeed in this unique opportunity to build a strong united Nigeria. The country could not afford sterile political strife and consequently no display of party flags or symbols or the shouting of political slogans would be allowed. There was optimism amongst the officials about the future, and George Dove-Edwin told me that centralised Government was well understood by the people and that his generation had grown up regarding the real seat of Government as Lagos.

The Nigerians were always asking, 'What of...?' What of Nigeria at this time? Things had fallen apart. The carefully balanced federal structure and political hierarchy had been destroyed by apparently idealistically minded and radical young Army officers. The Army had been the most unitary-minded, organised and most non-tribal of all the Federal institutions, but the predominantly Ibo plotters had severely shaken the fabric by murdering senior Northern and Western officers as well as politicans. The basic state of give and take between different Regions

13 Sir Joe, later Lord Garner, GCMG and the first head of the new Diplomatic Service.
14 Field Marshal Sir Richard Hull, KG, GCB, DSO.

and the people of the different Regions, who were previously able to live peacefully in each other's areas, had also received a rude shock. People therefore sought reassurance and healing and placed great hopes in the National Military Government of Ironsi.

But Ironsi could not rise to the formidable challenge and these hopes began to evaporate. When on 24 May Ironsi proclaimed a unitary state and the unification of the Civil Service, fuel was added to dissatisfaction in the North. The 'murderous majors', who organised the January coup and assassinations, had received no punishment beyond detention, and general resentment against the Ibos for their success both in government and commerce ran deep. Northerners also anticipated a raw deal if Civil Service unification resulted in more 'smart' Ibos holding high positions. Religious differences between the Muslim North and Christian Ibos became accentuated, Northerners being particularly incensed that Ibos had openly played banned records insulting the memory of the Sardauna, a religious as well as a temporal leader.[15] The North then began seriously to consider secession under the slogan 'Secession for the North unless the future constitution is federal'.

The country was thus left troubled and insecure after the January coup and a Northern reaction was predicted. The serious and simultaneous violence, which broke out in the North on 28 May 1966, was therefore not a total surprise. The towns of Kano, Kaduna, Sokoto, Zaria and Gusau were worst affected and the results devastating. Six hundred Ibos may have been killed and the Northern People's Party (NPC) was suspected of organising these massacres. Whatever the cause, the result was a rapid exodus of the two million Ibos living in the North, many of whom held important positions especially in the technical field. It was a particularly unfortunate coincidence that the trouble started the very day after Francis Cumming-Bruce's return from a tour in the North. Totally false assumptions that a British hand had been at work were therefore inevitably made and our position was uncomfortable for a while. Jim Treadwell, our Deputy High Commissioner in Enugu, had a particularly difficult time as Ibos could not bring themselves to believe that their own insensitivity towards Northerners and Northern aspirations could have had so dire a consequence. It was in fact both our policy and our personal hope that the Nigerians should

15 Feelings were further inflamed by leaflets attributed to Egypt (UAR) and other Arab countries.

themselves find a way of holding Nigeria together. After these massacres the Ironsi regime was unable to find a formula or means of reuniting the country and, lacking direction, ran out of steam.

There were still to be troubles, however. I was awakened by a telephone call from the duty officer at the High Commission at 5 a.m. on 29 July. 'The Army are at it again,' he said. There had been another mutiny and it proved the end for General John Ironsi who, with Colonel Fajuyi the Military Governor of the Western Region, had been murdered in Ibadan. Two Ibo officers were also murdered at Abeokuta. Lagos airport at Ikeja was seized by Northern troops under Lieutenant Suleiman, an Air Force officer and member of the ruling House of Sokoto, and moves towards secession by the North began. The BOAC VC10 which had just landed was impounded. Concrete steps towards Northern secession were taken rapidly in the next two days and Northerners, who had commandeered the aircraft of Nigerian Airways as well as the VC10, despatched their families to the North as quickly as they could. After our representations, the VC10 was allowed to proceed after making one run to Kano. Brigadier Ogundipe, commanding in Lagos in Ironsi's absence, sent out a small detachment of troops to retake the airport. Running into an ambush, however, they were defeated in an exchange of fire in which a British man and a German were caught and killed.

He had earlier sent Lieutenant Colonel Jack Gowon,[16] the Chief of Staff – whom we already knew well on the 'cocktail circuit' between the coups as a very bright, pleasant young officer – to negotiate with the rebels. The rebels also regarded him highly and, keeping him like Roman Praetorian Guards, sought to make him their leader. Finding himself, as he himself revealed later, in a strongly secessionist atmosphere, he tried in long telephone conversations on Saturday 30 July to persuade Ogundipe to take over the central Government in place of Ironsi, but it was in vain. The troops remaining in Lagos had no further stomach for fighting and Ogundipe himself was left as Commander without any credible force or support. Meantime a group of Permanent Secretaries, all strongly opposed to secession by any part of Nigeria, went out to parley with Gowon at Ikeja. My tennis friend Ben Okagbue, the Ibo Permanent Undersecretary at the Ministry of Health, later told me how proud he was to have been one of this small group. At this difficult time he played a significant role in a quiet way, particularly as

16 Though his name was Yacubu, he was always known as Jack.

Chief Scouts Commissioner and as such able to keep links between the Regions open.

Early on Sunday 31 July two of the most influential Permanent Secretaries, Abdou Attah (Finance) and Ayyida (Economic Development), called on me at home. They earnestly requested that we and the Americans should use our influence to deflect the group in control at Ikeja from secession and to persuade Gowon to move into Lagos 'to save Nigeria'. In the High Commission we prepared a paper in consultation with the US Ambassador, Bert Matthews, and Clinton Olsen, the Deputy Head of Mission, and this was taken out to Gowon by Tom Hunt, our Defence Adviser. Happily a change of heart took place. Ogundipe stood down and the remaining members of the Supreme Council all supported Gowon who thus became the Head of Government. Ogundipe left the country to become High Commissioner in London.

Serious shooting had occurred near other Army Commanders' houses and Ironsi himself was dead. Living next to Ogundipe at such a time was therefore uncomfortable. It was the only time during my diplomatic career that I ever seriously considered and planned where in the house the family would be safest if shooting started. I had real cause. On 29 July we gave a farewell party for a High Commission couple. A guest was told in a deep bass voice by a soldier guarding Ogundipe's house to 'keep out of my field of fire'. Soldiers breaking from discipline roamed the town with weapons, vindictive killings were all too many and bodies of soldiers and civilians floated down the creek near our house. The era was a strange mix of normality and abnormality and one night a soldier with a gun stood in the middle of the road signalling us to stop as we were returning from a dinner party. Conscious of the danger of becoming separated from the tiny Sara and her nanny Comfort, I was in two minds what to do when I noticed that the soldier was swaying and that a girl, clearly a girlfriend, was standing close by on the pavement. I decided, therefore, to drive on rapidly and forced him to jump out of the way, and there was no further reaction. We had been lucky, however, as my decision could have proved all too wrong.

The squash racket proved a useful weapon of diplomacy in Nigeria. After the first coup in January 1966 I became friendly with Major Mobalaji Johnson, the Sandhurst-trained Military Governor of Lagos, and played squash with him once a week. We went on with our games after the second coup in July and, as he continued to speak as freely as ever, I was able to learn some of the military regime's thinking in these crucial and dangerous times.

Prince William of Gloucester was at this time Third Secretary in Chancery. The British press had unkindly, if typically, suggested that his appointment to the Diplomatic Service was due solely to his royal status. In fact we had been specifically instructed that he was to be treated according to his diplomatic rank and not as a Royal Prince and he was very able, fully up to the standard of his contemporaries as well as a modest and dedicated member of the High Commission.

The Duchess of Gloucester arrived on a visit just before the second coup. When news of this broke, a *Daily Mail* reporter rang and said he assumed that Prince William was with his mother comforting her. I reassured him about the Duchess's safety and said that Prince William was in the office working, though it was long after official hours. The situation did not prevent the Duchess from presiding over a big charity ball at the High Commissioner's residence 6 Marina, a highlight of which was six talking drums[17] played by the Timi of Ede and his people demonstrating how messages could be conveyed over considerable distances. The ball was a good morale booster for Nigerian and British alike and the large turn-out included a number of Ibos.

Prince William was not only able in his chosen career but a keen pilot and all those who had known him in Lagos were deeply saddened by his death a year or two later in a light aircraft crash.

Jack Gowon, having moved into Lagos and reluctantly assumed the burden of office, made his first broadcast on 1 August as Supreme Commander and Head of Government. He faced problems of daunting magnitude, the first of which was to bring all the Military Governors into line. This was relatively easy with Hassan Katsina, the Governor of the North, Adekunle Fajuyi, Governor of the West and David Ejoor, Governor of the Mid-West, who all immediately recognised Gowon as Supreme Commander. It was another story with Emeka Ojukwu, the Military Governor of the East, who withheld support from Gowon; the latter was one junior to him on the Army List. Though the North had abandoned its secessionist aims, the East under Ojukwu, who by now was rightly or wrongly regarded as the architect of the January plot, seemed from now on to be moving in that direction. The next few months were difficult and tragic and the question of whether Nigeria

17 Talking drums probably explain how news of the Battle of Omdurman in 1896 reached the West Coast of Africa within forty-eight hours, as it undoubtedly did.

would fall apart or not hung over everything, though surprisingly many things went on seemingly as before. The Army and other service officers in Lagos believed fervently that Nigeria should remain a single country and the Permanent Undersecretaries also worked hard to this end. Ojukwu on the other hand began to speak openly of Eastern secession and addressed his communications to Gowon as 'Chief of Staff of the Army' and not as 'Supreme Commander'. Herein lay the seeds of the future short-lived state of Biafra.

Nigerians were facing the truth about themselves and, despite disposition, particularly in the East, to blame former 'Colonial masters' and others for their ills, realism prevailed and Gowon's administration in Lagos, though weak, provided a framework for constitutional discussion. Determined to civilianise the Government quickly, he ordered the release of all political detainees, including the old politicians imprisoned under Ironsi.

Members of the Supreme Council, even including Ojukwu initially, worked for a constitutional solution and in August Regional representatives met in Lagos. Ibo soldiers were withdrawn from the North, Northern soldiers from the East thus 'putting the safety catch' on the Army for a while. In September however, soldiers of 2nd Battalion, withdrawn from Ikeja, attacked Ibos in Kaduna. The situation then deteriorated rapidly and Northerners mounted new, simultaneous and coldly systematic attacks on Ibos there and at Jos, Zaria, Kano and Minna, almost certainly instigated again by old NPC politicians. I recorded in my diary, 'The way in which these wretched Ibos have been killed passes description and this is probably the nearest thing we have seen to genocide in Africa.' Expatriates in the North were not much affected except by the pitiful things they witnessed.

The Army were quite out of hand and, though discipline had held in the multi-tribal police, soldiers killed five Ibo policemen in the barracks in Kaduna. Gowon determined to gain control, vowing to restore law and order or die in the attempt. Meantime Ibo civilians from the North and Northerners from the East left under an exchange of populations, somewhere between 200,000 and 500,000 people becoming refugees. The Ibos, rich, clever, successful and industrious, prided themselves on being 'the Jews of Africa', specifically comparing their sufferings with those of the Jewish people. Hassan Katsina, the Military Governor of the Northern Region, broadcast movingly on the terrible shame of events in his Region, but there was surprisingly and alarmingly little public sympathy for the Ibos in other parts of Nigeria.

Perhaps it was natural that the Ibos should then play hard to get. Yet after a while the situation in much of Nigeria had returned to near normality and all was quiet. Two thousand Ibo policemen serving in Lagos and the West were helping maintain order and carrying out ordinary police duties. One calm young Ibo constable even accused me of a parking offence outside the High Commission, though I successfully pleaded diplomatic immunity! During the next few months, however, increasing pressures were applied to them and Ojukwu's administration apparently encouraged Ibos at home to urge their police relatives in Lagos to leave; and gradually they all did. It was seen by many as a cynical act by Ojukwu to gain 2,000 men trained in arms.

Ojukwu's position throughout was at best equivocal. Nevertheless many attempts were made to find political solutions by consensus, and Gowon and Ojukwu had long telephone conversations, though they never met. Ojukwu still refused to recognise Gowon as Supreme Commander, however, and withdrew the Eastern Region from the jurisdiction of the Supreme Court. On 19 September Gowon asked Francis Cumming-Bruce and Bert Matthews, the US Ambassador, to intervene to dissuade Ojukwu from secession and, on 22 September, Ojukwu assured them he 'had no intention of seceding and talk of the East's desire for secession was mischievous'. Nevertheless he rejected all efforts to bring him to the Supreme Council anywhere in Nigeria despite elaborate assurances as to his safety. Largely through the conciliatory efforts of Malcolm MacDonald he was, however, persuaded to attend one meeting of this body held on 4 and 5 January 1967 at Aburi in Ghana. This was the only meeting attended by all the Military Governors. Ojukwu came with a strong delegation in a military aircraft provided by the Ghanaians, having rejected a Nigerian HS182 which, he claimed, might have been tampered with in Lagos.

The Aburi meeting decided that Nigeria should remain one country and that force should be ruled out as a means of solving problems – a sad and pious hope in the event. A further meeting of the Supreme Council in Nigeria was also envisaged and the Regional Solicitors-General were to discuss the necessary amendments to the constitution to revoke all the unitary measures taken since January 1966. Military representatives were to discuss Army problems. The Army would stay in power but Regional Governors would have operational control within their Regions and there would be a Commander-in-Chief instead of a Supreme Commander. This was widely assumed to be a device to get Ojukwu to recognise Gowon.

However, though the Solicitors-General and the military representatives met and reached substantial conclusions, doubts about what exactly had been agreed at Aburi were too great for the proposed new constitutional decree to be issued on 21 January as envisaged. One reason might have been a fundamental difference of approach. Gowon had refused a Ministry of External Affairs briefing, wishing to concentrate on a cordial reconciliation between brother officers and inspiring a new spirit into the Supreme Council. Ojukwu on the other hand went well briefed and considered he had won an intellectual battle at Aburi. On his return Gowon was advised that there were considerable objections to the 'Accra decisions', in particular to dropping the title of Supreme Commander without adequate provision for the Commander-in-Chief to have overall command of the Army throughout the country. By the end of the month Lagos and Enugu were impatient with each other.

Malcolm MacDonald[18] was now well accepted by the Nigerians and was increasingly drawn into a very personal and determined mission of mediation. At one point it looked as if he would be successful in broking an understanding between Ojukwu and Gowon and their followers. Had he been, the tragic civil war would have been averted.

Though there was a strong tide of passion running in the East, a formula might, I believe, have been found had it not been for Ojukwu's own personality. The son of a successful millionaire businessman, he was educated at Epsom College and Lincoln College, Oxford. Undoubtedly able, he joined the Administrative Service and served as an Assistant District Officer. A quick look round Africa, however, convinced him that the route to power lay in a military career; so he joined the Army, passing successfully through Sandhurst. As a schoolboy he had confessed an ambition to occupy State House as ruler of Nigeria and it infuriated him that chance had led Gowon, his junior on the Nigerian Army List, to become Supreme Commander. Gowon himself, as a practising Christian, turned the other cheek to Ojukwu on numerous occasions and his brother officers considered him a gentleman. Much bloodshed, though there was all too much of it, was saved by his patience and constant seeking for peace. He could not, however, prevail with Ojukwu.

18 Malcolm MacDonald came to Nigeria initially to explain the British position over Rhodesia.

Our second daughter, Caroline, born on 16 January was, like her elder sister, destined to start life in what the Chinese call 'interesting times'. Ruth had decided, despite the uncertain conditions then prevailing, to have the baby in Lagos and was admitted to the Teaching Hospital at Surulere. It was a condition that they could use her case to teach their students, and that I gave a pint of blood. Another British wife preferred to go home for her baby. Ironically she had a Nigerian midwife in a West Country hospital in England whereas Ruth was attended by Dr Thompson, Head of the Teaching Hospital and a former Master of Rotunda in Dublin, and a splendid Irish matron, as well as impressive Nigerian nurses with ten years' or more experience in British hospitals. Before Caroline's christening I asked Chief H.O. Davies, a well-known Yoruba politician and lawyer, for his choice of name for a little girl just born in Yorubaland. 'Aduke,' he said, which means 'the little girl loved by all the world'. We took the Chief's advice by giving Caroline, whose birth was surrounded by portents of which the ancients would have made much, the second name of Amanda. Two white lilies suddenly flowered in a pot on the doorstep of our house, representing perhaps our two daughters, and a shooting star appeared just before the delivery. A freak rainstorm occurred on the following night and her birthday was the only free day between two days of national mourning for officers killed on 15 January 1966 and the three days for Ironsi.

The Nigerian situation was something new in post-colonial experience. British thinking hitherto had concentrated on reducing our presence and direct involvement in our former colonies. It had been essentially a 'phase of withdrawal' since 1947. Many Nigerians, however, had lost confidence in themselves and their ability to solve their country's problems and, despite the winds of change, many hoped Britain would play a more active role again at least for a while. On 14 November Hamzet Ahmadu of the MFA said nostalgically that in the old days the Colonial Secretary, having allowed the dust to settle, would summon the parties to a Lancaster House Conference. There was even talk in high Nigerian quarters of requesting British military and training assistance, and some saw a need for an independent force for a while.

A response to Nigerian needs seemed desirable and in May 1967 I wrote a paper advocating positive action to give support. It was clearly in our interest that Nigeria should be a stable independent country where British and Western investment was comparatively safe and where the good relations between black and white which prevailed could have a part in improving race relations all over the world. It could also be an example of a country where the 'rich' could play an effective and profitable part in helping the 'poor nations'. There was no shortage of Nigerians of the highest intellectual calibre but competent and honest administrators and able police and service officers capable of tackling the toughest situations were in short supply. Here British officers could very acceptably have lent a hand.

In the 1966 crises Nigerians had relied much on expatriates still in Government service who loved the country and had devoted their careers to it. Not only had the policemen Leslie Marsden and Stacey Barham largely drafted Ironsi's first proclamation, but other British people held important posts in the Government. Sir Nigel Brett and Sir Ian Lewis were key figures in the Judiciary. In the North there was still a large number of administrators and departmental officials who quietly exercised a steadying influence. Many, however, were on the point of retirement or resignation. There was a real need for an imaginative scheme of continued partnership which would appeal both to Nigerians and British and other administrators and experts. Such an initiative obviously depended on a Nigerian request and might have been launched under a Commonwealth umbrella to minimise opposition from the left wing and from the ever vocal Afro-Asian and non-aligned nations. Nigerian trades unionists were, perhaps surprisingly, among those who hoped for such a new British initiative.

In fact this was not followed up. It would have been an ideal situation for HMOCS to operate in the way originally foreseen for it. However, administrative considerations militated against this, as the modest funds necessary to enable British officials to continue to serve in ex-Colonies and to stay on where the local Government wanted them without loss to themselves, were not forthcoming. In the absence of an imaginative scheme which might have helped Nigeria in its predicament, British officials still serving there who would have liked to stay, and whom the Nigerians wanted, began to leave. The basic problem was that politically the Nigerian Government could not pay discriminatory rates to expatriates whilst the individual officials could not afford to stay with such significant loss to themselves. This, however, is a general observation and this particular problem did not appreciably affect Nigeria's immediate situation.[19]

19 See *From Empire to Commonwealth* by John O'Regan on this point.

When Francis Cumming-Bruce came to leave in February 1967, Jack Gowon gave a small dinner party for him at his house in the Dodan Barracks; he did not move into State House. It was a delightful informal occasion. When we had sat down at table I saw Jack Gowon, who was a practising Christian, chatting conspiratorially with Francis Cumming-Bruce. Then suddenly out of the blue, Gowon said, 'Donald, will you say grace?' Taken by surprise, I gave them 'Benedictus benedicat'.[20] Gowon in his graceful speech of farewell said that it was his mission to hold Nigeria together and he would do his best to do so. I remarked in my diary, 'It was quite obvious that he was sincere and he is a very reluctant hero. It is presumably this sincerity and integrity which Ojukwu cannot stand and caused him to say to the US representative he could not understand why the Americans always supported mediocrities like Gowon.' Nevertheless Ojukwu too paid Francis Cumming-Bruce a handsome public tribute before he left. An aristocratic intellectual with something of a genius for negotiation, Cumming-Bruce played a very important role in a quiet way during Nigeria's difficult times in 1966.

David Hunt took over as High Commissioner in February 1967. He had been a Staff officer with Montgomery in the War and was author of *A Don at War* and other books. Very genial, he also had a formidable intellect, displayed by his being winner of Mastermind on television in 1977 and Mastermind of Masterminds in 1982. He had previously been High Commissioner both in Cyprus and Uganda and still earlier Deputy High Commissioner in Lagos. When Iro Myrianthousis, who edited the social magazine *Lagos this Week*, heard he was coming, she told me that he was her 'best friend'. I took this with a grain of salt but was wrong, for they were married shortly afterwards. I enjoyed serving under him, but did not have long, because in May 1967 we were transferred.

This time it was to Academia in Durham as I was given a year's sabbatical at the Middle East Centre at Durham University. It was this which enabled me to do the necessary research for my book *The Trucial States* as well as to deliver the prescribed course of twelve lectures on the Middle East. I also had the privilege of being a Visiting Fellow in the Department of Geography under Professor Bill Fisher with Professors Howard Bowen-Jones and John Clark as colleagues, and of being a Fellow of the University College. It also started my long association with Durham.

20 The others there from the High Commission were Nick and Nancy Larmour and Tom and Linda Hunt. Commodore Wey the Commander of the Navy, and Mrs Wey, Major Mobolaji Johnson, the Governor of Lagos and his wife and Dr Elias the Attorney General were the Nigerian guests.

At the time we left Nigeria, there seemed just a little hope that the National Conciliation Committee, comprising distinguished Nigerians from all Regions, including Chief Awolowo, Mbanefo and Ibiam, might find a formula with Ojukwu. However, there were in effect two Military Governments – one in the East headed by Colonel Ojukwu and the other covering the rest of Nigeria, headed by Colonel Gowon. The writing on the wall, foretelling the civil war and unsuccessful attempt to establish an independent state of Biafra in Eastern Nigeria in August 1967, was growing ever larger and the words of the Nigerian National Anthem seemed to have a peculiar irony.

> Nigeria, we hail thee,
> Our own dear native land.
> Though tribe and tongue may differ,
> In brotherhood we stand
>
> O God of all creation
> Grant this our one request;
> Help us to build a nation
> Where no man is oppressed;
> And so with peace and plenty
> Nigeria may be blessed.

Though we had lived through terrible times, we left behind many close Nigerian friends. It was a special delight that on the morning of our departure the 'anti-British' Abdou Attah and his wife came to our house to see us off. We departed by air for Cairo on leave and arrived there as Nasser's troops rolled through the city to Sinai in the prelude to the fateful 1967 Arab-Israeli war.

7
Baghdad

The Arabian Nights, Haroun al Rashid and the mysterious Orient apparently gripped the minds of the 150 girls who responded to our advertisement for a nanny. They thought Baghdad, my next posting, sounded 'fabulous' and clearly had no idea of the revolutionary Iraq of the 1960s. The search for the perfect candidate wasted time and we took Martha, the charming and level-headed Dutch girl already with us, who suddenly suggested interrupting her university studies and coming too.

In June 1967 Iraq, in the last days of President Abdul Rahman Aref, broke diplomatic relations with Britain on account of Israel's victory in the Six Day War and Britain's perceived attitude to it. Our Ambassador, Dick Beaumont, left. In 1968, however, relations were restored much more quickly than expected and in May Trefor Evans went to Baghdad as the new Ambassador. I was to be his number two as Commercial Counsellor and consequently my departure from academic life was premature. I had first to attend a commercial course in London, on which Prince William also happened to be, and sadly we missed the summer term and long vacation in Durham.

Britain's lead in November 1967 in framing Security Council Resolution 242 – which provided for Middle East peace within secure and recognised frontiers, Israel's withdrawal from conquered territories and provision for the Palestinian refugees – altered Iraq's attitude, and the door was opened for restoration of relations. The West's general support for Israel and the underpublicised injustices to the Palestinians, however, was to remain both a matter for reproach and an inhibition on Britain's relations with the Arabs generally as Resolution 242 was flouted.

The 'approved route' to Baghdad curiously combined elegant old-fashioned travel by train and boat with an air journey. In September 1968 we left Victoria for Dover in the Pullman car with its chocolate and cream livery and sped across France on the Rome Express to Genoa in a blue Wagons-Lits carriage. After lunch with the Consul-General we sailed on the *Ausonia* to Beirut, calling in at Naples where Ruth and I made for Pompeii, leaving Sara and Caroline with Martha.

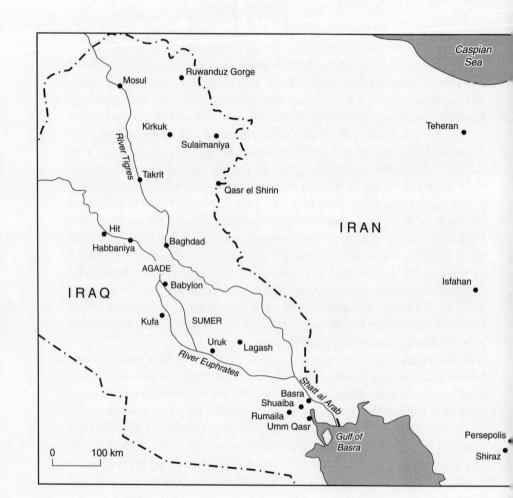

Iraq and Iran

Unlike most Italians, our taxi driver drove agonisingly slowly on the return journey but happily the goddess Fortuna came to our aid and we arrived at the ship's side just before the gangway was, to our horror, about to be drawn up. Sara, succumbing to the charms of the Italian waiters who showed the normal Italian tenderness for little blonde girls, referred to the most attentive as 'The one I like so much!' The Embassy 'Fixer' met us in Beirut and the last leg of the journey was no longer by Nairn bus across the desert, as in former days, but by air to Baghdad.

Trefor Evans and his wife Nest gave us a warm welcome. Philip McKearney was the other Counsellor. A tall Welshman, a good Arabic speaker and a Balliol man – with a rather military toothbrush moustache – Trefor Evans was a former member of the Levant Consular Service, who had served mainly in Cairo, Beirut, Damascus and other posts in the Levant.[1] He was able to keep up his Welsh as the presence of Welsh members on the staff gave him the chance to hold Welsh-speaking parties from time to time. He had the knack of moving quickly through a reception giving the impression that he had spoken to everyone there, and also the rather bizarre habit of insisting that every scrap of paper coming into the Embassy crossed his desk. Perhaps he had been let down in the past but no one was allowed to process a document unless it had his blue tick on it, though I persuaded him to modify this odd procedure. He was succeeded by Glen Balfour-Paul, a very old friend from the Sudan which made Baghdad a specially happy post for us. It was a happy post for others as well, despite the nature of the Iraqi regime and periodic tensions, and proved a remarkable place for inducing matrimony; no fewer than four of the girls who worked for me were married there.

My post as Commercial Counsellor made it easier for me to operate than the Political Counsellor, Philip McKearney, and it so happened that as Chargé d'Affaires for quite prolonged periods I had unusual responsibility.

The Embassy, an old Turkish house on the banks of the Tigris with a courtyard and central fountain, contained a monument to Lieutenant R. B. Lynch and the other officers and men drowned in the Euphrates on 21 May 1836 when a sudden violent storm sunk the *Tigris*. This was one of the two steamers which Colonel Chesney had with much labour brought overland in separate parts from near Alexandretta on the

---

1 Baghdad was Trefor's last post and he then became Woodrow Wilson Professor of International Affairs at Aberystwyth, publishing the diaries of Lord Killearn under whom he had served in Cairo.

Mediterranean to Bir on the Euphrates, to make trial of a route to India through the Persian Gulf. The loss of the *Tigris* inspired an epic poem at the time. My own office had in the 1920s been that of Gertrude Bell, when she served in the High Commission with Sir Percy Cox and Sir Arnold Wilson, and one or two older members of the local staff remembered the 'Khatun' well.

The fine residence of the Ambassador, also on the Embassy site and acquired from Haidar Pasha, had been burned down by rioters in July 1958. The Chancery alone remained, but the extensive Embassy grounds enabled us to to play cricket and football matches there. The Ambassador subsequently lived in the former house of the Managing Director of the Iraq Petroleum Company – known as 'Todd Hall'.

We had a pleasant spacious house in Mansur with marble floors, good woodwork and a garden, where the children were happy and we entertained freely. We had excellent Assyrian servants from Northern Iraq. This small people, being Nestorian Christians, had been squeezed politically in the modern Islamic state of Iraq and many had found safety in serving the British, particularly in the large former RAF bases of Habbanyia and Shaiba.

The US was not represented in Baghdad because of her support for Israel in the 1967 war, and her interests were looked after by the Swiss under the Chargé d'Affaires, Pierre Dumont, who with his elegant wife Madeleine became close friends. We often had a community of interest with the French, however, particularly over oil matters, and the Ambassador and I frequently exchanged information with M. Gorce or his successor M. Pierre Cerle.[2] On account of the Shell interest, we were even more often in touch with the Dutch Ambassador Paul de Lavalette and his wife Hilda, who also became lifelong friends.

The Turks had a special position as a result of their possession of Iraq in Ottoman times and many of the older Iraqis still spoke Turkish fluently. We had good relations with the Turkish Ambassador and his staff, and played a notable soccer match against the Turkish Embassy on the Embassy ground. I was captain of our side and the Turkish captain, the Counsellor, told me he wanted to begin the game ceremonially. So we led our respective teams on to the pitch and stood facing our opposite numbers along the centre line. The Turks then suddenly produced small bouquets of roses from behind their backs and presented us

---

2 Who, very unusually for a French Ambassador, often showed me his telegrams on oil affairs.

each with one. It was perhaps appropriate after such a polite and charming gesture that we drew the match!

Iraq is a large and potentially very rich country with a land area of 167,925 square miles – mountainous in the Kurdish north and very flat to the south. In 1968 it had a population of some 12 million. The Euphrates and Tigris rivers flow through it, joining streams south of Baghdad, down to the Shatt al Arab, the marshes and the Gulf, called 'Persian' by Iran and 'Arabian' by Arab States. For much of the year the land, sky and river adopt a uniform dun colour, relieved by marvellous light in the desert in winter and the blooming of wild flowers of every hue during spring. With very intelligent people and immense physical advantages of place and resources – land, people, irrigation schemes, industry, oil and gas – Iraq is a country of promise but disappointing through lack of its realisation.

Iraq is also an ancient land, one of the cradles of civilisation, with a history dating from the fourth millennium BC recorded on cuneiform tablets. Many dramas of history were played out there. Uruk was the home of the hero Gilgamish. Sumer found its way in to the Bible as 'the land of Shinar' and Abraham left his home in Ur of the Chaldees to journey westwards and father the Arab and Jewish peoples. Gudea established his empire in Lagash, and Sargon his in Agade. Hammurabi in the eighteenth century BC gave Babylon and the world its first known code of commercial, criminal and civil law, long foreshadowing the Code Napoleon. A thousand years later the people of Israel were held captive by King Nebuchadnezzar 'by the waters of Babylon' and the cities of Nineveh and Nimrud in the North were capitals of the Assyrian Empire from the thirteenth to the seventh century BC. Famous kings like Tiglath Pileser, Sennacherib and Shalmaneser commemorated their achievements and victories not only by massive and magnificent monuments but also by pyramids of enemy skulls. The violence which the present generation of Iraqis has seen is nothing new. The Kurds are probably descendants of the ancient Medes and a few descendants of the ancient Assyrians also remain.

Iraq, fought over for many more centuries, conquered by Alexander the Great in 332 BC, disputed militarily between the Great King of Persia and the Roman Emperors, later became subject to the Persian Sassanian Empire with its capital at Ctesiphon near Baghdad, and then the anvil of Islam. After the death of the Prophet Muhammad, the succession was fought out there between Ali bin Abu Talib, the prophet's cousin and son-in-law, and the Caliph Muawiya, before Ali was killed at Kufa in AD 661. At the Battle of the Camel in AD 680, Ali's son Hussain was killed near Kerbala. Thus the division between the Sunni and Shia in Islam was originally created there. The Iraqi Shia are now some 65% of the total population, and many hope to be buried – carried there in wooden box coffins on the top of taxis – at Najaf, Ali's burial place or Kerbala where Hussain was entombed.

Basrah then became famous for learning and trade, and the *point d'appui* for the Muslim conquest of Zoroastrian Khorasan and Persia. The round city of Baghdad, created by the Caliph Mansur, Abu Ja'far Abdullah ibn Muhammad AD 734–754, became the seat of Haroun al Rashid and the Abbasid Caliphs, who made Baghdad famous for culture, science and literature. This first round city and much else were destroyed, however, with the invasions from the steppes of Taimur and Genghiz Khan. When the Ottoman Turks obtained the Caliphate in 1517, ruling the greater part of the Muslim world, Iraq was part of their dominions and thus it remained, seeing prosperity and hard times for several hundred years, divided into the three *wilayats* of Mosul, Baghdad and Basrah.

Despite this long and rich history, Iraq, known from Roman times as Mesopotamia – the land between the two rivers – is not rich in surviving buildings. In every age most were built of mud brick and whole cities and towns have been reduced to mounds with thousands of 'Tells' dotting the country.

Modern Iraq was a British creation after the First World War. With the Turkish entry into the war, it was inevitable that British troops – largely the Indian Army controlled by the Imperial Government in Calcutta – should invade. The Turks were defeated after a very tough campaign and General Maude's victorious troops entered Baghdad on 11 March 1917. With the demise of the Ottoman Empire, the whole of Iraq came directly under British influence, although the *wilaya* of Mosul was for a while disputed with the French. Iraq became a British Mandate from the League of Nations with a British High Commissioner, and King Faisal I took the throne as the first King of Iraq in 1921. In 1932 it was recognised as an independent country and itself became a member of the League of Nations.

It nonetheless still remained much in the British sphere of influence, despite a short-lived period during the Second World War when actively pro-Axis elements with Rashid Ali al Gailani as Prime Minister gained control. Thereafter it was a close ally – one of 'our friends in the Middle East' – until the revolution of July 1958, when King Faisal II, who had very shortly before paid a State Visit to London, his uncle Prince Abdulilah and the Prime Minister, Nuri al Said, were murdered. Strong Arab nationalist sentiment was then running against the British and the French following the Suez debacle in 1956, compounded by the Arab nationalism of Gemal Abdel Nasser. The Balfour Declaration of 1917 also remained the source of constant reproach of Britain in view of the increasing strength of Israel. The growing strength of Soviet influence through Russia's strong position in the region, as well as very successful anti-'imperialist', anti-'colonialist', propaganda, further complicated the scene and the long Anglo-Iraqi honeymoon ended with the 1958 revolution.

There followed the Communist-inclined regime of Abdul Karim Qasim, who was President of Iraq from 1958 to 1963. Even when Abdul Rahman Aref succeeded him, the relatively free and easy relations of pre-revolutionary days were not restored. Personal relations between British and Iraqis, however, continued to be warm[3] but official relations fluctuated, as in most Arab countries, and personal relationships were inevitably complicated by politics and rising nationalist feelings.

By the time we arrived in Baghdad there had been two recent coups. On 17 July, Abdul Rahman Aref was overthrown by General Ahmed Hassan al Bakr, supported broadly by the Baath Party and on 30 July an inner core of Baathists took control, many of them kinsmen from Takrit on the Euphrates. Their names thus all ended 'al Takriti' and this confused visiting business men who would tell me that they had met an influential Mr Takriti, without knowing which of the large clan it was. This often made it difficult to advise them.

The Baath have maintained their grip on Iraq ever since. Saddam Hussein, the nephew of the President and Secretary-General of the party, was at first a shadowy but immensely powerful figure behind the veil. It was not until after our departure from Baghdad in April 1971 that he emerged as a public figure, having in the meantime engineered the murder of several rivals, including his cousin, the amiable General Hardan al Takriti and Karim Shaikhly, the Foreign Minister in our time.

The Baath aspired to leadership of the whole Arab world, as demonstrated by their writings and posters and maps widely displayed, showing the Baath over the whole of the Middle East including Egypt, the Sudan and Palestine. Thus they declared themselves as a socialist Arab

3 Some of our best Middle Eastern friends were Iraqis.

nationalist party in contention with President Nasser for pride of place. Often the impartial observer could detect little difference in practice between them on declared doctrine or reaction to events in the Arab world but, as Nasser Orabi in the UAR Embassy told me, Nasser disliked the Baath because they had frustrated the union of Egypt, Syria and Iraq in 1963. The age-old rivalry between the Nile and Tigris still lived on, though the Iraqis were not as successful as Nasser in spreading their influence. The Iraqi wing of the Baath were further handicapped by being constantly at odds with the Syrian wing, and the philosopher founders of the Baath party, Michel Aflaq and Salah al din Bitar, frequently visited Baghdad to attempt reconciliation.

The Iraqi Baath were strongly anti-Communist – perhaps in intent the most anti-Communist party in the Middle East – and many members were pro-British. Behind the scenes, however, there was a perceptible tug of war between Western-inclined members of the Baath and those who favoured the Soviet Union. As a Government, they demonstrated their socialist credentials early and immediately attacked the private sector, working apparently on the principle that, though the *petite bourgeoisie* was permissible, the *grande bourgeoisie* were as much an enemy of the regime as feudalists were of the French and Russian revolutionaries. In the course of 1969 new State organisations, notably the State Organisations for Trade and for Industry, began to show their muscle and a struggle ensued between public and private sectors, reflecting differences of philosophy within the regime. Senior officials in the Ministry of Economics opposed aggrandisement by State organisations because, though greedy for import licences, they did not use their allocations fully; consequently, to the detriment of the public, foreign goods authorised by the Government were not imported.

We strove to keep relations smooth and the auguries seemed good, as many Iraqi ministers and officials expressed pleasure at our return to Baghdad. Theoretically, therefore, the Baath should have been easier to deal with than their predecessors. This did not prove to be the case, however, though no one then foresaw that in 1990 Britain would be at war, among others, with an Iraq governed by that same regime. From the outset there were difficulties. First Iraq remained a police state. Secondly our relations were complicated by the past, by the mercurial character of the Iraqis and by diplomatic issues on which it was impossible to give them satisfaction.

Their method of government and attitude to human rights – though this term was not then in general use – also complicated our relationship and storms could brew up unexpectedly. For instance, in January 1969 the bodies of twenty Iraqis convicted of spying for Israel were displayed hanging in the central Tahrir Square. Another group had been tried in Basra and their bodies were displayed there on the very morning that HMS *Vidal* arrived to pay an official visit of friendship, which naturally had to be cancelled. These spectacles were intended as an awful warning to demonstrate the ruthlessness with which the regime was prepared to deal with opposition, ruthlessness which has preserved it to the present day. Large number of Iraqis gathered to view the gruesome scene and officials left their offices to do so. The Iraqis were not unaccustomed to such apparent cruelty and the pretty wife of one of our neighbours invited Ruth to go and view it on the television. However, Western opinion as a whole was outraged and the British Secretary of State for Foreign and Commonwealth Affairs, Michael Stewart, issued a condemnatory statement. This touched Iraqi pride and they took it as interference in their internal affairs, provoking a very large demonstration against us outside the Embassy.

It started early and, as Trefor Evans was unable to reach the Embassy because of the size of the crowd, I was the senior person there. It was a noisy affair with fierce chanting of anti-colonial and anti-imperial slogans. With still fresh memories of the attack on the Embassy in 1958, it was an uncomfortable situation which lasted the whole morning, though becoming a little calmer after I went out to meet two or three of the leaders and received a petition enumerating their political grievances against us, not least over Palestine. In the end they all went away peacefully and Iraqi friends and diplomatic colleagues offered the ex-*post facto* comforting view that the regime would not have allowed anything untoward to happen because they liked us so much. Indeed a number of tanks had been placed in strategic places outside the compound by the Defence Minister Hardan al Takriti and it seems that the trades unionists, teachers and students who formed the demonstration may have acted partly on their own initiative. At all events the Foreign Minister expressed anger that they had anticipated Government policy, though it is likely that some elements in Government had a hand in the organisation.

In the horror generally expressed in Britain and elsewhere over the hangings and display of corpses, it was easy to forget that the last public hanging in the United Kingdom was in 1868 and that until then our forebears had attended such hangings in large numbers – a point which I made in a despatch. But the Iraqis held it against us, as well as the other Western embassies, that no friendly overtures were made to them after these hangings.

It was to be expected under a totalitarian regime that our telephones were constantly tapped, but this had its lighter side. The Assistant Defence Attaché's wife, Anne Crocombe, having complained that their telephone was always out of order, was told brazenly by a Posts and Telegraphs official that, as there were not enough 'tapping machines' to meet demand, their number would have to remain 'out of order'! Ruth, attempting to telephone me in the Embassy, often found herself abruptly cut off. Demanding strongly of the void following the cut-off click to be given a line, she would hear the Security man reply in a thick, strident voice, 'No!' Other diplomats, speaking German or French on the telephone, were interrupted and instructed sharply to speak English or Arabic. I was tempted from time to time into making political remarks with the deliberate intention of being overheard.

I complained about these telephone abuses and, at a Bulgarian Embassy reception, the Foreign Minister Karim Shaikhly, with whom I got on well, opened the conversation by asking how our telephone was working. I was able to report an improvement. Then, demonstrating the paradox in Anglo-Iraqi relations, he took me on one side and asked for help in placing two nephews in boarding school in England.

Only Iraqis who had been cleared by the Security Services were allowed to have social contact with us. Fortunately there seemed to be large numbers of these, including Ministers, senior officials, academics and merchants. We therefore had quite a wide circle of friends and were often invited to their houses. On the other hand some neighbours were so afraid under the Baathist regime of being seen to associate with British people that the distinguished Iraqi eye surgeon who lived next door left it until our penultimate night in Baghdad before inviting us in for a drink, with profuse apologies for his enforced lack of hospitality.

The Iraqis are a very talented, intellectual people and have no lack of world experts on many subjects. They have a tendency, however, not to agree with one another and are no strangers to violence. Late at night after several strong whiskies, they could be very frank on many subjects, including themselves, and would sometimes grow quite maudlin. We are a very bad people and very difficult to govern. Did we not kill Ali? Did we not kill Hussain? Very few have successfully dominated us. Did not Al Hujjaj, Muawiya's Governor, succeed by his strength after he had been pelted with filth in the mosque at Kufa giving the Friday sermon? Did he not call us a "people of faction and troublemaking"? Did he not carry out his threat to cut off the necks of the recalcitrant? There was a man!' 'Nuri Said too knew how to govern Iraq,' they would say. It is an Iraqi trait to admire strength and to respect it for the stability it can give.

I decided once to use quiet strength diplomatically. The Iraqi Foreign Ministry was prone to send messengers to our Consul even late at night demanding a UK visa because some Iraqi VIP was travelling next day. At the same time the Iraqis were very awkward and dilatory about giving visas to bona fide British businessmen. I had no authority from the Foreign and Commowealth Office, but I instructed the Consul next time he received an urgent and inconvenient visa request to say it would only be available after a week. The Iraqis understood the concept of reciprocity very well and visas for our business men immediately became easier to obtain.

The Security services – apparently staffed only by short fat men who bulged out of the ill-fitting suits under which their firearms were clearly visible – suffered from such paranoia that all the Iraqi businessmen who attended the opening of our new British Commercial Office in the centre of Baghdad were arrested, even though some of the Baathist establishment wished for friendly relations with Britain. The Iraqi Government, though, was already much indebted to the Soviet Union and such, in practice, was the atmosphere of suspicion in which we worked that our overall relations were in a constant state of 'might have been'.

Three threads ran through our relations between 1968 and 1971. The Iraqis looked for a more positive attitude towards the Arab/Israel problem and development of the initiative taken by our sponsorship of Security Council Resolution 242, which emphasised the inadmissibility of acquiring territory by war and called for a just and lasting peace in the Middle East. Secondly they sought British intercession with the Shah to stop Iranian interference, mainly carried out through Mullah Mustafa Barzani, in Iraqi Kurdish affairs. They also requested our support to maintain the status quo on the Iranian/Iraqi boundary in the Shatt al Arab, which unusally left the whole of the waterway between the two banks in Iraqi sovereignty, even though they later agreed with Iran that the frontier should lie midstream.

The respective rights, duties and expectations of the Iraq Petroleum Company (IPC) and the Government of Iraq was the third matter over which the Government looked to us for assistance. This was thorny and centred round relations with the Iraq National Oil Company (INOC), the exploitation of the Rumaila oilfield in the south and the Iraq 'take' from oil operations. The largest concession had been held by IPC since 1931, the shareholding in which was 23.75% BP; 23.75% Shell; 23.75% Compagnie Française de Petroles; 23.75% the American Near East Development Corporation and 5% Gulbenkian (later Partex). Oil had been exported via pipeline to the Mediterranean at Tripoli in Lebanon since the mid 1930s and the Iraq Government received royalties, taxes and a share of the profits. During the British period many Iraqis received a liberal British education and the IPC, which was British-managed, gave training and university education to many Iraqi engineers, at one time sending 200 to the UK every year. Not a few married British wives and most such marriages were successful.

The Iraqis demanded a larger slice of the cake but amicable solution of the oil question was complicated by the existence of five shareholders in the IPC. Resembling a five-headed Hydra with heads often facing in different directions, they found it hard to agree on policy and their immediate interests seemed seldom to coincide.[4] The Managing Director of the IPC in Iraq was 'Cocky' Hahn, a large, amusing and totally dedicated man originally of South African origin. Formerly a diplomat, claiming quite wrongly a 'rag bag of a mind' and full of interesting pieces of information, he was very able in negotiating with the Iraqis and in his own idiosyncratic way nearly achieved a breakthrough. All those involved with the IPC problem became friends but, despite numerous comings and goings and the closest collaboration between Embassies and shareholder companies, no solution emerged, although agreement did seem likely at one stage in early 1971. The Iraqi Oil Minister was Saadoun Hamadi and his lemon-like sourness may have had something to do with the failure.

The ambivalence in our relations sometimes worked to our advantage rather than disadvantage and on some occasions the Iraqis showed us special favour. British offficers had founded the Iraqi Army and, when in January 1971 celebrations were held to commemorate its fiftieth anniversary, the British Army and the RAF were invited to send representatives. Relations at the time, however, were such that it was only deemed appropriate to send a brigadier and a group captain. Despite this the Iraqis gave them pride of place and showed much goodwill

4 When Shell wanted a settlement, BP for its own reasons did not, or vice versa. When CFP (Compagnie Française de Petroles) saw the need for a particular course, Standard Oil of New Jersey had another agenda.

towards them. It was an opportunity to improve bilateral relations and Corran Purdon, the Brigadier, made a very good impression and helped the work of Jake Sharpe, the Defence Adviser, in developing links with the military.

The events themselves were a strange mixture of British drills and uniforms and of revolutionary manifestations. The Military College cadets wore 'blues' exactly on the Sandhurst model and were very smart. I was Chargé d'Affaires at the time and several officers came up to me spontaneously introducing themselves as 'Old Sandhurst boy, sir!' On the other hand, at the grand parade on 6 January when the mechanised, infantry and cavalry units rolled, marched or trotted by, the commandos passed at a double 'knees up Mother Brown' pace accompanied by loud blood-curdling revolutionary roars. The Abu Dhabi delegation to this event included Colonel Faisal bin Sultan, son of a former Ruler of Ras al Khaimah, one of the first Trucial States officers to be fully commissioned in the Trucial Oman Scouts during my time there, and it was good to renew acquaintance with him.

We were given preference too on another occasion. The two Kurdish factions – supporters respectively of Mullah Mustafa Barzani, Chairman of the Kurdish Democratic Party, and Galal Talabani – reached a historic, though sadly short-lived, agreement with the Baathist Government in Baghdad and, declaring a three day holiday, the Revolutionary Command Council announced on 11 March 1970 the 'complete and constitutional settlement of the Kurdish issue'. The agreement provided for measures to re-establish peace and security throughout the North: the recognition of Kurdish nationality, and adoption of the Kurdish language as official in Kurdish-majority areas, together with Arabic. Kurds would have an equitable ratio of ministerial, governmental and Army appointments while in Kurdish areas officials were to be Kurds or Kurdish-speaking. Following this, Ruth and I were able in the spring to visit all the Governorates of the North, hitherto closed to diplomats. We were the first given permits to travel widely, though we had already visited Mosul and Kirkuk, the main oil-producing area.

We had a very hospitable reception from the Kurdish Governors in Mosul, Sulaimaniya and other northern areas, and they all expressed particular pleasure at a British visit. We spent one incredible night in the resort of Sarsang, where we could only keep warm under a huge heap of bedclothes with a smelly oil stove burning all night, but our trip was rewarded by seeing the majestic scenery of Northern Iraq and the drive through the spectacular Ruwanduz Gorge. The Kurdish Minister

of Northern Affairs in the central Government in Baghdad was even
warmer than the Northern Governors in his reception when Glen Balfour-Paul and I called on him later. He upbraided us, however, for
Britain's 'failure to colonise' the Kurdish region after the First World
War, thus leaving them backward compared with Iraqis living further
south. Signs of nostalgia for safer times in contrast to the hazards of life
in Baathist Iraq also sometimes appeared among even intellectual Iraqis
and one – not a Kurd – exclaimed, 'What would I not give to see General Maude riding in to Baghdad again on his white horse!'

Nostalgia also affected the Mutasarrif, the Governor, when Ruth
and I paid the first official visit to Basra in 1968 after the resumption of
diplomatic relations. Very cordial in his welcome, he urged that the
Consulate-General and the British Council, both closed in 1967, be
reopened. But this was never to be. The Consulate-General was sadly
closed for good in 1970, ending a very long British presence in Basra,
and the elegant furniture we had used there on our first visit was all
shipped elsewhere. The last link was broken when Mr Padiyath, who
during the break in diplomatic relations had kept the British flag flying,
was moved to Baghdad, though he later joined the Embassy staff in
Muscat in my time there. This continued a tale of loyal family service
with the British for this 'Paddy' was the nephew of the President of the
Indian Association in Dubai, who had bounced me into speaking
impromptu at the Indian National Day.

It was not always plain sailing for a diplomat in Baghdad. On the
way to visit a factory with a British Manager and British plant near
Hillah I had to pass through several checkpoints. No problem arose.
On the return journey, however, one of the checkposts was unmanned
and my driver Esho and I, after making sure that the box usually occupied by Security Police was empty, proceeded on our way. A few miles
further on, a crowd of Iraqis in rural attire stood blocking the road,
thumping it with thick staves. We were compelled to halt and a uniformed Iraqi appeared, brusquely demanding that I get out and go to
see his officer. I asked why and he accused us of failing to stop at a
checkpoint. I told him who I was, claiming diplomatic immunity,
saying that, if his officer wished to see me, he should come to the car.
The man continued to demand that I get out. Equally stubbornly I
refused. Esho then played his trump card, whispering in a low voice to
the soldier, 'Be careful. This very important man.' The soldier reluctantly disappeared and his officer appeared a moment or two later. I
explained smoothly in Arabic what had happened, saying we had no

intention of transgressing. The officer immediately invited us to take tea with him and, after being treated with typical Arab courtesy, we were sent on our way with an apology.

Sometimes a situation could be defused by direct confrontation in an acceptable way. When Chargé d'Affaires I had to authorise a third person note to the Ministry of Foreign Affairs and, owing to the Iraqi usage of 'Arabian Gulf' rather than 'Persian Gulf', which we used officially, I thought it prudent merely to refer to 'the Gulf'. At a reception on the following day, the Undersecretary Abdul Hussain Jamali, a close friend from when we served together in Cairo, warned me that the Foreign Minister was very angry. Approaching Karim Shaikhli boldly, I said I understood he was angry with me and asked why, to which he replied, 'You know.' I retorted by saying he must know that I had used the term 'Gulf' merely out of deference to Iraqi sentiment. The British Government officially called it the 'Persian Gulf' and I had known it as that at school, as I suspected he had. He roared with laughter and said, 'No. We called it the Gulf of Basra!'

We still retained a rather special position and the Queen's Birthday Party was always attended by senior Iraqis from the two Vice Presidents downwards. The Iraqi Army Band attended and played good imperial tunes like 'The British Grenadiers' and a long selection from *HMS Pinafore*. A number of sofas were set aside for the Iraqi VIPs and coversation with them on such occasions was always easy and informal. The Iranian Ambassador and Counsellor sometimes joined in and it was notable that the representatives of countries, so much at loggerheads politically, enjoyed such easy personal relations.

Between 1968 and 1970 the Iraqis for a variety of reasons showed an increasing inclination towards the Eastern Bloc although political ambivalence and the secret but palpable tension within the regime between those wanting closer relations with the West and those seeking alliance with the Communist Bloc still continued. When a deal was struck on a visit to Moscow by Vice President Ammash on exploitation of the North Rumaila oil field the Minister of Oil was not happy, begging the Italian Ambassador to find an Italian or other Western company to execute Iraqi plans to keep the Russians out. Nonetheless, even if Iraq were to become increasingly dependent on Bloc loans for development, we had some commercial successes.

Iraqis still had an in-built desire to buy British, if possible, and the Government ordered a large consignment of Bedford trucks from Vauxhall. During leave at home I went to the Luton factory to see how the order was being carried out and was delighted to find every vehicle destined for Iraq carrying a special Baghdad sticker. A bid for a considerable number of modern refuse collecting trucks with automatic grinding gear was also successful and we celebrated this with the Iraqi agent, who provided champagne from 8 p.m. till after midnight and then a cold dinner – a diplomatic penance! In another respect we were not so successful. Nearly all the cars in Iraq were then of British make and, like other Commercial Counsellors in the Middle East posts, I recommended that British manufacturers put air-conditioning into even small models. The Japanese were already doing this and Iraqis increasingly demanded it. Unfortunately British manufacturers were incensed, even accusing us of 'knocking the British motor industry' and we lost the market – a sad blow for members of British Embassies who worked hard to see more British cars on the road.

Sometimes political circumstances inhibited sales. Baghdad was notable for its British red buses, which operated in the same way as London Transport, and the Iraqi Government wished to place a new order to the value of £4m to renew their fleet. Iraq, however, was assiduously applying the Arab Boycott of Israel as directed by the Boycott Office in Damascus and AEC, like other British motor companies, had been incorporated into the British Leyland Motor Company. This merger unfortunately had the effect of 'tainting' all the companies in the new group, including AEC, on account of Leyland's association with Israel, in particular their assembly plant at Askelon. The Brigadier appointed Director-General of Transport was always poring over the latest edition of *Bus and Coach* when I visited him and, pointing to particular models, sought to identify a British manufacturer unassociated with Leyland. There was not a single one and, although we thought of formulae to overcome the strict boycott rules, none satisfied the Iraqis. On the other hand, if the military wanted Land-Rovers – which fortunately for British employment they often did – military need took priority over the boycott.

Other military needs also proved advantageous and, summoned to see an Iraqi general at the Ministry of Defence, I was asked to arrange the supply of 10,000 Sam Browne belts and 10,000 pairs of good brown shoes for officers. The Iraqi military had been so impressed by the Crown Prince of Bahrain's turn-out on an official visit that they had decided to smarten the Iraqi Army in similar style.

The Baathist Government was not content merely to indoctrinate their own people with their ideas. Sara went to a kindergarten school called Mickey Mouse, run by a French lady, where she learned a song with which she regaled us on car journeys. I gradually pieced it together and it ran:

> *Baba Adani hadiya*
> *Rushasha bunduqiya*
> *Hatta asir jundi kabir*
> *Fi Jaish et Tahrir*
> My father gave me a present, a Tommy gun
> so that I can become a big soldier
> in the army of liberation [meaning of Palestine]

I told Madame of the concern this caused me. She understood, but claimed she had to adopt 'suggestions' made by the regime in order to live. Not long afterwards we were invited to the school speech day and children's show. Sara not only participated in a patriotic communal song, during which they pointed to the Iraqi flag – '*Alami, Alami*' ('My flag, my flag') – but also gave a solo recital in faultless Arabic. The Iraqi parents enthused over this performance by a small blonde girl with blue eyes in her spotless white robe. Sara was a talented child with an inquiring mind and, after coming to church one Sunday and observing the vicar, the Revd Colin Davies, at drinks with us afterwards, asked, 'Daddy, why does God smoke a pipe?' Caroline, the cynosure of the Assyrian servants' eyes and christened '*bazoona*' (meaning kitten) by them, started her schooling with Sara, but could not stand having her lovely blonde hair fondled by fascinated Iraqi teachers and girls.

Another parent, a personable young man called Hindawi who became quite a close friend, was in the Information Department and was probably an Intelligence Officer. One evening we were together eating *masquf* – a Tigris fish cooked by being opened up, then skewered and placed in a circle round a fire of tamarisk wood to cook in a manner dating from Sumerian times – and an argument ensued about how President Nasser had defined the Arab world. I remembered his 1956 speech distinctly and his use of the phrase 'from the Persian Gulf to the Atlantic'. Hindawi maintained his words were, 'from the revolutionary Gulf to the Atlantic'. When we became slightly heated, an Iraqi lady asked us to be calmer and we agreed to wager 100 fils. on it. Hindawi kindly telephoned next day to say I had won the bet!

The Iraqis were hard liners on Palestine and did not accept the ceasefires of 1948 or 1967, perhaps because they were not directly involved. After the June war they did not for some time come out strongly against a peaceful solution, both Government and people giving us considerable kudos for Lord Caradon's sponsorship of Resolution 242. However, in 1969 Shaikhly, the Foreign Minister, specifically rejected a peaceful way forward and after that Iraq openly supported the Palestine Commando movement. Both Yasir Arafat of Fatah and George Habbash of PFLP (People's Front for the Liberation of Palestine) visited Baghdad on many occasions. There was much popular support for Fatah but the Baathist regime for a while became special protégés of the extremist and Marxist PFLP.

Iraq was directly concerned with events in other Arab countries, supporting revolutionary activity in South Arabia and elsewhere, including Libya. On 3 September 1969 when I was Chargé d'Affaires, I was summoned at very short notice by N'ima N'ima, the Undersecretary in the Ministry of Foreign Affairs, and told – amicably – that Iraq would not 'stand with its hands tied behind its back' in the event of interference by the UK or others in Libya, where King Idris had just been overthrown by the regime of Colonel Gaddafi.

A year later they were much involved in support of the Palestinian cause in Jordan, where the Palestinians had established a very strong position. The country was in a precarious state. There was an assassination attempt on King Hussein on 1 September and fierce fighting took place between Royalist troops and Palestinian Commandos. Negotiated ceasefires did not hold, although King Hussein and the Chief of Staff Masshur Hadithi did their best to calm things. The Palestinian Commandos, who feared extinction, however, had in effect set up an *imperium in imperio* and from this they were endangering both the King himself and the legitimate Jordanian Government. The Iraqis impetuously and imperiously issued an ultimatum calling on the Jordanian Government to cease action against the Commandos or the Iraqi Army would 'take all necessary measures to protect commando activity in accordance with the dictates of nationalist duty'. I was again Chargé d'Affaires and was talking to Shaikhly, the Foreign Minister, at a Libyan Embassy party when the President telephoned him and a moment or two later the Jordanian Ambassador was summoned to a room inside and given the ultimatum. The Iraqis already had their Salahuddin force in Jordan and its Commander conveyed a similar ultimatum to the Jordanian Chief of Staff.

The Iraqis were playing the Middle East maverick in the eyes of the West, the USSR and of Arab countries which favoured the plan for a Middle East settlement put forward by William Rogers, the US Secretary of State. This involved *de facto* Arab recognition of Israel in the area it held immediately before the 1967 War, which was roughly four fifths of Palestine as mandated to Britain after the First World War. The *quid pro quo* was justice for Palestinian refugees and Israel's withdrawal from areas just conquered, though only if Palestinian guerrillas were controlled. Nasser accepted the proposals and Israel did likewise, if unwillingly, for a short time, though few believed that Israel would easily give up its conquests. In the light of subsequent events, perhaps the Iraqis were justified in being as sceptical as they were.

A series of events then took place which caused the Iraqis to moderate their policies, particularly towards the more extreme Palestinian organisations. On 6 September 1970 four aircraft bound for the US were hijacked by Palestinian Commandos of the PFLP and two of these, a Swissair and a TWA plane, were taken to Dawson's Field in Jordan.[5] The hijackings were at first greeted with a paean of praise by the Baghdad press, though many ordinary people were horrified and one Minister asked the French Ambassador to intercede for the Arabs in their predicament saying, 'We are not savages.'

On 9 September a BOAC VC10 – the very aircraft which had brought Ruth and the three children[6] out from home after leave – was also hijacked on the return journey between Bahrain and Beirut. There was a full load of homebound passengers including many schoolchildren. After some alarm that it might come to Baghdad, it was, like two of the other hijacked aircraft, flown to Dawson's Field, where passengers and crew were held hostage in the aircraft for a day or two, a very grim experience in the scorching heat. One Palestinian involved was Leila Khalid and by a curious chance Ruth had not long before sat next to her at a Red Crescent sewing party to aid the Palestinians, observing that she was wearing a gold ring adorned with a grenade.

This time the Iraqi press, indulging in no fulsome praise about hijacking the BOAC aircraft, reported the event factually, leading the always speculative and inventive Lebanese press to attribute this to the Iraqi Baathists being pro-British. The British Secretary of State, Michael Stewart, had made representations to all the Arab Ambassadors in London urging their Governments to exert every effort to obtain the release of passengers and crew as well as the aircraft. All the Arab Ambassadors had expressed regret for the hijacking except Kadhim al

5 A PanAm aircraft had been flown to Cairo where the hijackers blew it up and the attempt on an El Al plane had been thwarted.
6 Our third daughter, Susan, was born on 1 January 1970.

Khalaf, the Iraqi. As Chargé d'Affaires I went at 11.30 a.m. on Thursday 10 September to ask Abdul Hussain Jamali, Director-General of Arab Affairs, who in the absence of the Undersecretary was the senior official in the Ministry,[7] to explain the Iraqi Government's formal position. Jamali said he would find out, and this gave me the opportunity to repeat the Secretary of State's request for intervention with the Palestinians concerned. President Bakr himself was personally presiding at the time over a full-scale meeting of the Revolutionary Command Council to consider the situation.

Two hours later I was summoned to the Ministry and very formally ushered up the front steps. I seriously thought I might be about to be declared *persona non grata* or that some fearful ultimatum would be delivered. Shown this time into the Undersecretary's own office, I was greeted again by Jamali, who seemed a changed man – very buoyant. 'Good news!' he said, going on to announce that the Iraqi Government disapproved of hijackings on principle and would do their best to obtain the release of all the 'civilians'. I asked for clarification and he said this meant all the passengers and crew without regard to nationality. I wondered at the time if the word 'civilian' had any special connotation and wondered still more on Saturday 12 September when the PLO said they would release all the detainees except Israelis with military potential. However Jamali on that day reiterated that his previous words were the correct interpretation. In the event the passengers were released but the three aircraft at Dawson's Field were blown up.

In the background there had evidently been a resolution of differences between pragmatic moderates and doctrinaire members of the regime. This was probably due to the influence of Bakr himself and Saleh Mahdi Ammash, who had sent a personal message to our Secretary of State giving the same assurances as Abdul Hussain Jamali had given me. It is not clear what line Saddam Hussain, who was already beginning to emerge as a key figure, took over this but on 12 September there were rumours that he had been shot, or was under arrest or had resigned.

The Revolutionary Command Council remained in something of a cleft stick but decided on a moderate line in support of the PLO when the PFLP were expelled from that organisation because of their involvement in the five hijackings. The Iraqis did not want to see a Commando government in Amman instead of King Hussein and they

7 He had just been promoted to Ambassadorial rank.

continued to deal with the Jordanian Ambassador in Baghdad even after Palestinians had occupied his Embassy and hoisted the Palestinian flag. The Iraqis nonetheless expected the Ambassador to exchange messages with the Royalist government in Amman, even though, ousted from his own premises, he had to rely on the radio facilities of the UAR (Egyptian) and Kuwaiti Embassies.

The Iraqis with their fresh viewpoint were severely embarrassed by the hijackings, which switched world sympathies away from the Arabs at a time when the West was showing signs of losing patience with Israel because of the recalcitrance they increasingly showed over the Rogers proposals. Iraq reduced their commitments in Jordan. They were concerned at direct interference there by the new Syrian regime under Hafez Al Assad, and also not unmindful of the presence of the US Sixth Fleet in the Mediterranean, US aircraft in Turkey and British aircraft in Cyprus. At the back of their minds they saw themselves as remaining in contest for leadership of the Arab world and tried to score tricks off Nasser whenever they could.

Another Rogers concerned the Embassy at about this time. Cecil Rogers, the senior representative of the British consultants Sir Alexander Gibb, had been refused an exit visa and held for several weeks as a sort of hostage – albeit free to move in Baghdad – until the final accounts were cleared up of a particular consultancy job over which the Iraqis were making unreasonable difficulties. I wrote to Ammash, the Vice-President, about the case and he immediately arranged for me to see the Minister of the Interior, a well-disposed cavalry officer who had served on Luneburg Heath on secondment to the British Army. By gentle but extreme persistence and insisting on not leaving his office until a framework for settling the problem was set up, I achieved this. A firm appointment for me to see the Minister of Works and Housing, who had been singularly unavailable previously, was made for the same day. He greeted me, saying, 'We like Mr Rogers very much.' I retorted, 'Yes, Minister, you like him too much and we want you to let him go. Will you please give him an exit visa.' He agreed fairly readily and formalities were completed in two more days, after which Cecil Rogers got safely away. In my experience toughness was required in dealing with Iraqis, but the Ministerial reaction in this case demonstrated a degree of goodwill towards Britain and was perhaps another example of Ministerial empiricism in the face of bureaucracy and party doctrine.

Earlier in the year the state of Arab-Israel relations also brought our most memorable visitor – George Brown, who had been Secretary of

State for Foreign and Commonwealth Affairs under Harold Wilson but was no longer in office. Perhaps in the spirit of his extraordinary public attempt at the Lord Mayor's Banquet in 1967 to get the Egyptian and Israeli Ambassadors to shake hands in front of the television cameras, he arrived on 8 January 1970 on a self-appointed 'peace mission of goodwill' to Middle East countries claiming the support of the Labour Government. He had sent word to us of his coming and this had been conveyed to the Iraqi Ministry of Foreign Affairs, but they made no concrete plans. He was met at the airport by the Undersecretary and one or two others from the Ministry of Foreign Affairs, and Glen Balfour-Paul and I were there too.

In the VIP room George Brown asked the Iraqis for a copy of his 'programme' only to be told that nothing had been prepared. They wished to know what he wanted to do. A tirade from George Brown ensued and he protested that Baghdad was the first place he had visited in Middle East where there was neither a programme nor an appointment fixed with the Head of Government. Glaring through his glasses, he turned to the Iraqi press correspondents present and said, 'Write that down and publish it!' The Swiss Chargé d'Affaires, who had looked after our interests during the break in diplomatic relations, believed in taking a strong line with the Iraqis and grunted his approval. George Brown then mellowed and said that, despite this bad beginning, he would proceed with the visit in a spirit of goodwill.

The Iraqis did not rush things and George Brown had to wait for many hours before news came of an appointment with the President, General Ahmed Hassan al Bakr. Immediately after this Ruth and I held a lunch for him, and the guests included the Permanent Undersecretary, N'ima N'ima, and the most senior officials in the Ministry of Foreign Affairs. On George Brown's return from the Palace the Iraqi guests asked politely how the meeting with the President had gone only to receive the reply, 'He is a nasty little man. I didn't like him at all. Less than any of the other Heads of Government I have met on this tour.' N'ima and the others were shocked, defending their President by saying that he was 'perhaps a little unsophisticated but . . .'. George Brown would have none of it. We sat down to lunch hosted by Ruth, who had given birth only six days before to our daughter Susan. He conversed provocatively in a near monologue with the Iraqis and, meeting only politeness in return, he turned to Ruth saying, 'Your dinner's lovely, darling, but the conversation's lousy.'

After lunch we went in to the drawing room. As was customary in those days, brandy, liqueurs, coffee and cigars were offered and George Brown filled his brandy balloon fuller than I have ever seen one before or since. He then sat down – on the floor rather than the sofa – and when all were seated he glared round the room from behind his horn-rimmed spectacles and said, 'You Iraqis! You're all a lot of bloody "Commies".' They sighed. 'Oh Mr Brown!' 'You are a bunch of "bloody Commies", though you don't know it, but I know a Commie when I see one,' he retorted. He went on to a very frank exposition of the regime's short-comings and the errors, dwelling on its totalitarian nature and close association with the USSR and the Communist bloc. The Iraqis listened and the party broke up in a spirit of surprising goodwill. George Brown later met a very large number of Iraqis including General Saleh Mahdi Ammash, the Vice President, with whom he had a friendly and fruitful dialogue, but broke virtually every rule in the diplomatic rule book and all advice on how to behave in an Arab country. His special style and charisma, however, enabled this brilliant maverick to get away with it and for weeks after his departure we had tender inquiries. 'How is dear Mr Brown? What news have you of him?'

In our time in Baghdad, our leisure consisted of tennis at the Alawiya Club with Iraqi and British friends, picnicking on the banks of the Tigris after trips in the Embassy launch and, in the cooler months, pic-nics in the desert. Then we often went 'telling' to see what we could find on the surface of the thousands of tells all over the country – sites of former towns and villages and poignant reminders of the mutability of human affairs. Sara and Caroline developed eagle eyes for pretty sherds and fragments of glass.

Iraq's archaeological riches brought experts from several countries to work there. David Oates was the Head of the British School of Archaeology, who numbered Leonard Woolley and Max Mallowan, husband of Agatha Christie, among his predecessors. Dr Schmidt led a German team digging at Uruk, one of Iraq's oldest sites which he described to us in fascinating detail on a visit. We dined well with him and his colleagues, though I did not have to wear a dinner jacket as his German predecessor would have insisted. The Italian archaeologist Paolo Costa and Germana, later to be his wife, were also active in Iraq and with them we visited Ur and other sites in the South. Later both went to Oman to open up new fields of archaeology there.

Baghdad was very significant for our family. First my mother and father came out to stay – exactly forty-nine years since they had been together in Baghdad in 1920 when the railway from Basra to Baghdad was a military one and the stations had only tented accommodation. Though much had changed, there were still parts, especially where the old Turkish houses still stood, which they found easily recognisable. My mother had often described the blooming of the desert from her much earlier visit and at Hatra, the ruins of the ancient town allied with Rome on the marches with the Persians, we all walked through the beautiful wild flowers of every colour – tulips, anemones and alpines – which had that year bloomed everywhere in the desert. Much to my botanist mother's delight, Caroline – later no botanist! – was enthralled and picked posies.

Secondly, our third daughter, Susan, was born in Baghdad, though Ruth at one moment wondered whether she might not arrive during a picnic at Babylon on 1 January 1970. In fact I took Ruth to the hospital at about 10 that same evening. Susan's arrival was speedy and at 2 a.m. next day Ruth herself telephoned to announce that she had just been delivered of a beautiful girl. We had somehow expected that it would be a girl, but the Scottish matron of the Haidari hospital – mindful of Iraqi disappointment at the birth of a girl if a son is expected – seized the phone and said with Scottish forthrightness, 'It's not her fault, Mr Hawley!' We ourselves were delighted with the new arrival, who had plenty of the very dark hair which she much later redeveloped after early years as a blonde. She was christened at our local church in Little Gaddesden in Hertfordhire during our home leave in 1970 but as a baby was also dipped in the Tigris by her godfather, Glen Balfour-Paul, on a river picnic.

We took leave in October 1969 and toured Iran. Good friends in the Iranian Embassy gave us letters of introduction before we set off for the frontier town of Qasr el Shirin. At the border Iraqi guards hospitably provided us with tea and gave cold drinks to Sara and Caroline, and we then thought we were on the broad road to Shiraz. We were wrong. At the Iranian frontier post we were stopped and, rather than offered hospitality, told we must be quarantined. They said that all travellers from Iraq, where there was allegedly an outbreak of typhoid, must be subjected to this. Diplomatic immunity availed us nothing, which was galling as the alleged 'outbreak' might well have been largely 'political'.

We spent an uncomfortable night and most of the next day there, during which we managed to get a message to the Iranian Embassy with a British traveller from Teheran to Baghdad. They sent immediate telegrams and the Governor of the Province was instructed to release us at once, though his message only arrived after we had satisfied the health authorities by physical proof that we were all clear of infection. In fact Caroline, who at the age of two and a half had inevitably scrabbled in the dust of the quarantine camp, promptly fell ill – fortunately very briefly – with gut trouble just as we arrived at the hotel in Qasr el Shirin.

The journey on to Shiraz was also eventful. I was pressing on at some speed on the rough road, despite some protest from the prescient Sara, to get the children to the hotel at a reasonable hour. Power was suddenly lost when we were some miles from Dizful. A large stone had knocked out the sump of my Jaguar and we came to a halt in the middle of nowhere. Fortunately only a few moments passed before we were rescued by French contractors' men working on the Shiraz-Dizful pipeline, who took us to their camp where the British consultants were also based. The kindly British engineer in charge generously made his own caravan available and gave us a good dinner, at which his colleagues quizzed me on many subjects saying they did not often have the chance of speaking to a 'real politician'! The car was repaired perfectly in the workshops overnight by a marvellous Iranian mechanic, who resolutely refused any reward.[8] The British engineers were extremely impressed with the skills and accuracy of the Iranian welders on the pipeline, finding it almost impossible ever to fault their work. After the initial traumas of the trip we enjoyed the splendid sights of Shiraz, Isfahan and Teheran, and saw friends there.

On another occasion we, like other members of the Embassy, visited Kuwait for shopping. Esho, the Assyrian driver, was astonished at the physical aspect of Kuwait and exclaimed, 'Really, sir, in Kuwait I see only cars – no people; no animals.' A neat summing up.

During my sabbatical leave at Durham University, Denis Healey, Minister of Defence in the Labour Government, had persuaded his colleagues that Britain should withdraw from military commitments east of Suez. This led to a nearly farcical situation over the Persian Gulf, making me thankful that I had no role in decision making at the time. Goronwy Roberts, a Minister at the FCO, was charged with two diametrically opposed missions within three months in 1967/68. First he visited the Gulf Rulers to assure them that, 'in the interests of stability

---

8 I was able to remedy this by sending a donation later from Teheran.

in the Gulf region', the British military presence would be maintained at all its traditional bases and, though there would be a term to Britain maintaining her responsibilities under the Treaties of Protection, there were no immediate plans to change the *status quo*.

Within a few months, charged with performing an unenviable diplomatic backward somersault, he informed the Rulers of the Government's intention to withdraw all British forces from the Gulf and to end the Treaties of Protection at the end of 1971. This caused consternation as the existing long-standing but flexible relationship with Britain was relied upon and highly valued. The Rulers attempted to change the Government's mind and Shaikh Zaid bin Sultan, the Ruler of Abu Dhabi, offered to pay the £12 million a year which it was said the withdrawal would save. The Labour Government was unmoved.

The Conservative Opposition was unhappy and undertook to reverse the situation on returning to power, though in fact they proceeded more cautiously when they won the election in 1970. Alec Douglas-Home, the Foreign and Commonwealth Affairs Secretary, appointed Bill Luce[9] as his Special Representative to carry out a formal consultation with the British-Protected Gulf States and their neighbours in September 1970. It was almost inevitable that Iraq, Iran and Saudi Arabia would, for reasons of national pride, not feel able overtly to recommend a continuation of the British presence, whatever their private feelings, and this proved to be the case. Meantime Iraq was naturally amongst the States to be visited.

As Chargé d'Affaires I conveyed news of Luce's impending arrival in Baghdad to Abdul Hussain at the Ministry of Foreign Affairs. It caused consternation at first but the Iraqis then said he would be welcome, though he would be received at official and not Ministerial level. This was another example of Iraq's maverick behaviour, as he was received by King Faisal of Saudi Arabia, the Shah of Iran, the Amir of Kuwait, the Sultan of Oman, all the other Gulf Rulers and the Egyptian Foreign Minister.

It was a particular pleasure to meet an old friend and colleague again but the scene at the airport had elements of farce. The Iraqi Undersecretary, N'ima N'ima, by chance arrived on the same plane, but I was astonished to see General Hamid Shehab, the Minister of Defence, General Shanshal, the Chief of Staff, and the Director of Military Intelligence all waiting in the VIP room. Abdul Hussain Jamali was equally

9 Sir William Luce.

astonished when he came in. Some rapid whispering between civil and military officers ensued, and the military withdrew in some disarray. It transpired that they had come to meet Vice President Hardan al Takriti off the same plane, though he was not due until a later flight.

I telephoned the Ministry of Foreign Affairs the following day at 10 a.m. to be told the Undersecretary was still sleeping, and a number of increasingly embarrassed telephone calls from Abdul Hussain continued through the morning. Next day the Head of Protocol telephoned to say that, as the Undersecretary was still sick, Jamali would receive Bill Luce on behalf of N'ima. We went to the Ministry at 10 a.m. and were received by Jamali in the Undersecretary's office with considerable courtesy. We pressed for a meeting with one of the Vice Presidents and Jamali said he would try personally to approach Saleh Mahdi Ammash who happened to be in the building. Bill Luce explained the object of his visit, stressing that his calling on various capitals was a necessary courtesy and prelude to the British Cabinet making its decision.

Jamali then stated Iraqi policy from a carefully prepared brief. Iraq did not intend to export their revolution. Though under pressure from the more extremist groups, they did not support the policy of the People's Front for the Liberation of Oman and the Arabian Gulf – PFLOAG. Iraq favoured the Union of the Nine Gulf States and did not want to see Bahrain go it alone. They had counselled the Rulers in this sense. Iraq considered that the Union of the Nine should become a member of the Arab League and of the UN before there was an question of association with Oman or of frontier rectification. Saudi claims could be dealt with at that stage. As for the islands, Tunbs and Abu Musa, Iraq looked to us to keep them in the UAE and to reject Iranian claims. Iraq did not favour any political or military alliance for the Nine and Iraq 'insisted' that the British Government should not change its predecessor's policy over withdrawal.

Jamali did not manage to contact Ammash but the Acting Minister, Rifai, suggested that N'ima should be dragged from his bed to see Bill Luce! In the event, Alec Douglas-Home's Personal Representative decided that, having done all he could, he should leave on the afternoon plane to Beirut. Jamali then astonished me by saying the visit had been a success and a beginning had been made. It was difficult to decide why Iraq behaved in this fashion, but perhaps they feared we were resolved to stay on in the Gulf and did not wish to be seen to be in collusion with us. Alternatively they might have been making a point since no British

Minister had visited Baghdad since the Baath Government had assumed office.[10]

There was some ambivalence in Iraq's policy towards the Gulf States. Abdul Hussain Jamali reiterated to me that Iraq did not intend to 'export its revolution'. At the same time, however, other parts of the Iraqi establishment, working in Aden, were actively supporting the Dhofar Liberation Front in their rebellion against Sultan Said bin Taimur in the southern part of the Sultanate, as well as giving military training to Omani rebels at Shuaiba in Southern Iraq. The tug-of war between the two opposing doctrinal blocs was reflected in this sphere also.

Iraq in any case took an increasing interest in the Gulf. They had already developed a port at Umm Qasr near Kuwait to give them direct deep water access to the Gulf, and were increasingly concerned about freedom of navigation in the Straits of Hormuz. Relations with Kuwait varied somewhat, particularly over development of the Rumaila oilfield on the border, but no serious problems arose. Shaikh Zaid bin Sultan, the Ruler of Abu Dhabi, was accorded a full-scale State Visit in 1970,[11] and the Crown Prince of Bahrain also paid a high profile visit. The Rafidain Bank was established in Bahrain and there were numerous visits of Chambers of Commerce, insurance establishments and bankers to develop closer links.

On 24 July 1970 Sultan Qaboos seized the reins of power in the Sultanate from his father. At first Abdul Hussain thought the Iraqis would not want to receive a goodwill mission sent by the new Sultan, led by Shaikh Abdulla al Tai, to Arab countries. Here again they performed a somersault and in the event welcomed them, even expressing willingness to help the new Oman. This was a very positive decision as there was an Imamate Office in Baghdad, as in Cairo, Damascus and other Arab capitals, and they still recognised the Imam Ghalib as ruler of at least part of Oman. They were willing to overcome this considerable political problem, however, perhaps because the pragmatists were managing to gain the upper hand over the Intelligence Officers' more sinister tactics. From this time Iraq's support for revolutionary movements, as well as the Imam Ghalib, gradually diminished.

10 Perhaps too they believed that our new Gulf policy was connected with our support for the Rogers plan, which they continued to reject, and we intended to squeeze the Baathist regime in order to bring it down.
11 I saw him and renewed friendly contact.

When we left Iraq in April 1971, it was with much nostalgia for a country which we had enjoyed very much more than we had ever expected, and for the many friends there. I was to take up my new appointment as Ambassador to the Sultanate of Oman.

8
Oman

Aspects of my new appointment were unusual. In May 1970 I was told I was to be appointed Ambassador to His Highness Sultan Said bin Taimur, Sultan of Muscat and Oman, in a last attempt to persuade him to move more energetically into the modern world. Previous British Representatives had been Consuls-General and it was hoped that the upgrading would make the Sultan more receptive to advice. A pregnant silence followed and on 23 July 1970 Qaboos, Said's only son, seized the Government and proclaimed his faith in his country's future by giving the country a new name – 'The Sultanate of Oman'. It was a bold step, for the country was then far from united. The discreet connivance of the British Government, perhaps surprisingly, earned it more kudos than opprobrium in the Arab world.

A few months later His Majesty Sultan Qaboos bin Said, as he had become, gave his 'Agrément'.[1] Thus, accredited to the son instead of the father, I became the first Ambassador in Oman – at least since the Great Mogul sent an Embassy there in the 1780s. The Sultan was away for three months and, instructed to be in Muscat by May 1971, I spent two months until his return as the last British Consul-General. This quirk of circumstance caused an unexpected difficulty over my preparatory briefings in London. The Heads of Mission Section, which very efficiently made all official appointments for newly appointed and established Heads of Mission, was run by Nancy Fisher, a lady who refused point blank to have anything to do with mere Consuls-General, however exceptional the circumstances. An awestruck and embarrassed Head of Personnel Department kindly made other arrangements for me

Oman, with an area of some 309,500 square kilometres, is the largest country in south-east Arabia, its people now numbering more than two million – about 750,000 in 1971. It is a land of stark beauty and contrasts. Magnificent mountains of many shades of red, grey and green stand out jagged against the clear blue sky. Neat villages girded

---

1 The technical term for a Head of State giving his assent.

by extensive groves of date palms nestle serenely in barren *wadis* or stretch along the ocean shore. Flat plains stretch as far as the eye can see and deserts roll away eastwards into the Rub' al Khali, the Empty Quarter, with its waves of dunes rising to 600 feet or more. Bedu tribes, whose hitherto spartan lives have now been much changed by prosperity, live with their camels and goats to the west of the great Hajar mountain range running down the centre of Oman with peaks rising to some 10,000 feet. The plain on the sea side is known as the Batinah (or stomach) and the opposite side as the Dhahirah (or back). People on the 1,000-mile-long coast have traditionally made their living from seafaring, fishing, or agriculture.[2]

The hills of Dhofar in the south catch the south-west monsoon from May to September, turning them green like no other part of Arabia, and the majestic cliffs rise imposingly along Dhofar's coast. Oman's neighbours, with which it now has agreed boundaries, are the United Arab Emirates (UAE) to the north-west, Saudi Arabia to the west and Yemen to the south. Possession of the Musandam Peninsula gives Oman control, with Iran to the north, of the strategically important Straits of Hormuz.

Lying roughly between 16° and 26° in latitude, Oman's winter climate is almost idyllic though so hot in summer that the fourteenth century Arab geographer Abdul Razak wrote, albeit with huge hyperbole, 'The heat was so intense that it burned the marrow in the bones, the sword in its scabbard melted into wax and the gems which adorned the handle of the dagger were reduced to coal. In the plains the chase became a matter of perfect ease, for the desert was strewn with roasted gazelles.'

A palpable sense of the continuity of a long history characterises Oman. Known from the fourth millennium BC as Magan, it exported – according to Sumerian cuneiform inscriptions – copper and diverse other goods, including 'Magan chairs'[3] and onions to Iraq. Numerous archaeological sites dating from 3300 BC testify to a common culture in Oman and the UAE with connections with the Jemdat Nasr culture (2800–2600 BC) in Mesopotamia and sites in eastern Iran.

Magan's ships and shipwrights were mentioned in third millennium tablets just as the Arab author Ma'sudi commented in the tenth century

2 The long coastline changes from hundreds of miles of flat beach to the rocky inlets around Muscat and the dramatic mountains and inlets of the Musandam peninsula, which have been called a 'tropical Norway'.

3 The form of these chairs, meriting special mention, can only be guessed at.

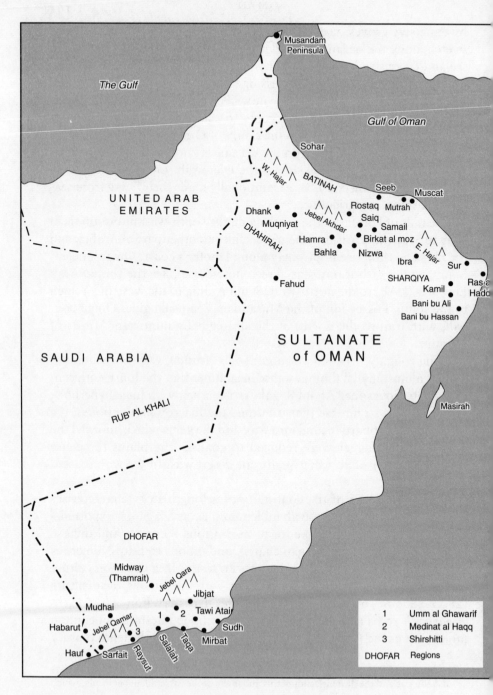

Sultanate of Oman

on the shipwrights of Oman. Craft of up to 500 or 600 tons were built in the port of Sur. Thus, with their 1,000–mile coastline on the Indian Ocean, Omanis were seafarers who colonised much of the east African coast from some 2,000 years ago, later reaching Madagascar and Sofala. In the ninth century AD they reached Canton to the east, inspiring tales such as Sindbad the Sailor, and al Muqadissi[4] described Sohar as 'the hallway to China, the storehouse of the East and the stay of Yemen'; a major seaport and richer in fine buildings and foreign merchandise than any other in the Islamic world. Hundreds of years later, from the seventeenth to the nineteenth centuries, Omani fleets were formidable in size and strength and Singapore still has a Muscat Street in testimony to Omani sea power and widespread trading interests – only stifled by the arrival of the age of the steamer and European dominance.

Oman, under Persian rule for nearly 1,000 years from the time of the Achaemenids in the sixth century BC until after the advent of Islam, was mentioned by Pliny, Strabo and Ptolemy and in later centuries was subject not only to Persian influence but also permanent settlement from Yemen and South Arabia. The conversion to Islam of the large population practising Christianity, Judaism and the worship of the trinity of Sun, Moon and Venus was early, quick and relatively free from strife and, from the seventh century AD, Omanis were prominent intellectually and militarily in the development and expansion of Islam, participating in the conversion of Khorasan in Persia.

The mountain villages of the Interior depended on the clever *falaj* system, identical with the Persian *qanats*, by which a water source is tapped and the water channelled for long distances underground to the cultivated fields. The people were traditionally settled and at various periods in the past prosperous. For long periods the ruler of the country was an Imam elected for his personal qualities, and Nizwa and Rostaq were both at one time capitals of Oman, with seats of Islamic learning and libraries. Much of Oman's rule by Imams, Sultans and Meliks has been faithfully recorded by Omani historians.

The majority of the Omanis follow the Ibadhi precept, of which an Omani historian has said, 'The true religion has been compared to a bird; its egg was laid in Medina, it hatched in Basra and flew to Oman.' They believed that the Caliphate should not necessarily go to a member of the Prophet's family but that the best man available to lead the people should be chosen as Imam. In practice the Omanis have

---

4 Like Ma'sudi writing in the tenth century.

throughout history been a largely tolerant people, who have on occasions given refuge to others fleeing persecution elsewhere.[5]

The existence of two traditional factions – the Hinawis, representing the Qahtan or Adnan tribes who emigrated from Yemen, and the Ghafiris representing the Nizar tribes from further north – has affected much of Omani history, but a different, long-standing and paradoxical dichotomy between the coast and the Interior in northern Oman has also been strong. As a consequence of these divisions the rulers of one part of the country have not always exercised effective rule over others. The earlier name of Muscat and Oman perpetuated this division and suggested, rightly, that the previous Sultan's hold on the people of the Interior was tenuous.

A satisfactory but delicate balance between Sultan and Imam had been upset when the Imam Shaikh Mohamed Al Khalili, who governed the Interior, died in 1954 and Shaikh Ghalib bin Ali was elected as his successor. This led to separatist military and political campaigns against the Sultanate instigated by Talib, the Imam's brother, Shaikh Sulaiman bin Himyar of the Bani Ryam tribe and Shaikh Salih bin Isa leader of the Hirth tribe of the Sharqiyah area. An important goal was control of the oil which was believed to exist in the Interior, but Talib's forces, under the banner of the Oman Revolutionary Movement, had been defeated and dislodged from the high Jebel Akhdar area in 1959. The leaders were forced into exile in Saudi Arabia but the 'Imamate of Oman' was recognised by a number of Arab countries and 'The Question of Oman' came up on the agenda of the General Assembly of the UN every year.

This was the situation in 1971 and a serious rebellion was also raging in the southern province of Dhofar. Many young Omanis had gone abroad to seek education, the country's three schools being totally inadequate to meet aspiration and need, and the country enjoyed virtually no international recognition. Conditions were therefore not very auspicious for the young Sultan Qaboos's aims and ambitions. It was my fortune and privilege to see the start of his reign, during which Oman, with the help of increasing oil revenues, has against the odds been unified, transformed, and modernised.

On 27 April we left Baghdad *en famille* and flew to Bahrain to stay with Geoffrey Arthur,[6] the last British Political Resident in the Gulf. He

5 For example Iraqi Jews fleeing from Baghdad in the nineteenth century.
6 Sir Geoffrey Arthur, earlier Counsellor in Cairo, Ambassador in Kuwait and later Deputy Undersecretary of State. After retirement he was Master of Pembroke College Oxford until his death in 1984. He was also our son's godfather.

and I easily evolved a working relationship for the delicate period of overlap, which would last only a few months. It was delicate because the Sultans, as completely independent rulers, had not fully recognised the Political Resident as having jurisdiction in Oman, where Britain had traditionally been represented by a Consul or Consul-General.

On 2 May we flew to Muscat on a BAC1–11. Richard Anderson, the portly and affectionately labelled 'Major Drum', whom I had known as a slim young adjutant in the Green Howards in Khartoum in the 1940s, was on the same flight. Gulf Aviation had overbooked, as they did too often, and an Omani lady passenger had to take her child on her knee. Richard typically rose to defend her rights and soundly berated the steward for the airline's bad habits. Not long afterwards, my wife Ruth, by then Ambassadress, was asked to do the same!

The approach to Bait al Falaj airstrip – now the site of the Central Bank and other major banks in the main commercial area – was spectacular and alarming. It seemed as if the aircraft's wing tip must surely touch rocks on either side as it negotiated the surrounding mountains. We landed safely nevertheless and were met by John Shipman who was holding the fort in the Consulate-General. Hugh Oldman, the British Defence Secretary to the Sultan, an old friend from Khartoum days, and Colin Maxwell, the Deputy Commander of the Sultan's Armed Forces and also an old friend from Trucial States days from 1958 to 1961, were also there to greet us.

I awoke on 8 May to hear gunfire. In my dreamlike state I imagined we were still in Baghdad and another coup had started. Looking out of the window, however, Ruth and I saw rings of smoke and balls of fire belching from the muzzle-loaders on the saluting platform of Fort Merani, fired by police wearing khaki uniform and the French-style blue *kepis* introduced by the former Sultan. It was the Prophet's Birthday and this was the way the battery always announced Muslim feasts and fasts.

Our new residence looked out over the Muscat Cove and the same magnificent seascape as a line of British representatives – Political Agents, Residents, Consuls and Consul-Generals – had enjoyed since 1800. Chinaman's Cove, an attractive rocky bay to the east, brought pleasant breezes to the enormous verandah. At the entrance to the harbour facing the Embassy, two identical buildings, originally British and French coaling stations, testified to the compromise solution found to an Anglo-French dispute at the turn of the nineteenth and twentieth centuries when in 1900 the British authorities frustrated French attempts to establish a coaling station at Bandar Jissuh to the east.

The palace of the former Sultans still stood on the waterfront and, between it and the Embassy, a small customs area and tiny quay received all the material for the early stages of development of Oman. The scene was soon to change, however, with a much larger and more striking palace where its demolished predecessor had been. The most dominating features in the meanwhile were the two forts built by the Portuguese in the sixteenth century – Merani on the left, and Jalali on the right, then a jail from which prisoners in chains emerged to work or, liberated as an act of mercy at Ids, whooped with joy as they came down the steps.

Muscat was then small and close-knit. Everyone, Omani, British and others, knew one another and mutual visits were frequent. There were less than ten saloon cars, and their owners were immediately identifiable by the model or number plate. Behind the old palace was a small modern building, erected by Sultan Said, and there I called on the whole Government in one morning, an easy task as each Ministry had only two rooms – one for the Minister and the other for his whole staff.

Sayyid Tarik bin Taimur, the first Prime Minister and the Sultan's respected senior uncle, lived and worked in a modern house opposite Bait Garaizah, a large and beautiful house in traditional Omani style built on the site of the sixteenth-century Portuguese cathedral,[7] which adjoined an Augustinian priory at the same period. I called on him there frequently, my visits often lasting several hours. He was not only a fascinating talker and spinner of ideas, but had a brilliant command of English; though he was by now less a man of action than in his earlier days. When, as frequently happened, he proclaimed his democratic principles and then complained of things happening of which he did not approve, I urged him to speak personally and frankly to the Sultan. He was after all his nephew's appointee. He would not countenance this, however, and insisted that it was I who should speak to Qaboos. I would press him on why he could not or would not, but he simply replied, 'Because he is the Sultan.' Such was the aura of respect.

Sayyid Thuwaini bin Shihab, Governor of the capital and the Sultan's Personal Representative as his father had been before him, also had his seat in Muscat and other members of the Royal Family were also beginning to take on increasingly important roles in the new Oman. Sayyid Fahr bin Taimur[8] was in the Defence Department, which

7 Garaizah is an Arabic corruption of Ecclesia.
8 Another uncle of the Sultan.

was to remain his area of endeavour and interest until his death in 1996. Sayyid Fahd bin Mahmoud was in Foreign Affairs and Sayyid Faisal bin Ali held several Ministerial posts before he came to epitomise the nation's heritage. Sayyid Shabib bin Taimur, the Sultan's youngest uncle, was also introduced into the Government circle.

Sayyid Shabib, who had been brought up abroad, called on me one day shortly after his arrival in the country, impeccably dressed in spotlessly white Omani costume and wearing his curved *khanjar* at his waist. Hamdan, our Omani butler, offered him coffee, tea and *halwa*[9] in the Omani tradition and, when Shabib came to take his leave incense was produced, followed by rose-water, which was sprinkled with the liberality which his rank merited. Shabib looked highly astonished at his drenching and later confessed that it was not till he came to the British Embassy that he had experienced the full effect of old Omani customs!

Four members of the Royal family in particular – Sayyids Tarik, Thuwaini, Fahr bin Taimur, and Faisal – as well as all the Ministers were frequent visitors to the Residence and the weekly film show at the Embassy, which was for a year or two after 1970 one of the few forms of evening entertainment. Tarik and Thuwaini often came to play tennis too on our very hot concrete Embassy court and we had a weekly four. The Sultan's great-uncle, Sayyid Abbas bin Faisal, who had been a good cricketer, hockey and tennis player in his day and was well known to crews of visiting ships, was also prominent on the social scene, always recording events with his camera as he had in the former Sultan's time. Sayyid Ahmed bin Ibrahim, the most senior member of the Al bu Said family and Minister of the Interior under Sultan Said, had a traditionally long white beard and the impeccable courtly manners of Omanis of the old school. Though advanced in age, he was very lively with a merry twinkle, rejoicing in his nickname of Father Christmas. Remarkably shrewd and well-informed, he was a mine of information about the past and like another elderly scholar, Sayyid Mohamed bin Ahmed, taught me much about Omani history and religion.

The *suq* in Muscat was small but lively, extending to the western edge of the Embassy compound, and the merchant community was very friendly. There were three British banks, the Chartered Bank, Grindlays and the British Bank of the Middle East presided over by Peter Mason – principal bankers to the Government. The Bab al

---

9 A special Omani sweet, made of starch, ghee, honey and cardomom.

Kabir, the great gate,[10] was no longer shut at night as it had been in the days of Sultan Said after the evening gun 'Dum Dum' was fired. There had been virtually no physical changes since the new Sultan's accession. Heads were full of plans, aspiration and hope, however, particularly with the prospect of the tiny revenues from the oil discovered at Fahud, growing consistently more substantial.

The largest and best-organised concern in the country was Petroleum Development Oman (PDO) – a company owned 85% by Shell at that time, 10% CFP[11] and 5% by Partex, though the Government was later to acquire an increasing stake. On this were centred all hopes for the wealth to open the way to development and Oman benefited in the early 1970s both from increasing production and also a fourfold rise in world oil prices. The production was at Fahud and the oil piped to the coast at Mina al Fahal, where the company's headquarters was situated. Rudi Jackli, who had replaced Francis Hughes,[12] was the Managing Director, and John Jennings, who himself later became the Chairman of Shell in London, became his deputy. George Band, who had been the youngest member of John Hunt's 1953 expedition which conquered Everest, also joined the staff as a senior executive.

Communications were primitive. PDO had graded the road from Mina al Fahal to Fahud, but otherwise the only made up road in the country ran for about eight miles from the Embassy through Mutrah, past the Sultanate's only traffic policeman standing on his pedestal at a crossroads in his blue *kepi*, and on to the Sultan's Armed Forces Headquarters at Bait al Falaj. When Ruth and I made our first journey to Nizwa to call on the Wali and stay with Fergus Mackain Bremner and the Muscat Regiment, the journey took five hours over an appallingly bumpy road. Our first visit to Buraimi over the bedrock of the Wadi Jizzi took twelve hours. Seeb airport was still at the planning stage and on a short flight in a Skyvan with Hugh Oldman, Curly Hurst, then commanding the Sultan of Oman's Air Force, pointed out where it was to be. Such was the Sultanate in 1971.

In July the young Sultan, heir to the oldest dynasty and monarchy in Arabia,[13] returned from abroad after his first absence from the country

10 It was later much widened.

11 The French Compagnie Française de Petroles. Partex was the famous 5% held by C.S. Gulbenkian and stood for Participations and Explorations Corporation.

12 An important figure at the time of the change of Sultan and the immediately following period.

13 The Al bu Said dynasty, which replaced the Ya'ruba dynasty dates from 1741.

for many years. I was asked to leave the country to enable the Omanis to receive me properly in my ambassadorial capacity and, after a brief visit to Dubai, made my second entrance, on 21 July. This time Sayyid Fahd bin Mahmoud on behalf of the Ministry of Foreign Affairs and Omar Barouni, the Libyan Adviser, were there, though they had a long wait as the plane was delayed. Gulf Aviation having overbooked again, the question of who should and should not leave the aircraft in Dubai to avoid standing room only was hotly and protractedly disputed before a solution was found.

Britain had formal relations with Oman from an early date and, as early as 1646, the first treaty dealing with trading relations was signed; the Treaty of Friendship made in 1800 has governed relations ever since. I referred to this when I presented my credentials to HM Sultan Qaboos on 22 July 1971, the day before the first anniversary of his accession, on which I immediately became Dean of the Diplomatic Corps. Tim Landon[14] attended as Equerry and the formal ceremony took place in the Sultan's temporary palace, formerly the house of Leslie Chauncy, Adviser to the old Sultan. It was a historic occasion and, wearing white tropical uniform, I read my formal speech recalling, 'It was 171 years ago that a treaty was concluded which envisaged friendship between our two countries lasting until the end of time, and also provided that an English gentleman of respectability should always reside at the port of Muscat. I shall endeavour to the best of my ability to maintain and strengthen the very warm and historic relations between my country and Oman on the basis of mutual respect and equality.' It was not until 25 July 1972, however, when we were on leave in England, that I went to Buckingham Palace with Ruth and formally 'kissed hands' with our Queen. After that Miss Fisher spurned me no longer and we became firm friends.

The treaty of 1800 envisaged the friendship of the two nations enduring 'till the end of time or the sun and moon cease in their revolving careers' and it had been the custom over many decades for the Consul-General and Sultan to address each other in official correspondence as 'Dear Friend'. The traditional part of me wished to keep this charming and meaningful custom alive, but the political and practical part spoke louder; it was no longer appropriate and would have raised terrible dilemmas for ambassadors of other countries. Consequently I quietly dropped the practice. The very long history of friendship

14 Tim Landon had been at Sandhurst with Qaboos and played a much more important role in Oman than his official position suggested.

between Oman and Britain had thereafter to be expressed in other ways.

Geoffrey Arthur paid a visit to Oman from 25 February to 1 March 1972. This ended the delicate 200-year relationship between the Sultanate and the Political Resident ('PRPG' to generations of Service people). It was a poignant few days as there was particularly warm personal rapport between Qaboos and Geoffrey Arthur. A first-class oriental and classical scholar and linguist and a brilliant conversationalist, Geoffrey was also wise, charming and amusing. Qaboos made the Royal Yacht, the *Al Said*, available to him for a final visit to Sur and the Sharqiyah. Ruth and I went too, though we nearly came to grief in the dinghy crossing the tricky sand bar at Sur in a heavy swell.

We called on the Walis – local Governors – in Sur, Kamil, Bilad Bani bu Hassan, Bilad Bani bu Ali and Ibra, our tour being greatly facilitated by the Sultan's Armed Forces and Oman Gendarmerie. At the little-visited Bilad Bani bu Ali we failed to identify the scene of the battle where Captain T. Perronet Thompson's troops had been defeated in 1820 during the disastrous campaign against the 'pirates', which followed the successful operations against Ras al Khaimah and the conclusion of the 1820 treaty with the Shaikhs of the Emirates. Although this defeat resulted in his court-martial, this remarkable and enthusiastic man later became a general, a Liberal MP for Bradford and a doughty champion of subject peoples.

Ruth and I gave a farewell dinner at the Embassy for Geoffrey Arthur, which the Sultan himself attended. Our butler Travasos – commonly known as 'Travers' – excelled himself for the occasion, laying the table with napkins stretching from glass to glass and meeting in the middle, thus making a series of perfect Gothic arches. When asked where he had learnt this singular skill, he immediately quoted chapter and verse of a naval manual, having in his earlier days been a chief petty officer steward in the Royal Navy.[15] The following day, after a final cordial audience with HM, the last Political Resident left. It was then that I inherited the RAF Andover which had been at his disposal for official flights – the only time in my life I had a nearly private aircraft.

The change in British representation from Consulate-General to Embassy helped to symbolise the beginning of the new era in Oman. Although the Sultanate had been juridically independent and not under

15 He was previously butler to the Political Resident.

British Protection by treaty, as the Gulf states were, it had been under the broad shadow of the British Empire in India from the beginning of the nineteenth century until India's and Pakistan's creation in 1948. Sultan Said never made any effort to assert Oman's independence internationally, with consequent annual embarrassment for Britain at the United Nations as 'The Question of Oman' was dealt with as a colonial issue, involving not only the Imamate's claims against the Sultanate but also Britain's alleged 'colonial' role *vis-à-vis* the Sultanate.

Terry Clark, later himself to be our Ambassador in Oman, became my number two as Head of Chancery[16] and Barry White, the Commercial Secretary, who lived in a newly built house called by the British community, in their typical way of rolling English and foreign words together, 'Whitebait'.[17] John Shipman, who had greeted us on arrival, remained a linchpin in our small set-up. Courtney Welch later became my Defence Attaché with a pivotal military liaison role.[18]

The change in status to an Embassy also stirred British officialdom and a letter arrived announcing that the Residence was now entitled to a variety of extra comforts – crockery, plate, pots and pans etc – denied to a Consul-General. Acceptance of plans to improve the building and furnishings also became easier. A very talented official of the Department of the Environment (later lost to the private sector) drew up a plan for the furnishings. A large drawing room looking out over the sea was created out of a small drawing room, a study and a lobby, and the narrow dining room was greatly extended by taking in verandah space. It became a lovely house to live in.

The old and new blended in the Oman of the early 1970s. The exchange of gun salutes and mutual courtesy calls when visiting ships of the Royal Navy came into port[19] were still a regular feature, though the muzzle-loading cannon at Fort Merani, which had so startled me on first arrival, were withdrawn in 1973 in favour of more modern saluting guns. This modernisation, though much safer for all concerned, deprived us of the sight of the gun crews preparing their ancient

16 After a brief period when 'Geoff' Coates was Consul.
17 *Bait* is Arabic for a house.
18 He was succeeded by Colonel Pat Allardyce and Terry Clark was succeeded by David Tatham, who later held such diverse posts as Ambassador in the Yemen, Governor of the Falkland Islands and High Commissioner in Colombo. John Shipman was followed by Dennis Gallwey.
19 And warships from other nations, though these, with the exception of the occasional US Naval visit, were few and far between.

weapons and the occasional ramrod floating through the air with the rings of smoke into the cove!

In the Embassy itself we said fond farewells to two of Muscat's 'oldest inhabitants', Cyril and Eileen Cooper. Captain Cyril Cooper, who had been awarded the MBE and the Papal Cross, had served in Muscat for twenty-five years and left for retirement in Australia. A nice, round, quietly-spoken man with a good sense of humour, he was a walking encyclopaedia on the country and a familiar figure to many as he walked his dog on the beach every day wearing a crumpled pair of shorts. His successor Mr Padiyath, 'Paddy', also served the Embassy subsequently for many years after his earlier service with us in Basrah and Baghdad. Another old 'Anglo-Indian' link was broken too when in February 1973 Mr Gokaldas Khimji Ramdas, whose firm had supplied the Sultan's Armed Forces for decades, retired to India, though his sons continued to live and trade in Oman.

Another historic and symbolic event occurred in November 1972. An enormous flagstaff stood in the middle of the Embassy compound; it was a ship's mast sunk into the ground to the depth of a fathom or two, shown on the naval charts and used for generations as a leading mark for navigation by day. At night a lantern, placed on the hill behind the Embassy by an elderly Omani guard, was aligned on a bearing with the light on the flagpole itself. The mast was said to be a trifle higher than the mast at the old palace, which was later replaced by an infinitely taller one. In the meantime this troubled Sayyid Tarik, who also thought it wrong for a British flagpost to stand on 'Omani soil', though in this his case was not sound and many Embassies and High Commissions round the world fly the flag from a pole in the ground.

The Royal Navy had traditionally kept this flagpole painted and when HMS *Andromeda* paid a courtesy visit in that November, I asked Captain Richard Franklin whether his crew could do this. He readily accepted and the sailors climbed the mast. Unfortunately one yardarm was rotten and a serious accident was averted only because naval discipline had ensured the proper use of protective harness. The courtyard was spattered with white paint, and Richard Franklin, not having the time or resources to replace the whole wooden superstructure, offered to take it down. I agreed immediately, reckoning I could weather any objections by any remaining diehard imperialists. A small plaque was later put in place to commemorate the mast, which had the additional significance of having been clasped many times in the past by slaves seeking manumission[20] by the Consuls. Thereafter the Union flag flew from the Embassy roof.

After the Sultan's return it was abundantly plain that he intended to rule his country, at least in the early stages, very personally. Consequently I had frequent and always refreshingly frank and open audiences with him. They were sometimes in the North and sometimes in Dhofar and on one occasion, having arranged to travel to Salalah on the new Viscount service operated by the Sultan of Oman's Air Force – SOAF – I arrived at Bait al Falaj airstrip on time, only to see the aircraft at the end of the runway about to take off. The transport officer hastily recalled it and the pilot, a smiling and apologetic Squadron Leader Lechmintoff, hoisted me up the back steps. It was nearly a diplomatic disaster; had he not turned back 'Lech' might not later have become the Captain of the Royal Flight!

Qaboos had been much influenced by his famously conservative father, who unfortunately gave him very little to do on his return from education abroad. In fact he was kept in virtual house arrest in Salalah until 1970 and his own assumption of power. It was sad that father and son never met again after Sultan Said bin Taimur's deposition, especially as plans had been made for such a meeting in 1973. But on 19 October 1972 Said died suddenly in London where he was living in exile. He was a remarkable man who had been educated with Indian princes at Mayo College in India, and I regret not having had the opportunity to meet him personally. It was a tragedy that, having rescued his country from virtual bankrupcy, he had been unable after the arrival of oil revenues in 1967 to abandon the habits of economy and careful husbandry, developed over a lifetime, and to inititate development schemes at a speed sufficient to satisfy his people.

Another early influence on Qaboos was his English tutor, Philip Romans, and his wife Laura,[21] from whom he obtained a broad general education in England before going to Sandhurst which, unlike some other future Heads of State, he enjoyed. It was there that he not only met Tim Landon, later to become his Equerry and Adviser, but also developed the growing interest in classical, organ and military music

20 When a slave was freed, he or she was given a document in English and Arabic with two crossed Union Jacks at the top, and reading: 'Be it known to all who may see this that the bearer, ..., aged about ... years, has been manumitted and no one has a right to interfere with his/her liberty. [dated and signed]'
21 Typically he repaid their early kindnesses to him by generously making a house available to them in Muscat.

first acquired with the Romans. After receiving his commission, he served with the Cameronians on Luneburg Heath in Germany and was then seconded to the Local Authority in Warwick to observe the workings of local government. He later went on a world tour with the Chauncys. At Sandhurst he had to endure a stern physical test when attempts were made to teach him to swim. All were unsuccessful, including 'walking the plank' from the diving-board at the Sergeant Major's command. He merely sank to the bottom of the pool and had to be rescued with a pole. In retrospect he found this hilariously funny, particularly after his bodyguard had succeeded in teaching him the art.

Qaboos, who always spoke naturally and openly, stated both publicly and privately that his ambition was not merely to bring his country into the comity of nations but to bring peace and to unify and develop it. Always thinking on a large scale his ideal was to see good triumph, and his commonsense and concern for his people have resulted in Oman's emergent success and the special regard in which he is held.

One of Qaboos's aspirations for his country was of an exceptional nature – and certainly unusual in Arabia or Asia. In early 1972 he astonished me by saying he wished to have a military band which would appear at the Edinburgh Tattoo. My normal aptitude for diplomatic response deserted me. There was no one in Oman at the time who could blow a note. A week or two later, however, he introduced me to the new bandmaster. I asked this tall and fine-looking Sikh how things were going and he replied that at present his bandsmen could play nothing, though after a month they would certainly be playing something. What, he did not yet know. From this extraordinary beginning Oman's splendid military and police bands have sprung and on the fifteenth anniversary of the Sultan's accession, not only did his band appear at Edinburgh, but, as Ruth and I witnessed, it stole the show with manœuvres largely devised by Qaboos himself. Not content with this musical achievement, Qaboos later – in 1984 – founded the Royal Oman Symphony Orchestra, all the players being young Omani men and women with no previous training. Oman is thus now unique in Arabia in having a first class orchestra, which frequently plays with international solo artists.

Early in his reign Qaboos displayed a gift for oratory, delivering the first of his series of National Day speeches at the parade on the old airport at Ruwi on 18 November 1972, his birthday.[22] Demonstrating his

---

22 Celebrated as the National Day every year since.

powers for the first time in sonorous rounded Arabic phrases, he showed his capacity to hold a crowd. The occasion was slightly marred as the planned fly past of Skyvans – Oman's Air Force was at this stage very small – failed to materialise, through no personal fault of the British Commander, Les Phipps.[23] Qaboos showed his reasonable displeasure, however, by requiring Phipps as Commander to absent himself from the celebratory tea party held in his simple palace which, despite the contretemps, was a delightfully relaxed and informal affair.

Qaboos was very conscious that as Head of State it was difficult for him to entertain other Heads of State until there was suitable accommodation, and it was a great relief to him when the new palace at Seeb, the first of his new palaces, was completed in 1973 and he was able to hold his National Day tea party there. The bands played and a choir sang an Ode to the Sultan in celebration. Id al Adha fell on 4 January 1974 and the Sultan received me and other members of the growing Diplomatic Corps at the new Seeb palace when we paid our Id call. It was a colourful ceremony, with servants in white *dishdashas* and cummerbunds offering *halwa*, coffee, rose-water and incense. Sayyid El Mu'tasim, whose father I had known in the Trucial Oman Scouts, had by then become the Sultan's ADC replacing Colonel Said Salim who had assumed a broader role in coordinating Palace affairs.

The Sultan's National Day parade on 18 November 1974 was held for the first time in the police stadium and the style of it set the general pattern for future celebrations. The troops on parade were extremely smart and their drill much improved. Qaboos himself was mounted on a grey, attended by his ADCs and escort, also mounted, and he later drove round the perimeter of the stadium in a Land-Rover, saluting his people before leaving.

At the very beginning of his reign Oman had a long way to go to gain international and internal acceptance. Sultan and Prime Minister therefore took immediate steps to change perceptions of the Sultanate by despatching goodwill missions to Arab countries, where there were Imamate offices, and offering an amnesty and encouragement to return to exiles and dissidents. Applications for membership were made to the Arab League and the United Nations for membership but even Sayyid Tarik, an optimist, was doubtful of success at the first attempt. In the event, however, the new regime got off to a good start with Oman's

23 A group captain seconded from the RAF, who later became Air Vice-Marshal L. W. Phipps, CB, AFC.

admission to the Arab League in September 1971 and to the United
Nations on 7 October. 'The Question of Oman' was then taken off the
agenda of the General Assembly. The neighbouring United Arab Emirates (UAE) was likewise admitted to the Arab League on 6 December
and the United Nations on 9 December after the individual treaties of
protection were terminated.

Shortly afterwards, Qaboos himself embarked on a series of State
Visits abroad with the encouragement of the British, US and other Governments, and also the help of two figures of the *demi-monde* whose
visibility in Oman was low but influence strong and enduring – Yahya
Omar, a Libyan, and Ghassan Shakir, a Saudi. These two were well
rewarded.[24]

Qaboos's uninhibited impressions of his overseas visits were always
lively. He set out in late 1971 for his first, to Saudi Arabia, with some
trepidation, particularly as this neighbouring country had originally
opposed Oman's admission to the Arab League and United Nations. As
the aircraft approached Ryadh, Qaboos looked anxiously out to see
whether King Faisal would grant him the full honours of Head of State.
But seeing the guard of honour, the red carpet and King Faisal himself
with many dignitaries drawn up to meet him on the tarmac, he was
reassured. This visit was, therefore, a significant turning point, particularly as it finally dashed the pretensions and hopes of the Imam Ghalib
and his supporters. Ghalib in fact cooked his own goose by rudely
refusing recognition to Qaboos as Sultan, thereby greatly angering the
King. This was the end of the 'Imamate Question' and the Imamate
Offices in Arab countries were all soon dismantled. Deciding then to
take advantage of Qaboos's policy of pardoning former rebels and welcoming them to the new Oman, Ghalib and his followers themselves
sought accommodation and many were given Government posts.

Qaboos was one of the many Heads of State who attended the Shah
of Iran's magnificent 2,500 Years anniversary celebrations at Persepolis
in 1971. On this occasion the Shah offered Iranian aid in the fight
against the rebels in Dhofar, an offer he later honoured by providing
substantial forces. I had a hand in the first formal request made to the
Shah after Persepolis. Shown informally a draft communication and
finding it somewhat bald, I proposed a more flowery diplomatic document to address to His Imperial Highness.

24 An American, Robert Anderson, was also much involved behind the scenes at this
stage.

In April 1972 I visited Iran myself and was summoned to an audience with the Shah within two hours of landing in Teheran. I travelled with Peter Ramsbotham, our Ambassador, to the Niavaran Palace and had over an hour's conversation, briefing the Shah fully on the war in Dhofar and listening to his concerns about Soviet activity in the Gulf and Iraq. He expressed his interest in the Sultan being successful as well as a desire to visit Oman personally, and was adamant that Britain should remain strong east of the Straits of Hormuz and retain the RAF stations in Masirah and Salalah, despite having pulled out of the Gulf militarily.

Qaboos also visited Egypt, Jordan and Libya in 1972 and these visits brought dividends. Abdel Qader Hatem, the Egyptian Minister of Information, followed up with messages of support from President Sadat and undertakings to explain the Omani case in the Arab world, a policy reiterated by Mahmoud Riad, the Egyptian Minister of Communications. Prince Sultan bin Abdul Aziz, the Saudi Defence Minister, and Shaikh Khalifah bin Zaid, the Crown Prince of Abu Dhabi, arrived with promises of financial support. Tunku Abdul Rahman, the first Prime Minister of Malaysia who had become Secretary-General of the Islamic Conference, visited Oman in that capacity.

Thus Oman emerged rapidly from its shell and India and Pakistan, with which Oman had long historical connections, were amongst the early countries to show renewed interest. It was Swaram Singh, the Indian Foreign Minister, who was the first Foreign Minister to come, and India responded to the Sultan's original request, conveyed through Hugh Oldman as Defence Secretary, to second officers for the Sultan of Oman's Navy (SON). Pressure from Muslim countries, however, later caused the Sultanate to turn to Pakistani officers instead, an arrangement more acceptable to Iran which, like Pakistan, was a regional member of the Central Treaty Organisation (CENTO).[25]

Iran's role became increasingly important as its support for the Sultanate grew and the Shah, mindful both of the very ancient historical ties and geography, influenced China to withdraw its support from the rebels. This was significant because some of them, including one who earned the military sobriquet of 'Peking Pete', had been trained in China. King Hussein visited in 1973 and the Jordanians also provided some technical military assistance.

The Sultan himself, who by then had already blazed a number of trails, stepped up his overseas visits and, visiting the Shah again in

25 See preceding chapter.

March 1974, held particularly important meetings which resulted in further significant Iranian military assistance for the Dhofar campaign.

Foreign Heads of State began to show an interest in coming to Oman. Colonel Gaddafi, the quixotic Libyan leader who at an earlier meeting had suggested to Qaboos that he should style himself President instead of Sultan as it was 'more trendy', was at one stage expected to arrive at an hour's notice. The Omanis rose to the occasion and had a guard of honour ready for him on parade at Seeb airport but, with predictable unpredictability, Gaddafi failed to show up. Dom Mintoff, the Prime Minister of Malta, paid a two-day visit, also at very short notice, but President Siad Barre of Somalia, announcing his visit only as he was flying into Oman, put Omani powers of improvisation to an even severer test. As Oman gained increasing respect internationally, support for the Dhofar rebellion from other governments continued to fade; despite this, it still remained a tough nut to crack.

The rapidity of Oman's international acceptance was demonstrated not only by visits from international statesmen but also by the exchange of diplomatic relations with other countries. Early in Qaboos's reign, Omani envoys were sent to the capitals of most importance to Oman and they went off like explorers entering fresh territory, with very little preparation. One Omani Ambassador told me he had been given an Omani flag, wished good fortune and despatched without further ado. However, 'great oaks from little acorns grow' and the Omanis with their innate courtesy and distinctive dress quickly began to cut notable figures in new places.

Meantime in Muscat itself there was a growing number of ambassadors accredited to the Sultanate. On our arrival in Oman there had only been one other resident diplomat – Mr Suri, who became the Indian Chargé d'Affaires when I presented my credentials. We were also joined by a resident Pakistani representative, who also became Chargé d'Affaires. It was the US Ambassador, Bill Stolzfus, who was next to present credentials after me but, as he was resident in Kuwait, Pat Quinlan came to live in Muscat as Chargé d'Affaires. Next came the Indian Ambassador, Nirmal Jat Singh, followed by the Iranian, Dr Zand – a descendant of the eighteenth-century ruler, Karim Khan Zand of Shiraz. Egypt and other Arab countries and then France quickly followed suit, despite severe accommodation shortages in Muscat. The Egyptian Ambassador, Hassan Salim, was particularly engaging; having as a young man acted with the Old Vic, he was dramatic, even melodramatic, in manner and, with his strong Egyptian sense of humour, introduced an attractive note of levity into the Corps.

Iraq, a country which had previously shown scant sympathy for Oman, sent an Ambassador in a breathtaking example of diplomatic cheek and discourtesy without either negotiating an agreement with the Omanis on the setting up of a Mission or putting forward the Ambassador's name for approval by the Sultan. The Omanis reacted robustly and required him to leave after searching the packing cases which accompanied him, though without finding anything sinister. Later relations were established on a proper and regular basis.

Meantime, in Muscat the new Government of appointed ministers – representative institutions were to follow much later – was taking a grip. None had experience in government but they manfully took on their own portfolios using their own administrative, technical or political skills to guide them, subject to the Sultan's orders. Apart from the Al bu Said Ministers, the most prominent were Dr Asem Jamali as Minister of Health, for which he was well qualified after his service in the Trucial States;[26] Karim al Harami as Minister of Posts and Telegraphs; Shaikh Saud Al Khalili, whom we visited at his home at Samail on our first Friday in Oman, as Minister of Education.

There was, however, a serious hiccup when Sayyid Tarik decided, despite strong efforts to dissuade him, to resign from the office of Prime Minister on 21 December 1971. He kindly wrote me a personal letter announcing his decision and for a while he left the country, though he later returned as Chairman of the Central Bank. Tarik appointed Dr Asem Jamali, who had been closely associated with him in exile, as Acting Prime Minister but Asem lacked any political constituency and the Sultan did not confirm the appointment, taking the Prime Minister's portfolio himself.

Although some members of the Al bu Said family believed that Ministerial posts should largely be held by the family, Qaboos himself was not only a realist but a believer in meritocracy. His policy, therefore, was to draw on a wider field for competent Ministers. Khalfan Nasir, who had had a promising career with PDO, the oil company, was given successively one or two portfolios and Abdul Hafidh Salim Rajab, a Dhofari educated in Moscow with a Russian wife, was Minister of Agriculture but given wider responsibilities for a while after Tarik's resignation. During 1973 Sayyid Fahd bin Mahmoud moved to Legal

26 Working for the Trucial States Development Scheme.

Affairs, his own expertise, later becoming a Deputy Prime Minister. Thus Qais Zawawi, whose nature made him a natural diplomat, came from the private sector to become an urbane and successful Minister of State in the Foreign Ministry and travelled widely in that capacity. Another merchant, Mohamed Zubair, a man who was always able to get things done, was also given Governmental responsibilities. Ahmed Mekki, later to become Oman's Representative at the United Nations and Ambassador in Paris, was Undersecretary at the Ministry of Foreign Affairs[27] with Abdulla Ghazali as Chief of Protocol. Omani Ministers and senior officials began to play increasingly important roles internally as well as externally and, though this was originally intended as a temporary measure, Ministers were allowed to retain or indulge in their own business interests provided they were not considered incompatible with their official duties. The Police Force was reorganised and greatly expanded under Felix de Silva, an officer who had had many years' service experience in Ceylon[28] as Inspector-General. The Police, like the military, developed a first class band with the Sultan's strong encouragement.

In 1971 and 1972 Bill Heber-Percy, who had previously served in the Colonial Service in the Aden Protectorates, was initially in charge of the Development Department in the North, responsible to Sayyid Tarik, and the first signs of physical development began to appear there. Although the former Sultan had inaugurated some small-scale development schemes, they were not of much significance and not enough to satisfy the Omani people. Sayyid Tarik, therefore, set more ambitious projects in hand, including a much larger port at Mutrah than the modest one envisaged by Sultan Said. This was opened on 20 November 1974 by the Sultan as Port Qaboos during that year's National Day celebrations. The strangely limited system by which Sultan Said allowed only a few Walis and Shaikhs to have Land-Rovers was ended, and cars and trucks arrived in increasing numbers. A major road was constructed to the new airport at Seeb and other roads and tracks were improved by grading.

In June 1972, after Heber-Percy left, John Townsend was appointed Economic Adviser to the Government with a wide brief, and Dr Riad Rais became Adviser on Planning and Development. At the same time the Sultan set up a Supreme Planning Council, which resulted in greater

27 In the 1990s he became Minister of Finance and the National Economy.
28 Later Sri Lanka.

coordination of the development effort. The two external Advisers, Yahya Omar and Ghassan Shakir, also played a part in this. As Oman grew, the rapidity of development stretched its resources and a series of five-year plans were introduced as a framework for policy on finance and development. Omanis, including many returned from exile and those from East Africa, whose arrival in the country was accelerated by the revolution in Zanzibar, began to fill official posts on an increasing scale as Government expanded. These Zanzibaris were of Omani origin and related to people in Oman itself, Omanis having colonised and settled on the east coast of Africa for many generations. They had the initial advantage of a superior education and of speaking English well, but the disadvantage of speaking Swahili rather than Arabic.

The speed of growth in education was one of the most remarkable phenomena of the time as the three schools for boys in the Sultanate – Muscat, Mutrah and Salalah – were augmented by an increasing number of schools for both girls and boys. The hunger for education amongst young and older people was intense and initially during 1971 and 1972 many schools were started up in tented accommodation.

Developments in health were equally swift and dramatic. The British Consulate had run a hospital just outside the compound for decades and this was handed over to the Omani Government shortly after Sultan Qaboos's accession; it was put under Dr Hamad al Ryami, who frequently played tennis with us with Sayyid Tarik and Sayyid Thuwaini, the Governor of Muscat. The main hospital was then run by the American Mission under Dr Bosch who, with his wife Eloise, had served for many years in Oman. They, too, often played tennis with us.[29] With slender resources and dedicated doctors and nurses, the hospital had provided devoted medical care to the people of Oman since the turn of the century. The work of two Dr Thomses, father and son who had a countrywide reputation for selfless service, was of particular note and deeply appreciated by the people. But plans were taking shape for the expansion of Government medical services, including hospitals and dispensaries, and a new hospital at Nizwa was opened. We were ourselves made acutely aware of the need for this when, on our first visit to Nizwa, Ruth and I had found a patient lying on a bed under a thorn bush, from which a drip was suspended to keep him alive.

29 The Bosches maintained their connection with Oman and the Sultan recognised their special contribution by building a house for them with a room to house their notable collection of Omani sea shells, about which Dr Bosch has published books including *The Sea Shells of Oman* (Longmans, 1992).

Generally development was fast and the physical aspect of the capital began to change. The Sultan opened Seeb International Airport in the autumn of 1972 and the new corniche in Mutrah on 4 May 1973. On 19 November he laid the foundation stone for Medinat Qaboos, which was built by two British companies – half by Cementation and the other by Taylor Woodrow Towell which, with Yahya Costain, was an early Anglo-Omani partnership in the private sector.

Before the international system was improved, the internal telephone service worked well but communication with other countries was through Cable and Wireless, whose office was for some years after 1970 still within the Embassy compound as it had been since the laying of the first cable in the 1860s.

Above all else, however, the prerequisite of Oman emerging as a strong and influential power in the region was an end to the war in Dhofar. This was the most crucial issue. The British Government gave a considerable amount of assistance and much of my time was spent in dealing with military affairs. The background to this war was dissatisfaction in Dhofar with the old Sultan's rule, leading to a low scale rebellion organised by the Dhofar Liberation Front breaking out in 1965. This movement was then given strong external support by the People's Front for the Liberation of Oman and the Arabian Gulf – PFLOAG.[30] This situation gave the People's Democratic Republic of Yemen (PDRY) – formerly Aden and the British Protectorates but by then an independent Communist state – an excuse for intervention. PDRY had support from a number of Communist states, including particularly the Soviet Union, China and East Germany, and, as we have seen, from Iraq.

The headquarters of the Sultan's Armed Forces, the Army, Air Force and Navy – SAF – was at Bait al Falaj, a wired encampment set up around one of the many old Omani forts which characterise the country, with whitewashed stones lining the rough roads in the best traditions of British military camps. The more senior officers, some seconded from the British Armed Forces and others on contract with the Sultanate, were then virtually all British. Hugh Oldman,[31] the Defence Secretary, had his house and offices there in a long low building. John Graham,[32] then commanding SAF and consequently a key figure during the Dhofar war, also had his office and house in this area.

30 The National Democratic Front for the Liberation of Oman and the Arabian Gulf – NDFLOAG – was also involved.
31 Later Sir Hugh Oldman, KBE.
32 Brigadier J. D. C. Graham, who later became Major-General, CB, CBE.

Like Oldman he had played an important and delicate role in the transition of rule from Sultan Said to Sultan Qaboos.

John Graham first took me to Dhofar on 2 June 1971, to see the situation there for myself. We travelled on a Caribou so noisy that, wearing the required ear muffs, we were unable to converse during the three-hour journey. Mike Harvey,[33] briefed us at the Umm al Ghawarif headquarters and a drive in Land-Rovers over the incredibly dusty plain left us looking as if tins of curry powder had been poured all over us. There we visited the site office recently established by Taylor Woodrow, the contractors for the first tranche of civil development – a small harbour at Raysut to enable heavy equipment to be landed at a quay rather than over a beach through the surf, and improvement of the runway at the RAF Salalah, which was used by aircraft of the Sultan of Oman's Air Force (SOAF) as well as the RAF.

The Consul-General's house, painted in yellow and black camouflage like a zebra, was inside the RAF station and we stayed there. We dined, however, in the mess at Umm al Ghawarif, to which we were taken by armed escort. The town of Salalah was under siege, with the rebels dominating the mountain area of the Qara range to the north, and firing periodically into the RAF station. SAF had neither the manpower nor the capacity to remain during the monsoon in this mountainous terrain – generally known as the Jebel – on which they campaigned in the dry season. The British Army Training Team (BATT) were having a significant effect working with the *Firqat* of Dhofaris loyal to the Sultan. These were groups of tribal fighters augmented by fellow tribesmen who had deserted from the rebels. Another hopeful sign was the recent recapture of the small coastal town of Sudh, which John Graham and I visited by helicopter, where the local people were manifestly grateful.

On the following day I called on the Wali, Shaikh Biraik bin Hamoud Al Ghafiri, a good man who had succeeded his father as Wali and played an important part in Dhofar in the early days of Qaboos's reign.[34] I also saw the civil development schemes being organised by Robin Young,[35] Michael Butler and his very active wife Robin. Although I diagnosed a slightly 'squeaky hinge' between the military

33 Colonel M. Harvey, OBE, a formidable judo 'black belt', who was then commanding the Sultan's forces in the south.
34 Later he was sadly to be killed in a road accident.
35 Robin Young had earlier been in the Sudan Political Service and later in the Aden Protectorates under the Colonial Office.

and civilian efforts, Qaboos's 'Hearts and Minds Campaign', which offered amnesty to as many people discontented with his father's regime as possible, was gradually winning some of the rebels over. These civilian efforts, augmented by the valuable work of the Civil Aid Teams (CATS) run by the British Army, were in conjunction with the military operations an important arm of this policy.

Despite encouraging signs, I concluded nonetheless that the situation remained serious and that HMG's interests demanded greater military assistance for Oman to help end the rebellion. Shortly afterwards, during the summer monsoon of 1971, the rebels became even more active than before, giving further alert to the danger to Salalah. I recommended deeper British involvement, even though this appeared against the trend in a year when Britain was ending its former treaty commitments in the Gulf and withdrawing British Forces from Gulf bases. It was not surprising that the initial reaction in the Ministry of Defence was negative, expecially as an open-ended commitment was feared. With the full support of Geoffrey Arthur and officials and Ministers in the Foreign and Commonwealth Office, however, I made the case before the Chiefs of Staff Committee in September 1971 and they fortunately took a favourable view, deciding on a number of positive measures, the most significant of which was that two Squadrons of BATT should operate for a period. It was this which enabled Johnnie Watts[36] to lead an effective sweep through the rebel-held Wadi Darbat, north of Salalah, in late 1971. Another consequence was that Colonel Courtney Welch, an admirably tough and active soldier, joined me as Defence Attaché.

Meantime the planned withdrawal of British naval, military and RAF forces from the Gulf was being smoothly carried out under the direction of Roly Gibbs,[37] who later became Chief of the General Staff. Britain continued to maintain the RAF stations at Masirah and Salalah. I went to lunch with Mike Carver[38] and David Williams,[39] the Admiral commanding, on HMS *Eagle*, one of the two aircraft carriers lying offshore near Masirah as part of the Gulf Covering Force in case of a repetition of the trouble of the last days of British administration in Aden and the Protectorates. Fortunately this was never called into action.

36 Later Lieutenant-General Sir John Watts, KBE, CB, MC and Commander of the Sultan's Armed Forces.
37 Major-General Roly Gibbs (later Field Marshal Sir Roland Gibbs, GCB, CBE, DSO, MC).
38 Field Marshal Lord Carver, GCB, CBE, DSO, MC, the Chief of the General Staff.
39 Vice-Admiral, later Admiral Sir David Williams, GCB.

It was fortunate that, at this time of ebb and flow, the British Government was headed by men who understood the Arab world and the Gulf area. Ted Heath was Prime Minister, but it was the Secretary of State for Foreign and Commonwealth Relations, Alec Douglas-Home[40] who had the prime responsibility; he and the Permanent Undersecretary, Denis Greenhill,[41] remained strong in support of British efforts in Oman. Equally happy and fortunate was the presence of Peter Carrington[42] as Secretary of State for Defence, as he took a personal interest and paid visits to northern Oman and Dhofar.

Once interest had been aroused in Whitehall and Westminster, the administration of British military aid became simpler. Previously – and curiously – when British military assistance was requested on however small a scale, I was requested to make a specific recommendation for each item that only 'extra' and not 'full' costs should be charged by the British Government. My own task in talking to key figures, including the Chiefs of Staff, was aided by the fact I had worked with or known several in the past. The Deputy Under Secretary (Policy) in the Ministry of Defence, a position more important than its name might imply, was my old school friend and fellow scholar, Pat Nairne. The Chief of the General Staff, Mike Carver, had been Army Director of Plans when in the late 1950s I had been liaising between the Foreign Office and the Joint Planning Staff, and Denis Spotswood, the Chief of the Air Staff, had been Deputy Director of Plans for the RAF at the same time. All visited Oman to keep abreast of progress. When Peter Hunt[43] succeeded Mike Carver as CGS, he continued his predecessor's direct interest and visited Oman himself. It was equally fortunate that the successive heads of the Arabian Department, Anthony Acland and Patrick Wright – both later destined to become Permanent Undersecretary – as well as the Undersecretary, Tony Parsons, knew me well and all proved stalwart in lending support.

Though there was still a long haul ahead, the high level British interest aroused led to increasing visits by Ministers, Service Commanders and others, as well as a Technical Assistance Grant of £250,000, a substantial sum in those days and appropriate in terms both of Oman's needs and still rather small oil revenues. The last Conservative Minister to come before the Government fell was Robin Balniel, Minister of

40 Sir Alec Douglas-Home, KT, formerly Earl of Home and later Lord Home of the Hirsel.
41 Sir Denis Greenhill, later Lord Greenhill of Harrow.
42 Lord Carrington, KG, GCMG, CH, MC.
43 General Sir Peter Hunt, GCB, OBE, DSO.

State at the Ministry of Defence, who visited Oman in October 1973. The new Labour Government continued the policy of support for Oman, however – to the relief of the Sultan and everyone involved – and Brynmor John, Parliamentary Undersecretary for the RAF, visited in May 1974 to demonstrate this.

This is to anticipate events, however. Back in early 1972 plans were made to inhibit rebel communications with the People's Democratic Republic of Yemen by occupying a commanding position at Sarfait, near Hauf on the border between the Sultanate and PDRY, and by holding the ground between that and the sea some 2,000 feet below. The first part of the plan, Operation Simba, was launched successfully in April 1972 by the Desert Regiment under Nigel Knocker.[44] This considerably boosted the morale of SAF and the people of Oman, dealing a corresponding blow to the rebels, PDRY and PFLOAG.

The attempt to secure the position between Sarfait and the sea, known as Capstan, was not so successful and PDRY continued aggressive tactics around Habarut on the border, where Oman and PDRY both maintained forts opposing each other. Retaliatory blows against PDRY were struck on 25 May by bombing and shelling Hauf with Strikemasters – Oman's most sophisticated aircraft at the time – and twenty-five pounder guns. All the pilots were British and the British Government, fearing hostile publicity, ordered that serving British officers seconded to the Sultan's Air Force should not participate after the first strike. In fact the action attracted little attention, but there was a strong response from the rebels who on 9 June made a serious attack on RAF Salalah, landing a shell on the mess and wounding eight SOAF officers, including the leader of the attack on Hauf, and one RAF officer.

As a family we were personally affected by these events. We had planned to go on leave on 5 July 1972, but I became somewhat apprehensive about doing so as both Hugh Oldman and John Graham were away. I felt strongly for some inexplicable reason that I should stay until John Graham's return on 19 July and so, after seeing the family off, I remained in Muscat. It was an incredibly quiet time but my hunch proved right as on the 18 July, the very day of my departure, the rebels suddenly attacked the small coastal town of Mirbat out of the mists. It was a decisive battle and proved a turning point in the war but might not have been won except for the chance that there were two

---

44 Colonel N. Knocker, OBE, who later became Defence Attaché in the British Embassy in Muscat and President of the SAF Association.

BATT teams there at the time, one relieving the other. The enhanced firepower was crucial to the victory.

When earlier in the year I had put forward the Ministry of Defence's recommendation for Brigadier Jack Fletcher to succeed John Graham as Commander of SAF, the Sultan surprised me by saying that he intended a major expansion of his forces and wanted a seconded general to command them. At home on leave in 1972 I told Mike Carver, the CGS, with some reservation that senior British officers in Oman thought he would meet the Sultan's request by seconding a general who had had his day. He assured me that on the contrary it would be one 'on his way up' and in the event Major-General Tim Creasey[45] arrived in Oman in the autumn with Jack Fletcher as Brigadier to command in Dhofar.

Jack Fletcher had a particular brief to oil the 'squeaky hinge' between the military and civilian efforts in Dhofar, and the upgrading of the two commanders signalled a more determined intention by Qaboos and the British Government to win the war which was still at its height. Tim Creasey's whole mien was authoritative. Tall and well built, he looked as military a figure as one could find, but his massive frame and 'simple soldier' camouflage concealed an astute strategic and political mind. He had served as a young man in the Baluch Regiment in the Indian Army and spoke Urdu which many people in Oman understood. We worked together very harmoniously and I had a great respect and liking for him. More importantly he was much respected by the Sultan, who later brought him back as his Chief of the Defence Staff in the 1980s.

It was obviously vital to maintain frequent contact between Ambassador and CSAF. Creasey was the Sultan's Commander, however, and it was neither appropriate nor necessary that we should meet too often. Courtney Welch, my Defence Attaché, therefore saw him every day and reported anything worthy of mention. On one occasion the consultation took place at the beach, and Welch's report referred to the General 'bobbing up and down in the sea like a Roman Emperor'. Military diplomacy had to go hand in hand with regular international contacts and Tim Creasey who, as CSAF, framed the strategy – following a pattern of visits by Hugh Oldman to Saudi Arabia and India – became increasingly involved in visits to Iran, Saudi Arabia and Jordan. It was

45 Later General Sir Timothy Creasey, KCB, OBE, who returned in 1981 as Chief of Staff of the Sultan's Armed Forces until his death in 1985, after being GOC Northern Ireland 1977–79 and C-in-C UK Land Forces 1980–81.

these countries which gave the most support, militarily or financially, to Oman.

Jack Fletcher made an immediate mark in Dhofar by his warm personality, sense of humour and capability, and started to build on the increased optimism induced by SAF's successes at Mirbat and in maintaining a presence on the Jebel throughout the monsoon.

By the autumn of 1972 the tide in Dhofar was just begining to turn. After Tim Creasey had made his initial assessment, we agreed upon recommendations, which the Chiefs of Staff Committee and Ted Heath's Government endorsed, and every quarter thereafter Creasey and I attended their meetings in London. Tim Creasey obtained the Sultan's approval for expansion of the forces to 12,000 and no difficulties arose over the increased number of British seconded officers for all three Omani services. More protection was given to RAF Salalah which stood on the plain between the town on the sea and the Qara mountains, from which the rebels operated. The firepower of the 'Hedgehogs', the sandbagged outposts of the RAF station, was increased; the RAF regiment was deployed more positively in defence and the field guns of the 'Cracker Battery', with the support of Royal Artillery officers and NCOs, were brought into action. The provision of a British Field Surgical Team was of especial assistance and comfort for casualties.

SOAF, commanded in a crucial stage of the Dhofar war from 1972 to 1974 by Les Phipps, played a vital part in the final victory both with their strike aircraft, initially mainly Strikemasters, and transport planes. The size of the transport aircraft grew and major transport tasks previously done by the RAF were gradually taken over by the Omani force, but the Skyvan, built by Shorts in Belfast, was the universal 'maid of all work' – invaluable in supplying military positions in the mountains. The increasing use of Augusta Bell helicopters also helped to tip the military balance. Meantime the Sultan's Navy (SON) was expanding under Philip Brooke-Popham.[46]

In 1973 there was a major change in the Omani Defence establishment in the departure of Hugh Oldman, the Defence Secretary who had in the 1960s commanded the Sultan's Forces and had spanned the reigns of the former Sultan and Sultan Qaboos. His role had become an anachronism but it fell to me to tell him of the Sultan's decision that he should go. Qaboos did not relish the thought of confronting Oldman himself and persuaded me that the kindest and most appropriate course

46 Captain P. Brooke-Popham, RN.

was for me, as a close friend since the 1940s in the Sudan, to tell him. It was one of the least agreeable things I have ever had to do, perhaps 'beyond the call of duty'.

A National Defence Council was then set up as the ultimate Defence Authority and the Sultan himself presided, retaining as he did the premiership and the portfolios of Foreign Affairs and Defence. Tim Creasey's personal influence grew and Sayyid Fahr bin Taimur, Qaboos's uncle, became Deputy Minister for Defence with Brigadier Fergie Semple, who had formerly commanded the SAS, as Undersecretary.

In Dhofar SAF gradually gained more key positions in 1972 and 1973 and began to squeeze rebel supply routes more tightly. The number and effectiveness of the Dhofari *Firqat*, tribal groups of fighters who were augmented by deserters from the rebels, increased with the continued assistance of the BATT, whose Commanding Officer, Peter de la Billière,[47] was a frequent visitor. Where key positions had been secured on the mountain, the Government started small development areas with a clinic, a school and a mosque together with a piped water supply for the mountain people and their animals. The first was called Medinat al Haqq, the 'City of Righteousness', or simply 'White City' in English. The name chosen by the Sultan personally was deliberately symbolic and the pattern was set for similar development in other places taken from the rebels.

In January 1973 I took the whole family to Salalah, where we enjoyed the warm hospitality of Jack and Mary Fletcher. Ruth and I were taken by SOAF helicopter to some of the Army's positions on the Jebel Qara and we visited Mudhai, a tribal centre, where on a later visit I met Salim bin Kabina, one of Wilfred Thesiger's guide companions crossing the Rub al Khali. We lunched with the Muscat Regiment commanded by Bill Kerr at the Simba position on the PDRY border, accompanied from time to time by 'outgoing' mortar fire, enjoying the splendid coastal scenery. At Midway, now Thamrait, the quantity of vehicles and equipment donated by Iran under Operation Caviar was already impressive, though there were later to be much more dramatic developments there. Flying back to Salalah by helicopter at dusk we took a look at the Omani fort at Habarut on the border from well inside Sultanate territory. Anti-aircraft guns from PDRY opened up, however, and tracer bullets flew in our direction, until we turned away.

---

47 Later General Sir Peter de la Billière, KCB, KBE, DSO, MC, who was Commander of British Forces in the Middle East during the Gulf War of 1990/91.

There was mild consternation amongst the military over this and I told them not to report it.

I continued to visit more exposed positions without Ruth and, accompanied by Richard Lea standing in as Defence Attaché, I flew to 'Condor', a position just occupied by the Sultan's Armed Forces where the helicopter pilot brought us down in a very tight loop, an operation repeated for security at 'White City'. It used to amuse the young British pilots, casting sly and wary looks at their passengers, to see how VIPs reacted to their aerial acrobatics. At Jibjat I met Mohamed Suhail, a *Firqat* leader whom I had known in the early 1960s as a bright officer in the Trucial Oman Scouts and who had completed his military training at Mons in Aldershot. He had served with the Scouts for eight years before he had been attracted, like may other Dhofaris in the TOS, into joining the Dhofar rebels. Now, disillusioned by these rebels, he had escaped and espoused the Sultan's cause. Another centre for development was Tawi Atair, a key position on the Jebel and renowned for its extraordinary and enormous 'erratic' hole in the ground, perhaps caused by a meteorite but providing plentiful underground water.

In Salalah itself, and at Mirbat and Taqa, there were encouraging signs of physical improvement in building and agriculture, the fruits of the civil development programme. The Sultan's distribution of building plots added to confidence and at Id there was joyful and colourful dancing outside the palace. Rebel mine-laying nonetheless remained a problem and Andrew Wilkinson, the Government archaeologist, was not long afterwards tragically killed by one near the ancient site of Samhuram, the old incense port.

Despite the increasing good news the rebels, with the continuing assistance of PDRY and other mainly Communist supporters, were still far from finished. Many measures were taken to inhibit their supply routes including long lines of wire barricade, but with their detailed knowledge of the terrain they still managed to move with some degree of freedom over the vast and rugged mountain area between Salalah and the PDRY border.

Early in 1973 the PFLOAG attempted to open a second front by starting a fresh rebellion in northern Oman, but it was nipped in the bud by the seizure of a large arms cache. An Omani court tried the perpetrators and a few ringleaders found guilty were executed. The Sultan pardoned or commuted the sentences of as many as he felt able to, thereby turning them into his ardent supporters. PFLOAG's efforts were not confined to Oman, for shortly afterwards attempts at action in

Dubai and Ras al Khaimah were forestalled by arrests. This was perhaps one of the turning points, for before long PFLOAG shortened their title, which neatly described their aims, to the People's Front for the Liberation of Oman. The 'Arabia without Sultans' of Professor Fred Halliday's book was by then doomed.

Disillusion grew amongst the rebels in Dhofar. Harsh Communist methods to compel obedience and anti-religious indoctrination impelled increasing numbers to desert and change loyalties. Such tendencies were further fostered by the obvious signs of real development in the coastal towns and liberated parts of the Jebel. To people whose livelihood was much bound up in their cattle, the wells provided by the Government attracted large herds of animals, visible to rebel tribesmen, and they also learned that Jebalis in the Government areas were able to sell their bull calves to the Government for RO46 a head. The hospital in Salalah had become an impressive health amenity and the benefits of the first class British Forces Field Surgical Team increased confidence among the fighting troops of all races. All these factors sowed doubts amongst the rebel tribesmen, who picked up the news from their relations with whom they found ways of being in constant contact. Many years later a palace driver told me that these were the reasons for his abandoning the rebel cause, to which he had been recruited as a young boy. Thus during 1974 the initiative was definitely passing to Qaboos's Government and encouraging signs both in the south and north were helping to begin a renaissance.

The Hornbeam Line to the west of Salalah had by then become, as I noted in July, 'a pretty formidable affair: 60 kilometres of barbed wire, mines and well placed positions ... proving very effective against the rebels'. At the same time a large and complex runway was being built to augment the base at Thamrait (Midway), for the easier supply of Sarfait in the west and also of troops committed to fresh operations. The work was commissioned in May 1974 to be ready by the end of the year and, during construction, the army of workers looked as if they were embarked on a work of Pharaonic scale. It was here that the Imperial Iranian Task Force, consisting of two strong battalions, a battery of guns and good support services – the fruits of the Sultan's visit to the Shah in March – arrived in C130 aircraft. The addition of these troops, combined with the increase in the Sultan's own forces, swelled the numbers available for fighting in the inhospitable terrain in which the rebels operated, and enabled Tim Creasey to commence operations west of the Hornbeam Line.

Another event of both military and symbolical significance was the reopening of the road through the mountains from Salalah to Thamrait, which the rebels had effectively closed for the previous five or six years. At about this time Qaboos decided to strengthen his forces with more sophisticated equipment and Rapier and Jaguar were ordered from Britain.

The autumn of 1974 saw the departure of Jack Fletcher, who as Commander of the Dhofar Brigade had contributed much to the improved situation, and his wife Mary, who had devoted her time in Salalah to nursing. They were much missed and there was general sadness when Jack Fletcher, who had been promoted to major-general, died of cancer not much later. His place as Brigadier was taken by another fine soldier, John Akehurst,[48] and he and his wife Shirley quickly made their own impact. John proved himself a very effective commander in the final crucial phase, when land and air attacks were made on the previously unreachable rebel strongholds at Rakhyut and their cave complex at Shirshitti. The first assaults on these vital positions took place in January 1975 with relatively high casualties, but it was the beginning of the real end of the war and the main actions against the rebels were over by May. In December 1975 Qaboos was able to announce with confidence that the war had been won. By then all the preliminary ground work in both military and civil spheres had been done to make Oman the strong unified country it became.

In 1970 the Sultan's Forces were strong neither in manpower nor sophistication and, under the former Sultan, very few Omani officers had been encouraged. Consequently British officers held the commands to a relatively low level. Qaboos himself was determined not only to win the war but also to train his men from relatively simple beginnings into first rate modern forces, using the latest and most sophisticated equipment. His family's long friendship with the British and his own experience at Sandhurst made it natural for him to rely on British assistance and British officers. In this he was supported, perhaps surprisingly, by the Egyptian Government and in most Arab countries, except of course PDRY itself and Iraq, there was little criticism. In SAF Omani officers worked, messed and fought alongside British officers in the Dhofar war and were gradually promoted to higher commands. The

---

48 Later General Sir John Akehurst, KCB, CBE, who became Deputy Supreme Commander Allied Forces Europe.

skills of Omani soldiers were considerably enhanced as the campaign developed and the size of the forces grew.

With Britain's withdrawal in the 1970s from all its main security commitments east of Suez, there were very few places left in the world where regular British officers could exercise the peculiar skills they had demonstrated over two centuries in providing leadership and inspiration to local troops – in the Indian sub-continent, South East Asia, Africa and elsewhere. Oman gave them a latterday opportunity owing to its special circumstances, and good officers were quick to seize it, some seconded from British forces and others on contract.

British seconded and contract officers holding executive command have now largely faded into history. They have been replaced by excellent and well-educated Omani officers from Commander-in-Chief down. In earlier and simpler times, however, including our period in Oman, a small band of British officers served Oman with devotion and were locally 'famous men'. They identified with the country and looked forward to a peaceful unified Oman with almost the same ardour as the Omanis themselves. The professionalism and character of British officers was appreciated in the Armed Forces and close personal friendships were forged. Omanis in rural areas also viewed them benevolently because of their welfare activities in distributing medicines, helping to transport the sick and giving material and physical help with small scale development schemes when, in the early days of Sultan Qaboos as well as under Sultan Said's regime, other authorities including the Wali had virtually no resources. The officers themselves relished this quasi-District Commissioner work, which helped to create mutual trust and friendship.

Two long-serving officers played vital roles in linking the old Oman with the new era. Brigadier Colin Maxwell, the Deputy Commander and 'Father of the Force', served in Oman from the early 1950s and probably knew every soldier in the Army, and everything about his background and family. Colonel Malcolm Dennison was an Intelligence Officer who had travelled to every corner of Oman and whose knowledge of and sympathy with the tribes and personalities was encyclopaedic. He was well known by the Walis, Shaikhs and people everywhere. Both were much respected and served Oman wholeheartedly.

The 1970s were an exciting time and the warmth and mutual respect between Omanis and British serving Oman led one to think that the prophetic words of the 1800 Treaty about the endurance of the friendship between the two states might be true.

Mutual courtesies were an important feature of life in more spacious times and a supreme example of this occurred at the time of the Imam Ghalib's rebellion in the 1950s. A British officer was ordered to take a small contingent of Sultanate troops to arrest a Shaikh in the Wadi Samail, as his village was suspected of involvement in mine-laying. The Shaikh, making no effort to resist arrest, insisted that coffee be brought to his 'guests' first. His duty of hospitality discharged, he then meekly allowed himself to be led away by his captors.

Such traditional courtesies continued in our time and, on Christmas Day 1973 and New Year's Day 1974, a few leading Omanis came to call, following the old custom when Muscat was a small close-knit community. The tradition had been that members of the British community called on Muslim notables and friends at Ids and on the Indians at Diwali. Reciprocal calls were paid on the Consul-General, who normally 'sat' on New Year's Day, and on other British friends. But as times changed, these agreeable courtesy customs were gradually becoming attenuated and modified.

Christians were able to practise their religion in Oman and there were weekly services at the American Reformed Church, often attended also by Anglicans; and the church was also used by other denominations, including the Mar Thoma – Saint Thomas – church of southern India, for their own services. I once had the agreeable task of giving a bride away in this church – a charming blonde American girl called Cindy who married the British Chief Engineer of the Defence Department, Chris Kennedy. An Anglican RAF padre also came to officiate in the SAF headquarters at Beit al Falaj from time to time, and Father Bart, a diminutive and lively priest in brown soutane, provided for the Roman Catholics. Later the Sultan made land available for the Anglicans and Roman Catholics to build separate churches in the ecumenical spirit of the age and place, and they shared 'church hall' facilities.

Ruth and I visited most accessible places in northern Oman officially, always calling on the Walis, whose capital towns and villages retained their dignified but crumbling and traditional beauty. I gravely disappointed the Wali of Dhank, however, who had invited me to lunch and was shocked that an Ambassador had only brought his wife and one or two other people rather than the retinue of forty or more, which he had anticipated and for which he had catered! On the other hand another Wali insisted on continuing to call me Consul rather than Ambassador, because the name of the 'British Consul' had long been one with which to conjure in the Interior.

Although Oman was changing rapidly and health and educational facilities were already reaching remote places, there was still a peculiar charm and beauty in many villages where time seemed to have stood still and where a way of life centuries old still endured. A typical example was Muqniyat to the north-east of the Hajar range. It was an ancient place with a dramatic fort standing out against a backdrop of magnificent red and dun mountains, wide areas of palms and a constantly flowing stream in the *falajes*. A visit to the nearby beehive tombs at Bāt which date from the fourth millennium BC[49] enhanced an already strong sense of the length of Oman's history. We had a similar experience on a visit to the Wadi Bani Kharus on 10 January 1975, which I described in my diary: 'Stopped at Istal: bright colours of girls' clothes and silver jewellery against a background of elegant mud houses, palms and towering mountains. *Falaj*, syphon under *wadi*, donkeys, flies and some sickness. A vision of how people have lived for so many centuries. Found a group making a new *falaj* with RO 3,000 provided by the Government. Up to Uliya. Did not find the Shaikh but walked up the valley and through the well-tended gardens. A lovely place nestling into the Jebel Akhdar range.'

Ruth and I took part in a memorable seven-day walking expedition on the Jebel Akhdar in November 1974 with Philip Horniblow, David and Kate Phillips and Ross Urquhart of PDO. David was a clever, witty and angular pioneer who had started up the British Council operation in Oman, living initially in a hot caravan in the Ruwi valley throughout the summer of 1971, and enduring warm beer. We climbed up from Birket el Moz to Saiq where the stocky and genial Graham Vivian, acting then as a sort of District Commissioner for the Jebel area, greeted us warmly. His assistant, Mohamed Said, taking us first to his own village nearby, became our guide for the whole trip. On the second day we caught our first glimpse of Jebel Shams[50] – the highest peak, for which we were heading – and there seemed something mystical about it. We strode over rocky ridges past Uqbat el Dhifr, where a battle had taken place in which the SAS were involved during the 1950s Jebel War, to Birket al Sharif. Walking on via Birket Dan al Gharr, from which there were wonderful views over the old towns of Hamra, Bahla and Nizwa, we reached Uqbat Ezoukia. We then climbed Jebel Shams, walking down to Al Nid – passing Masjid al Muala on the way on the

49 Archaeologists had not then begun their work there.
50 The mountain of the sun, though there has been considerable subsequent debate as to whether this is the proper name of this particular mountain.

following day – after a very wet night without tents during which there was a total eclipse of the moon. Ruth, who had climbed Oman's highest mountain once before, was the first British or foreign woman known to have done so and consequently one approach to the summit came then to be known as 'Ruth's Col'.

The sea and beautiful beaches provided another form of recreation and we used the Embassy launch, an old harbour boat from Singapore, for some of our expeditions as well as for naval visits. We often took picnic parties on this on our Friday holidays. On one occasion Susan, then aged about three, was walking precariously along the deck and I rushed to save her, precipitously falling in myself in the process. It only provoked peals of laughter from her at my plight, from which I was quickly rescued.

The size of the British community grew and, at my request, the Sultan granted a charter for the English-speaking school, of which our children had at one time comprised two-fifths, two out of five! Each Christmas Eve we had carols and mince pies on the top verandah of the Embassy for all members of the British community who cared to come – a tradition which became entrenched and was followed by our sucessors. I always conducted the singing, standing on a chair and using one of Ruth's knitting needles as baton. A child was heard to say, 'Who's that man up there telling us all what to do? You'd think he lived here!' The standard of music amongst the expatriate British community, which by then had grown to some 4,000, improved with more talented musicians arriving. Brenda Aitchison, a professional musician, who played the piano well and had a lovely soprano voice, performed in *Trial by Jury* and was a leading light. In 1974 for the first time her group of singers – which included Ruth and me – sang a few carols in the central courtyard below, in addition to the general singing. The acoustics were excellent and it sounded lovely – at least to us!

Among the many visitors was Bill Luce, the former British Political Resident in the Gulf, with whom I had served in the Sudan Government before Independence and whom I took on his initial tour of the then Trucial States. After a particularly relaxed and enjoyable joint audience and lunch with the Sultan in Salalah, we were each presented with large and beautiful Persian carpets. We both thought it appropriate that they should remain in the Embassy and I had them placed on the inventory. Another 'Sudani' visitor was Gawain Bell, whom I had recommended to Qaboos to write a report on the future of the *Firqats*. Shortly afterwards Eldon Griffiths, the Conservative MP, stayed with us when he came to see the new Oman. In those days men still used to wear Gulf Rig, white or black trousers, open short-sleeved shirt and cummerbund for summer dinner parties – very comfortable wear before the days of general air-conditioning. Eldon was bemused by the dress note on his formal invitation for dinner but was able to conform from his own wardrobe augmented by a cummerbund of mine. He later sent a charming thank you letter enclosing a cummerbund for the spare room in the Embassy 'so that Gulf Rig should never die'! Of course it has.

The year 1974 was an especially important one for us as Ruth was expecting a baby and Christopher Mark Frederick Hawley was the first baby to be delivered in the Khoula Hospital on 16 June 1974, the day after it was handed over by the oil company, PDO, to the Government. The birth of a son had been predicted by Bibi, Qaboos's mother and the Queen Mother of Oman, when having tea with us in England under the walnut tree in our Hertfordshire home. It was our tenth wedding anniversary and Christopher was the first child to be born to an 'English gentleman of respectability', as the British Representative in Muscat was termed in the 1800 Treaty. Shortly afterwards Ruth had to take him home to Great Ormond Street for a small operation and I was left in charge of our two younger daughters, Caroline, who was seven and Susan, four. I had to visit Dhofar to take stock and so these two small girls accompanied me, even visiting some of the less exposed military positions by helicopter.

By then it was time for changes in the *dramatis personae*. Tim Creasey, who had done so much for Oman, left with his wife Annette two days before we did in February 1975. He was succeeded as CSAF by Ken Perkins[51] with whom we only overlapped for less than a week; it fell to my successor Jim Treadwell, who had coincidentally succeeded me in my first District in the Sudan, to work with the new General. Peter Mason, the Manager of the British Bank of the Middle East, who was known to everyone in Oman after his three tours there, had left earlier in 1974 for Dubai with his wife Carol and two young daughters – a loss for our family as we had enjoyed many memorable picnics together.

We began on our own farewell calls and also visited favourite haunts outside the capital taking Susan and Christopher, the latter carried on Ruth's back in a home-made cloth 'papoose' as babies are in so many other countries. Erik Bennett,[52] the new Commander of SOAF, who

51 Major-General Kenneth Perkins, CB, MBE.
52 Air Vice-Marshal Sir Erik Bennett, KBE, CB.

was to build the Air Force up into a highly trained and sophisticated force, took us on a farewell helicopter tour, which included a dramatic visit to the Wadi Bani Khalid. Here the villagers – the women in their colourful dresses – took us to caves with a strong-running underground river. I asked the local headman where the water came from. To my astonishment he said, 'May God prolong your life; from the Shatt al Arab' – the combined Tigris and Euphrates running down to their mouth in the Gulf. I politely expressed my disbelief but he met this by claiming that marked sticks put into the Shatt had actually emerged in the Wadi Bani Khalid. Truth is no doubt stranger than fiction but this seemed difficult to reconcile with the geography. The Shatt al Arab is 800 miles to the north-west of this part of Oman.

In the very last days of my tour in Oman, David Ennals, the Minister of State in the Foreign and Commonwealth Office, paid a visit, the Labour Government having just won another General Election by three seats. He astonished me by saying, 'I do not expect, Ambassador, that you will let me, but I would like to see Dhofar.' I was in fact very keen that he should judge the situation for himself and so, accompanied by Qais Zawawi, we flew to Salalah. As the visit had been at short notice, the programme was somewhat improvised and Qais asked in a whisper on arrival what we should do. *Sotto voce*, I suggested going to the boys' and girls' schools, where we arrived totally unannounced. It was a great success as David Ennals found the children bright, charming, relaxed and very eager to learn. After further visits to military and other establishments, the Sultan hosted a lunch for him. He later met a large number of Omanis at our farewell cocktail party, to which about 300 people came, and I also took him to Samail, where we lunched with the Wali, Shaikh Mohamed bin Zahir, a jolly man of the old school. When David Ennals left on the morning of 8 February he carried away a very favourable impression of Oman and British activity there.

On this very day Ruth and I flew to Salalah to take our final leave of Qaboos at a farewell dinner. It was a special occasion as there were only the three of us. The band with the pipers and drummers in their swaggering finery and Glengarries – some wag had nicknamed them 'Wadi Darbats' – played a rich repertoire on the verandah as we ate. It had been selected by Qaboos himself and he had included one number called 'Daft Donald'. This typified his sense of humour which he demonstrated in another way at a very small dinner party in his little house near Salalah, by opening the front door himself so that we almost swept past him!

Just before our final departure on 14 February, St Valentine's Day, there were exceptionally heavy rains. Cars were washed away and deposited in contorted positions in the *wadi* at the foot of Fort Merani, but rain is a sign of blessing in Arabia and it was perhaps an appropriate moment to leave a country we had loved. Diplomatic life since our arrival had come to resemble that in other posts, with an increasing number of exchanges of calls with colleagues, dinner parties and more line-ups at the airport for visiting Heads of State. For me, however, it remained a splendid old-fashioned Ambassador's job because of Britain's special commitment to the Sultan and our final thoughts wholeheartedly echoed the words of the early nineteenth-century traveller, James Silk Buckingham; the Omanis are 'the cleanest, neatest, best dressed and most gentlemanly of all the Arabs ... inspiring ... a feeling of confidence, goodwill and respect.'

9

Return to the Foreign and Commonwealth Office

'This plant only flourishes in sandy soil.' In 1974 I suggested to Donald Tebbit, the Chief Clerk and Chief of the Diplomatic Service Administration, that in view of most of my previous postings some such label must have been attached to me. This was rebutted by my appointment as Undersecretary in 1975, with a ragbag of a portfolio of FCO departments to supervise. We had a very happy collaboration, with offices next to each other; and when Donald was succeeded by Curtis Keeble, things continued in the same vein.

Prima facie the list of my departments was not calculated to arouse the passion of a political animal – Finance, Accommodation and Services, Consular, Migration and Visa, Nationality and Treaty, Claims and the Passport Office, which was by far the largest with over 800 staff. In practice there was considerable interest and sometimes excitement. The defence against the incisive and initially often misconceived theses of the Central Policy Review Staff was one challenge. We could not for instance accept the concept of replacing conventional diplomatic entertaining with pub lunches and sandwiches in the cause of modernity and informality. Influential citizens abroad, not least in oriental countries, have very sophisticated ideas on cuisine and style in entertaining and, more often than not, there are no pubs. More importantly, informality itself is seen as bad manners in many countries and liable to silent censure or derision. Despite such canards, however, the CPRS's intelligent and provocative probing was probably good for the Service and for us individually.

I visited the main Passport Office in Petty France and the regional ones in Newport, Peterborough, Liverpool and Glasgow at least once. Most passport officials outside London had never seen an Undersecretary and one old man, who had served for over thirty-five years in the same office, charmed me by saying, 'It is nice to meet a real politician at last!'

I had to engage in horse dealing with the Treasury at the end of each year, which rather shocked me after the financial innocence of my life overseas, but mostly resulted in relatively fair settlements. The Treasury applied pressure at one point for part of the overseas diplomatic estate to be sold and, apparently at the instance of Joel Barnett, the Chief Secretary, specifically targeted the Villa Wolkonsky, the Ambassador's residence in Rome. We thought it a mistake (and so, predictably, did the Ambassador) to part with so historic a house, but the Property Services Agency, who then managed the overseas estate, put its value in the open market at many millions of pounds. Such a price, we thought, was not actually attainable for several reasons, particularly the planning restrictions imposed by the City of Rome and conservation of the Aurelian wall which ran through part of the garden. We agreed nonetheless that the market should be tested. Chance then intervened, and Joel Barnett visited Rome and stayed with Guy Millard the Ambassador. On his return he was said to have inquired, 'What is all this about selling the Villa Wolkonsky?' The pressure came off immediately and was not renewed.

Ted Rowlands, the MP for Merthyr Tydfil, a very courteous and open Welsh Minister, was the Parliamentary Undersecretary of State responsible for my part of the Office and I had a harmonious working relationship with him. I liked him the more for confessing he had come to the Office with some prejudice against stuffy diplomats only to find the reality very different. He threw an extremely successful party in his room, giving off the grand staircase, to enable similarly prejudiced parliamentary friends to meet officials.

Jim Callaghan, who had been the Secretary of State for Foreign and Commonwealth Relations before Harold Wilson's resignation as Prime Minister, was also won over by the Office. When he moved to Number 10, he gave a party there for all the people with whom he had had dealings in his former capacity – not neglecting his secretaries, chauffeur and messengers – and thanked everyone in a short speech for the support given him. It had been, he said, a 'Rolls-Royce service'. It was a graceful and much appreciated gesture.

In 1974 Turkey invaded the northern, mainly Turkish part of Cyprus following provocation by the Greek Colonels' regime in Athens. Considerable damage was done to the many houses owned by the large British community as well as to property owned by Greeks, who all fled to the more southerly part of the island dominated by the Greek Cypriots. For more than a year there was a severe refugee problem similar on a much smaller scale to the exchange of populations which had taken place in Anatolia in 1923 following the Lausanne Conference, though the Greek Cypriots with their ingenuity and capacity for hard work overcame their difficulties comparatively quickly.

I was asked to take a delegation to negotiate with the Government of Cyprus in Nicosia and the *de facto* Government in the Turkish area led by Raouf Denktash. I started in Greek-held Nicosia and then went through the barriers on the Green Line to talk to the Turkish Cypriots. On entering the Turkish area I was surprised to be welcomed to 'Cyprus' rather than the Turkish part or some such phrase. Both 'Governments' had friendly attitudes towards Britain and the atmosphere of the talks was relaxed, considering the trauma suffered by both sides. There even seemed hope at that stage that some settlement might be agreed.

Dealing with the British community in the north was at first another matter and a meeting with them was arranged in a hall in Kyrenia. The secretary of the Residents' Association, a man named Thornley, had insisted that all residents' questions should be given to him to pose, and he metaphorically barbed and poisoned his darts before loosing them. The main argument advanced was that HMG should assume liability for all damage to or loss of British property, since the British residents had settled in Cyprus in the confidence that HMG, which still had the British sovereign bases in the south, was a guarantor of the peace earlier negotiated for the island. However much individuals might have cause to regret Britain's much reduced will and capacity to interfere in overseas territories, it was an argument with little force. Nevertheless I had to think on my feet to put over an unpopular message, which might more properly have been a duty for a Government Minister. Asking the assembly if they had ever made stock purchases which had not turned out well, I said bluntly that their purchase in Cyprus was a precise parallel. At the same time I gave an assurance that we would do all we possibly could to help. This seemed to convince nearly all of them. Several were unhappy, however, about their secretary's aggressive and offensive style and two charming ladies came up immediately after the meeting saying, 'We're the Wolves – the Wolfe sisters – and we're not all like him in Cyprus!'

I toured the whole of the northern area with my team and saw the considerable, though fairly easily remediable, damage for myself. We were very hospitably received and one old lady invited me to tea. She had a classic strawberries and cream English complexion and provided an equally classic English tea. Pointing out the damage done to her neighbour's house a few days previously she said it had been raided by off-duty Turkish soldiers who had come in army lorries with number plates obscured by brown paper. She had, she said, rushed out to thwart them. When I asked her how, she replied, 'I went for the brutes with my umbrella and they went away.'

My call on the Foreign Minister of Cyprus, John Christofides, was well covered in the papers, but when I called on Denktash there were television cameras, press photographers and radio reporters. Denktash was in high good humour and said, 'I'm doing this partly to honour you but chiefly to annoy Makarios!' I asked him for a number of concessions to make life easier for the British community, not least the ability to cross through the Green Line in Nicosia to do their shopping. He agreed to them and honoured all he said he would.

The following year I paid another visit and again saw the Foreign Minister and the Permanent Undersecretary on the Greek side and Raouf Denktash and members of his Government on the Turkish. It became clear then that a deal might be done, arranged by Denktash on the one side and Glafcos Clerides on the other. The senior Turks told me that they trusted Clerides and, since he and Denktash had been friends at the same school and later as colleagues at the English Bar, there was a rapport between them which boded well for a political agreement. Any such agreement, however, needed the blessing of Archbishop Makarios, the President, who was out of the country. This unfortunately he resolutely failed to give and the inevitable happened. A whole generation has grown up in which Greek and Turkish Cypriots have been educated in separate schools on either side of the Green Line and the advantages of bonds and friendships forged by growing up together have been lost.

At least progress was made on more mundane matters and I secured further agreements to make life easier for our stalwart community. There was a tendency in Britain at the time to regard British people settled in Cyprus unsympathetically as tax exiles. Many had spent their working lives in Crown Service or business overseas – often in bad climates and primitive conditions – and I was impressed by them, sympathising with their desire to spend their retirement in the delightful climate of Cyprus. They were entitled, I believed, to compassion in their predicament and I urged David Owen, who was then Minister of State, to make a statement in Parliament expressing the Government's sympathy. He listened carefully but issued no statement.

Another interesting task fell to me when in 1976 I led a mission of Government officials and interested private sector parties to Uganda. Before setting out for Entebbe, I obtained a letter of commendation from Harold Wilson, the Prime Minister, to President Idi Amin. Relations had been stony since Amin's expulsion of Uganda's Asian community, the nationalisation of British plantations and other assets, and the arrest of Professor Dennis Hills, who perhaps trailed his coat by writing an uncomplimentary book about Uganda called *The White Pumpkin*.

President Amin received us at 'The Command Post', No. 10 Prince Charles Avenue, though all the other streets in the capital Kampala had been given Ugandan names. Assembled were his Ministers, Service and Police Chiefs and senior public officials, all crammed into a small room. I and my delegation sat on the left of his ceremonial seat. When he appeared, he was wearing a bottle green uniform and was accompanied by a small son. After initial greetings I handed him the Prime Ministerial letter and he took what appeared to be an age to read it. A pin could have been heard to drop and then, in a deep bass voice, he announced to everyone's palpable relief, 'This is very good letter.'

Amin then referred to the three matters which had been in issue between Uganda and Britain. 'The first', he said, 'is Mr Hills,' and that was finished because, as was true, 'I handed him over to your Foreign Secretary Mr Callaghan in this very place.' The second, the restoration of commercial relations, could be tackled that very afternoon under the presidency of the Ambassador of Zaire, President Mobutu having previously been helpful as an intermediary. 'The third matter, compensation, can be deferred until later.' I pointed out that I had been specifically charged with negotiating on compensation as well as trade and, after I had argued the case strongly, he agreed to its inclusion in the afternoon's talks. We parted with mutual compliments.

It was, therefore, disconcerting to hear on the Ugandan lunchtime radio broadcast, to which Jim Hennessy, our amiable and persevering High Commissioner, was listing avidly, that, despite what President Amin had said in the talks with Mr Hawley that morning, the Government had decided that compensation would not be discussed. Nevertheless, talks did start and I had to reply off the cuff to the set piece and propagandist speech made by the Ugandan Minister responsible. After an adjournment, officials on both sides got down to negotiating with no politicians present. I had succeeded in getting compensation talks reinstated but we wrangled over whether commercial relations or compensation should take precedence. When I agreed to deal with commercial matters first, however, the atmosphere became positive.

Despite this, by the tea break on the second day the Ugandans had been unwilling – presumably on higher instruction – to discuss compensation at all and sought to postpone it yet again. I then made it clear that my delegation would withdraw and return home next day if there were no progress. In the long break for tea I approached several Ugandan members of their delegation and begged them to consider my predicament. What would happen to me, I asked, if I returned and told my Prime Minister I had not carried out his instructions and had discussions on compensation? I was, I reminded them, a family man with four young children. This struck an immediate chord with the Ugandans, who well knew the consequences of frustrating higher authority in their own country, and I was thus able to carry my point when formal discussions were resumed after tea.

Next day, the Ugandan delegation did not appear on time but some thirty minutes later the Ugandan Solicitor-General, staggering in with a great pile of official papers, handed us copies of legislation covering compensation – hastily enacted and printed overnight. It was totally impossible, however, to negotiate on this document which failed to meet our needs, and I asked for a pause to consider the new move. When the session resumed we did agree on a fresh round of talks in two or three weeks at which the knotty compensation question would be tackled substantively. Amin was apparently so pleased at the outcome that, until restrained by his Ministers, he proposed to come personally to the airport to see our delegation off! These further talks, with some promise of ameliorating the situation, never took place as an Israeli aircraft was hijacked and landed at Entebbe. It happened that Mrs Bloch, a dual British and Israeli national, was killed in the course of action, which then led to the famous and daring Israeli raid on Entebbe – re-enacted in a popular film. All initiatives for settlement with Uganda were abandoned and I never saw Amin or Uganda again.

On 24 May 1976 the Secretary of State's Private Secretary rang to say that Enoch Powell was at that very moment on his feet in the House of Commons quoting long gobbets from a report I had written on immigration from India, Pakistan and Bangladesh. The Home Office was responsible for immigration policy but staff dealing with immigration cases, whether they came from the Diplomatic Service or the Home

Office, served in High Commissions and Embassies in those countries. Alex Lyon[1] had visited them all – incidentally not finding himself in harmony with British officials on the spot – and had given certain directions about the handling of immigration cases, the most important of which was that an immigration application had to be judged on the balance of probabilities, as in a civil court case, rather than requiring proof of entitlement beyond reasonable doubt. This was clear if controversial. On assuming my new office I was encouraged to go to Islamabad, Karachi, Delhi, Calcutta, Bombay and Dhaka to assure myself that ministerial instructions were being carried out, to look into any problems including the very long queues building up for entry certificates and the physical conditions under which applicants had to wait at the different posts, and to write a report.

My findings were largely factual but recommendations included a proposal that a definitive list of applicants should be drawn up with a closing date. However, the report, reinforced by the opinions of missions in the three countries as well as the views of the many Indians, Pakistanis and Bangladeshis interviewed, challenged the Home Office view that sub-continental immigration into Britain had a finite end. One particular reason for doubt on this was a recent Government decision that young women from the sub-continent settled in the UK could bring male fiancés to Britain to settle as well as the other way round. The males in Jullundur in the Punjab, which I visited, welcomed the measure almost to a man when I questioned them, but not for any sentimental reason. 'Because you get more Punjabis to UK,' was the almost universal answer. It was widely believed that, apart from legal immigration, entry into the UK with forged documents or by smuggling could be secured by payment of about 20,000 rupees – £1,100 – to one of the many agents operating in all three countries. Immigration officers themselves, who already had a very difficult and responsible job in deciding on people's life destiny, were also puzzled at the rationale of Alex Lyon's discretionary decisions under the Crown Prerogative in the Home Office itself and needed direction on this to help in reaching their own decisions.

The report was widely read in Whitehall both by officials and Ministers and there was considerable demand for additional copies. In consequence, when the leak occurred – and it was acutely embarrassing and awkward for me as the author – it became extremely difficult to

1 Then Minister of State at the Home Office.

trace the culprit who had leaked it. To me, as to every official at that time, leaking was anathema.

On the evening of 24 May and the following morning, the press pursued me to West Pulridge, our home in Little Gaddesden in Hertfordshire, and early in the morning a photographer appeared on our doorstep and asked to take my photograph. My face was covered with shaving soap but I invited him to do so there and then. He declined and asked politely if he could come back later. Rashly I agreed. He was only one of many, however; as I drove the car away from the house after breakfast, a dozen or more journalists and cameramen leapt out of the bushes. They thrust microphones in my face and one of them said, 'They say you are racist', to which I replied, 'Oh no. If I were, why would I have spent so many years of my working life with people I liked and admired in Africa and Asia?' Like others later they tried to push me into a pugilistic posture with Alex Lyon, who had gone on the record describing the report as 'rubbish'. I resolutely refused the challenge and would not be drawn, although, when it was suggested I had not visited the places in the sub-continent that he had, I explained where I had actually been – more places in fact than he. When told Alex Lyon had said I did not know anything about immigration law, I pointed out that, like him, I was a member of the Bar. One consolation was that Tony Crosland, the Secretary of State, personally congratulated me later on my handling of the affair.

One press man was particularly intrusive, however, and even Ruth was not spared embarrassment. He rang the bell after the others had disappeared, commented favourably on the house and made guesses openly about its value, remarking that it was a 'nice place'. He went on to speculate on Ruth's life and leisure, asking what she would be doing if he were not there. She took the wind out of his sails by replying, 'Revising for the A level exam in Sociology which I am about to take.' He departed nonplussed. Ruth, who was looking for intellectual exercise at the same time as looking after small children, passed the exam with an A grade.

The report made headline news for some days. I was mentioned in *Private Eye* in an extremely contentious light, suggesting that I was the stool-pigeon of David Ennals, Minister of State in the Foreign and Commonwealth Office, who was supposed to be a political enemy of Alex Lyon. When I threatened to sue the magazine, my colleagues restrained me, maintaining that a mention in *Private Eye* was the hallmark of success! However I was relieved that the press generally took the report seriously. Comment was more favourable than not and I received a number of letters of congratulation, including some from Indians resident in the UK. One outcome was that Alex Lyon left his post at the Home Office. I had to appear before a Parliamentary Committee but Evan Luard, the Parliamentary Undersecretary who had replaced Ted Rowlands, kindly insisted on attending too to give me political protection. It was he who answered most of the difficult questions. One Labour MP took a particularly hostile stance but, after the formal session, genially asked me to tell him what was really going on.

My visit to the West Indies with Tony Brennan, my opposite number in the Home Office, was less dramatic than that to the subcontinent but equally interesting. We went to Guyana, Trinidad, Barbados, Jamaica, St Lucia and St Kitts and discovered very few problems in the immigration procedures and practice anywhere. All the local authorities received us well and we learned much about the pattern of immigration into the UK and the reasons why some people returned either temporarily or permanently to their countries of origin. The most surprising discovery was the extent to which West Indian parents in the UK, if they could afford it, sent their children back home to be educated because they regarded the system of education there as better, more disciplined and more suited to their temperament. This confirmed the reports, which I later read, by a number of Parliamentary Select Committees which commented on the manner in which the British education system had let down the children of West Indian families settled in the UK. The relationships between West Indian men and women outside marriage but resulting in children, who were thereafter often looked after only by the woman and grandparents, were also described to us by West Indian women sociologists and put into the context of immigration politics.

Although this did not specifically impinge on my work, I was surprised to hear Alex Lyon and others arguing that Britain was a multiracial society and that it was incumbent on the Government to take special measures for ethnic communities. The number of immigrants from Africa and Asia was then much less than now and I think that most people felt that legal immigrants were welcome but should be expected to conform generally with local ways of life and not to look for special privileges. The British electorate was never consulted or balloted in any way on whether they wished to become a multiracial society and I suspect that more than twenty years later one of the causes of 'racism', which is very ugly both as a doctrine and cast of mind, is a latent feeling amongst many ordinary people that a multiracial society has been gradually imposed on them without such a fundamental change being openly debated. My own belief is that, once immigrants and their families are legally part of our society, they should enjoy all the rights and privileges of being British but that measures of positive discrimination are wrong and unhealthy.

Another matter which came within my scope was the new British Nationality Act and I served on a joint Ministerial/Official Committee. The main object was to remove the anomalies of the British Nationality Act of 1948 and subsequent measures aimed at correcting these. This earlier Act had been visionary at a time when the British Empire was turning into the British Commonwealth. It envisaged that Commonwealth countries – the old Dominions of Australia, Canada, Newfoundland, New Zealand and South Africa as well as India and Pakistan, which had just become independent – should enact parallel legislation. The idea was that there should be a common category of 'British Subject' and thus, under the United Kingdom's 1948 Act, those domiciled in the United Kingdom or one of the Colonies or Protectorates did in fact become 'British Subject. Citizen of the United Kingdom and Colonies'. If the concept had taken root, other citizenships would have become for example 'British Subject, Citizen of Canada (India, Pakistan, Australia etc)'. However, no other Government introduced the envisaged parallel legislation, which would have conferred reciprocity throughout the Commonwealth, and the arrangement had become lop-sided. The time was ripe for a review and the work which the Labour Government then did was substantially adopted by the subsequent Conservative Government. It was an interesting and technical assignment, for which my earlier legal training came in useful.

During this period at home I was appointed an Adviser on Foreign Relations to the Archbishop of Canterbury, Donald Coggan, and went to Lambeth Palace from time to time for meetings followed by services in the chapel. It was a privilege to work with this Archbishop whose spirituality, humour, charm and humanity made a deep impression; he was a patently good man. The main issue of the time was the progress of the ARCIC talks – Anglican Roman Catholic International Commission – on the reconciliation of doctrine between the two Churches. There was a perhaps surprising measure of agreement even on the knottiest of problems such as the legitimacy of priests, but it was clear that there could no agreement that the ordination of women should be permitted, although this was not the burning issue in the Anglican Church which it later became. There was one particular historical difficulty. The Papal Bull of 1570 excommunicating Queen Elizabeth I had never been rescinded and, even though it had fallen into desuetude and Archbishops of Canterbury and Popes had held cordial meetings, it remained doubtful whether it ever would be. Similar talks were also held with the Orthodox Church, but the possibilities of reconciliation there were considerably more remote. My involvement with Anglican Church affairs also included membership of the Church's Board for Social Responsibility, then chaired by Maurice Chandler.

In 1975 I joined others in founding the Anglo-Omani Society and became the first chairman – a rewarding task at the time and worthwhile in the longer term as the society has been going strong ever since. In general these three years in London were a happy interlude, of being well-informed at the centre of things and enjoying the company of stimulating colleagues in the Foreign and Commonwealth Office – officials and politicians. Living at home, too, and seeing more of all my family was a special pleasure in view of the years I had spent abroad. I only had three or four more years, however, before my sixtieth birthday and my last assignment in the Diplomatic Service was approaching.

10

Malaysia

The posting to Malaysia was a complete surprise.[1] The Chief Clerk, Curtis Keeble, had asked one day whether I would like to become Governor of Bermuda. Though Ruth feared it might entail too much formality including frequent wearing of gloves, stockings and hats, I expressed keenness. A short while later, he came into my room again. 'I'm sorry,' he said, 'you have been trumped.' David Owen, the Foreign and Commonwealth Secretary, wished to send Peter Jay to Washington as Ambassador and the Prime Minister, Jim Callaghan – incidentally Peter Jay's father-in-law – had agreed. This led to Peter Ramsbotham's[2] controversial move from Washington to Bermuda as Governor. An uncertain pause ensued. Then out of the blue, on 5 May 1977 Curtis Keeble told me I had been selected for Malaysia.

My delight in this was enhanced by its very unexpectedness, although the appointment had some logic. Malaysia was a multiracial society with a very large Muslim population, and much of my own service had been in the Islamic world and two partially Muslim countries, the Sudan and Nigeria, which like Malaysia had been left on independence with democratic institutions on the British model.[3] I had met many Indians and Pakistanis in the Gulf and Oman, but dealing with the Chinese was to be a new and fascinating experience. It was an enticing prospect.

Ruth and I 'kissed hands' with the Queen on 11 October and had a delightful twenty minutes of informal talk with her. On 20 November we flew to Kuala Lumpur and Caroline Wilson, the daughter of very old friends, came with us to help run the house and look after Christopher, then aged three.[4] We arrived by night, and by the headlights of the large Daimler – which friends later said looked like a Tamil taxi when

---

1 Kuala Lumpur had always been the preserve of former members of the Commonwealth Service.
2 The Hon. Sir Peter Ramsbotham, GCMG, GCVO.
3 Unlike Malaysia both had sadly lost them through military intervention.
4 Sara, Caroline and Susan were all at boarding school in England. Despite the aversion I had felt earlier in life to sending girls away to school, our circumstances in the Diplomatic Service had left us with little choice.

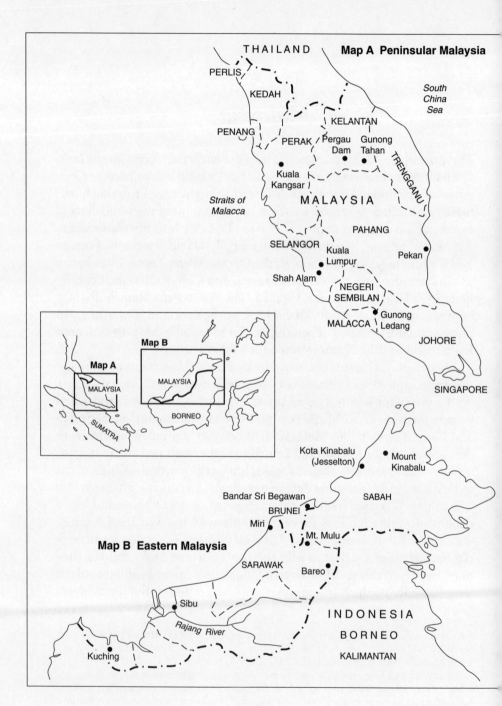

THAILAND **Map A Peninsular Malaysia**

PERLIS

KEDAH

South
China
Sea

KELANTAN

PENANG

PERAK Pergau Gunong
Dam Tahan

Kuala
Kangsar

TRENGGANU

Straits of
Malacca

MALAYSIA

PAHANG

SELANGOR

Kuala
Lumpur

Pekan

Shah Alam

Map A

MALAYSIA

Map B

MALAYSIA

NEGERI
SEMBILAN

SUMATRA

BORNEO

Gunong
Ledang

MALACCA

JOHORE

SINGAPORE

Kota Kinabalu
(Jesselton)

Mount
Kinabalu

Bandar Sri Begawan

SABAH

BRUNEI

Miri

Map B Eastern Malaysia

Mt. Mulu

SARAWAK

Bareo

INDONESIA

Sibu

BORNEO

Rajang River

Kuching

KALIMANTAN

Malaysia

Author's mother

Author's father

Author aged six

Author as bimbashi

Bill Luce (centre) and author at lunch given by Ruler of Umm al Qawain

Sudanese tea party: Grand Kadi in conversation with Paul Daniell on author's right

Author leading procession of judges at opening of first Sudanese Parliament, January 1954

Khartoum Station

LEFT Author with Shaikh Rashid bin Said, Ruler of Dubai RIGHT With Shaikh Shakhbut bin Sultan, Ruler of Abu Dhabi

LEFT Author with Shaikh Zaid bin Sultan, later Ruler of Abu Dhabi and President of the United Arab Emirates RIGHT With Colonel Stewart Carter, Commander of the Trucial Oman Scouts

LEFT Author with President Nasser at presentation of credentials by (centre) Sir George Middleton, 1964 RIGHT Wedding Day, 16 June 1964

Author with Geoffrey Arthur, Chargé d'Affaires, at signing of Anglo-Egyptian agreement on British property, with Dr Kaissouni, Minister of Finance, 1962

Author and Ruth with Chief Ben Oluwole, Lady Bishop and flanking nuns on SS *Apapa* on voyage to Lagos, January 1965

Sir Abubakar Tafewa Balewa, Prime Minister of Nigeria 1965

Lt-Colonel Yakubu Gowon, Head of the Nigerian Military Government 1966

Author in discussion in Baghdad with (centre) Abdul Karim Shaikhly, Foreign Minister, and Vice-President Saleh Mahdi Ammash, 1969

LEFT Author, first Ambassador to the Sultanate of Oman, presenting credentials to HM Sultan Qaboos bin Said, July 1971   RIGHT With Sultan Qaboos and Ruth at a National Day reception, 1984

Muscat in 1971, showing Fort Jalali and British Embassy to right of flagstaff

Author with Brigadier Jack Fletcher in Dhofar by a frankincense tree

Volume 1, No. 868   **Sh. 1/-**   Kampala, Wednesday, September 17, 1975   **ABC**

From the *Voice of Uganda*: with Idi Amin in Uganda, 1975

On a visit to Jullundur in the Punjab, 1976

With Tan Sri Vic Hutson at investiture with Tunku Abdul Rahman (on author's left), first Prime Minister of Malaysia, and Tun Sir Henry Lee, former Finance Minister

Author with Datuk Hussein Onn, Prime Minister of Malaysia, and Lord Carrington and George Walden

LEFT Dr Mahathir Mohamed, Deputy Prime Minister RIGHT Author and Ruth at Carcosa

Family at Carcosa with wife of Tunku Abdul Rahman: left to right, Caroline, Ruth, Christopher, Susan and Sara

Carcosa

Ruth as High Sheriff of Wiltshire, 1998/9

Honorary degree ceremony at Reading University 1994

our whole family was in it – we had our first sight of the extensive façade of the High Commissioner's Residence, Carcosa.

I had been told it was large but was still unprepared for its vastness. 'I shall need time to grow into this!,' I thought. It was a very fine house, probably the best in Britain's tropical Diplomatic estate. Surrounded by forest, white and magnificent, it stood in twenty-five acres of grounds on an eminence near the Parliament buildings, looking out over the beautiful Lake Gardens. Sir Frank Swettenham had built it for himself in 1896 when he was Resident-General in the Federated Malay States. Its name aroused endless speculation; Swettenham himself said he took the name from a mysterious poem about 'Carcosa' entitled 'The King in Yellow'.[5] Alternatively, he may have had 'Cara Cosa' ('dear/pet thing') or 'Cara Casa' ('dear house') in mind. A corrupted quotation from the Koran implying heavenly wisdom and grace has also been suggested as the name's origin. Be that as it may, the Social Secretary and large domestic staff were all waiting on the steps to greet our arrival warmly, and very soon we came to love our new home and the staff who enabled us to live there in memorable comfort and style.

Such was the ambience of Carcosa that it seemed almost unbelievable that any invitation we sent out should not be swiftly answered in the affirmative! Yet we had to work harder in Malaysia to make an impression than in any previous post. So many channels were already open between Britain and Malaysia that a High Commissioner was in danger of being regarded as a bird of passage.

KL – as Kuala Lumpur was generally known – was a beautiful garden city and, away from the busy centre, uniquely rural. Trees and rich tropical foliage lined the roads that followed the contours of the hills in the pleasant residential areas. A single crane was visible on the horizon, working on the first of KL's present forest of high-rise buildings. No dual carriage highways swept through the city to meet the voracious needs of the infernal[6] combustion engine in a prosperous society.

At first everything seemed auspicious. On the second day I called first on the Chief of Protocol, Encik[7] Kamaruddin Abu – later to become Malaysian High Commissioner in London – and then the Minister for External Affairs Tunku[8] Rithaudeen. My welcome could scarcely have

5 Published in 1895 by Robert W. Chambers, an American novelist.
6 Not a misprint!
7 A title much like 'Mr'.
8 Prince (also spelt 'Tengku' in some States).

been more friendly. On Friday 25th I presented my credentials to the Agong.[9] Greeted by a guard of honour provided by the Malaysian Army with their British-style drill, I entered the Istana Negara[10] in grey morning dress accompanied by senior High Commission staff. In the audience chamber the Agong stood impressively in full regalia with the mask-like expression worn by Malaysian royalty on formal ceremonies. When I had presented my papers and delivered my speech, Ruth and I had an informal audience at which the Agong was joined by his wife, the Raja Permaisuri Agong. Relaxed and in private a different persona from his public face, the Agong chuckled that, though Malaysia was a Muslim country, the people were 'civilised' and western in outlook – and they drank!

The whole occasion was supervised by the Grand Chamberlain, Tunku Mahmoud of Negri Sembilan, a delightful man of the old school who had been educated at St Edward's, Oxford. He accompanied us back to Carcosa with Tan Sri[11] Zakaria, 'Zak', the Secretary-General of the Ministry of Foreign Affairs and the Chief of Protocol. At the small *vin d'honneur* which we held, Henry Oakley, my Acting Defence Adviser, stood out wearing the full ceremonial uniform of a Gurkha officer. He so impressed my son, who was peering at us through the balustrade on the first floor knowing I was meeting the King that day, that Christopher afterwards confided that he too had seen 'the King'.

The Prime Minister, Datuk Hussein Onn, invited us to the wedding of his daughter that very evening. It was a colourful ceremony and graceful girls with beautiful black hair lined the drive in ankle-length dresses to greet the bridegroom on his arrival by waving ornamental silver palms. The bride and bridegroom later sat in state under a canopy, following the pre-Islamic Hindu marriage custom still prevailing, and were treated like a Royal Prince and Princess for the evening. Traditional rites were performed and yellow rice was thrown over the couple in blessing.

Throughout its long history Malaysia has had an inner core of strong indigenous Malay cultures blended with considerable influence in various ways from India and China. Lying between 1° and 14° north, with the independent island state of Singapore to the south, Malaysia is now a country of some 20.69 million people with a total area of 127,317

9 The King – Yang di Pertuan Agong.
10 Literally 'State Palace'.
11 A title like a knighthood awarded by the Federation; 'Datuk' (or 'Dato') is awarded by a State (see below) or the Federal Government.

square miles, divided, as in Caesar's famous description of Gaul, into three widely separated parts – *tria juncta in uno*. Peninsular Malaysia, a forested club-shaped peninsula roughly the size of England with an area of 51,000 square miles, consists of eleven states formerly known as Malaya. The other two parts lie across the South China Sea on the East coast of the island of Borneo – the states of Sabah, formerly British North Borneo with an area of 29,388 square miles and a population of 1.5 million, and Sarawak, the former fief of the three White Rajahs of the Brooke family, with an area of 48,250 and a population of 1.8 million. The small independent state of Brunei – once a considerable empire giving its name to the whole of Borneo – is sandwiched between Sabah and Sarawak. The Malays and other indigenous people comprise the majority in the country as a whole – some 56% with 34% Chinese and 10% Indians, Sri Lankans and others.

The Malaysian rain forest dates from 130 million years ago and is notable for beauty and more species than India and Burma; its trees rise to 200 feet and there are over 9,000 different flowering plants and ferns. Despite heavy logging, it still covers about two thirds of the country. Gunong Tahan, 7,186 feet high, and Gunong Ledang[12] break impressively through the undulating forest mantle south of Kuala Lumpur. The forest yields figs of many varieties and durian, which is said (rightly) to taste of strawberries and cream whilst smelling of drains; it is much prized by Malaysians, who like Europeans to share their taste. The tawny orang-utan,[13] flying foxes and flying squirrels live in the forests of Borneo. Numerous islands surround the peninsula – home of the Orang Laut,[14] Malay seafarers who turned to piracy when legitimate trade failed. The landscape has changed appreciably in recent times, not only through widespread building and development but also because of the vast plantations. Malaysia is the world's foremost producer of rubber, palm oil, cocoa and pepper. It also has large oil and gas reserves and in recent years the industrial sector of the economy has grown sharply, outstripping the agricultural.

Roughly equidistant between India and China, peninsular Malaysia has throughout history been involved in East-West trade as the sea passage between the Indian Ocean and the South China Sea was either

---

12 Europeans called it Mount Ophir. The Malay Peninsula has been identified by some scholars as 'The Golden Chersonese' of Latin and Greek geographers.
13 This is a Malay name meaning 'Man of the Woods'. This creature is found only in Borneo and Sumatra.
14 'Man of the Sea'.

through the Straits of Malacca or the Straits of Sunda. The only other
possibility for traders was transshipment of cargoes across the peninsula near its narrowest point – the 35-mile-wide Kra isthmus. Malaysia
also lies at the centre of the spice countries.

Two thousand years or more ago, Malays migrated from the north –
western China – to the peninsula and Borneo, bringing with them a
culture similar to that of Indo-China. Its chief characteristics were
splendidly carved wooden buildings on stilts, knowledge of the sea and
navigation, the cultivation of rice, and the Malay language. The courts
of the Malay rulers then adopted Hindu and Buddhist customs spread
from India and Sri Lanka, many of which still prevailed even after
Islam, brought by Indian and Arab Muslim traders, became their
religion in the fourteenth century.

The greatest Malay Sultanate, Malacca, flourished from 1403 to
1511, and was the successor of the sea-based empires of Funan, Sri
Vijaya and Majapahit. When the Portuguese broke into the Indian
Ocean to initiate nearly 500 years of European influence, they captured
Malacca in 1511 and made it their key port. It was a considerable prize
for, as Tomes Pires wrote in 1512, 'Men cannot estimate the worth of
Malacca of account of its greatness and profit ... a vast fair, where
products of China and the Far East are exchanged for those of western
Asia and Europe. Whoever is Lord of Malacca has his hands on the
throat of Venice.'

In the seventeenth century the Portuguese were eclipsed by the
Dutch, who in their turn were ousted from the peninsula by the British
during the Napoleonic wars. Francis Light, a young Suffolk sea captain
acting for the East India Company, acquired Penang for Britain from
the Sultan of Kedah in 1786,[15] and Singapore was founded by Thomas
Stamford Raffles in 1819 on land acquired from the Sultan of Johore.
Sarawak was ceded to James Brooke by the Sultan of Brunei in 1841.[16]
British North Borneo was acquired in the late nineteenth century.

Singapore, Malacca and Penang were governed as a Crown Colony –
the Straits Settlements – and the Malay states of the peninsula progres-
sively came under British protection. Sir Frank Swettenham formed
'The Federated Malay States' comprising Selangor, Negri Sembilan,
Perak and Pahang. Johore, Kedah, Perlis, Kelantan and Trengganu did

15 Penang was initially called Prince of Wales Island with Georgetown as its capital.
16 From then on it was ruled by the three 'White Rajahs' of the Brooke family until the
Second World War.

not join this grouping and, remaining unfederated, came under looser protection.

The formation of the modern state of Malaysia was a complex process. Immediately after the Second World War, during which the country was occupied by the Japanese, the British attempted, in the cause of modernisation and placating US opinion, to install a unitary Malayan Union. This was resisted fiercely by the Malays, and in consequence the Federation of Malaya, with Malacca and Penang included, was brought into being in 1948 under a constitution preserving the religious as well as the secular position of the Rulers; the Union concept would have destroyed this position. The Federation of Malaya obtained Independence – 'Merdeka' – as a parliamentary democracy in 1957 and the Malaysian crown was neatly substituted for the Queen's with a unique constitutional monarchy providing for an Agong (King).

Singapore remained a separate self-governing Crown Colony until 1963, when Malaysia was formed from the independent Federation of Malaya and the three territories which had still remained under British rule: Singapore, Sabah and Sarawak.[17] Singapore, however, left the federation in 1965 after differences between Tunku Abdul Rahman, Prime Minister of Malaysia, and Lee Kuan Yew, who became Prime Minister of Singapore as an independent state. The Malaysian coat of arms tells this story simply for, incorporating the separate arms of all the States, it still contains Singapore's shield standing empty. Despite this break up, Malaysia and Singapore deserve the same credit as India for having preserved, unlike all too many former colonies, the parliamentary democracy created by the 1957 and 1963 constitutions, and subsequently holding proper elections every five years.

The Malaysian constitution specifically provided that the powers of the Rulers of individual States should be preserved. As heads of Islam as well as constitutional heads of state, they formed an important part of the weave of Malaysian society, although Dr Mahathir, when he became Prime Minister, was later to curb these powers somewhat in the 1980s. At the apex stood the Agong elected from among their own number every five years by the Conference of Rulers of the nine royal States – Johore, Pahang, Selangor, Negri Sembilan, Kedah, Perak, Kelantan, Trengganu and Perlis.[18] The two Agongs in our time were the

17 The new nation was formed – not without controversy – following the recommendation of the Anglo-Malayan Commission under the chairmanship of Lord Cobbold.
18 The other four states, Penang, Malacca, Sabah and Sarawak, having Governors and not traditional Rulers, have no part in this election.

Sultan of Kelantan, who died in office on 29 March 1979, and the Sultan of Pahang, known to his friends as 'Eddie', who succeeded him.

Though the Prime Minister of the Federal Government was and is the key figure in Malaysian politics, the offices and institutions of each State, with their Executive Councils and elected Assemblies, reflect – and incidentally predate – those of the Federation. In practice there is considerable local autonomy as all the powers not specifically assigned to the Federal Government rest with the States. Just as the Prime Minister and all Federal Cabinet Ministers must be members of Parliament, the Chief Ministers[19] and State Ministers must be elected members of the State Assembly.

Between 1977 and 1981 most States were controlled by parties, which were members of the Barisan Nasional, the National Front. The main members of this coalition – then as now – were the United Malay National Organisation (UMNO), the Malaysian Chinese Association (MCA) and the Malaysian Indian Congress (MIC). Kelantan in the north-east was the exception and was controlled by the Islamic Party (PAS), though UMNO defeated them there in the election held in 1978. Candidates from different parties within the Barisan could stand against each other in elections, but all the main parties, including the rather different ones of the Borneo States, were represented in the Cabinet.

These were the bare constitutional bones. Nevertheless a moral may be drawn from the Malay national weapon, the *kris*, with its mystical and religious significance. It is kept in a beautiful sheath, often finely wrought with ivory or wood and decorated with silver and gold. The weapon itself, however, has a tortuous sinuous blade with a distinctive shape, and is often given a name of its own.[20] Symbolically perhaps this demonstrates that in Malaysia things cannot always be judged by external appearances.

Thus behind the parliamentary democracy lay a more complex pattern, largely due to the country's racial mix and a historical compromise made at the time of Merdeka in 1957. Earlier attempts to found successful multiracial parties having failed, the leaders of the main communities – the Malays through UMNO, the Chinese through the MCA and the 'Indians'[21] through the MIC – then worked out an agreement

19 Called Mentri Besar in the nine States with hereditary Rulers.
20 Cf. famous swords with names like Excalibur, and Samurai swords.
21 The term here includes people not only of Indian, mainly Tamil origin, but also those originally from Sri Lanka, Pakistan or Bangladesh.

based on political realities. The 'special position of the Malays' – and later in 1963 the 'Natives of Borneo' – was to be constitutionally safe-guarded, which meant a dominating role in Government with some special consideration to alleviate their relative lack of prosperity. As a *quid pro quo* the Chinese and 'Indians', many of whom were first-generation immigrants, were given citizenship in the new independent state and it was tacitly agreed that the three main races would stick largely to their former 'lasts' – the Malays with the lion's share of posts in Government, the Forces and the Police, and ultimate political con-trol, and the Chinese dominating the banking, trading and entrepre-neurial sectors. The Indians would remain strong in the professions, especially medicine and the law.

The historic compromise ran into difficulty when several hundred Chinese were killed in Kuala Lumpur in 1969 in riots fomented by a disappointed Malay politician. The underlying cause – and not the excuse – for this was strong Malay feeling that, still owning only some 7% of the corporate sector, they had not as *bumiputras*, sons of the soil, enjoyed a fair share of Malaysia's rising prosperity. Consequently the Government introduced the New Economic Policy, the object of which was to eradicate poverty throughout Malaysia, irrespective of race or creed, and to give the Malays 30% of the corporate sector – out of growth and not expropriation – by 1990. 30% was to be for foreigners and 40% for other Malaysians – in practice mainly Chinese.

The policy of gradual positive economic discrimination for a limited time was matched by preference for Malays in the university sector. It produced tensions and frustration amongst young and able Chinese but was generally regarded as nationally fair and indeed necessary. All Malaysians, still very mindful of the race riots in 1969 and determined that nothing similar should happen again, recognised the need to work together. So at times of tension, leaders of the main communities, look-ing down into the abyss, decided that compromise was best – political maturity in a country where no race was strong enough to dominate the others. No one culture could dominate – as it did in Thailand or Indonesia – and the necessary cement in this multiracial society was provided by a combination of indigenous and British-inspired institu-tions, not least the legal system and a spirit of fair play. Malaysia was fortunate that the first generation of post-Merdeka leaders of all races were men of ability and integrity.

The country, therefore, which was fast modernising during our time there, possessed many obvious blessings. The Judiciary was multiracial and absolutely independent. The press was relatively free, though Tunku Abdul Rahman, who had been the first Prime Minister, felt able to use his *Star* newspaper to take greater liberties in comment than others. The Royal Malaysian Police was generally regarded as a fair and efficient body and educated people of all races including expatriates mingled easily socially and in business. Extremists of all races were held in check. True there were still several hundred Communist terrorists, CTs, in the jungle, but their activities were well contained.[22]

Thus the Government's main tasks were to maintain security, ensure justice between the communities and to encourage the growth in the private and public sectors necessary to maintain contentment and to give hope. They also had to take account of 'fundamentalist' – better described as extremist or fanatical – attitudes. Chinese 'chauvinism' was one cause of concern but extreme attitudes to Islam, which in the past had taken a very moderate and liberal form, were still more worrying. Concern increased in Malaysia's multiracial and multi-faith society when enthusiasm for the revolution against the Shah in Iran in 1978 spread even to Malay *kampongs* (villages).[23] The Malaysian Government accordingly sought to 'ride the tiger', proclaiming their belief in moderate Islam's orthodoxy against extremist 'heresy'.

I had never been in a country with less 'post-colonial neurosis' than Malaysia at that time. Malaysians felt they had a very special relationship with Britain and contacts between the two countries had been long and deep. There was no British organisation not mirrored there, including many voluntary bodies such as St John Ambulance, the Red Cross – latterly known as the Red Crescent – and Cheshire Homes. Education in England gave a considerable number of influential Malaysians an affection for us. Many judges and lawyers were members of the English Bar and a very close tie remained between the judiciaries of Malaysia and England after Merdeka; appeals from the Federal Court, Malaysia's highest appellate court, still lay in civil cases to the Agong and through him to the Judicial Committee of the Privy Council for an advisory opinion. Similarly close contacts existed between members of the medical, veterinary, agricultural, accountancy and other professions.

22 An important task of the Police was to prevent them establishing influence again in urban communities.
23 This was surprising as most Malays, like other Muslims in South-East Asia, are Shafi's and not Shia.

All shades of the Christian Church were represented in Malaysia. There were strong links, too, between British and Malaysian trades unions – Len Murray, the Secretary-General of the TUC, gave me a book on Malaysian unions. Ties between Malaysian universities and British academics were many and varied and about 18,000 Malaysians – some Government scholars and others, particularly Chinese, sent at their parents' expense – were studying in UK universities and colleges, where they were highly regarded. Malaysians followed British football with keen interest.

British forces had fought alongside the Malaysians to achieve stability during the 'Emergency', an insurrection started on 16 June 1948 by mainly Chinese Communists, and later '*Konfrontasi*' with the Indonesians in the 1950s and early 1960s. All the Armed Forces – Army, Navy and Air Force as well the Royal Malaysian Police – had been trained by British officers, many of whom had served in the Malaysian Forces in command positions, and strong links of personal friendships remained. Thus joint collaboration had been particularly strong in the field of defence and General Sir Gerald Templer, combining the supreme civilian and military offices between 1951 and 1954, established an especially high reputation for bringing the Emergency substantially to an end, thus opening the way to Merdeka in 1957. A small legacy of Templer's period was the clear briefing – with blackboard and pointer – which Malaysian official bodies give to visitors, every institution now having its own special room for the purpose.

Moreover British military withdrawal under the 'East of Suez' policy inspired by Denis Healey in 1967, when he was Secretary of State for Defence in the Labour Government of Harold Wilson, had been as much opposed by Malaysia as by Lee Kuan Yew, the Prime Minister of Singapore, who had flown specially to London to plead with Harold Wilson against it.[24] The handover of power on Independence in 1957 had been extremely smooth. Britain had helped to train Malaysian diplomats to prepare them for their role after Independence and I personally, when Head of Chancery in Cairo, had done what I could to help the first Malaysian Chargé d'Affaires in Cairo – Jamaluddin bin Haji Bakar, later destined for high office. He and his wife had become good friends and on our arrival at Carcosa we found a large spray of orchids from 'Jamal and Rahma'.

---

24 The Rulers and Governments of the Persian Gulf States also argued strongly, and unsuccessfully, against withdrawal from their area.

The ceremony of the Opening of Parliament[25] was another illustration of the happy blending of British and Malay traditions. The Agong,[26] dressed in royal yellow, arrived and inspected a very smart guard of honour performing British-inspired drill movements. A twenty-one-gun royal salute was then fired by the 'gunners' before the Agong proceeded under a yellow umbrella to the Chamber, where he read the speech from the throne. The judges wore full-bottomed wigs, and ministers and senior officials neat uniforms with round black *songkoks*[27] on their heads.

Britain still retained treaty obligations for Malaysian and Singaporean defence under the Five Power Defence Arrangement (FPDA) in the late 1970s and early 1980s,[28] and the Permanent Undersecretaries for Defence of the two countries met every few months, with the High Commissioners and Defence Advisers of the UK, Australia and New Zealand. Australia was especially closely involved in the defence of the peninsula with a large contingent of RAAF fighter aircraft at Butterworth, on the mainland opposite Penang. The Royal Australian Air Force in Malaysia was commanded by an air vice-marshal.

Golf was always an adjunct of official meetings. When my old school friend Pat Nairne congratulated me on my 'marvellous appointment' to KL, he inquired 'But is your golf good enough?' He had a point, but it proved to be adequate. The FPDA meetings were invariably followed by golf matches and the six High Commissioners – of Australia, New Zealand and the UK in KL and Singapore – had other regular meetings which also involved golf. Although there were many other occasions when the game featured as part of official functions, Government business itself was no longer conducted in the dressing room of the Royal Selangor Golf Club, as it had been in the days of Tunku Abdul Rahman. Hussein Onn, by now the Prime Minister, played only once a week and Dr Mahathir, the Deputy Prime Minister, not at all.

A few days after our arrival on 29 November 1977, there was a frightening crash during a violent thunderstorm. The tall flag pole standing in the garden of Carcosa was struck by lightning. A large hole appeared in the lawn at the bottom of the wire guy ropes but the flag itself continued to fly – perhaps a portent predicting trouble through which we would pass safely. It was not long afterwards that a crisis in

25 I witnessed this with other members of the Diplomatic Corps on 20 March 1978.
26 The Sultan of Pahang, Haji Ahmed Shah.
27 Traditional Malay head caps.
28 This was still in force in 2000.

British-Malaysian relations blew up in what had appeared to be a clear sky. The immediate cause was the supersonic aircraft Concorde and it came to affect many aspects of British-Malaysian relations.

A joint service by BA and Singapore Airlines was planned from London to Bahrain and Singapore, and from there over Indonesia to Australia. No service to Kuala Lumpur was offered. In a routine exchange of third person notes between the High Commission and the Malaysian Ministry of Foreign Affairs, Wisma Putra, clearance had been given earlier in the year for Concorde flights over Malaysian airspace. Subsequently official talks took place over mutual air traffic rights as the Malaysians sought increased access to London for their national airline, MAS.[29]

The British negotiators naturally opposed this except on terms putting British Airways at no disadvantage. The problem was complicated. When Singapore left Malaysia in 1965 it was broadly agreed that Singapore should take over the international routes, while the Malaysians should have the regional ones. After a while, however, Malaysia predictably wanted their own international destinations as well and they decided to use approval for Concorde to fly over Malaysian space as a bargaining counter for extra MAS DC 10 services into London.

Indonesia had already given permission for three flights of Concorde a week, but on 7 December Tan Sri Manickavasagam, Malaysia's Minister of Communications – the most senior Indian in the Cabinet and President of the Malaysian Indian Congress – dropped the bombshell without warning. He told me that the Cabinet had decided for 'environmental and other reasons' not to give permission for Concorde's flight over Malaysia. Specific details of Concorde's inaugural flight to Singapore planned for 9 December had only been notified a few days before. This, combined with the routine nature of the earlier clearance for Concorde's overflight, was, he claimed, an attempt to bounce them.

Moreover our action was only one of many instances of Britain 'taking the Malaysians for granted'. They felt 'sore' that British negotiators had given them a rough deal over a Memorandum of Understanding on the number of permitted flights into London and that Singapore was thus being given unfair advantage. Manickavasagam also felt slighted that he had not been received at equivalent ministerial level when he was in London earlier for medical treatment (his British

29 Malaysian Air Services.

'opposite number' happened to be away from London at the time). He added, as further cause for the Government's decision, that Britain had let Malaysia down in negotiations, ended inconclusively in Geneva, over a proposed Common Fund for Commodities. As a final point he claimed that the environmental lobby and Muslim 'fundamentalists' might exploit the Concorde issue in the forthcoming State election campaign in Kelantan.

The Malaysian Cabinet had clearly taken up an entrenched position and even a letter from our Prime Minister, Jim Callaghan, to Hussein Onn failed to move them. On 8 December Gordon Davidson, Director of Concorde, and Captain Brian Calvert, BA's chief pilot – coincidentally the brother of Mike Calvert, the Manager of the Hong Kong and Shanghai Bank in Malaysia – came to discuss a way forward, and on 10 December Concorde arrived in Singapore without overflying Malaysia. Gordon Davidson wished me to make the strongest protestations to the Prime Minister, though by then I was convinced it would take time to resolve the problem.

I was, however, very sympathetic. In Nigeria I had taken a strong line and made personal representations to the Nigerian Prime Minister when BOAC were faced with a difficult situation caused by PanAm's competitive activities.[30] Gordon Davidson continued to press me so forcibly that it almost seemed that he wanted me to make the modern equivalent of Lord Allenby's gesture when, after the murder of Sir Lee Stack in Cairo in 1924, he had driven to the Palace of King Fuad accompanied by a troop of British Lancers and issued an ultimatum. I had no Lancers and saw no way of making successful demands of Hussein Onn. Patient negotiation was required.

My response must have struck Davidson as a diplomat's predictable weakness.[31] He said he would go and see the Prime Minister himself – an understandable reaction in view of the embarrassment and disappointment. I cautioned him against doing so, but he decided to ignore my advice and arrived at Hussein Onn's house in the evening, demanding to see him. This was seen as a gross breach of manners – a grave matter, in the light of the chilling Malay proverb, 'It is better even that a child should die than that manners should be forfeited'. The incident, reported on adversely in the press, did nothing to assist settlement.

30 When for a very brief period I was Acting High Commissioner.
31 In fact I was the only High Commissioner after independence who had been a 'Colonial' administrator in my days in the Anglo-Egyptian Sudan!

The importance of manners in Malaysian society was perhaps accentuated by the ceremonies at the courts of the Rulers, though the Malaysians liked a delicate balance between formality and informality notwithstanding their taste for titles and honours.[32] A Tun was the highest conferred honour comparable with a life peerage, whereas Tunkus – or Tengkus – were born princes or princesses of their particular States more akin to hereditary peers but without the right to sit in the Senate. A Tan Sri was a conferred federal title, whereas Datuks – synonymous with Datos – might be created by the Federal Government or a State. Malaysian jokers liked to think that a Tan Sri was 'Sir Plus'.

In view of the complications over Concorde, my first meeting with Hussein Onn was postponed until 12 January 1978. The Prime Minister had several Ministers with him – Dr Mahathir Mohamed, the Deputy Prime Minister; Tunku Rithaudeen, the Minister for External Affairs; Tan Sri Ghazali Shafi, the Minister for Home Affairs (familiarly known as 'Guzz'), and Tan Sri Manickavasagam – and it was clear that the stage was set to give me a diplomatic 'wigging'. On Christmas Day, however, I had twisted my ankle by stepping on a ball when playing tennis with the children and my leg had to be put into plaster. A fresh plaster had been applied on the very day of my call and I therefore arrived at the Prime Minister's Office on crutches, making an entry which evoked both surprise and considerable sympathy.

Nonetheless, Datuk Hussein and Dr Mahathir repeated the message that Britain was 'taking Malaysia for granted' both generally and over Concorde and air traffic rights. On Concorde they were more hurt than angry but had been upset about the way the DC10 negotiations had been handled. The trouble, he said, was partly a 'question of style' and a 'new breed of British official' now apparently dealing with Malaysia. Malaysian Ministers wanted to solve the Concorde problem quickly, though this would entail some commercial trade off. Asking me to pass this on to the British Government, Hussein said he would now reply to Jim Callaghan's letter. It was clear that an element of polite blackmail had crept in.

Thus my early days in Malaysia were neither simple nor trouble free and the theme of Britain's attitude towards Malaysia was to recur often over the next few years. I did my best to ameliorate the situation, but this was the beginning of the rumbling which led, after my time, to the 'Ice Age' – Mahathir's policies of 'Look East' and 'Buy British Last' –

32 There were some parallels between the honours systems of Britain and Malaysia.

and the subsequent 'spat' in 1994 over the Pergau Dam. The British media, which seldom gave Malaysia due credit for its achievements, had some direct responsibility for complicating relations.

In the first half of 1978 both the British and Malaysian Governments – and BA and MAS – remained at odds over Concorde and mutual traffic rights. The British negotiators maintained, correctly in law, that the Malaysians were in breach of the Chicago Convention on Civil Aviation in denying overflight to Concorde, and that the two matters should not be linked. Though no British Minister had visited Malaysia for two years, the Duke of Kent came out in March as Vice-Chairman of the British Overseas Trade Board at Jim Callaghan's suggestion, and stayed with us. George Rogers, an Undersecretary in the Department of Trade, whom the Malaysians regarded as a hard man, had made several visits but failed to reach agreement on air matters. I hoped he would be in Kuala Lumpur over the Duke's visit, but he demanded to see me at 11 p.m. on the preceding evening to say he was leaving within two hours and it was up to the Duke to solve the problem of traffic rights.

The Duke's visit was essentially one of goodwill and it went well. He himself had visited the country several times in the past and his whole family were both respected and liked. The Prime Minister and other Malaysian Ministers received him warmly. Some specific contracts were discussed but, comparing our attitude with the aggressiveness of some other countries, Datuk Hussein advised – evidently not referring to Concorde – that in commercial rivalry with our competitors we should 'play rugger and not cricket'! The Duke's audience with the Agong, to which I accompanied him, was easy and friendly although Datuk Hussein was not himself present and was represented by Dr Mahathir, the Deputy Prime Minister.

The Duke – on my perhaps misguided advice – referred to the generous gesture by which Tunku Abdul Rahman and the Government of Malaya in 1957 had made a gift of Carcosa for the use of the British High Commissioner in recognition of Britain's help militarily and diplomatically in the period leading up to Merdeka. The house would otherwise have been handed over, in accordance with normal practice on Colonies becoming independent, with other Colonial Government property. The Agong graciously accepted the sentiment expressed by the Duke, but Mahathir muttered, 'The greatest mistake we ever made!' I felt a chill wind and my gut told me that Mahathir might later take action over this, as indeed he did when he became Prime Minister in 1981. From then on, too, I felt that on taking over he might spring some unwelcome surprise on us. It was perhaps significant that, although the Prime Minister, virtually all the other Cabinet Ministers and many Deputy Ministers came to the house in our time, Mahathir never accepted an invitation, thus perhaps remaining true to his own principles.

Carcosa was not under immediate threat in our time, however, despite its prominent position, and many older Malaysians took pride in the generous 1957 gift. Nevertheless there were faint rumblings of the sort that eventually led to its surrender to Malaysia. On the Malay side there had always been some who had been antagonistic to the gift and in the early 1980s, after our departure, pressure built up from UMNO Youth, then led by Anwar Ibrahim who later became Deputy Prime Minister. Dr Mahathir by then Prime Minister himself was not minded to resist it.

On the British side, too, there was a growing body of opinion that it was no longer appropriate for a British High Commissioner to live in so large a residence which was costly to keep up. A remarkable amount of paint was required, it is true, to keep the place smart and trim, together with a staff of twenty, including four guards. The cost was a mere bagatelle, however, compared with the value of the site and the cost of a small replacement plot of land with no building on it. Moreover I wonder why we lack pride in our very rich British heritage abroad, of which Carcosa was a fine example, when we guard our heritage at home so assiduously.

One small item of this heritage was a Hanoverian coat of arms, which had apparently originally come from the High Court in Penang, hanging above the stairs in Carcosa. The face on the lions was said by older members of the British community to be Swettenham's. I was sceptical and consulted Tom Barlow, founder of the plantation company Highlands and Lowlands, who had persuaded Swettenham after retirement to become the first Chairman of his company. Gazing at the picture with hands folded behind his back, he pronounced that, without question, it was the face of Frank Swettenham. This seemed conclusive and I presumed that at some stage a joker had been at work in restoring the picture. I believed this until in 1997 I looked closely at the lions on a similar Hanoverian coat of arms in our own village church at Little Cheverell. There I saw the same anthropomorphic faces, raising doubts whether tradition about such faces long predates Sir Frank Swettenham.

In the event Dr Mahathir was personally very helpful over Carcosa when the handover took place in the later 1980s, and he authorised a

complicated scheme of land exchange, beneficial to Britain and resulting in a new High Commission office and a new Residence. This is built
where the Defence Adviser's house formerly stood overlooking the
Royal Selangor Golf Club, but the site is rather small in relation to the
impressive house designed by a Malaysian architect, Hisham Bakri.[33]
Carcosa itself became a VIP Government Guest House and my efforts
to persuade Mahathir that it should become a museum of Malaysian-
British history did not prevail. It was a graceful gesture, however, that
in 1986 the Queen and Prince Philip were the first visitors to Carcosa in
its new, much modified, form.

The Concorde problem was not solved quickly. I did my best to persuade Whitehall and BA that if they wanted a quick solution there
would have to be some *quid pro quo*. Otherwise it would take time.
Though I was given no straw to make bricks, fresh instructions arrived
every few weeks urging me to solve the problem. I kept gently pushing
the case with Manickavasagam, Tunku Rithaudeen and Hussein Onn
himself, who was always looking for a way out. I argued throughout
that it would be fair to give it a trial, even though the environmental
lobby, led by Gurmut Singh, intensified their claims that Concorde
would kill the fish in the Malacca Straits. Talks continued at official and
airline level but were inconclusive. The Malaysians had persuaded
themselves, rightly or wrongly, that the British line was stubbornly
hard.

My idea of a purely goodwill meeting between British and Malaysian
Ministers misfired badly. Dr Mahathir was to visit London privately in
early 1978 and I recommended that Edmund Dell, then Secretary of
State for Trade and Industry and thus Mahathir's 'opposite number',
should receive him personally for a courtesy call. Mahathir agreed on
the clear understanding that no business would be discussed and I recommended very strongly in a telegram that Concorde should not even
be mentioned. According to the Malaysians, Edmund Dell, who was
accompanied and advised by several officials when the meeting took
place, did not offer coffee or tea to Mahathir but lost no time in pitching in to him over Concorde. Mahathir, who only had the Malaysian
High Commissioner with him, regarded this as a breach of courtesy
and was highly put out. Datuk Abdulla, my opposite number in
London, later confided that this meeting actually stiffened Malaysian
resolve in the Air Traffic rights negotiations. A later visit by Edmund

33 Hisham Bakri's wife, Valerie, is English.

Dell to Malaysia was planned and might well have mended fences but sadly had to be cancelled. By way of pleasing contrast, Tunku Rithaudeen, who anyway had none of Mahathir's prickliness, was well received in London by David Owen, the Foreign and Commonwealth Secretary, in November 1978 after attending the EEC/ASEAN ministerial dialogues in Brussels.

Eventually – and it had taken almost exactly a year of my advocacy – Hussein Onn persuaded his Cabinet that Concorde should have a six-month trial and, after some prevarication due to resistance by officials in his ministry, Manickavasagam announced this publicly on 15 December 1978. I was invited by British Airways to travel on the 'rein-augural' flight from Singapore to London on 25 January 1979. Having obtained permission from the FCO, I had early morning tea at Carcosa and breakfast on the flight to Singapore – where there was time for me to visit my colleague John Hennings. The pilot from Singapore to Bahrain was Brian Calvert, the airline's chief pilot, and he invited me to the cockpit, where I was able to send a message of greeting to Sultan Qaboos as we overflew Oman. Having had an excellent lunch between Singapore and Bahrain I had an equally excellent one between Bahrain and London. On its 7,000 mile eastward journey Concorde contracted time and, when my sister Enid met me at Heathrow, she also asked if I would like lunch – it would have been my third. I declined. She had anyway already lunched herself, and so we went to her home in Hertfordshire for tea.

On the return flight from London a few days later I was sleeping when I was awoken by 'Fasten your seat belts, ladies and gentlemen, as we are shortly about to arrive in Kuala Lumpur.' I thought I was dreaming as I had been instructed in pressing Concorde's case to argue that Subang, Kuala Lumpur's airport, would never be used except in an emergency. I was not convinced incidentally that it was a good argument because, if one or two Concorde flights a week into Kuala Lumpur had been offered, Malaysian objections might well have vanished. A moment or two later, however, the landing announcement was repeated and the hostess came to see if I was awake. We really were about to land at KL, Singapore airport having been blocked by a Jumbo 747. It was early morning and the Malaysian airport staff were tremendously excited by their first sight of the 'great bird'. By vigorous telephoning I managed to persuade Manickavasagam and the Director of Civil Aviation that passengers destined for KL should leave the plane without proceeding on to Singapore. This was a generous decision as there was no agreement in force entitling Concorde passengers to land at KL.

This whole saga ended sadly as the joint BA/SIA Concorde service to Singapore was cancelled after only a few weeks of operation. Higher fuel costs, combined with a series of diversions and zigzags on the route, insisted on by countries approving overflights, reduced the passenger load owing to the need to carry extra fuel, and made the route uneconomic.

The Concorde/Air Traffic rights problems clouded many, but fortunately not all aspects of Anglo-Malaysian relations. On 3 April 1978 Hussein Onn gave an evening party at his private residence for Sir John Wilson, the inspiration and prime mover of the Royal Commonwealth Society for the Blind, and Lady Wilson. At this Hussein, responding to a personal letter from me about Concorde, assured me he would do his best to solve our problems. Musa Hitam, the Minister of Education, also took me on one side and said he wanted 200 British teachers for a 'crash programme' to teach in the classroom and raise the standard of English again; it had declined alarmingly since the early 1970s following the introduction of Bahasa Malaysia, the national language, as the main medium of instruction.[34]

Next morning early I took John Lawrence, the British Council Representative, to call on Musa and this resulted in the Centre for British Teachers (CfBT), an independent educational charity, being engaged to provide the teachers. A technical supervising officer, Jim Kerr, was appointed by the British Council but the bulk of the very valuable work was done by CfBT under the direction of Tony Abrahams, its founder.[35] This important and successful programme ran for several years and incidentally resulted in several Anglo-Malaysian marriages.

Another bright spot was Ted Heath's visit in November 1978 with members of the Brandt Commission. This body, led by Willi Brandt, was set up by Robert McNamara, the President of the World Bank, to examine the interests of both the developed and developing countries – a study of the 'Rich and Poor Countries'. We entertained Ted Heath to lunch and Abdel Latif Hamad, the talented and charming Kuwaiti Finance Minister, came with him. Other members of the Commission on this visit to Malaysia were Katherine Graham of the *Washington*

34 One of its objects was to help create unity between the races.
35 A few years after my retirement from the Diplomatic Service I became Chairman of this body.

Post, and Khatijah Ahmed, a successful Malaysian businesswoman; she had come back to her own country to represent the developing world while Katherine Graham represented the developed. Ted Heath was very genial, recalling the 'breakfast incident' in Dubai, and when I asked him whom to watch in the Labour Party he presciently named John Smith.

Members of the Commission were invited to dinner by Hussein Onn and by chance I arrived first. It was then that Hussein told me that the Cabinet had agreed to a six months' trial period for Concorde. I was, he said, to regard this information as personal and to feign surprise when Manickavasagam informed me officially. He seemed reassured when I told him I had done some acting in my younger days. After dinner Hussein asked Ted Heath and me to stay and we talked for over an hour in a very frank and relaxed way. The occasion turned into a sort of pleasurable *conversazione* with a number of Malaysian Ministers – Mahathir; Tengku Razaleigh the Finance Minister; Ong Kee Hui from Sabah, the Minister for the Environment; Leo Moggie from Sarawak; and Datuk Amr Taib also from Sarawak who was Minister of Information. Zak represented Wisma Putra.

I was fortunate in having to deal with Hussein as Prime Minister. I liked him immensely as a man and we had an easy rapport. What is more I could talk to him as a fellow barrister, sometimes appealing to his sense of justice and fair play.

Although not wishing to cast him as the villain of the piece, I have little doubt that Dr Mahathir, then the Minister of Trade and Industry as well as Deputy Prime Minister, took the lead in proposing retaliatory action against Britain, including the handling of Concorde, for 'taking Malaysia for granted'. He was of a different stamp from his three predecessors as Prime Minister, who were all old aristocrats educated in England and members of the English Bar. The first Prime Minister, Tunku Abdul Rahman, was a prince of the house of Kedah, the son of a previous Sultan who knew well how to score his nationalist points with the British and to lead the country to Independence. Tun Razak, whom I met when he was passing through Muscat in the early 1970s, likewise came from a notable family of Pahang and sent his son Najib, now himself a senior Minister, to Malvern. Hussein Onn, the son of perhaps the most prominent pre-Independence politician, came from a Johore family closely associated with the Sultan's court.

Mahathir was not a member of the English Bar and, atypically for a senior Malaysian at that time, had no part of his education in Britain or the West, having qualified as a doctor, as his wife did, at the Medical School of the University of Malaya in Singapore. Even amongst his own Malaysian colleagues he had a reputation for 'shooting from the hip' and for being maverick. An example of this occurred in 1978 when the tragic Vietnamese 'boat-people' were arriving in Malaysia and, although this imposed great strains, 50,000 or more were efficiently 'processed' for onward transit to recipient countries. The press reported Mahathir as saying that, as Malaysia could not cope with a greater influx, the naval forces would have to 'shoot' them away. He later said that he had actually used the term 'shoo'.

In 1970 he had written a book called *The Malay Dilemma* analysing with great insight the specific problems of the Malays in a multiracial country. It was judged at the time to be provocative to Chinese and Indian Malaysians and consequently banned. It was not until several months after he became Prime Minister in 1981 that the ban was lifted. In the meantime he must have been the only Prime Minister in the world whose book was banned in his own country!

If there was any anti-colonial reaction in Malaysia, it came from Mahathir – and even then that was twenty-five years after independence. On 5 February 1979 he was invited to open a seminar in Kuala Lumpur attended by a group of senior figures in the City of London led by Charles Denman[36] who had all flown out specially for the occasion. In the event he was unable to come, and Musa Hitam, the Minister of Education, read his speech. It was more bitter than welcoming and criticised City reaction and press coverage of Sime Darby's bid – then owned by Malaysians[37] – for the plantation company Guthries. Musa, embarrassed, whispered as he sat down, 'I never like reading other people's speeches. That was Mahathir. Nice to be able to disclaim what you do not like!' Other senior Malaysians schooled in traditional Malay courtesy – including Tun Ismail Mohamed Ali, the Governor of the Bank Negara and Mahathir's own brother-in-law – were shocked, but a warning note had been sounded.

However, merely to brand Mahathir anti-British, as some people have, is wrong and too simple a diagnosis of a remarkable and complex personality. Though he did sometimes give this impression, and despite sometimes trying sensitivities, he was in many ways Anglophile. For

36 Lord Denman, a merchant banker – Tennants – with wide experience of the Middle East and Asia, was then the Chairman of the Invisible Exports Committee.
37 It was originally a British company involved in and associated with plantations and trading in South-East Asia.

instance, immensely keen on British theatre and humour, he never missed one of the plays which Derek Nimmo brought periodically to Kuala Lumpur – for the first of which in 1979 the furniture was borrowed from Carcosa. Furthermore he sent his children to Britain to be educated and has always enjoyed spending time in London unofficially. When he thought praise was due to a British company or individual for assistance to Malaysia, he would not hesitate to give it in public. Always genuinely pleased as Minister of Trade and Industry to see British efforts and successes in the industrial investment sphere, he would happily open a new British factory, such as one in Perak in 1979. Whenever I accompanied leading British businessmen to see him, he was courteous, helpful and effective in solving problems. More generally Mahathir was determined to make investment in Malaysia easier and less cumbersome, and he welcomed new initiatives from any source. He fought obstruction by officials and set up a 'one-stop' section in his Ministry to help and encourage investors.

My task in dealing with Malaysian sensitivities in the early days of my tour would have been helped by a visit by a British Cabinet Minister, particularly as no Minister at all had come for two years. As I have mentioned, it was the Duke of Kent who in the event broke the ice, though he was followed shortly afterwards by Goronwy Roberts, Minister of State at the Foreign and Commonwealth Office[38] who paid his first visit on 22 March 1978. A learned and charming Welshman, he claimed that only two men in the House of Commons could be turned to for classical quotations – Enoch Powell and himself. Persuaded on his first visit of Malaysia's importance, he came back several times and was well received by the Malaysians although they were very conscious that he was not a Cabinet Minister. He made his particular mark one night when staying with us. Intending to summon a servant because he had left his glasses downstairs, he pressed a button in his bedroom which he mistook for a bell. Instead he set off the alarm and within moments police cars rushed up the drive with screaming sirens. He blushed a little and in his Welsh lilt remarked on the 'positive malice of the inanimate'.

It was not until 6 January 1979 that a Cabinet Minister came – this time a Scot, John Smith the most junior member in the Cabinet who had just been appointed Secretary of State for Trade and Industry. He stayed with us, was a charming guest and made a very good impression

---

38 Lord Goronwy Roberts, whom I already knew from my time in London.

on the Malaysians. For them, however, one belated swallow did not make a summer. For me it was gratifying because John Smith, whom I came to respect and like greatly, inflated my already bloated ego by telling British businessmen that the Concorde service had been due to my diplomacy!

The Opposition sparked earlier than Cabinet Ministers, and John Davies, the Shadow Secretary of State for Foreign and Commonwealth Relations, came with his wife Georgie in 1978 and made friendly and positive calls on senior Ministers, a gesture which was generally helpful to my mission. He had been a colleague and friend of my father in BP in his earlier days but sadly died prematurely shortly after this visit.

On 4 May 1979 the Callaghan Government fell and Margaret Thatcher became Prime Minister. Cecil Parkinson as Minister of Trade came out to Kuala Lumpur in June, stepping elegantly in to John Smith's place. He and Norman Tebbit, both of whom I saw later in London, the latter being a former airline pilot, cleared up the long-standing question of MAS flights into London sympathetically, helped by an Undersecretary, Stewart Sutherland, who had a much easier manner than his predecessor. In early July Peter Carrington, the new Foreign and Commonwealth Secretary, paid a brief visit, for which I had been recalled from leave. He was very cordially greeted by Hussein Onn, Ghazali Shafi and the acting Foreign Minister, Taib. This visit so early in the new administration's life created a very good impression, especially as the Malaysians tended to feel more at home with a Conservative Government. I returned with the Secretary of State on his aircraft via Delhi and Baghdad – and thus had the unexpected pleasure of seeing several old Iraqi friends.

In September Hussein Onn visited London – his son was at Cheltenham – and Peter Carrington gave a lunch party at No. 1 Carlton Gardens. Malcolm MacDonald and Gerald Templer headed the list of distinguished 'Anglo-Malaysians' at this historic and nostalgic occasion. (Sadly both were to die not long afterwards.) Margaret Thatcher entertained Hussein to tea at No. 10, gracefully pouring it herself from a silver tea pot, with the Malaysian High Commissioner and myself as the only other guests. It was a pleasantly informal occasion. In January 1980 Peter Blaker, the Minister of State at the FCO, came and so it went on with more useful Ministerial visits until, in the days before our final departure in 1981, there were more visits than I could easily cope with. Dearth was, as in the natural order of things, followed by glut.

But the good done by increased contacts was partially undermined when the Government in 1979 withdrew subsidies for overseas students' fees. These amounted to some £200 million a year *in toto* and the decision took immediate effect. The Malaysians, with their 18,000 students in Britain, were consequently hit harder than any other country and this aroused a feeling that the measure was particularly aimed at them. It was in fact nothing of the sort but it was an own goal on Britain's part and caused disproportional damage because of its suddenness. Despite having been given no warning – for the measure had slipped through the British Cabinet without any real debate owing to a technicality of presentation – I did my best to explain our action, pointing amongst other things to Britain's poor economic situation at the time.

The Malaysian Government was particularly embarrassed, because the hardest hit so unexpectedly were the Chinese middle class with no great wealth. Their children were at a disadvantage over university places because of preference given to Malays in Malaysian universities under the policy running parallel with the New Economic Policy to give them their 'fair share of the cake'. Musa Hitam, the Minister of Education, was particularly concerned and said to me, summing up Malaysian Government sentiment, 'High Commissioner, your Government like ours is free and sovereign, and we have no official comment on their actions. But Donald, why are you doing this to your friends when French, Germans, Japanese and others are constantly knocking on my door to gain entry here?'

The situation might have been mitigated if a scheme for transitional funding, with contributions from the British and Malaysian Governments and the private sector, had been adopted. Ungku Aziz, the Vice-Chancellor of the University of Malaya, and I actively advocated it and many senior British businessmen resident in Malaysia agreed. It was to no avail because the seriousness of the situation was not fully grasped at first, though the British Government later found £4m to alleviate the situation – known as 'Pym Money' after Francis Pym.[39] 'Pym money' did help to build up relations again.

'Buy British Last' started about nine months after we left Malaysia in February 1981. The rubrics of journalism, and to some extent Whitehall, attribute this and the 'Look East' policy to the British Government's decision on overseas students fees. This thesis has attractions to Academia and some journalists but is inaccurate. The timing does not

---

39 Foreign and Commonwealth Secretary succeeding Peter Carrington who, to the regret of many, had honourably resigned over the Falklands issue in 1982 and no longer held office.

fit. 'Buy British Last' started at the end of 1981, whereas the British decision on overseas university fees was taken towards the end of 1979. It is true, however, that in April 1980 Mahathir did attack British 'racialism' over the increase in fees for overseas students and the 'high and mighty British professional institutions which refused to recognise Malaysian qualifications'. It was an unjust attack and, asked for my reactions by the *National Echo*, I gave a strong riposte, explaining why our policies were not 'racialist'. Mahathir to his credit bore me no grudge for this and my easy personal relationship with him was unaffected. Nonetheless the fees issue was an irritant and Mahathir, who succeeded Hussein Onn as Prime Minister in late 1981, maintained that it was a further example of the Malaysians being 'taken for granted'. Different interpretations in implementation by various UK Local Authorities prolonged this irritation and confusion amongst ordinary Malaysians.

Another incident affected Anglo-Malaysian relations. It was Malaysian policy in furtherance of the NEP to acquire foreign, particularly British, plantation and trading companies and in 1981 Guthries was obtained in a legal but controversial 'dawn raid' on the Stock Exchange. It was carried out by Rothschilds on behalf of the National Equity Corporation, Permodalan Nasional Berhad – a Malay Unit Trust. This action, with which Mahathir was closely associated, provoked critical and patronising leading articles in *The Times* and *Financial Times* about him as the new Prime Minister, and accusations of 'backdoor nationalisation'. Mahathir told me himself that this was the final straw, and it, rather than the fees issue, pushed him to his retaliatory 'Buy British Last' policy. He particularly resented the implication that Malaysia was a sort of banana republic and that the high price Malaysia actually paid to shareholders was not mentioned. The attitude of the City to such dawn raids and changes to regulations, which Malaysia saw as particularly directed against them, compounded the sense of outrage. It was ironical that it was during one of his usually enjoyable private visits to London that Mahathir read the offending articles which sparked off his hot-headed 'Buy British Last', complementing 'Look East' policies.

Mahathir's attitude to Britain was not based merely on this and the university fees issue, however. He had for some time challenged the almost automatic Malaysian assumption that what came out of Britain was good and he sought in his 'Buy British Last' policy to make Malaysians look carefully at alternatives first. Even worse for us, having no direct ties forged during residence in the UK, he began to conclude that the British had departed from their former *gravitas* and increasingly embraced values as repellent to Muslim society as to an earlier generation of British people themselves.

The style of British journalism was not the least thing to nettle him and in a lecture at All Souls College in Oxford in April 1985 entitled 'Holier than Thou – A Mild Critique', he analysed and criticised the Western media in general. Much of what he said struck a chord with his audience of professors and dons – and indeed me – though with the politesse of Oxford Academia they questioned whether he had spoken in the right forum. After the lecture, Raymond Carr – then Warden of St Antony's College – hosted a small lunch in Trinity, culminating with a brief speech in which he said, 'May I say, Prime Minister, how much nicer you are in person than in public.' This amused Mahathir hugely and his wife, Datin Seri Siti Hasmah, who was sitting next to me, burst into spontaneous and irrepressible laughter, saying, 'Everyone says that about my husband!'

Combined with his distaste for Western journalism was a feeling that Britain did not want Malaysia to take its place in the modern world and he often expressed, with a strange degree of intellectual paranoia, his view that the Western world generally did not want Asia to succeed. I believe this was and is very misplaced but it is one explanation of his later strong advocacy of 'Asian Values'. In any case he admired the dynamism of Japan, Korea and Taiwan – and indeed Singapore – and wanted a similar ethic of hard work to motivate Malaysians, particularly the Malays. As soon as he assumed the Prime Minister's office he insisted that Government officers should clock in on time and wear an identity label, as he himself did, in the office. Visitors were surprised to see his 'Mahathir' label on being greeted officially by him but his lead undoubtedly affected Malay attitudes to their work.

Despite all this Mahathir was – though it might seem paradoxical – determined that very bright young Malay boys and girls should be given a first-rate education in Britain. The newly formed British Malaysian Society, of which I was the founding chairman, was asked at short notice in 1985 to obtain fifty places in 'Britain's best public schools' for A level students, 'so that they could go on to Oxford and Cambridge'. Although it was impossible to guarantee the university aspiration, places were found in good schools through the influence of members of the Society, particularly Tony Abrahams who was chairman of the Harpur Trust, and the scheme prospered with an increasing number of such students being sent at the expense of the Malaysian Government every year. They shone in their schools, several becoming prefects or even head boy or girl as well as doing well at games, and many succeeded in obtaining places at Oxford and Cambridge entirely by their own efforts. Virtually all achieved very good university placements under the scheme, the name of which the Malaysian Government changed, at the society's suggestion, from 'The Oxford and Cambridge Scheme' to 'The Top Universities Scheme'. A complementary Host Families Scheme was arranged by Ruth, and in the first few years British people welcomed the girls and boys into their homes for half terms and short holidays. It was Mahathir who personally promoted this unique scheme for bringing young Malay and British students together and that was certainly no 'anti-British' act.

Mahathir's achievement lies in presiding for nineteen years over Malaysia's impressive economic growth and, despite his maverick tendencies, putting Malaysia prominently on the world map. His 'Vision 2020' after he became Prime Minister in late 1981, combined with his pragmatism, impelled Malaysians of all ethnic groups towards a diversified 'Tiger' economy, thus changing a country relying on primary commodities to a principally industrial one. Even so Malaysia remained the world's largest exporter of rubber, tin, palm oil and pepper, with oil and gas production both on the east coast and Sarawak. Presiding over a stable, prosperous and economically blessed country – until the late 1990s – with a sound Central Bank and other institutions inspiring the confidence of foreign investors, he became the architect of a Malaysia with high aspirations epitomised by the Dai Bumi building, the tallest in the world in 1997, though at the cost of the country losing something of its earlier and simpler delights and charm.

He might at one stage have seemed unlikely to cut an international figure, for in the early 1980s he was totally unconvinced about the value of the Commonwealth. The Ministry of Foreign Affairs, Wisma Putra, were dismayed that he did not listen to their arguments on this. Later, however, veering through 180°, he decided to play a prominent role both in Commonwealth and international affairs. In this he was encouraged by Margaret Thatcher, with whom he established a close personal rapport and agreement on political philosophies from the time of their first meeting as Prime Ministers in 1985. The chemistry between them proved exactly right on that occasion – a great relief to everyone quietly involved in encouraging a meeting beforehand – and subsequently they developed a warm mutual regard.

In my time I found that the Malaysians for their part not infrequently 'took us for granted' – the very offence of which they accused us. I was able to make some play with this diplomatically. But there were acts and omissions on Britain's part in the post-colonial period which undoubtedly caused hurt to a proud people, the worst of which was apparent official indifference. 'Were the Malaysians over-sensitive?' I often asked myself. 'Were they unreasonable in negotiation?' The answer was undoubtedly 'yes' in both cases, but it is the task of diplomats, exercising their art and craft, to deal with the characteristics and idiosyncracies of the people in whose countries they are serving.

Malaysian feelings were succinctly explained several years later when Ruth and I visited Kuala Lumpur in the early days of Mahathir's 'Buy British Last' policy, during which with the active encouragement of my successor Bill Bentley[40] and the FCO, I had some unofficial meetings with the Malaysians. We were entertained to lunch at the Royal Selangor Club by Zak, who was still Secretary-General of the Ministry of Foreign Affairs, and his wife Razmah. He explained that the Malaysians were not anti-British; on the contrary they regarded themselves as very close friends of Britain and felt wounded by our lack of consideration – not least over university fees.

British investment was the largest in the country by a long way, though much of this was transferred to the Malaysians by their acquisition of the plantation companies. However, even then British investment was substantially greater than any other country's. British companies already established in Malaysia continually increased their investment, reinforcing their success, but unfortunately new British exporters and small manufacturers did not always take advantage of all their special opportunities. The Americans, Germans, Japanese, Taiwanese, Singaporeans and Koreans were much more active in investing in Malaysia – especially in the Free Trade zones.

With the many British-originated institutions in Malaysia, it might have seemed that everything was straightforward and many British businessmen coming for the first time told me how easy and familiar they had found everything. The 'Britishness' of institutions and the friendly nature of the people always gave this impression. I had to warn them that appearances could be deceptive and that Malay politeness could conceal their aspirations and real intentions, reminding them of the nature and shape of the Malays' *kris*.

40 Sir William Bentley.

The aims of the New Economic Policy with its concept of raising the Malay stake in the corporate sector to 30% could not be achieved entirely out of growth, and this affected our interests. The Malaysians had to look to the largely British-financed plantation companies to reach their target. This put unexpected pressures on these companies. Their directors took me into their confidence and I did my best to help in their affairs wherever I could. The concerns of Guthries and Harrisons and Crosfields – great and historic names – took much of my time, and Henry Barlow initiated me into the Byzantine problems of Highlands and Lowlands, and Barlow Boustead. Henry Barlow, the first member of the Barlow family to make Malaysia his permanent home, lived on a small and beautiful former tea plantation at Genting outside KL. There was a wrong-headed tendency in Britain – perhaps based on impressions from Somerset Maugham's stories – to regard the plantation industry as old-fashioned. Nothing could have been further from the truth. This might have applied to some individuals' attitudes, but there was much foresight, careful research and innovation as well, and the plantations were extremely well managed. If they had not been, the Malaysians would not have been so keen to acquire them.

The problems of new investors in Malaysia often loomed large as there were many hurdles to be cleared, including dealing with bodies such as the Foreign Investment Committee (FIC) and the Capital Issues Committee (CIC) which were concerned with adequate Malay equity being available to further the NEP. The bureaucracy was sometimes unnecessarily complicated – a fact well appreciated by Dr Mahathir as Minister of Trade and Industry, who never tired of making strong and successful efforts to overcome difficulties caused by officialdom.

With a view to encouraging further trade with Malaysia and investment in the country's development, I succeeded in obtaining a grant from the British Government of 2.25 million ringgit for a review of Malaysia National Airport Plan. More significantly, in January 1981 I signed an agreement for a mixed credit loan of £77 million, which was a combination of a development loan from the British Government and an officially backed line of credit provided by commercial banks. It was the first such loan offered to any country and the first unspecific aid loan to Malaysia for some years. Its object was to finance a wide range of projects in the transport, mining, energy, telecommunication and agricultural sectors. The first tranche of £20 million was interest-free and repayable over twenty-five years while the rest was credit on a ten year basis. It was potentially of very significant mutual benefit, but proved to be a damp squib because any drawing down was lost in 'Buy British Last'.

On foreign policy, there were few contentious specific issues in British-Malaysian relations. Like other ASEAN States, Malaysia was almost always moderate and helpful to the West in the counsels of the UN. This made for very close, easy and genuinely warm relations with Wisma Putra, many of whose members were charming and became good personal friends. Malaysia at that stage placed much emphasis on the economic nature of ASEAN and less on the political, though in practice it became increasingly significant as a moderate political grouping, and the members maintained solidarity against the Communist countries to the north, especially as Communist terrorists were still posing a low-level threat in Malaysia and elsewhere.

Far from the US withdrawal from Vietnam being welcomed as a victory for local nationalism, the Communist victory there worried the Malaysians deeply and Hussein Onn voiced a widely-held view in complaining that the Americans had let their natural regional allies down by withdrawing. US prestige was not high, though we shared a broad community of interest and I maintained very close contacts officially and socially with the warm and friendly American Ambassador, Bob Miller, and his wife Kaity. The US reputation under the Carter administration was dented further, however, by the unsuccessful raid in April 1980 to rescue US hostages in Teheran.

There was nevertheless one tricky issue in Anglo-Malaysian relations: Brunei. I often discussed this with Zak, and with Ghazali Shafi, the Minister of the Interior, himself an earlier Secretary-General of Wisma Putra. In the late 1970s Brunei was still an independent state under British Protection but, like the Gulf States, it was not a formal Protectorate.

Brunei's relations with Malaysia had been tangled and hostile since 1962. At this stage it was envisaged that Brunei would become part of a Malaysia formed from Malaya, Singapore, British North Borneo and Sarawak. In 1962, however, elections were held in Brunei on the recommendation of the British Government and the Parti Rakyat Brunei (PRB – National Party of Brunei) under A. M. Azahari won convincingly. This party favoured Brunei's incorporation into Malaysia, but only if Brunei, Sarawak and North Borneo were first unified under the Sultan of Brunei, Sir Omar Ali Saifuddin. The PRB had a militant wing, Tentera Nasional Kalimantan Utara (TNKU) or North Kalimantan

National Army, which was a violent 'anti-colonialist' liberation movement. This was supported by Indonesia, perhaps because the Indonesian struggle for independence against the Dutch had been a bloody
affair unlike Britain's peaceful and amicable handovers to new nations.
They planned rebellion against the Sultan, who might have been
tempted into Malaysia on certain terms but was much more inclined to
keep Brunei separate under British Protection. The uprising started on 8
December 1962. It was put down by British troops and the Sultan himself was saved by Gurkhas, for whom he formed a lasting admiration.
Thus Brunei did not, as envisaged, come into the Malaysian union but
remained under British Protection. Later Sir Omar abdicated in favour
of his young son Hassanal Bolkiah,[41] while retaining great influence as
the 'Seri Begawan' – a name now commemorated in the capital of the
State.[42]

Brunei was convinced that Malaysia had given help and encouragement to the PRB leaders Azhari and Yassin Affendi, who continued
their opposition, and was particularly suspicious as the PRB sometimes
operated from Limbang – the strip of Sarawak which divides Brunei
into two halves. This was especially sensitive because the Bruneians
strongly resented the loss of this to Sarawak in the last century.

In 1978 the British Government wished to withdraw Protection from
Brunei. The Sultan and Seri Begawan were unhappy and enlisted eminent voices to their cause, including Hartley Shawcross[43] who told me
he wondered why the Labour Government was being so 'doctrinaire'. I
too had found it difficult to understand. The Malaysians, themselves
used to the electoral process and mindful of pre-Independence procedures in other former British territories, opposed independence for
Brunei without a formal act of self-determination. I pointed out to Zak
and Guzz that the independence in 1971 of Bahrain, Qatar, and the
UAE, which had been Protected States like Brunei, had been recognised
by the Arab League and the UN without 'self-determination'. Zak
found this persuasive and asked me to give him chapter and verse,
which I did. I hope this may have helped the Malaysians to modify their
entrenched stance.

I was keen to visit Brunei myself and Jim Davidson, our High Commissioner there, encouraged me. Hussein Onn asked me to convey

41 His Majesty Paduka Seri Baginda Sultan Haji Hassanal Bolkiah Mu'izzaddin Wad-
daulah. His full Malay title is much longer.
42 Bandar Seri Begawan.
43 Lord Shawcross, GBE, PC, QC.

greetings to the Sultan and the Seri Begawan and at my audience on 30 May 1978 I assured them both that Malaysia had no designs on Brunei and hoped for friendly relations. The Sultan listened attentively. The Seri Begawan, who did most of the talking in Malay translated by Pehin[44] Isa, the senior Court official, said that, though they did not want to be in Malaysia, they wished to be on good terms with all their neighbours including Malaysia and Singapore. The meeting was very cordial and I was able to give my own favourable impressions of Malaysia and its Government. The Seri Begawan emphasised his trust in Hussein Onn and accepted that Ghazali Shafi – about whom he had had grave reservations since Ghazali served on the Cobbold Commission examining the future of the Borneo States in the early 1960s – had now probably 'followed Hussein's good example'.

The Seri Begawan thanked me warmly for coming and said that I was the first British High Commissioner in Malaysia to come for seventeen years. Jim Davidson swiftly deflated me afterwards by saying he had refused to see any of my predecessors. Nonetheless my visit may just have helped to break the ice. Shortly afterwards a compromise agreement about independence was reached in London providing that the Treaty of Protection would not end until 1983. It was signed at the Sultan's and Seri Begawan's insistence on a 'propitious day' settled by the diviners. Hussein sent a mission to congratulate the Bruneians and to mend fences. Tunku Rithaudeen the Foreign Minister, a Prince of Kelantan well versed in Malay courtesies and court procedures, was an ideal envoy.

A gradual easing in relations followed, assisted by 'polo diplomacy' between Brunei and Pahang. The Sultan and the Seri Begawan attended the Installation on 19 July 1980 of the new Agong, the Sultan of Pahang – the Sultan of Kelantan having died in office earlier on 29 March. The grand, glittering and dignified occasion – involving *inter alia* a white tie dinner – was attended by the Rulers and Governors. The Sultan, granted exceptional courtesies at this essentially Malay occasion, was seated with the Rulers and before the Governors and was the only head of a foreign State there. Both Sultan and father were visibly delighted and the Agong was invited to pay a state visit to Brunei.

On my second visit to Brunei in October 1980, relations had visibly improved and already there was talk of Brunei joining ASEAN, though Sir Omar was somewhat mystified and quizzed me closely about this organisation. I offered to help Brunei set up an office in Kuala Lumpur

---

44 A title much like 'Lord'.

and to train Brunei diplomats in our High Commission, and the invitation was accepted with gratitude.

During our time in Kuala Lumpur we were fortunate to have many interesting visitors. Clarissa Avon, the widow of Anthony Eden, came on a private visit and met her many Malaysian friends. John Hunt, leader of the first successful Everest expedition, visited in his capacity as President of the Royal Geographical Society and Eddie Shackleton, another former President of the RGS, also returned to Malaysia particularly to revisit Mount Mulu in Sarawak, having been one of the first to climb it with the Oxford University Expedition to Sarawak in 1932. On a jungle walk with Ruth to the appropriately named Gunong Bunga Buah (Flower and Fruit Mountain), he was so excited by the sight of the summit when the mist suddenly cleared that he threw his arms round her and kissed her. Peter Scott with his wife Philippa paid a visit as Chairman of the World Wild Life Fund and he opened our eyes to jungle birds as well as painting beautiful bird pictures in our children's autograph books. All these visitors renewed friendships and contacts with influential Malaysians.

Wilfred Thesiger, another well-known traveller, became one of our very first guests in December 1977. He was an old friend more associated with the deserts of Arabia, and I had first met him in the bar of the old Shepheard's Hotel in Cairo in 1942. In the summer of 1977 he left for South-East Asia with Gavin Young in the steps of Conrad and, meeting him on the steps of the Travellers Club in London before this, I invited him to visit us. On the very day our three girls were arriving for the Christmas holidays and the heavy luggage was being delivered, he rang from Singapore. Ruth told him he would be welcome.

Next day – I was out at an official function – she gave a small lunch party for him. Henry Barlow, one of the guests, asked how long he would be in Kuala Lumpur, to which Wilfred replied, 'Well, my next firm engagement is in Delhi in April.' Ruth is reputed to have blanched. In the event, though, he stayed only until the end of January. He was a welcome guest who, despite his reputation for misogyny, took to Caroline our second daughter, then aged ten, and enjoyed arguing fiercely over politics with Caroline Wilson, our housekeeper-cum-nanny who was a recent graduate in politics from Reading University. On departing he asked if he could come again. I said he would be very welcome on condition he wrote at least 4,000 words a day as he still had at least two good books in him![45]

45 NB: He did not come, but did write more books.

Distinguished British judges visited Malaysia from time to time – a particular pleasure for me as they revived my earlier involvement with the law. In 1979 references to the Privy Council came to an end and thus the formal links between the Malaysian and English Judiciaries were severed. Kenneth Diplock[46] visited in June of that year and Hussein Onn gave a big dinner for him, at which all the males present were members of the English Bar. Warm personal and professional relations continued. Desmond Ackner[47] stepped into Kenneth Diplock's shoes as the liaison judge with Malaysia in the new circumstances.

A visit in 1979 from an England B soccer team to play a representative team excited people in KL and we gave a reception for the teams and officials of the Malaysian Football Association. The players were all good ambassadors for Britain but it was a surprise to discover that several of them, all of course professionals, had university degrees. A lighter note was struck as people left the reception. A Chinese, who had evidently had his leg pulled by his friends on modes of address, said in farewell salutation, 'Well thank you very much Your Excellency His Knibs. Very nice party!'

Royal visits always had particular significance in this country with its Agong and hereditary Rulers, and in May 1980 Princess Margaret came as guest of the Malaysian Government, accompanied by her ladies-in-waiting, Fiona Aird and Elizabeth Paget, and her equerry Nigel Napier. She made a round of visits to Malaysian institutions, with which she had particular associations both in KL and Penang, and at her request we gave a small after-dinner reception. Originally she asked to be seated for the occasion and we planned to bring people up to her throughout the evening. In the event she insisted on going round the whole party, talking to everyone, and members of the British community, initially a trifle blasé about her visit, were greatly charmed. When she returned home after the visit she wrote me a delightful letter of thanks in her own hand.

Princess Margaret also endeared herself to the six-year-old Christopher. We were fortunate in having a beautiful swimming pool, put in at the instance of Anthony Head, one of my predecessors who insisted on this in preference to salary. The Princess had tea with us there and Christopher announced that he was looking forward to seeing *The*

---

46 Lord Diplock, 1907–85, was a very distinguished judge with a reputation as one of the very finest legal brains of his time. He was appointed a Lord of Appeal in Ordinary in 1968. He had previously had special responsibility for Malaysia.
47 Lord Ackner who was appointed a Lord of Appeal in Ordinary in 1986.

Incredible Hulk that evening on the television. Princess Margaret's eyes lit up and she said she wanted to see it too. A 'television dinner' was rapidly arranged by Carcosa's inimitable staff and Princess and small boy sat watching the film together, the Princess describing how the 'Hulk's' eyes would have changed colour dramatically if only we had a colour and not merely a black and white television. Two years later Christopher became a chorister at St George's Windsor, where he sang at many fine services taken by the Dean[48] including the Commemoration of the Queen's sixtieth birthday, the Christening of Prince Harry, and the funeral of the Duchess of Windsor, and he ended up as Head Chorister and Head Boy of St George's School.[49] I often wondered whether Princess Margaret recognised the same small boy when she came to the chapel, as she often did.

The dominant Malaysian character of our time in Malaysia was still Tunku Abdul Rahman, the first Prime Minister of Malaya and then of Malaysia, whom remarkably I had first met in Muscat when he visited as Secretary-General of the Islamic Conference. 'Tunku', delightful and charismatic, retained a special place in people's hearts as 'Baba Malaysia'[50] and I was fortunate to see him on many occasions. He had the great gift of commonsense and was not averse to using humour to deal with extremism.

One vehicle for his views was his daily newspaper, the *Star*, published in Penang. In 1979 and 1980 a few Malaysians, including academics, advocated Muslim penalties for crimes rather than what was provided for in the Penal Code. 'Tunku' responded by drolly asserting in his weekly article that if the Muslim penalty for adultery were introduced, he feared there would not be enough stones in the whole of the Malay peninsula! Similarly he told me that when he was Prime Minister the Opposition had proposed a motion in Parliament to ban the serving of alcoholic drinks. He had stood up and, to the astonishment of all present, said 'The Government accepts the Opposition's motion,' and immediately sat down again. At the next large Government reception, he clapped his hands and announced 'Tuns, Tan Sris, Datuks and their ladies, ladies and gentlemen, the Government has accepted the Opposition's motion that alcoholic drinks will not be served. They will not be. However, you are free to help yourselves!'

48 The Right Revd Michael Mann.
49 He was also taught the trumpet so well by Mortimer Rhind-Tutt that he obtained a place in the National Youth Orchestra of Great Britain.
50 Father of Malaysia.

Towards the end of his life he confided to a group of friends at the launch of a book in his honour that the twenty years he had spent in London before passing his Bar exams had caused many people to brand him as a playboy wasting his time. But, he said with evident nostalgic satisfaction, the Twenties had been a wonderful time to be in London and he had learned there to distinguish between good and bad people. His aristocratic style did not mix easily with Mahathir's modern and somewhat aggressive approach, however. 'Tunku' did not approve, for instance, of the pressure on Britain over Carcosa.

'Tunku' invited Ruth and me to dinner at his house in Penang and it was an occasion which typified his individual courtesy and charm. In the course of the evening he told us he had purchased and cooked the meat himself. From his many years in England he knew that the English liked roast beef and Yorkshire pudding and he had also learned how to cook it there.

The only other guests were Dr Lim Chong Eu, the Chief Minister of Penang and his wife. Dr Lim had been educated at Cambridge and had actually travelled to London with Tun Ismail, the Governor of the Bank Negara, on the same boat before the Second World War. They became lifelong friends. He was very Anglophile and a warm reception, therefore, always awaited us in Penang where the Georgian centre, the Christian cemetery with its haunting inscriptions to British people who had died young, the large ornate houses of the rich Chinese in spacious gardens, the Peak with its cable railway and the lovely beaches exercised a special charm. The kindly Governor Tun Sardon and 'Lady Sardon' made their beach bungalow available to us. I was made an Honorary Member of the Penang Club and used to have a haircut and massage at the long-established and old-fashioned E and O Hotel next door. The small British community was lively and hospitable.

Dr Lim as Chief Minister of Britain's oldest foothold in the area would frequently chide me because the British Deputy High Commissioner had earlier been withdrawn and the British Council 'closed down'. There was no remedy for his first complaint – our diplomatic representation in such posts had been reduced everywhere in the world, probably to our disadvantage. But on the second count my defence was good; the British Council had in fact remained open under a local officer. Dr Lim swept that plea aside, asserting that a British resident officer was needed. All I could do was to encourage more visits from the Representative and his KL staff, but I was able to pursue with Dr Lim other ways in which Britain could become more involved again especially in the commercial sphere.

'Tunku' himself kept up his old friendships and when Alan Lennox-Boyd, who as Colonial Secretary had been personally involved with Independence negotiations, visited Malaysia in January 1980 with his wife, he gave an intimate dinner party for them. The only other guests were Tun Sir Henry (H.S.) Lee and Tun Haji Omar Yok Lin, the first Speaker of the Malaysian Parliament, their wives, Ruth and I. Former times were discussed with great frankness and we drank brandy congenially well into the night.

'Tunku' had a very early engagement next morning. It was the opening ceremony of the Islamic Dakwah (Missionary) Conference for South-East Asia and the Pacific. He not only held the view that alcohol taken in moderation was not inconsistent with being a good Muslim but, having a strong constitution, was none the worse for wear and played a prominent role throughout the ceremony. The conference was opened by the Agong, the Sultan of Pahang, who preached moderation with the message that Malaysia's need was for true and not fanatical Islam – emphasising that Islamisation in Malaysia and South-East Asia generally had been achieved by peaceful conversion by traders and not the sword of Islam.

Somewhat incongruously I had been invited to this conference to represent Brunei, which was then still a Protected State, and was probably the only non-Muslim there. There was a welcoming line of men and women including Dr Aishah, the wife of Tun Omar Yok Lin who had been at the dinner on the previous evening. She was incidentally of Chinese origin and had a Roman Catholic convent upbringing. I held out my hand to greet her in the normal manner in Malaysia but she said, 'Please excuse me, Sir Donald, but you know the custom.'

This was not an example of traditional Malay moderation and thereupon Datin Leila, the wife of Datuk Amr Taib, the Minister of Information, who was standing next to her, said very firmly, 'You had better shake hands.' Leila was a tall lady of a Polish family who had been Muslims for many generations and she won the day. Nonetheless this incident did reflect the increasing Muslim sensitivities of the time. There were also other examples. Malay girls of quite tender age had been permitted, even encouraged, to exchange their pretty light blue 'gym slips', worn with a white shirt, for long skirts covering their legs and to adopt the headdress of other parts of the Muslim world but previously rare in Malaysia.

The Governor of the Bank Negara, Tun Ismail Mohamed, was a towering personality in the banking and investment world and bankers, expatriate and local, trembled before him. Small and almost gnome-like with bald head and glasses, he had complete integrity and was one of the main architects and executors of the New Economic Policy. Educated at the Malay College at Kuala Kangsar, he went to Cambridge in 1938. When his studies were completed, he was caught in Britain by the war, during which he worked for several years with the BBC.

He was a perfectionist as I found out in 1980 when he led a mission of senior Malaysian bankers and businessmen to the City of London. He insisted that I should come home too and the FCO granted me leave. In London I asked one of his team how things were going. He said it had been very tough living up to Ismail's standards. He was apparently quite determined that each member of his team should show himself or herself – there was one woman member – fully up to the standards of the City in their public presentations. Consequently he had insisted on seeing all their drafts, correcting them as he thought fit and often complaining about their English usage!

He and his wife Maimunah dined with us at Carcosa quite frequently. Once, just after his retirement from the Bank Negara in 1980, she came alone. Ismail was ill. I asked after him and she replied, 'Oh, Sir Donald, the only trouble is he has got no office to go to!' Shortly after this, he was appointed Chairman of the PNB, National Equity Corporation, and took on a new lease of life. This was an institution he had fostered as Governor – an all-Malay investment trust, through which ordinary *kampong* Malays became shareholders in the corporate sector, thereby contributing substantially to increasing the percentage held by Malays in equities. Mahathir was married to Ismail's sister, Dr Siti Hazamah.

Tun Suffian bin Mohamed was the Lord President and Head of the Judiciary – so called because the first British holder of the office, Tun Sir James Thomson, was a Scottish rather than English lawyer. The son of a religious judge, 'Suff' went after his Malay education to Gonville and Caius College, Cambridge.[51] Here he met his English wife Toh Puan 'Bunny' – a diminutive mistress of the nudge and the wink and a popular eccentric figure in Kuala Lumpur. They frequently came to our parties and I very much liked and respected him. Suff himself, with round face, horn-rimmed glasses and ever-present pipe, was a distinguished lawyer with whom I found it easy to be on terms of close

---

51 Most Malaysians of that generation who went to Britain went to Cambridge, because Oxford required a knowledge of both Latin and Greek, whereas Cambridge only required Latin. Neither language was normally taught in Malayan schools.

friendship as I was with many of the other Malaysian judges educated in England.

The Chief Justice, Raja Azlan Shah, who succeeded 'Suff' as Lord President, became Sultan of Perak on the death of his cousin and was then elected Agong, in which capacity he paid a state visit to the UK in 1993. Ruth and I attended the State Banquet at Buckingham Palace, as well as the Banquet at Guildhall and the Agong's return Dinner.

Omar Yok Lin, one of those present at 'Tunku's' dinner for the Lennox-Boyds, was President of the Senate. He was a man of many parts, liked the company of diplomats and, with his charming younger wife, Dr Aishah, whose children were of the age of our younger ones, was a frequent visitor to our house. Earlier in life he was involved in the formation both of independent Malaya and Malaysia and, after accompanying Tunku Abdul Rahman to London in 1957 to finalise the Federation of Malaya's Constitution, he was a Minister in his first Government. In 1961 he led a Malayan delegation to Kuching for a meeting of the Solidarity Consultative Committee prior to Sarawak's incorporation into Malaysia, and in 1963 was a signatory in London of the Agreement establishing Malaysia. After that he became Malaysia's first Ambassador to the US, Canada and Brazil – with which Malaysia had a common interest in tin – and Permanent Representative to the UN.

Other Chinese and Indian Ministers and senior figures in Malaysia's past history also became good friends. Prominent among these was Tun Tan Siew Sin. He and his wife Catherine came from Malacca and were leading members of the Chinese 'Baba' community[52] which had been established there for centuries and, speaking Malay rather than Chinese, were very much rooted in the country. Siew Sin had been President of the Malaysian Chinese Association, one of the leading parties in the National Front Alliance, and a former Finance Minister and member of Tunku Abdul Rahman's first Cabinet. He later became Chairman of Sime Darby after its acquisition by the Malaysians. We visited him and his wife in Malacca, driving to their house past the red buildings which were a legacy of the Dutch period from the seventeenth to the nineteenth centuries. It was 15 April 1980, Chinese All Souls Day, and we watched their act of ancestor worship. Catherine was a practising Christian but, like Siew Sin, waved burning tapers before the family altar, on which there were offerings of duck, chicken, pork, cuttlefish, wine, tea and other items. They then knelt in obeisance.

52 The ladies of this community were called Nonyas.

Siew Sin had strong views about China itself, believing that Communism had destroyed the innate capacity of the Chinese for hard work and enterprise, contrasting the spirits of those still in mainland China with the exuberant success of the overseas Chinese. Catherine was a passionate and successful gardener and once asked me whether I 'scolded my plants', claiming she often did so to good effect.[53]

H. S. Lee was one of the Grand Old Men of the Chinese community. Born in 1901 and educated in Hong Kong and at Cambridge, he won a golf Blue, as did his son Alex later. By the 1970s he was Chairman of a considerable number of companies and organisations. During the war he had been a colonel in the British Army, after which he was a member of the Merdeka delegation to London and of the first Cabinet of independent Malaya. He and his wife, Choi Lin, were frequent guests. He remained prominent in the Oxford and Cambridge Society, which had a considerable number of members and held a big dinner on Boat Race night every year. A reception was also held after the Annual General Meeting, at which each President tried to get through the business faster than his predecessor. A very good recipe for quick and efficient meetings, this tradition was also an open field for gamesmanship. In 1980 I was President and the AGM was held at Carcosa. My attempt to finish the meeting in less time than Henry Lee's record failed, as he persistently raised lighthearted points of order to thwart me. He himself had a formidable reputation for despatch in business with bodies he chaired and remained very nimble and fit into his eighties. When asked how he was on arrival at a party, he invariably replied in a quick mumble of contracted words – 'Very well, thanks. Eighteen holes of golf today.'

The custom of calling on Ministers and Muslims at Hari Raya, the Id al Fitr, provided opportunity to meet many Malaysian officials and friends informally. There were also similar celebrations for Chinese New Year and the Indian Diwali festival. On these occasions soft drinks, tea, and coffee were offered with a wide selection of delicacies to eat, one particular delicacy being *halwa Muscat*. This was a brown sweet differing somewhat in consistency and taste from the *halwa* of Oman but an interesting reminder of maritime ties between Oman and South East Asia – similarly attested by Muscat Street and Arab Street in Singapore. Ruth and I made the long journey between Malaysia and

53 Other frequent Chinese ministerial guests at our table were Richard Ho, Paul Leong, and Dr Goh Chong Cheik.

Oman rather more speedily when in November 1980 we flew to Muscat to attend at his personal invitation the impressive Tenth Anniversary celebrations of Sultan Qaboos's accession.[54]

The most important aspect of the High Commission's work was bilateral relations with Malaysia – political, economic, trade, aid, defence and, with the British Council, cultural. Perhaps the cultural high point was a performance of *Swan Lake* by the Royal Ballet, attended by the Agong and the Cabinet. However there was a monthly meeting of EEC Heads of Mission to exchange views, and the EEC/ASEAN dialogue and periodic meetings involved us all.

The Diplomatic Corps was large and included representatives of countries enjoying no relations with each other. My seniority in the Corps was of some special significance. Having presented my credentials after the Ambassador of Vietnam and before the Chinese, my place at formal functions was between the two. If, however, I was unable to attend a ceremony – where we were of course placed in order of seniority – the Malaysian Protocol had to take special measures as Chinese and Vietnamese were unwilling to sit side by side. The same was true of the Ambassadors of North and South Korea, who, placed next to one another at a magnificent white tie banquet given by the Sultan of Selangor for the marriage of his daughter, had to be rapidly separated.

Our Dean, in whom we were fortunate, was the High Commissioner of Singapore, Wee Kim Wee, a shrewd and sunny man who later became President of Singapore. He had earlier been a distinguished journalist. The French Ambassador, André Travert, who had spent many years in Hong Kong and spoke excellent English without a French accent, was something of a card. Asked at a party not long after his arrival what he 'did', he replied, 'First I am a jockey and secondly l'Ambassadeur de France.' He was indeed an amateur jockey and looked like one both in height and mien. His hero was Lester Piggott, who rode in Malaysia from time to time. He chided me for not having invited 'the greatest living Englishman' to Carcosa but it was well nigh impossible to find out when Piggott was coming or to get hold of him. In any case he did not enjoy the reputation of being one of the world's liveliest conversationalists.

The Egyptian Ambassador, Adil Guenena, and his vivacious wife Leila had been the first to greet us at the wedding of Hussein Onn's

54 The FCO readily granted permission for this special visit to Oman.

daughter. We were already old friends from Cairo where we had lived in the same block of flats in Zamalek; he was then Private Secretary to the Egyptian Foreign Minister, Mahmoud Fawzi. The German Ambassador and Ambassadress, Willi and Gisela Ritter, were very good company. He had been a participant as a young cavalry officer in the Pentathlon in the 1936 Olympic games and was Chief of Protocol for the Olympic Games in Munich in 1976. My Soviet colleague was Boris Koulik, whose wife Gallina was somewhat formidable both in style and intellect. When the Soviet Union invaded Afghanistan in 1980, the Malaysians were almost as much concerned as Western countries and I was much minded to send him Kipling's warning about the Afghans in 'Private Ortheris's Song':

> Ho! don't you aim at an Afghan
> When you stand on the skyline clear.

In the light of subsequent developments it would have been a salutary warning.

I was fortunate in my own staff. The Defence Adviser, Bill Copinger-Symes had served as a young officer in a battalion of the Malayan Army. Tim Gee and Gerry Hayward were experienced Counsellors who knew Malaysia well. Peter Joy and Jeremy Varcoe, who later became Ambassador in Somalia and an Undersecretary in the FCO as well as my Deputy High Commissioner, succeeded Tim Gee as Counsellors.

The Deputy High Commissioner during the first part of our time was Rex Hunt. He had started his overseas career in the Colonial Service in Uganda and then joined the Commonwealth Relations Office, having postings between 1964 and 1967 in Borneo, first in Jesselton – as Kota Kinabalu then was – and then in Brunei and Kuching. The closing of Kuching as a Deputy High Commissioner's post was much regretted by people in Sarawak. In 1979 I received a cypher telegram addressed to me personally. I was asked to find out whether Rex Hunt would accept the Governorship of the Falkland Islands. I put it to him. Believing that he had finally left the Colonial Service he was surprised, although he had been expecting promotion, but said he would consult his wife Mavis.

The following day he returned accepting it and I informed the Office. I then said, 'Rex, may I be the first to congratulate you. I believe, however, that HMG have gone out of their minds.' He looked shocked. 'Did you not have to leave Uganda prematurely on independence?' He conceded this was so. I then said, 'Were you not Head of Chancery in

Saigon and last out when the Viet Cong took it?' He confessed he was, and I said, 'QED?' I was not to know that lightning would strike again with the Argentinian invasion of the Falklands and bring Rex Hunt so much into the limelight.

The transition from the British period to modern Malaysia was smooth and seamless. Many British people stayed on after Independence. With a very happy blend in society of Malays, Chinese, Indians and British – including members of the large business community largely centred on Kuala Lumpur – those who 'stayed on' did not face the troubles of those in Paul Scott's novel about India. In an atmosphere of mutual regard between British and Malaysians and a general freedom from racial prejudice relationships were easy and happy and a number of British people obtained Malaysian citizenship.

In 1977, twenty years after Merdeka, there were still over 300 British planters – a phenomenon which resulted from an agreement between the Government and Claude Fenner,[55] who was the Representative of the Rubber Growers Association, that British planters should be allowed to continue working up to their normal retiring age of fifty-five. The last British Commissioner of Police before and first Inspector-General after Independence, Fenner was perhaps the most prominent of the 'stayers on'.

He was a tall and commanding figure, though he had not been able to get the plantation companies to work out a joint long-term policy in the light of the NEP – something he deeply regretted. 'I told the b......s', he said, 'that, if they did not stick together, they would hang alone!' Given to strong words, he was nonetheless correct in his prediction. I believe that a common policy with British Government backing would in fact have proved advantageous to all parties.

Claude Fenner died very suddenly on the morning of 15 May 1978. We knew him and his wife Joan very well and it was a sad loss to Anglo-Malaysian relations. The Royal Malaysian Police made all the arrangements for his funeral, starting with a service at St Mary's on the Padang.[56] He was accorded full honours in the military style and his coffin was draped with the Police flag – which incidentally he had himself designed. There were beautiful flowers and Malaysian officers in their best white uniforms were the pall bearers. The traffic was halted

55 Sir Claude Fenner, KBE, also Tan Sri; he had served in the Police before the Second World War, during which he was in Force 106, returning to the peninsula behind enemy lines in a mini-submarine.
56 Square.

for the journey to the crematorium, where Tan Sri Mohamed Haniff bin Omar, his successor as Inspector-General of Police, and all the senior officers were assembled. The guard of honour fired a salute of three rounds as the coffin descended and the whole occasion demonstrated the affection and respect in which he was held by the force which he had done so much to build up.

Claude Fenner had commended me to Haniff, who generously took me not long afterwards with the Singaporean High Commissioner, Wee Kim Wee, to visit the police forts in the jungle among the Temiar[57] people. These forts had been set up as a defence against the Communist terrorists,[58] who, though defeated, had not entirely given up their increasingly vain struggle. It was not until 1985 that their leader Chin Peng, by then fattish and looking like a prosperous Hong Kong businessman, signed a peace agreement with the Government. Haniff took me again to the same area in 1980 with Dickie Franks[59] and on each occasion we were warmly received by a reception of children in their school uniforms, and required to dance with the local people, wearing crowns of plaited palm. A local unit, the Senoi Praq, had received specialist training from the British Army – a fact of which they were very proud.

The planting community was present in strength at my first public appearance as guest speaker at the St Andrew's Ball on 26 November 1977, at which the Sultan of Selangor and Tengku Ampuan were guests of honour. The Scots abroad were at their most colourful. The male members of the Society, some of whom were of enormous stature including the Chieftain, Ken Stimpson, wore their full kilted 'evening fig'. Their ladies were in white with the tartan sashes of many clans. The haggis was piped in by pipers of the Malaysian Police. 'Amazing', as I noted in my diary, 'to see an expatriate gathering of this size and nature still going so strong. There are not so many ex-Colonies where it could be!'

It is only possible to mention a few of those who stayed on. One of those who became Malaysian citizens was a former Justice of the Court of Appeal, Donal Good. It was significant that he was Chairman of the review body set up by the Government to consider the cases of those

---

57 One of the tribes, known as Orang Asli (original people), whose presence in the peninsula predated the Malays. They lived in the thick of the forest and CTs brought pressure on them to give them food and other assistance.
58 Known generally as CTs.
59 Sir Dickie Franks, KCMG.

detained under the Internal Security Act. The continuance of this measure introduced under British rule during the Emergency was justified in Malaysian – and many objective – eyes by the continuing Communist activity still prevailing, albeit at a reduced level, and Malaysians considered criticism of it in the British press as hypocritical in view of Britain's own Prevention of Terrorism Act. Moreover the number so detained was small and constantly and rapidly diminishing – from a few hundred to a handful.

Another Irish 'stayer on' was Mubin Sheppard, who had served with distinction in the Malayan Civil Service – MCS.[60] He was educated at Marlborough and Magdalene, Cambridge, and joined the MCS in 1928. He was a prisoner of the Japanese in the war and, *inter alia*, wrote *Taman Budiman: Memoirs of an Unorthodox Civil Servant*.[61] In retirement he became not only a Malaysian and a Muslim but an expert on Malay customs, arts and crafts, which he promoted vigorously.

Tris Russell was proud to represent the fourth generation of his family to live in the country, owning and running the Boh Tea Estates in the Cameron Highlands, in which his children, the fifth generation, also played their parts.

Another Irishman who remained in the country and took Malaysian citizenship was Vic Hutson,[62] an Irish planter who, arriving in the country in 1946, had served in the French company SOCFIN. On retirement he became a major prop of the Zoological Gardens in KL, of the Royal Commonwealth Society's large and flourishing Malaysian branch and of the Outward Bound school at Lumut, which I visited more than once and found very impressive. He had close relations with all the major figures of the early days of Independence and several of these attended the investiture I held at Carcosa when Vic Hutson was awarded an Honorary CBE. The guests included H. S. Lee and Khir Johari, one of the first Ministers who later involved himself with many charitable causes, and 'Tunku' himself. At the champagne reception after the ceremony, which was a very relaxed and chatty occasion, 'Tunku' and H. S. Lee quietly advised me strongly to go to Hong Kong and discover the joys of 'perpetual youth' by taking an infallible elixir – snake's gall bladder in brandy. I never found opportunity to try it!

60 Tan Sri Datuk Haji Mubin Sheppard, CMG, MBE – who also had many other Malaysian decorations.
61 Heinemann, 1979
62 Tan Sri Dato Victor Massey Hutson – holder of a number of Malaysian decorations.

Harry Traill was an intellectual planter, who was made a Datuk. He was a keen naturalist and became a local historian and an authority on the *Hikayat Abdulla* – the disarming autobiography of Abdulla bin Abdul Kadir, who worked with and described Raffles and other Europeans living in the early part of the nineteenth century. In Kelantan there was another small group of 'stayers on'. Of these Mike Wrigglesworth was a lawyer and always known as 'Datuk Lawyer'. Bill Bangs, also a high-ranking Datuk of Kelantan, was a former planter completely absorbed in local society. Ray Hall was a schoolmaster well supported by the ruling family, and ran a private school for the disadvantaged.

John Skrine had long practised as a lawyer and was a wise observer of the contemporary scene – Hussein Onn had at one stage been in his firm. Norman Marjoribanks was also a lawyer of long standing and he and his wife Peggy were ubiquitous on the KL social scene, where she supported various charities like the Cheshire Homes with a vigour belying her age. A familiar and genial figure was Colonel Phil Bennett, who had been the last British officer serving in the Malaysian Army, a pillar of the St George's Society – all the 'loyal Societies' flourished in KL – and every year during our time in Malaysia and for several years after he gallantly sent Ruth a bunch of red roses on St George's Day.

Penang too had its own old British community. Sjovald Cunyngham-Brown, who had been in the MCS, was a witty, amusing, and learned man – a keen historian. Hugh Watt and his wife had lived on the Glugor estate since just after the First World War, giving tennis parties every Saturday over this long period. The two Borneo States of Sabah and Sarawak also had their share of old hands and a lady member of the Sabah Government was the daughter of a British official and a wife from the local people.

Malaysia was still well endowed, therefore, with rich British characters and among them was Dr Reid Tweedie, a remarkable Scottish doctor who had practised his medicine at Sungei Siput in Perak for many years. Much loved locally, he had been accused by some during the Emergency of having – albeit true to his Hippocratic oath – on occasion treated terrorists as well as those on the Government side. Be that as it may, his reputation was formidable and people liked his amiable eccentricities, accentuated by living for a long time in near isolation. He was very hospitable to us and our children, taking especially to Ruth. He was also very kind to me, seeking to prove that I must be a Scot not merely because of my first name but because he had found a reference to a Donaldus Hawley killed in the Drummond-Murray feud at Monzievaird in 1490 in *The Surnames of Scotland*! He had been so long in the country that, sitting round our swimming pool in the heat of the day, when everyone else was bathing, he wore two cardigans and a woollen cap.

Ruth and I visited all the States at least twice officially and some more often unofficially. The official visits involved formal calls on Rulers, *Mentris Besar* (or Chief Ministers) and other leading personalities, and a particular advantage was that people outside Kuala Lumpur often spoke more frankly about federal politics than those in the capital. Malaysia was an interesting mixture between old and new ways as two contrasting examples illustrate. A senior police officer in Perak asserted that his most serious problems were; first the seven Chinese secret societies, who organised smuggling, protection rackets, drugs and prostitution; secondly, fighting between inshore Malay and deep-sea Chinese fishermen; and thirdly smuggling and piracy carried out even by Indonesian naval vessels. On the other hand, the manager of a new British factory showing me the latest machinery, extolled the multiracial work force for their skill and motivation – a representation of the modern Malaysia, on which Dr Mahathir with his vision of Malaysia 2020 has been able to build the 'tiger economy'.

On our first call in Trengganu, the Sultan and Tengku Ampuan kindly invited us to lunch. The setting was lovely, the table elegant but conversation did not flow as easily as elsewhere. Ruth and I found ourselves doing most of the talking. Two years later we returned to Trengganu for our farewell call by which time there was a new Sultan, his predecessor having died. The conversation was no more lively and once again we did most of the talking but I was knocked slightly off balance when the State Secretary, one of the guests on both occasions, remarked, 'You said that last time.'

Our first call on the Sultan and Sultanah of Kedah on 13 February 1978 was more relaxed. Only a few months earlier he had completed his five years as Agong, and he and his wife were urbane and easy to talk to. Both had been educated in England, he at Wadham College, Oxford and she, a member of the Negri Sembilan family, at Nottingham University. I asked how he had felt on stepping down from the kingship and returning to his own State and he replied with a smile that he had had no problems of social adjustment. He and the Sultanah were both sociologists!

The call on the eighty-three-year-old Sultan of Johore on 16 May 1978 was a unique experience. Educated in England where he had stayed from 1903 to 1920, he returned to Johore, never to cross the sea again – in respect for an old tradition. He spoke beautiful English in an old-fashioned way and Malay – so it was said – like an Edwardian English gentleman. A tour round the Istana, which was built in 1864 by Sultan Abubakr, the 'Father of modern Johore', preceded lunch. Standing in a superb position overlooking the straits with a park in which eighty Angus cattle were grazing, it was full of interesting objects including exchanges by letter and telegram with our own Royal Family. The Audience Chamber contained enormous contemporary portraits of Queen Victoria, Prince Albert, the Prince of Wales – later King Edward VII – and Princess Alexandra, and the Duke and Duchess of York.

At lunch with Sultan Ismail and Sultanah Nurah the Private Secretary was requested to bring a selection of letters from the Sultan's large circle of friends in England. These included Beverley Nichols, who had been an Oxford contemporary of his at Christ Church, Oxford, Barbara Cartland and Somerset Maugham. He was singularly well-informed about London life of the 1970s and knew how different it was from the society he had known. Nevertheless he kept asking about various dukes and peers, when it must have been their fathers or grandfathers he had known himself.

We saw most of the Rulers close to Kuala Lumpur such as the Sultan of Selangor, out of whose State the federal capital had been carved in the 1970s. The Yang di Pertuan Besar and Tunku Ampuan of Negri Sembilan, with whom we had served as diplomats both in Cairo and Lagos, would greet us by our Christian names. Their family all had the endearing quality being talented performers at informal functions – willing to play and extemporise at a moment's notice.

The Sultan of Pahang used to give enormous birthday parties at his Istana in Pekan, the State capital, to which he would invite personal friends and a selection of members of the Diplomatic Corps. It would be a mixture between an oriental and occidental occasion, with the personal guests placed close to the Sultan and the Tengku Ampuan. The dining room was reputed to be the largest in Asia with the exception of one in Beijing, and could accommodate some 2,000 people. The Sultan expected the whole room to be filled, and so it was – with the Malay men in formal dress and ladies in coloured woven dresses of *kain sonket.*[63] No alcoholic drink was served at the dinner itself, but the personal guests were offered every kind of liquor, including the finest champagne and whisky, in a separate room both before and after dinner. The guests were expected to keep dancing to the band playing Eastern and Western dance music until the Sultan himself withdrew, which might not be until three or four in the morning. It was very enjoyable but a 'hard day's night'!

The ceremony for the initiation of a new Ruler, after the decease of his predecessor, took differing forms in the various States. The first Ruler to have a formal 'coronation' was the Sultan of Johore in the early years of the century. The Sultan of Selangor followed suit with a coronation in 1912 and Kelantan had its first coronation in 1921. The former Sultan and Agong at the time having died, Ruth and I were invited to the Coronation of the Sultan and Raja Perempuan of Kelantan on 30 March 1980. The previous night we were guests at a private party given by Tengku Razaleigh, the Finance Minister and uncle of the Raja Perempuan.

It was still dark when we set off next day from the hotel for the Istana Balai Besar with Encik Mohamed Ismail and Nik Asiah, our Protocol Officers. The streets were bright with decorations and arches lit by the crown of Kelantan. The Istana itself was already thronged. Most Malay men were wearing traditional dress with apron of black and gold *sonket* and matching turbans. Their *krises* were stuck into their cummerbunds and they were decked out with the sashes, badges and medals of a fine array of orders. Other men were in smart official uniforms – white tunic and black trousers – with the round *songkok* on the head and more colourful orders.

The audience chamber was set with chairs – almost in cathedral style – and, after being greeted by the Deputy Chief Minister, the diplomatic guests were shown down the long blue and gold carpet towards the raised dais, on which stood two thrones. We were seated with several Federal Ministers to the right facing the thrones. The brown wooden thrones with 'four poster' canopy were beautifully carved, a traditional skill in Kelantan. They were ornamented with seat coverings and drapings of yellow, the colour of royalty in Malaysia, Thailand and Brunei. Flags of Kelantan, blue and white, red and yellow, fluttered with the movement of fans, which stirred the huge chandelier into a

---

63 The traditional Malay woven cloth made, with extensive use of gold thread, mainly on the east coast.

gentle swaying movement. At 6.50 a.m. the representatives of the Rulers of other States – mainly Rajahs Mudah[64] – arrived in brightly-coloured Malay suits, followed by the Governors of Penang, Malacca, Sabah and Sarawak. Last came Datuk Hussein Onn, the Prime Minister representing the Agong. The time of the Coronation had been fixed by the Mufti of Kelantan as the most propitious in accordance with an Islamic astrological computation. This did not prevent a brief power failure, however, which sabotaged lights, air-conditioning and fans.

The Sultan and Raja Perempuan arrived to the beating of drums and Malay music played on traditional instruments by a band sitting on a low dais. Opening with prayers in Arabic and Malay, and gun salutes, the ceremony itself was quite short. The regalia were placed in round silver stands before the royal couple. Removing his own turban, the Tengku Panglima, who had officiated for the previous two Sultans, crowned the Sultan and then the Raja Perempuan with golden crowns. The Tengku Sri Utama Raja bore in the royal *kris* signifying the beginning of the Sultan's rule and a traditional ceremony with betel nuts – important on most Malay occasions – was then conducted.

Kelantan had a special character and charm, though Mohamed my Malay driver protested difficulty in understanding the local dialect. Women played a more prominent role there than elsewhere and were dominant in the markets and the commercial sphere. One came across some delightful names, such as Pantai Cinta Berahi, the beach of passionate love (Islamic pressures have recently caused the name to be changed), and the Nilam Puri, Palace of the Blue Fairy, which had been handed over to an Islamic foundation. I surprised the Director there by speaking in Arabic and on a second visit presented them with a collection of works on Islam by British authors for their library.

The investiture of seven new Datuks at Shah Alam in Selangor on 1 March 1978 demonstrated the continuing strength of Malay custom and tradition. The Sultan and Tunku Ampuan wore complete suits of royal yellow and the Rajah Muda and his beautiful wife were clad completely in green from turban to shoes. The ceremony lasted about an hour and a half, and the Malay Datuks clad in very colourful costumes had to perform an elaborate twisting and grovelling ceremonial in approaching the Sultan, originally designed to reveal any hidden *kris*.[65]

---

64 Heirs presumptive.
65 Those Datuks of other races were spared.

We participated in ceremonies of a very different kind on our first visit to Sarawak on 6 March 1978. Having flown to Sibu on the great 'grey green' Rajang river, we went by launch to Bawang Assan, a group of six Iban longhouses. We were accompanied by Abang Amin bin Abang Hashim, the Assistant District Officer – the local officers held the same posts as the British in the former Brookes' Administration, later the Colonial Government. The area Chief, Temenggong Bangan, welcomed us. Little girls and boys, mustered for the occasion in their school uniforms, sang the Sarawak anthem and we proceeded under a welcoming arch to the Temenggong's longhouse. At the bottom of the steps a small pig was tethered. I had been forewarned of the signal honour to come and steeled myself to a duty which was clearly obligatory when the Temenggong invited me to kill the poor creature. My hand guided by him, I pierced its jugular with a sharp spear. Death was fortunately instantaneous. A man waved a captive cockerel over my head and a pretty and very nubile girl, wearing a beaded mantle and jewelry of silver coins, garlanded me.

The longhouse was a finely built wooden structure with a long verandah and doors leading off. At the top of the steps the wife of each separate family stood with a tray of rice wine in small glasses. A glass had to be drunk from each tray, though as I had been briefed by the Temenggong the first glass had to be poured away as a sort of libation. Then there was handshaking all round – with men and women – and we were conducted to seats at the end of the verandah, the 'village street' of the longhouse. This was decorated with Ming jars, Christian religious pictures and the shrunken skulls of slain enemies – the Iban having, like other Borneo tribes, been until recent times headhunters. Here the 'Meering' ceremony took place, which involved offerings to the spirits. As instructed, I placed plates with offerings of food on a high wooden ledge outside the Temenggong's 'house'.

Ruth and I were presented with gifts and a cockerel was placed in my hands. I was told to wave it over my head, which I did, though the bird squawked in protest. A bard then came and, kneeling in front of us and sweating with concentration, delivered a long impromptu poem for several minutes commemorating the visit – an amazing *tour de force*. We all then joined in dancing wearing ceremonial headgear. There was play with swords and shields and much beer and conversation. We then retired into the Temenggong's house for the night and slept till dawn despite the background of creaking, coughing and nocturnal animal sounds.

This was the traditional life of Borneo. Next day, however, we saw another aspect. There had been Chinese people in Borneo for many centuries who had intermarried with indigenous people, as well as many others who had come in more recent times. Such was the population of Sibu, where the the Ding brothers ran their impressive sawmills and furniture business, with 75% of the machinery British made. The Chinese in Sibu, whose nocturnal capacity for drinking brandy was phenomenal, all seemed to have rhyming names such as Ding, Ling, and Ping. On our second visit in 1980 we were surprised to find that the former heavy drinkers were content with soft drinks and coconut milk. Their change of heart had apparently been on grounds of health rather than the influence of the local Christian Fathers, one of whom rejoiced in the name of Hyacinth.

We flew back to Kuching, to be met in the tiny VIP room at the airport by Temenggong Jugah, perhaps the most influential Iban on the Rajang and a friend of Malcolm MacDonald when Commissioner-General in South East Asia. He had adopted MacDonald and his sister, who was married to a professor at the Sains Universiti[66] at Penang, into his tribe. He had of course aged but Malcolm MacDonald's description still fitted: 'His manly face, swift to break into a laugh or pucker in a frown, was a faithful expression of his vivid personality.'

Back in the capital, Kuching, we called on the amiable Governor, Haji Muhamad Salahuddin, who showed us round the museum in the Istana containing many relics, portraits and photographs of the Brooke period in the nineteenth and twentieth centuries. The Istana, home and headquarters of the three Brooke Rajahs, stands on an eminent site over the Kuching river – an English period piece, with Gothic tower dating from 1870. Another outstanding building is the Sarawak Museum built during the period of Sir Charles Brooke, the second Rajah, and set up by Alfred Russel Wallace, who independently evolved the same thesis as Darwin about the origin of species without achieving Darwin's fame.[67].

On first arrival in Sarawak a few days before, we had held a reception at the house of our Honorary British Representative – the equivalent in a Commonwealth country of an Honorary Consul. Alan Deverell, the Manager of the Standard Chartered Bank, and his wife

66 As it sounds, the University of Science.
67 Alfred Russel Wallace, OM, FRS and Darwin published a joint paper on the modern theory of evolution in 1858 and he also wrote *The Malay Archipelago* in 1869 about the area where he had carried out his researches.

Helen were already well known to us from our days in Muscat. Having been advised that we should lose face badly if we offered anything less in quality, we had brought VSOP brandy and Black Label whisky. The party was supposed to be from 6.30 to 8.30 p.m., after which there would be a small dinner party given by the Deverells. It did not work out like that and the guests, particularly the Chinese, enjoyed themselves so much – incidentally mixing our precious spirits with every form of fizzy drink - that at 11.45 Ruth and I felt obliged to say good night and retire. By this stratagem the guests were dispersed and we were able to sit down to dinner at about 12.15!

On other trips to Sarawak we visited the Royal Geographical Society's expedition to Mulu in 1978, led by Robin Hanbury-Tenison. It was the largest scientific expedition which the Society ever mounted, with over fifty scientists of various disciplines involved, and consequently a most important contribution to the study of Sarawak. We happened to be there when the 'cavemen', the speliologists, saw the limestone caves for the first time and immediately pronounced them some of the most enormous in the world. Ruth, ever eager to conquer any incline, later climbed Mount Mulu, which rises to some 8,000 feet, with a splendid guide from the Punan tribe who remain hunter-gatherers and have incredible skills with the blowpipe.

We were made welcome on more than one occasion at the Shell operation at Miri, which had been producing oil since its discovery there in 1895 and was a major contributor to Malaysia's economy. Hans Brinkhorst, the Managing Director, was a colourful Dutchman who had the distinction of being made a Datuk of Sarawak. From there we visited the Niah caves with their traces of human habitation over a 40,000–year period and saw Chinese recovering the nests of myriads of swiftlets living in these caves by climbing unbelievably high and rickety bamboo scaffolding. We were spared bird's nest soup for our lunch near the caves but instead had bird's nest pudding, still full of down.

Pro-British sentiment was strong in Sarawak less on account of the short Colonial period (the first Governor, the inoffensive Sir Duncan Stewart, had been stabbed to death by a fanatic) than of the Brooke family rule. This had lasted from 1840 until the Second World War, a hundred years compared with the eighteen year Colonial period from 1945 to 1963.

Romantically called 'The Land below the Wind', Sabah, the former British North Borneo is dominated by Mount Kinabalu, which is the highest mountain between the Himalayas and New Guinea. The

Mount Olympus of Sabah, it is held in awe by the local people as the resting place of departed spirits and seat of a dragon. The capital, Kota Kinabalu, is closer to Vietnam than to Kuala Lumpur and 1,200 miles equidistant between Kuala Lumpur and Hong Kong – and only 1,500 miles from Darwin in Australia.

In Sabah the redoubtable Chief Minister, Datuk Harris Saleh, poured out a constant stream of ideas at once inspirational and tiring. He was President of the Berjaya Party which, having defeated Harris's tough predecessor, Tun Mustapha, was within the 'National Front' coalition. The Honorary British Representative was Brian Rogers, Manager of the Hong Kong and Shanghai Bank. It was customary that each of the two British banks should hold one or other of these honorary posts, by no means sinecures, in the Borneo States.

Brian and Gillian Rogers had a beautiful house and garden with a panoramic view overlooking the island of Gaia. They were also very good company and we made a number of expeditions with them – the most memorable of which was the climb of Mount Kinabalu on 10 and 11 March 1979. We set off after an early breakfast from the power station, which stood at some 7,000 feet, accompanied by four graceful Kadazan girls, who carried our kit in locally-made round baskets strapped to their backs. We climbed to the Sayat hut at 12,500 feet with its ten bunks. We all had a great sense of achievement, particularly as some of us went higher that evening and nearly reached the summit. As we came down to the hut again, the pink evening sunlight brightened the crags. Later, as a nearly full moon shone, the Kadazan girls sang very sweetly together. Early the following morning we all climbed to Low's Peak at 13,455 feet, reaching it around 7.30 a.m., sitting on the top in the sun and enjoying the marvellous views all around over the lower mountain folds to sea, islands and inlets. We descended all the way to our starting point for lunch, our legs increasingly wobbly, and it rained.

Henri Fauconnier in his book *The Soul of Malaya* describes the Malays as a very poetic and imaginative people with a strong belief in spirits; and, despite the advent of Islam, sympathetic magic is still practised by many Malays. Belief in ghosts, *hantus*, is widespread. It is a complex subject, but much folklore surrounds such apparitions. Nazidon, the senior Malay bearer at Carcosa, was definite about the existence of ghosts and lucid in his descriptions of those he had seen at Carcosa and elsewhere. Belief in the powers of a *bomoh*,[68] credited with

---

68 Sort of 'witch doctor'.

special spirituality and power to keep rain away, was also general and deeply rooted in tradition. It was therefore common practice, especially though not exclusively amongst Malays, to call a *bomoh* to prevent a party or important event being washed out.

It is easy to be sceptical but the success rate was astonishing. For instance Tan Sri Jamal Abdul Latif, the Chairman of SOCFIN, gave a farewell party for us on the lawn of his house on the neighbouring hill to ours – there was always friendly banter about which house stood higher. As the guests arrived to a grey unpromising evening, it started to rain with gradually increasing intensity. Jamal called the *bomoh*, who, already resting in the house, went out on to the grass, Koran in hand, accompanied by an acolyte. There he started to pray and read aloud. The rain quickly stopped and, when the guests reemerged from the shelter of the house, the party proceeded outside as planned. On another occasion when a *bomoh* had been called to the stadium to prevent the final of a football match being washed out, the sight of heavy rain-shedding clouds hanging round the stadium until the match was over was said by witnesses to be uncanny.

Another witness to the efficacy of the *bomoh* was the professional at the Royal Selangor Golf Club, Norman von Nida – a hard-headed Australian as well as a distinguished international golfer. He swore to me that one year the rain was pouring down all round the periphery of the golf course but not on it. As the last flight went down the 18th, the rain followed them, holding off until the prize-giving was finished whereupon it immediately started raining cats and dogs.

The Indian festival of Thaipusam was another strange phenomenon. Invited by Tan Sri Manickavasagam, the MIC Minister, on 10 February 1979, Ruth and I had to fight our way through a colourful throng of people to the Sri Maha Mariamman Temple at the Batu Caves. There on a special wooden stand sat 'Manicka' and other VIPs overlooking a crowd whose origins lay in southern India or Sri Lanka. They were well-behaved and clean – though they left mountains of litter. Many of the men were very handsome; many of the women outstandingly beautiful. About 10,000 devotees of the God Subramanian mortified the flesh in various ways after a month's preliminary purification, involving fasting, a vegetarian diet and total abstinence from sex and drink. The first ceremony began at the flowing river, where with accompanying music some appeared to go into a trance, inducing them to extraordinary acts. Some helped by their families put on the *kevada* – a heavy harness, supporting a superstructure, decorated with many coloured fabrics and tinsel. Chains falling from the frame ended with half-inch hooks which were embedded in the flesh of the penitent to hold the *kevada* in place.

So, burdened with their garish and – to European eyes – tawdry sacrifice of the flesh, they danced and whirled to the accompaniment of drummers, chanters and other musicians. Long spears up to four feet in length with sharp spikes at either end had been inserted through the cheeks and tongues of some, and they advanced slowly, pirouetting towards the 200 steps leading up to the temple cave. None showed any sign of suffering from this apparent torture. There was no blood. Some uttered strange shouts, some grunted but the majority proceeded in silence. One man walked firmly, yet mysteriously totally unharmed, all the way from the river and up the steps to the cave over razor-sharp axe blades, which would sever a limb, embedded in wooden blocks placed alternately before him by his attendants. We witnessed this unbelievable sight from a distance of a mere two feet. It was indeed a day of wonders.

Inside the massive cave, to which a sympathetic young Indian guide accompanied us, the throng was immensely thick and smoke arose from piles of burning incense. The flames cast a lurid light on the wonderful complications of the rock roof and, at the far end, people on a higher part of the cave floor looked down on the scene below. Dante's inferno and the Last Judgement came to mind. Each penitent brought his particular burden of the flesh to the priest, who removed it. In removing the spears, the priest first spat on each cheek, where the metal had pierced them, and, moistening the metal, withdrew the rods. Then, holding his hands on the wounds for a moment, he covered them with ash. In many cases no blood at all flowed; in others a very little. Some devotees, who were all male, went away as if nothing had happened. Others fell down in a faint. Those who had adequately prepared themselves by fasting, prayer and exercise, we were told, did not suffer but those who had not succeeded would try again in the following year. All traces of a wound disappeared and every cheek healed without scar. Nonetheless the first aid services of St John Ambulance and the Red Crescent, staffed by Malaysians, were available and clearly necessary for the several men carried down the steps on stretchers.[69]

The official tours enabled us to see much of the country, and to learn about its inhabitants, industries and history, as we tried to cultivate and

69 This description is taken from the author's detailed note made at the time.

improve relations with the many-faceted Malaysians. But there were other joys – trips to the jungle and bathing in the streams with the children, delightful lunches followed by walks round his fruit orchards with Henry Barlow; stays in the Guthrie bungalow, appropriately called 'Eden', at Port Dickson at the invitation of Bernard Lewis; stays in the Camerons with Tris and Joan Russell and their family on the Boh Tea Estate; and weekends at The Lodge at Fraser's Hill, the Prime Minister's house, which he generously allowed Ambassadors and High Commissioners to use. This had been the house of the British High Commissioner before Independence and Sir Henry Gurney was on his way there when on 6 October 1951 he was ambushed on the winding jungle road and assassinated by Communist terrorists.

It had old-world charm and its fires were often welcome in the chillier atmosphere of over 4,500 feet. Perhaps we had more than our fair share of it but the Prime Minister and his Office did not seem to mind and the other Heads of Mission seldom used their privilege. In that house, where there were 1950s *Who's Who*s and *Whitaker's Almanac*s in the bookshelves, I felt some sort of continuum with the former British Colonial Administration.

There were opportunities for golf in many places in addition to the Royal Selangor, where I played two or three times a week, and trips with the children to Pangkor Island with its beautiful coastline and lovely beaches and to the east coast and its islands. At Carcosa we not only played tennis frequently but enjoyed our pool, around which much of our entertaining was done. In many ways our life was idyllic.

At Christmas we always had an evening party for our UK-based staff, starting with carol singing, which I conducted, nearly raising the churchlike roof of our home. The Elizabethan Club was the High Commission staff club and a house in the grounds of Carcosa had been allotted to them. In pre-Independence days it had been lived in by the Private Secretaries to the Chief Secretary – Mubin Sheppard had lived there in that capacity. Each year the Elizabethan Club put on a show in the winter and Rex Hunt persuaded me in 1978 to make a surprise appearance. I had rehearsed some Gilbert and Sullivan songs with the pianist for the show without anyone knowing, and on the first night I walked into the dressing room. No one took any notice at first and then one of the girls suddenly exclaimed in surprise, 'What are you doing here?' 'I'm next on!' I said.

As our time in Malaysia drew to its end, I became conscious of what I would miss – not least the splendid variety of food: the Chinese, with fresh fish, prawns and other seafood and fresh vegetables; the Malay with the spicy beef *rendang* as favourite; the hot sub-continental curries complemented by that 'queen of puddings', *gula malacca*, made of sago with the milk of coconut and dark sugary syrup from the Nipa palm poured over it.

There was the usual round of kind farewell parties in KL but Ruth and I were very touched when the Royal Malaysian Police gave us a special farewell dinner, demonstrating the strong ties which still continued. We also visited all the States on farewell calls and received much kindness, including the help of the Royal Malaysian Air Force who, on the directions of the Chief of the Air Staff, made a helicopter available and thus enabled us to get round the country quickly. A highlight was our visit to Sarawak on 31 January 1981. We flew in the RMAF helicopter 'Nuri' to Mulu to visit the British-Sarawak caving expedition. We descended into a small clearing, the vertical descent giving the impression of going down in a lift with huge trees at the sides. We then approached the caves themselves by going in small boats up the River Melinau with its jungle-clad banks and logs sticking out of the stream in eerie shapes past which gushed the dark green and brown stream. The 'Deer Cave' dwarfs any cathedral but the 'Cave of the Winds' and the 'Clear Water Cave' with its rushing river are also magnificent.

We flew up to Bareo at 3,500 feet on the plateau. The Penghulu, tall slim and dignified in an impeccable grey suit with a single medal, met us with a group of fine-looking men with long dangling ears weighed down by rings of brass or carved hornbill ivory. They were of the Kelabit tribe which, until rescued in the 1940s by the Borneo Evangelical Mission, had been destroying themselves through drink. Some wore distinctive caps of coloured straw. We walked up the path to the Penghulu's house between a long line of people including many schoolchildren who shook hands with us – the girls in their attractive light blue school gym tunics. The school bamboo band, the sound of which was vaguely reminiscent of a Swiss mountain village, played tuneful and haunting music in greeting.

A good lunch was served based on the excellent rice of Bareo, preceded by a Christian grace in Bahasa. The Kelabit are now an upright and lovely people and have produced very distinguished sons and daughters. Freda was one such: she was the beautiful and talented Personal Assistant of the Shell Managing Director, George Band, who, having succeeded Hans Brinkhorst, was with us on this visit. After lunch we walked through the mud to another longhouse where a large

crowd was assembled. The Penghulu made a warm speech with gra-
cious references to the old British connection, and I replied.

Then there was traditional dancing by men and women wearing
their heirloom caps of beads, some of which were of old Venetian glass.
The ladies in pink *bajus*[70] did a neat and very fast dance between two
long boards clapped together under them by tough-looking men, deftly
avoiding injury to their ankles. Some women, including the Penghulu's
daughters, danced individually and others in groups. Old men sang in
chorus about our visit, praising British times nostalgically and congratulating the Malaysians on going on with what the British had started.
The final act was a long conga all round the longhouse before we
departed for the helicopter. As we took off we waved and waved out of
the window in final farewell to these wonderful friendly people. They
had asked me for the *Encyclopaedia Britannica* and I persuaded my
successor, Bill Bentley, to present it to them.

Meantime thoughts about the 'afterlife' became increasingly important. I did not feel ready to retire, even if a letter addressed to 'Sir Ruth
Hawley' at Carcosa could have been a hint that I was running out of
steam! I had, however, reached the mandatory age of sixty. Some are
ready to retire then; others not. Malaysia was a very happy last post,
full of varied interest. It was a country already moving fast and the
Malaysians since Independence had built effectively and impressively
on the foundations bequeathed to them. The administration was strong
and efficient and this boded well for the future.

The British-inspired institutions, combined with the sensitive
manner in which the leaders of the three main races handled their
mutual relations and forged a Malaysian identity and style, created the
cement which held the people and country together. It had been a great
experience. My love of the country and its people had left a good taste
in my mouth and I left for the unknown of retirement with a feeling of
pride in what Britain and Britons had done for good in this diverse and
burgeoning country, and a profound respect for Malaysians of all races.

---

70 A long-sleeved, high-necked, long jacket with buttons, worn by Malay and other
indigenous women over a straight skirt.

11

'Afterglow'

The Diplomatic Service was very precise over retirement. Strangely I only discovered a few months in advance that it was obligatory to retire, having taken all the leave due – with any untaken forfeited – on or before one's sixtieth birthday. Therefore, whereas we had originally planned to leave KL in May 1981 we actually left on 18 February. This had the advantage that, sad as we were to leave, there was no time to be 'killed with kindness' at too many farewell parties, of which there were plenty anyway.

We made presentations and said farewell to the marvellous staff at Carcosa, whom we regarded as 'extended family'. It was very emotional and Ah Lin, the cook and peacemaker of the household, was greatly upset at our parting. I did my best to keep the traditional stiff upper lip, but Christopher burst into floods of tears. Mohamed, who had driven for all the Diplomatic High Commissioners since Independence, drove us away from Carcosa for the last time, and Sidik and the other guards in their police uniforms all waved their hats in the air in final salute. At the airport Mohamed, who had been my remembrancer on the way to the office each day as well as driver, said to Ruth, 'Lady, who will look after HE when I am not here? You will have to, Lady.'

In the airport VIP room, there was a large crowd to see us off on the 1 p.m. flight to Bangkok. Sam, Nazidon and Ah Lee had set up a bar and we said our last farewells to these delightful and faithful people there. I wrote in my diary, 'How we shall miss lovely Carcosa, which I have been appreciating especially keenly these last few days – situation, flowers, orchids, trees and lawns.'

We to visited several countries on the way home, beginning with Thailand. Peter and Rosemary Tripp revived us from our pleasantly exhausted state in the Embassy in Bangkok during a short stay. We went on to Burma, where we stayed with Charles and Gillian Booth at the Embassy; then to Calcutta, from where we went to Darjeeling, staying in the Windermere Hotel – redolent of the British Raj with porridge still served for breakfast! Introduced by the Bands, we saw Tenzing, who kindly gave Christopher a copy of his book *Tenzing after Everest*, and his wife, Daku. Her brother Phenjo became our guide for a five-day trek, and we stayed the first night at Tongla in a draughty resthouse. When Christopher, then aged six, walked very nearly the whole of the twelve and a half miles on the following day to Sandakphu, we were immensely proud of him. We went on to have superb views of the 'roof of the world' from Everest to Kanchenjunga and away into Tibet.

After this we went on to Delhi, where we stayed with John Thomson,[1] the High Commissioner. Then, after visiting the splendours of Rajasthan, including a stay in the Lake Palace in Udhaipur, we had a final fortnight on a houseboat in Kashmir, to the awakening of spring. This memorable journey inspired us to later travels in India, Pakistan, Bhutan and elsewhere.

On return to England I was appointed to the London Advisory Committee of the Hong Kong and Shanghai Banking Corporation and also became their Special Adviser on Middle Eastern and South-East Asian affairs. There were two other diplomatic advisers, my old friend Geoffrey Arthur and John Addis, the adviser on China – a distinguished collector of porcelain whose collection is now in the British Museum. I was also appointed a non-executive director of Ewbank and Partners Ltd, eminent consultants in the power sector whose headquarters were in Brighton, and a consultant to the Centre for British Teachers Ltd, an active trading educational charity. My main office was at first in the bank in Stanhope Gate, which was under the charge of Peter Mason. His whole career had been in the British Bank of the Middle East and, a close friend from Muscat days, he was now Chairman's Representative. On 7 April 1986 Ruth and I attended the opening of the new HSBC building designed by Norman Foster in Queen's Square in Hong Kong.

Events were to change the emphasis of my work. After I had been with Ewbanks for a few months, I was asked if I could help them with a merger with Preece Cardew and Rider (PCR), an old-established consultancy firm of about the same size and also based in Brighton. They were competing with each other in world markets, which did not make much sense for them or for Britain. Both sides wanted my involvement and the first step was to talk confidentially to each and then to report to the board of Ewbanks, whose chairman was Michael Ewbank, the son of the founder, and to the owning partners of PCR, of whom Brian Goodman was the senior partner.

1 Sir John Thomson, GCMG.

I began this in May 1982. Although there was some overlap in functions, the firms complemented one another in many ways. For instance whereas Ewbanks had strength in oil and gas, which PCR did not, they had no capacity in telecommunications or mass transport, whereas PCR did. Indeed Preece Cardew and Rider had been founded in 1899 by Sir William Preece, the former Chief Engineer of the Post Office, and a letter of introduction to Sir William about 'an interesting young man called Marconi' hung in the boardroom. PCR had been much involved in the Colonies and other parts of the world and amongst other things were responsible for establishing the general power supply both in Malaysia and Jordan. They had long tradition and a first class reputation. Ewbanks on the other hand had been founded by Harry Ewbank shortly after the war when the power industry in Britain was nationalised. Formed as a limited company it was regarded as very go-ahead and innovative in obtaining work and had designed power stations not only at Kingsnorth in Britain but in a number of countries in the Middle East and Asia.

My 'cloak and dagger' work was not seen as unusual in either firm; both had known me in Malaysia and my comings and goings were put down to giving advice on South-East Asia. My report was accepted by both sides and virtual agreement was reached to go ahead with a merger at a dinner at Handcross in the summer. However a valuation of the two businesses had to be undertaken by objective assessors – Ernst and Whinney, who concluded after minute examination, but conveniently, that the two firms were approximately equal in value. The merger was thus much less complicated than it might have been.

Apart from the principals on both sides, the only people party to what was happening were a very small number of secretaries, who were sworn to secrecy. On the day in September 1982 that announcements were made simultaneously to both firms at special meetings, no one had any inkling of why they were being summoned. The only man who had perhaps got some wind of anything was the driver who ferried me between the two firms, and on the day before the merger he asked me whether I was going to consult 'the troops as well as the officers'! We gave a special dinner for the secretaries who had preserved the security of the merger preparations so effectively.

I became the first Chairman of the Ewbank Preece Group as an executive director. It was a role which I greatly enjoyed. Many of the engineers were outstanding in their fields, and I came to hold them in the highest esteem. A good spirit prevailed within the group, though at times I likened my task to conducting a choir of prima donnas. Mergers always have their difficulties and the most difficult aspect was to change the culture without people losing their justifiable pride in and loyalty to their original firm. The process of integration was helped because a number of engineers had already served in both firms and knew both cultures. I gave up the chairmanship in 1986 to Alan Plumpton and remained a consultant to the group for a further ten years, including a short period after Ewbank Preece was merged into Mott MacDonald and lost its independent identity. Thus I had ample opportunity to keep up links with old friends and contacts in the Middle East and Malaysia.

I lived during the week in the Old Ship Hotel, which had been acquired by Ewbanks before the merger. John Bacon, whose family had owned the hotel for generations, was still a director of the hotel, which stood on the sea front between the two piers. It had coincidentally been rather a favourite of my grandfather's, when Brighton was a little more elegant than it is now. It is one of the oldest hotels in the country, having been founded by Nicholas Tettersell, the owner of the *Surprise*, who took King Charles II across the Channel to Fecamp in 1651 – an event now commemorated in an annual race of sailing boats to Fecamp starting opposite the Old Ship. It has splendid Assembly Rooms dating from the Prince Regent's love affair with Brighton, and Paganini played there from the small balcony in the ballroom. It is therefore just possible that Michael Faraday, who was a friend of his, heard him play there, though there is no record of this. If he did, it would have been a happy precursor to the Old Ship being owned by a firm of mechanical and electrical engineers.

Meantime the family settled happily into Little Cheverell House in Wiltshire, which we had bought in 1980 after selling West Pulridge in Little Gaddesden in Hertfordshire. This was a former rectory sold by the Church at the time of the Great War. Just before making an offer to Joyce Crossley, I remarked that the house had a good feel and there must have been nice people living in it. It seemed a happy chance when she asked whether I knew the Luces, and it transpired that it had been bought in the 1920s by Admiral John Luce, the father of Bill Luce with whom I had served both in the Sudan and the Persian Gulf.

My time after retiring from the Diplomatic Service was very full. However in 1983 relations with Malaysia had deteriorated on account of Mahathir's 'Buy British Last' policy and I was approached by the Chairmen of SEATAG, the South East Asia Advisory Group, the London Chamber of Commerce and the CBI and asked if I could get some sort of British-Malaysian Society going. I agreed to try, provided the aim was not too ambitious. There had already been moves in Kuala Lumpur to set up reciprocal organisations to help to keep strong links going between the two private sectors, and Tun Ismail Ali, the former Governor of the Bank Negara and Neville Green, the General Manager of the Standard Chartered Bank, were both prominently involved.

On one of my business visits to Malaysia, I obtained Mahathir's general blessing for the concept of reciprocal societies. George Jellicoe, then President of the British Overseas Trade Board, and others had urged me to try to get Gordon Richardson,[2] who had just retired as Governor of the Bank of England, to head the British side. I held discussions both with him and Ismail and each agreed to take the task on if the other did, and at a lunch *à trois* at the Bank of England, the matter was clinched. Gordon Richardson successfully summoned the Chairmen of all the most important companies dealing with Malaysia to the foundation meeting in 1983, and the British-Malaysian Society came into being with Gordon Richardson as President and me as Chairman, and a very strong Council and Committee. Its first function was a luncheon given in honour of Ismail at which he announced that he would found a mirror image society in KL. Being a man of action and his word, he quickly did this and from then on yearly joint meetings were held alternately in Britain and Malaysia.

The twin societies were launched with the blessing of both Prime Ministers. Mrs Thatcher held a reception at No. 10 for the first joint meeting in Britain and Dr Mahathir was guest of honour at the dinner in Kuala Lumpur, an event attended by nearly 400 Malaysian and British people to celebrate the first joint meeting there. The two societies worked together in a unique way and Geoffrey Howe,[3] when Secretary of State, suggested to Gordon Richardson and me that it might act as a precedent for dealings with other countries.

The easy informal personal relationships which developed between a number of prominent and influential British and Malaysians in the private sector set the tone. After the initial meetings, Malaysians commented that, whereas we had started by each side having a 'delegation', the events turned into friends sitting around a table to discuss common problems. Of the three committees, the one on Trade and Investment proved a frank and useful forum for British investors and businessmen

2 Lord Richardson of Duntisbourne, KG, MBE, TD.
3 Sir Geoffrey Howe, later Lord Howe of Aberavon, CH, QC.

to explain problems facing them as well as for comparing notes on the two countries' economies and reviewing the world economic scene. The Education Committee's main achievement was administration of the A Level programme – or 'Top Universities Scheme'[4] – and between 1985 and 1993 (when the Malaysians took over its direct administration), over 500 of Malaysia's very talented boys and girls passed through first rate British schools and universities.

The Cultural, Social Affairs and Tourism Committee resulted in co-operation over cultural events. Among the most noteworthy was a joint exhibition of the work of modern Malaysian and British artists in Kuala Lumpur – mounted with invaluable assistance from the British Council – called 'Side by Side'. It was opened by Dr Mahathir's wife. There was also an impressive exhibition in Penang of Sir Frank Swettenham's paintings.

The twin society concept also had the advantage of acting as a shock absorber to supplement the work of the respective High Commissions, if difficulties arose between the two countries. An example of this was the row over the Pergau Dam in 1994, exacerbated in particular by articles in the *Sunday Times*, then edited by the sturdy and forthright Andrew Neil. I found myself on the Kilroy programme on television opposing Neil and dealing with the journalistic catch slogan, 'The dam that nobody wanted'. I pointed out robustly that the Malaysians, the people most concerned, emphatically did want it. Having decided that part of their national power supplies should come from hydro-electric schemes, the highly competent Economic Planning Unit (some of whose staff had degrees from British universities) had concluded, after exhaustive examination, that Pergau was the best place for the dam. Such was the prelude to the British Government's decision, after their own examination, to provide a loan for it. Whether my words cut any ice I do not know, but something had to be said.

After my retirement as Chairman from Ewbank Preece, I became Chairman of the Centre for British Teachers on a three days in the week basis. The headquarters of this was in Chancery Lane and it had been founded by Tony Abrahams, a barrister who was the nephew of the famous Harold. The essential philosophy was that teachers performed best if well managed – a good military principle which Tony Abrahams, a man of ability, foresight and sometimes charm, had learned in the Indian Army. CfBT had started with a very big project teaching English in Germany and had, as we have seen earlier, successfully managed the

4 Referred to above in chapter 10.

'crash' English teaching programme started by Musa Hitam in Malaysia. By 1986 their largest project, with well over 200 teachers involved on the ground, was in Brunei. There was also a reduced programme in Malaysia and possibilites for development in Oman and elsewhere. These projects were efficiently managed, but there was need for diversification. We also needed less expensive premises than those in Chancery Lane and, before I retired from the organisation in 1992, the headquarters had been moved to Reading. Neil McIntosh, formerly the Director of VSO and earlier of Shelter, had been recruited as Chief Executive. Under him, the centre has gone from strength to strength, using the expertise and good spirit built up in the organisation over the years, including becoming a major contractor to OFSTED for school inspections. It has also won a considerable number of contracts under Overseas Aid Schemes from the ODA, and has thus become a very significant educational institution in the UK.

On retirement from KL, I had been asked if I would sit on the Council of Reading University and in 1987 I became President of the Council in succession to Philip Rogers.[5] I found this unpaid job most satisfying and remained as President until my seventy-third birthday in 1994. Patterns in tertiary education were changing rapidly. The days of money available on demand were over and, as resources decreased and new formulae for funding were devised, the universities were faced with problems of great complexity. Often it appeared rather a matter of chance as to how a particular university would fare in the series of funding exercises, though the research assessment exercise became increasingly important in determining the allocation of funds. Reading was fortunate in its Vice-Chancellor, Dr Ewan Page, who was an excellent administrator and, while carrying on an ambitious building programme, he left the university on his retirement in 1992 in very good shape.

One of my most important and interesting roles was chairing the committee of selection for the new Vice-Chancellor. Our choice fell on Professor Roger Williams of Manchester University, who had been Scientific Adviser to the House of Lords. Under him, the university has made considerable further progress and gains in the research assessments exercises. The Chancellor for several years was Roger Sherfield,[6]

---

5 Sir Philip Rogers, GCB, CMG, a distiguished civil servant who had Permanent Undersecretary at the Department of Health and Social Services.
6 Lord Sherfield, GCB, GCMG, FRS.

a distinguished ex-diplomat who had ended up as our Ambassador in Washington. He had also been Permanent Undersecretary at the Treasury. When he went to the House of Lords he became *inter alia* the Chairman of the Lords Scientific Committee.

He shared the view that Peter Carrington,[7] whose home at Bledlow is not far from Reading, would be an ideal successor. He approached him but also asked me to add my voice. I therefore went to Christie's, where Peter Carrington was then Chairman, and urged him to accept the post of Chancellor. Fortunately for the university he did. And as Roger Sherfield was still so live and interested – he had a dance for his nine-tieth birthday – the unique post of Chancellor Emeritus was created for him.

I had a great deal of contact with the academics, especially the two Vice-Chancellors and Monty Frey the Deputy Vice-Chancellor, and enjoyed my relations with them. It was also comforting and amusing to have as Vice-President Jim Hamilton, who had been Permanent Undersecretary at the Department of Education and Science. The atmosphere in the university was very friendly, something on which Roger Williams commented favourably when he took over. I was awarded the Honorary Degree of DPhil there in 1994 and, to my added surprise, Durham University also granted me the Honorary Degree of DCL, which was conferred by the Chancellor, Peter Ustinov, in July 1997. I had always maintained contact about Sudan and Middle Eastern matters with that university since my sabbatical there in 1967/68 and after retirement had served on one or two bodies such as the Committee on Research and Development.

A special interest in Durham was the Sudan Archive, beautifully maintained in the library on Palace Green. It is a unique record of individuals' service under the Anglo-Egyptian Condominium.[8] An important conference was held in Durham in 1982, when a large number of people who had served in the Sudan, in Government and other capacities there, were brought together. Papers were presented, mine being on the law in the Sudan, and debates and proceedings were all recorded. After this I made an off the cuff appeal for funds for the Sudan Archive and, although I had only expected the proceeds of a 'retiring collection', several thousand pounds were subscribed. This enabled the Archive to carry on at a difficult time until the university

7 Lord Carrington.
8 Also see *Sudan Canterbury Tales* (Michael Russell, 1999).

decided that the Archive was unique and made provision for secure financing. Since then it has gone from strength to strength.

I was also made Chairman, as well as representative of the Luce family, of the Sir William Luce Memorial Fund. The object of this is to provide a fellowship for each summer term to enable a scholar from one of the countries in which Bill Luce spent his career to undertake post-doctoral studies at Durham and to deliver a significant lecture.[9]

In 1994 I became Chairman of the Royal Society for Asian Affairs. This was both satisfying and time-consuming with its fortnightly lectures and other events, the highlights of which were the annual dinners at the Savoy – notably in 1995 when the guest of honour was Malcolm Rifkind, the Secretary of State for Foreign and Commonwealth Affairs; in 1998 when Chris Patten was the principal guest speaker; and in 1999 when George Robertson, the Secretary of State for Defence, and Mark Moody-Stuart, the Chairman of Shell, were the guests of honour. Also particularly enjoyable were the Society's tours to northern Pakistan, following the path of Kelly's famous march to Chitral in 1895; to the south and west coast of Turkey on Alexander's path in 1997 in beautiful traditionally-built Turkish wooden boats; and to a rapidly changing Iran in 1999.

Our own association with Sultan Qaboos bin Said of Oman, which went back to the beginning of his reign, continued and we were privileged to be invited for many years to the annual celebrations of his birthday – the National Day. These involve spectacular displays by the military massed bands, which the Sultan loves, and by the children in charming colourful tableaux. We could only feel delighted for the people of Oman and their progress since 1970. In contrast the events in the Sudan, especially the fighting between northerners and southerners and the misery in parts of the country, have been dispiriting.

At home in Wiltshire Ruth was active in local affairs as the Chairman of the Parish Council for many years. She was also the County President of St John Ambulance and served two years as Commander, becoming a Dame of the Order in 1996. She sat on the Swindon Health Authority and became a director of a National Health Trust. In 1998 she became High Sheriff of Wiltshire and my role was to accompany her as a 'Denis'.[10] She had earlier become a trustee of a charity, Medical Support for Romania, and had driven a van of medical supplies out

9 Hooky Walker – Sir Harold Walker, KCMG who had first served with me in Dubai, became the other non-university member of the committee.
10 My consort's job resembled Denis Thatcher's in a small way!

there. This caused one local newspaper to report her appointment under the headline, 'Woman Van Driver Is New High Sheriff'. Ruth was only the third lady holder of this office in Wiltshire – which dates from about AD 900 when Gawdulf was Sheriff – the first having been Ela, Countess of Salisbury in the thirteenth century and the second, Anna Grange, in 1994/95. Over the centuries, six High Sheriffs have come from our small village of Little Cheverell, one being John Luce, former owner of our house.

Our children grew up and all went to Oxford – Sara to Corpus to read PPE, Caroline to Pembroke to read Arabic and Persian, and Susan to Worcester to read Theology – from which she proceeded, having spent a year among the Meskito and Sumu Indians of the Atlantic Coast of Nicaragua, to write a thesis for her DPhil on 'Does God Speak Meskito?'. Christopher followed his sister to Pembroke to read Arabic and led a full sporting and general life there. They all succeeded in obtaining good 'two/ones' and we could be proud of them. On 22 May 1999, my birthday, Ruth and I sat on the hard benches of the Sheldonian Theatre for several hours to see the BA conferred on Christopher in the morning and the DPhil on Susan in the afternoon. We had had the pleasure of being at home and following all the children's activities in school and were particularly fortunate to attend the services in St George's Chapel at Windsor when Christopher was a chorister there. I became a churchwarden of St Peter's, Little Cheverell – a suitable role perhaps for the inhabitant of the former rectory.

We have been fortunate in retirement and spared boredom – a great blessing – thus proving that there can be life after Government service for many an old diplomatic dog who has worn the Queen's collar. The rhyme about John Hawley in the event proved descriptive of my own life:

> Blow the wind high. Blow the wind low.
> It bloweth good to Hawley's hoe.

Index